MODERN MASS MEDIA

Second Edition

John C. Merrill
Emeritus, University of Missouri

John Lee
University of Memphis

Edward Jay Friedlander
University of Arkansas at Little Rock

HarperCollinsCollegePublishers

Acquisitions Editor: Daniel F. Pipp
Project Coordination and Text Design: Publishers Services, Inc.
Cover Design: John Callahan
Cover Photo: The Stock Market
Photo Researcher: Leslie Coopersmith
Production: Hilda Koparanian
Compositor: Black Dot Graphics
Printer and Binder: R. R. Donnelley & Sons Company
Cover Printer: The Lehigh Press, Inc.

For permission to use copyrighted material, grateful acknowledgment is made to the copyright holders on pp. 433–434, which are hereby made part of this copyright page.

Modern Mass Media, Second Edition

Copyright © 1994 by HarperCollins College Publishers

Library of Congress Cataloging-in-Publication Data

Merrill, John Calhoun, 1924–
    Modern mass media / John C. Merrill, John Lee,
Edward Jay Friedlander.
        p.   cm.
    Includes bibliographical references and index.
    ISBN 0-673-99025-7
    1. Mass Media. I. Lee, John, 1931–   . II. Friedlander,
Edward Jay. III. Title.
P90.M453 1994
302.23—dc20   93-31909
                                                            CIP

94 95 96 9 8 7 6 5 4 3 2

CONTENTS

PART 2 Practice and Support

Contents

CHAPTER 12 Public Relations 293

PART 3 Issues and Concepts

CHAPTER 13 Press and Government 315

CHAPTER 14   Freedom and Controls   345

CHAPTER 15   Media Ethics   373

PREFACE

Modern university students are already experienced media consumers. From the time they get up in the morning until they put their heads down at night, they are assailed by media messages that inform them, entertain them, persuade them and alert them to dangers. Information arrives through a variety of mass media vehicles, all competing for their attention: the clock radios that wake them, the newspapers that drop at their doorsteps, the pages of slick magazines, the television sets that dominate their living rooms, movies, books, billboards and more.

Some of the rush of information is valuable. Much is useless. Student media consumers, like other people, obviously can't pay attention to every message that comes their way. They might go crazy if they tried. So which messages are they to listen to? Which do they believe? How do they choose?

One objective of this book is to help answer these questions. Another is to provide students the opportunity to enhance, analyze and consolidate raw data they already possess. Whether they are preparing for media careers or hoping to become more sophisticated media consumers, students should be exposed to media problems of the past, present and future. They must understand media principles and concepts. They should learn to question, examine and solve media conundrums. The key to understanding is knowledge.

Modern Mass Media in the 21st Century

A contemporary media textbook organized to meet the needs of a changing mass-communication scene must be more than accurate and readable. It must examine the process of communication and show how the process works on a mass scale and how it affects the average consumer. Each of the major media must be carefully examined to clarify its purposes and its unique problems. Such basic issues as the relationship of media to government and the concepts of freedom and controls must be thoroughly investigated. *Modern Mass Media* was designed to update the best of this common body of thoughts and insights about media.

But more is necessary to meet the needs of the coming century. Like media consumers themselves, media are in a constant state of flux, and the mass media textbook that prepares students for the future must reflect and predict these changes. A full range of traditional information must be blended with analytical discussion and special features aimed at broadening knowledge in areas too often left undeveloped.

In assessing the rapidly altering interests of communication professors and specialists, the authors of *Modern Mass Media* encountered a growing insistence that certain areas of instruction be strengthened. University teachers want a meaningful study of evolving media economics and a stronger flow of media history than is available in most textbooks. They want to see current and newsworthy issues from the world's headlines used as teaching devices. They require an up-to-date look at swiftly changing media operating procedures. They demand a stronger focus on women and minorities. They expect knowledgeable predictions on the trends that will shape the 21st century. And they want textbook material couched in a gentle language that will maintain the interest of students and propel them forward.

But most of all, educators insist that two major media concepts—global communication and media ethics—have grown in importance and must be expanded and addressed more intensely to meet the complex demands of the next century.

Global Communication

The primary focus of any American media text naturally must be the American mass media. But the world continues to shrink, and national problems have a way of becoming international problems, causing knowledge and interest in other cultures to assume critical importance. Too many professional media personnel and American media consumers know little or nothing about the media systems of other countries. And that's a mistake. Parochialism, like so many other spheres of ignorance, is a dangerous indulgence.

Modern Mass Media not only offers a strong chapter on global issues, but international information is integrated throughout the text in the form of boxes called **Global Glances.** These special insights not only reinforce the importance of the international scene—they also provide a basis for comparison with American media practices.

Ethics

Another subject of great complexity and growing concern is that of media ethics. Ethical procedure embraces a respect for personal responsibility and the public welfare. Numerous codes of ethical conduct exist, but a number of media critics suggest that modern media practitioners, like politicians and government appointees, have shown faulty understanding of ethical behavior.

Are the critics correct? When one considers the potential power of mass communication, one must also consider questions of media conduct. Should there not be basic principles, values and obligations by which media personnel operate? Who is to set these norms? Who is to enforce them? Can they be enforced? Should they be enforced?

Quandaries and questions abound. At least half of all journalism and communication programs in American universities now offer some kind of course in media ethics. Those that do not offer a formal ethics course frequently introduce ethical discussion into the content of other courses. The conclusion is inevitable: American mass media cannot be properly explored for the coming century without an examination of ethical concepts. *Modern Mass Media* provides that examination.

Structure of the Book

Modern Mass Media, responding to the requirements and preferences expressed in a poll of university specialists, offers the latest data on media theory and practice, with anecdotal materials straight out of the world's headlines. Content is offered in three major sections:

- The first section, **Theory and Impact,** explains how the process of communication works, explores communicators and audiences, considers media functions, and probes the impact and effects of mass media messages.
- Part two, **Practice and Support,** examines the operating procedures, economics, and problems of each of the major media, as well as media support systems such as advertising and public relations.
- The final section, **Issues and Concepts,** studies important concepts such as the relationship of government to media, press freedom and controls, media ethics and vital concerns of international communication.

Throughout the book, the reader will find a variety of special-interest "insight" boxes, designed to enhance the learning process. These insights appear under four standing heads. **Global Glances** are provided to increase knowledge of comparative international media practices. **Past Pointers** offer unusual or important historical asides to supplement the historical timelines threaded through most of the chapters. There are also **Special Spots,** a freewheeling collection of pertinent highlights, discussion of the progress in treatment of women and minorities, and explanatory notes. And, finally, **Future Focus** boxes attempt to peer through the mists and see what the next century will bring.

The book contains sixteen carefully organized chapters, one for each week of the average college semester. Written in an easy, informal language, the chapters offer the expected traditional information, as well as fresh material unique to this book. Each chapter is also peppered with the special "insights." At the end of each chapter, the authors have included a brief retrospective, identifying and summarizing the most important points of interest. Readers will also find a list of summary discussion questions that are designed to solidify the student's understanding of major concepts and encourage thoughtful analysis. As a starting place for written reports and for students who want to explore individual topics more deeply, lists of both classic and innovative media books at the end of each chapter offer rich fields for further study. At the end of the book, a glossary provides useful terms for quick review.

For the instructor, a teaching manual is available. The manual contains a summary of the goals of each chapter, followed by a list of discussion questions, suggestions for class projects, and a collection of sample test questions, including 20 to 25 true/false, multiple choice, fill-in-the-blank and essay questions for each chapter, a total of more than 300 questions from which choices can be made to reflect the instructor's own emphasis in lectures. A computerized version of the test bank, *Test Master,* is also available free of charge. The *Test Master* computer version allows instructors to shuffle question order, replace or revise questions, or insert questions of their own choosing to reinforce important points made during lectures, analyses and commentaries. Results can be graded easily on a personal computer with an optical scanner.

Acknowledgments

The authors wish to express their appreciation to the hunderds of university professors who shared their thoughts and their comments on what they wanted to see in the media text of the coming century. We especially wish to thank a handful of dedicated university experts who spent so many hours combing the early drafts of both the first and second editions and offered detailed, much-appreciated refinements for our consideration. Those hardy souls included: Walter H. Brovald, University of Minnesota; David Clark, Colorado State University; John Doolittle, American University; Christina Drale, Southwest Missouri State University; William Elliott, Southern Illinois University at Carbondale; Stuart Ewen, Hunter College; Gilbert L. Fowler, Jr., Arkansas State University; Hal Fulmer, Georgia Southern College; Earl S. Grow, University of Wisconsin-Milwaukee; Kenneth Harwood, University of Houston; May W. Jones, University of New Orleans; Timothy L. Larson, University of Utah; Val E. Linburg, Washington State University; David N. Lowry, Pepperdine University; Maclyn McClary, Humboldt State University; Srinivas R. Melkote, Bowling Green State University; K. A. Neuendorf, Cleveland State University; Sondra Rubenstein, Hofstra University; Leonard Sellers, San Francisco State University; John P. Smead, Central Missouri State University; Roger Saathoff, Texas Tech University; Douglas Starr, Texas A&M University; Jacqueline Steck, Temple University; Joseph Turow, University of Pennsylvania, Annenberg School of Communication; and Tim Wulfemeyer, San Diego State University.

And, finally, we want to recognize the following friends and compatriots who offered special support, assistance and guidance when this book first began to form: Fran Matera of the University of Arizona; Deni Elliott of Dartmouth College; Bruce Garrison of the University of Miami; Sandra

Akridge of Southwest Texas State University; David Rubin of New York University; Bill Brody and Dan Lattimore of the University of Memphis, and Jeanne Norton Rollberg, Luther "Sonny" Sanders, Marilyn Wright and Stephen Zeigler of the University of Arkansas at Little Rock.

ABOUT THE AUTHORS

John C. Merrill, emeritus professor of journalism at the University of Missouri, has taught at seven universities in the United States and abroad. He is the author and editor of 20 books and has lectured in some 80 foreign countries. His academic degrees are in English (B.A.), journalism (M.A.), philosophy (M.A.) and mass communication (Ph.D.). He has been a newpaper copyreader, reporter, columnist and feature writer.

Edward Jay Friedlander is a professor of journalism at the University of Arkansas. He holds a bachelor of science degree in journalism, a master of arts degree in mass communication and a doctorate in education. Friedlander has worked as a newspaper reporter, a reporter for the United States Information Agency and a film publicist. His work has appeared in 40 newspapers and a dozen regional and national magazines. He has edited three book-length annual reports for the Federal Communications Commission and is author of two college-level texts.

John Lee is a professor of journalism at the University of Memphis. He has also taught at American University in Washington, D.C., the University of Arizona, New York University and California State University at Long Beach. Lee has a multimedia professional background, including newspapers *(Fort Worth Star-Telegram, Denver Post)*, magazines (articles for more than 30 consumer magazines), public relations (an international industrial company), television (he hosted a weekly public-affairs program on PBS) and books (six fiction and six nonfiction, including two best-selling novels). Two of his novels have been optioned for movies.

Theory & Impact

What is communication? How does it work? The process seems simple enough. We speak or we write or we smile. Someone listens or reads or watches, and there is understanding. Even children do it, right? But effective communication isn't always that easy. There are many potential barriers to proper understanding and any unexpected interference can actually make the process of communication quite complex.

Missed communication and misunderstandings are common. When the communication situation is a small, personal one—a woman speaking to a man or a parent to a child—a simple missed message may lead to momentary confusion, crossed signals, disappointment, and even anger. But when the communication process is extended to a mass medium and a life-or-death message is directed toward a mass audience, the possibility of misunderstanding is greatly compounded. And the results can be disastrous.

To understand the way modern mass media work, we must first understand the process of communication itself. We need to know how a message is transferred from one party to another. We should learn to recognize the many possible barriers to communication and seek ways to circumvent them. We should become acquainted with the types of communicators and their equally varied types of audiences. We should study the functions of mass media and try to avoid the roadblocks that sometimes cause these functions to go awry. And, finally, we should delve into the intricacies of mass media messages and begin to weigh their effects on mass audiences.

Only when we begin to understand the communication process may we fruitfully advance to an examination of the structure and operating procedures of the individual mass media.

CHAPTER 1

How Communication Works

Fire is a simple word. It means one thing to a toddler pointing to crackling logs in a fireplace. It means something else to someone sitting in a crowded theater, hearing it shouted out of the darkness. And it has a different, even more personal meaning for a blindfolded person standing against a wall, listening to the clink of metal as a squad of soldiers loads and aims weapons.

Fire. Four simple letters arranged to form a word that can suggest various meanings to anyone who sees or hears it. Put the word together with other words and the meaning changes like a kaleidoscope—forest fire, Yule fire, hang fire, open fire, fire a fast ball, fire up one's spirits, fire an employee.

Reuel Howe, in his book *The Miracle of Dialogue,* observes:

> To say that communication is important in human life is to be trite, but that bit of triteness witnesses to an invariable truth: communication means life or death to persons. A study of the nature of communication is needed in this day of mass communication. On a colossal scale never known before and with technical aids that surpass the wildest imaginings of yesterday's science fiction, man can bombard his fellow man's mind, feelings, and will with a subtleness and effectiveness that is frightening (1963, p. 4).

Should communication be frightening? Is a study of the nature of communication really so necessary? After all, what's so puzzling about the way communication works? We spend our lives, from cradle to casket, communicating, and we think we know everything there is to know about it. Actually, we know almost nothing.

We do know, of course, that we communicate some things to some people at some times. We know this empirically: We can see a glimmer of understanding in their eyes; we observe an expected response; or we get no response at all. Actually, we communicate at every turn in our daily lives. Messages are sent and received. Some reactions to the messages are observed, and those that are unobservable are probably of more interest to psychologists than to journalists and other mass communicators.

Communication is a broad concept, and people who are concerned with it are part of a very large area of academic concern. In fact, communication is basic to all academic disciplines, although it has been claimed largely by speech and journalism departments.

In this book we will concentrate on **mass communication:** institutionalized communication that flows out to large audiences in formal and largely impersonal ways. But even though we are dealing with mass communication in society, we must begin with the basic process of communication—with what is usually called *interpersonal* small-group communication—in order to understand the process. Only then can we proceed to the more complex structures of mass communication and the communication industries of society—such as newspapers, movies, and television—that specifically communicate to or with the masses.

What does the word *communication* mean? This is a difficult question with numerous answers. Communication can be defined as the establishment of a common understanding; as a transfer of meaning from one person to another; as the stimulation of common symbols in various minds through symbolic interaction; or as the creation of meaning in others through stimulus-response activities.

The word *communication* has the same root meaning as *community* and *common* (from the Latin *communis* or *communicare*). From this similarity we can infer that communication is related to some type of communion between or among persons—a kind of linguistic or symbolic sharing. One who participates in the communication process is called a *communicant* (one who communicates) and can be either the originator and sender or the receiver and interpreter of a message.

The dictionary tells us that even rooms can communicate—in the sense of being connected to each other or joined.

For us, as communicators of information, the importance of communication lies in its ability to connect symbolic meanings and create a common understanding. You mentally connect with someone else when you communicate successfully—that is, when you and another person have the same or similar meanings established by your mutual activities.

The goal of communication is to establish a community of understanding or a sharing of meaning through the most effective communication activities. The dictionary also tells us that communication takes place when there is an interchange of thoughts or opinions shared through "words, letters, or messages." *Sharing.* That's the key concept in communication. In simple interpersonal communication, such as two people chatting informally, the communicants must share information. But even in a relatively simple minicommunication process, this is not as easy as it sounds.

We can identify many kinds of communication. In a very broad sense, communication can be classified as effective/ineffective, focused/nonfocused, objective/subjective, informational (factual)/opinionated (discursive), devious/forthright, or articulate/inarticulate. For our purposes, however, we don't need to discuss the subject so broadly.

Let's look briefly at three sets of communication types that are basic to an understanding of communication: verbal and nonverbal communication, interpersonal and intrapersonal communication and small-group versus mass communication.

Verbal and Nonverbal Communication

When we speak, we use words. When we write, we use words. Both are forms of **verbal** communication. As we try to communicate, we verbalize our messages. We use standard spoken and written symbols that are generally understood by literate and articulate persons in our societies. In short, we use language, in its common meaning.

Most college instruction in communication focuses on verbal communication. You learn to improve your writing skills by studying grammar, punctuation and organization, and you learn to speak effectively by stressing diction, pronunciation and enunciation, emphasis and pauses, and organization. Whether you speak or write, you are generally thinking about words and sentences and the most effective way to put them together. Verbal communication is of basic importance to everyone because it is the main way we engage in social intercourse.

Most academic curricula emphasize verbal over nonverbal communication. Though you're likely to hear about the importance of eye contact and physical gestures in some speech courses and a few television news classes, verbal communication is the focus of the majority of communication courses, especially in the mass media. Nevertheless, we all do a lot of communicating without using words. We smile. We frown. We grimace, or shrug, or applaud. We raise our hands to answer a roll call or to vote or to signal that we have a question. We clench our fists or fold our arms in resignation. We wave good-bye. We use all kinds of body-language (**kinesic**) activities to communicate a whole range of emotions—disgust, merriment, affection. Sometimes we use nonverbal language by itself, and sometimes we use it to reinforce or supplement our verbal messages.

Interpersonal and Intrapersonal Communication

Inter is a Latin prefix meaning "between or among," as in intercollegiate athletics (one university playing against another). *Intra* is a prefix meaning "within," as in intramural sports (teams from the same university playing against each other).

Interpersonal communication, therefore, means communication between or among persons. It can take place one-on-one, face-to-face, or it can involve groups, both large and small. It can also take place through an artificial mass medium, such as radio. It can be formal or informal, personal or impersonal. When you talk with a friend, you are engaging in interpersonal communication. A district volunteer answering a voter's question, five people holding a lively political discussion, 500 people listening to a speaker in an auditorium, or 6 million people watching a political speech on television are involved in interpersonal communication. What is important to remember is that it takes at least two persons to start the process.

Intrapersonal communication is not what we normally think of as communication at all because it takes place within a single person. In effect, that person is engaged in self-communication. Intrapersonal communication involves encoding (formulating) a message—a process we normally call *thinking;* you communicate with yourself in a closed-system type of communication. Your interpersonal messages will depend on the effectiveness of your intrapersonal communication. It is impossible to communicate with someone else without first communicating within yourself. And just as you, the sender of the message, go through the intrapersonal process, so must the receiver of the message.

The Small-Group Interpersonal Process

Before tackling the extremely complex mass communication process, let's concentrate on the small-group interpersonal process. Here we have a relatively uncomplicated form of communication. The simplest type is the one-on-one, face-to-face situation (**dyadic**) in which one person attempts to communicate with another. A slightly more complex type is the **small-group** communication—for example, three or four students drinking coffee between classes and talking informally about the coming weekend.

At an even higher level—though still in the province of small-group interpersonal communication—is a professor lecturing to a classroom of 20 or 30 students. Now the situation becomes a bit more complex and difficult, but it is still relatively simple in that interaction—the possibility of sharing—is possible. Indeed, interaction can be easily accomplished in these smaller communication environments because the potential exists for return messages (**feedback**) to be sent very quickly from the message-receivers to the message-senders. For example, you listen to the professor and ask questions, allowing the professor to modify the message by repeating it using different words. Now you understand the message, or if you still don't, you can prompt the professor to explain further. The potential for *immediate feedback* is the main reason that small-group, face-to-face communication is the most effective communication situation.

Within a small group, there are certain ingredients—or what are called *facilitating factors*—that make this type of communication particularly effective. For example, if the communicants have similar backgrounds—a similar education, religion, economic status, ideology, race, sex, and so on—they should be able to establish communication more easily. Common experiences should also be helpful. Perhaps they've all been to Paris and can talk about that city, or they're all veterans and can discuss the armed forces. Having a common interest in the topic under discussion is another helpful factor.

And, of course, skill level of the various communicants, whether speaking, writing, listening or reading, is basic to any communication situation. A poor speaker is more difficult to understand than a good one who speaks with clarity, organization, knowledge and respect for both the substance of the message and the receiver of the message. Even in small-group situations, many people talk past one another. Messages go nowhere, and commonness of understanding is not established. We think we are communicating, but we aren't. It takes at least two to communicate. Even the best listener must have something to listen to, and even the best speaker must have a good listener.

Talk-show personalities such as Oprah Winfrey often engage in small-group and mass communication simultaneously

Mass Communication

The process of **mass communication** is formalized, institutionalized and impersonal. It consists of messages sent through some form of technology to large groups of people, or mass audiences (see Figure 1.1). Technology is always involved in mass communication; there is no face-to-face sharing of information. Messages are communicated to mass audiences via a variety of forms—the printed page, radio and television, movie screens, huge billboards and even mass-produced T-shirts.

In discussing mass audiences, we must consider their salient characteristics. Like so many basic terms in the field of communication, *mass* is an extremely difficult word to define. Each of its characteristics needs its own definition or clarification. The list that follows identifies the essential traits of mass audiences.

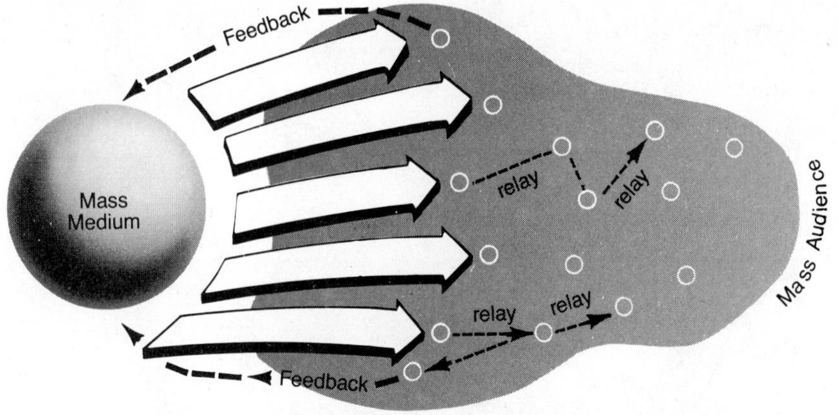

Figure 1.1
Basic Mass Communication
Model

○ Potential and actual mass message receivers (audience members)
⇨ Identical messages from mass medium
◄ ▬ ▬ Delayed feedback
◄ ▬ ▪ Message relayed from one receiver to another

1. *Large numbers.* Mass audiences are large. Just how large varies, but the numbers usually range from hundreds to thousands to millions of people.

2. *Scattered nature.* Mass audiences are widely scattered or dispersed geographically. Some audience members may be in one section of a city and other audience members in another. Some may be in different parts of a state or a region. Others may be dispersed nationally or even internationally.

3. *Anonymous nature.* Members of a mass audience are usually anonymous—unknown to one another and to the communicator. As you watch Dan Rather or Tom Brokaw on network television, you may know a few other audience members—your family or certain friends—but generally you don't really know the countless others who are watching. This is quite different from squeezing into a booth with a few friends at a local café for coffee and conversation.

4. *Heterogeneous nature.* A mass audience is not only large, scattered and anonymous, but it is also *heterogeneous.* It is made up of a wide variety of people with different backgrounds, ages, sexes, occupations, educational levels, interests and political persuasions. Audience members have little in common. The only common element among heterogeneous audience members might be that they are being exposed to the same message at the same time.

Considering all four of these essential traits together, we can get a clearer concept of a mass audience. And from each of these essentials, various other definers or characteristics can be derived. For example, the fact that such an audience is *scattered* would imply that little or no interaction can take place among audience members. And little or no feedback will come from the

Mass audiences are usually large, scattered, anonymous, and heterogeneous.

audience to the mass communicator. What feedback there is will be *delayed*, thereby not doing the communicator much good while the message is being encoded and sent.

As part of the mass audience, each of us is familiar with the *instruments* of mass communication—the mass media. These media come to us in three main types: print media, film media and electronic media. *Print* media are books, newspapers and magazines. *Film* media include still and motion pictures. And *electronic* media comprise radio, television and recordings.

Berelson's
Relativistic
Formula

Many variables make the communication process complex, and this complexity extends ultimately to the effect on the receivers of messages. In 1948, sociologist Bernard Berelson, in summarizing communication, put his finger on the difficulty of trying to predict very much about the outcome of communication. In contrast to the "social categories theory," in which broad aggregates of rather uniform people composed audiences, Berelson emphasized the relativity of the communication process and the individual differences among audiences.

Berelson's formula, which has capsulated the communication process and aided researchers, is "Some kinds of communication on some kinds of issues, brought to the attention of some kinds of people under some kinds of conditions, have some kinds of effects."

Source: Bernard Berelson, "Communications and Public Opinion," in *Mass Communication,* ed. Wilbur Schramm (Urbana: University of Illinois Press, 1949), p. 500.

These media, or at least their messages, are omnipresent and pervasive. You'll find them almost everywhere in your daily lives. And they are big businesses, selling information and entertainment. They even refer to themselves as "industries"—for example, the television industry. But before we get sidetracked by the size and power of the mass media in our society, let's return to the communication process itself and take a closer look at some of its fundamental elements.

Communication Elements

Even at its simplest levels, communication is a complicated business involving various basic elements (see Figure 1.2). To begin, someone must formulate the message. This person—the **encoder**—puts the message into a "code" or symbols that are thought to be understandable to the intended receiver—the **decoder.** At this point, the thought process of the message-sender (his or her *intrapersonal communication*) is very important. And, of course, when the decoder is exposed to the message, he or she begins interpreting (trying to understand) the message, which also requires *intrapersonal* communication (thought).

The Message. What is it that one person wishes another person to understand? A necessary element in the communication process is the **message** itself. Messages may be relatively simple, or they may be extremely complex. For example, you may want a visitor to have a seat when he or she comes into your room. It isn't difficult for you to get that message across. However, if you want to explain the Second Law of Thermodynamics to the visitor and to make sure the visitor understands it, then you have a much more difficult communication problem ahead of you. Messages can be *semantically difficult* (hard to understand) or easy to understand. They can be *informational* (factually based), they can be *analytical* (interpretively based) or they can be *opinionated* (subjectively based). They can even be some of all three.

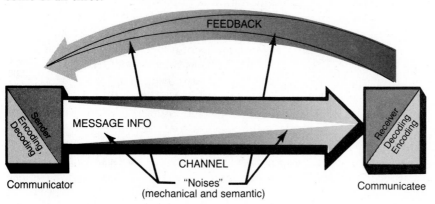

**Figure 1.2
Basic Communication Model**

The Channel. The mechanism by which the message is transmitted is the **channel.** You talk to a friend. Sound waves carry your words and constitute the channel. Your senses can serve as channels, for example when you smell something or feel something. If you write a note in class, a piece of paper is the channel. These channels for minicommunication (personal small-group communication) are quite different from megacommunication channels, such as newspapers, magazines, radio and television. So we see that channels can be considered in at least two ways; there are *basic* channels such as sound waves and there are more pragmatic, *instrumental* channels such as posters, newspapers and television stations.

Feedback. Once the message has been transmitted via its channel, the communicator can expect **feedback,** a return message from the receiver to the sender. Feedback is basically a response that tells the sender that the message is getting through and that it has been understood—or misunderstood. Feedback may be *immediate* or *delayed.* You raise your hand to ask the speaker a question: immediate. You write a letter to a newspaper in reaction to a story you liked or disliked: delayed. And your response may be either obvious to the speaker (overt) or not so obvious (covert). You may nod as a speaker talks to you or ask a question in response to something he or she says. You may even get up and abruptly leave the room. This reaction is *overt* feedback; the speaker can see it. Or you may say nothing overt in response to the message. You may just sit there and fret, responding surely enough but hiding your true response (boredom or irritation or whatever) from the speaker. The speaker may note this passive demeanor and *assume* something from your silence or passivity. He or she may *infer* that you are perhaps not interested in the message or that you are sleepy or not feeling well. This is **inferential feedback,** and its reliability is always questionable.

Like communication generally, feedback can be verbal or nonverbal. *Verbal* feedback is put in the form of words or meaningful symbols. The communicants use words, either spoken or written, to communicate. You are involved in verbal communication as you read these words. Underlining significant information in the text or answering questions on a test is your verbal feedback to our communication. Through nonverbal feedback, the communicants establish a commonness of understanding not with words, but with gestures, smiles, frowns, shrugs of the shoulders, and so on. If someone speaks to you and you throw your drink in his or her face, there is no need for words. Your action says, "I don't like what you said!" Or you may slam this book closed. Sometimes actions do speak louder than words.

Interruptive Noises. Another important element in the communication process is what communication specialists call **noises.** Noises tend to disrupt the communication, interject barriers to understanding, compete with primary messages, distract attention, and in general frustrate the communication process. Two main noises cause the trouble: mechanical (or channel) noise and semantic noise.

Mechanical noise is physical; it has to do with such things as static on the radio, lines of type missing from a newspaper story, the distracting hum of fluorescent light in a classroom, or coughing during a lecture. Modern technology, better acoustics, good public address systems and the like have helped diminish the effects of this kind of noise. Usually—though not always—the message comes through loud and clear; it can be heard or it can be read.

But then *semantic* noise interjects its silent voice. Just what is semantic noise? It is the degree of potential misunderstanding between sender and receiver. It is vagueness built into a message. It can lead to either no communication or to dysfunctional (flawed) communication. So it is not a real noise as we generally consider noise. Rather it is a kind of semantic (meaning) disharmony that invades the message—either in encoding or in decoding or in both. You have probably experienced semantic noise in this paragraph (or anywhere else in the book, for that matter). When you read phrases such as *"dysfunctional communication"* or *"semantic disharmony,"* the chances for misunderstanding rise rapidly. That is one reason there are so many parenthetical insertions in this chapter, giving you secondary or alternate meanings for words in an effort to help you understand a difficult topic. After all, if communication is generally difficult, think how much more difficult it is to explain (communicate) those difficulties.

Semantic noise is pervasive and largely unavoidable. It invades the messages of even the most skilled communicators, especially when the message is complex. It thrives on abstract words and concepts. It buzzes away in such concepts as "freedom of the press," or "patriotism," or "media responsibility," and it is quite likely to play havoc with such discussions as we have been having in this chapter or those that we will face in Chapter 15 on media ethics. Mechanical noise can be largely eliminated or negated, but semantic noise is insidious and will be with us forever. Good communicators and good listeners recognize this fact and work to reduce it as much as possible.

The Audience. The receivers of messages are, naturally, vital elements in the communication process. Presumably a message can be sent by a communicator without there actually being anyone to receive it. But this is not communication—it takes at least two to communicate. So the **audience** is important, though communication courses in colleges and universities usually place the emphasis on the sender of the messages.

In small-group, face-to-face communication, audience members are closely involved, probably know one another, and are part of a chain of communication action and reaction. In mass communication, the story is different: the formality and impersonal nature of mass communication isolates audience members from one another and from the communicator.

There are many different kinds of audiences and audience members, and you'll hear more about them in the next chapter. For now let's simply say that audiences are important and that any communicator should know as much as possible about his or her audience. In small-group communication, this is relatively easy. In mass communication, it is far more complex and difficult.

Barriers to Effective Communication

Most of us know from experience—from trying to communicate with family or friends, for example—that effective communication can be elusive. In this section, we'll consider some of the basic impediments to message sending and receiving. As we've already seen, it's easier to communicate in small groups where there is a maximum of interaction; mass communication is much more difficult and complex. But even face-to-face, small-group communication is filled with frustrating factors, each seeking to disrupt the effectiveness of the messages.

General Impediments to Communication

First, let's look at some of the main barriers to effective communication (see Figure 1.3). If two people are talking, these barriers come into play. If a person is reading a story in a newspaper or watching a program on television, these same barriers again are operative. They are, in essence, factors that tend to frustrate, impede or even halt communication—to keep a commonness of understanding from developing.

Personal Barriers. You are listening to a speaker (either face-to-face or on television) whom you don't like. Or maybe the speaker doesn't like you. Communication between you is damaged. Such personal feeling may seem inconsequential, but it is important. *Personal considerations* play large parts in helping or harming communication. Common respect among communicants will help; lack of common respect will harm. It's as simple as that, regardless of the message or the skill with which it has been encoded.

Figure 1.3
Barriers to Message Impact

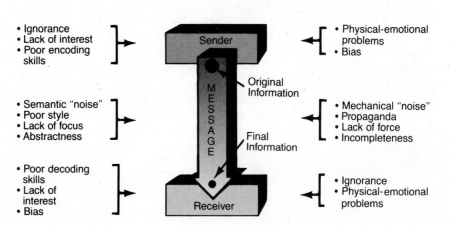

- Ignorance
- Lack of interest
- Poor encoding skills

- Physical-emotional problems
- Bias

Sender

Original Information

M
E
S
S
A
G
E

- Semantic "noise"
- Poor style
- Lack of focus
- Abstractness

- Mechanical "noise"
- Propaganda
- Lack of force
- Incompleteness

Final Information

- Poor decoding skills
- Lack of interest
- Bias

- Ignorance
- Physical-emotional problems

Receiver

Other personal barriers may be physical in origin. One of the communicants has a headache or is sleepy: communication suffers. The speaker has the sniffles, affecting clear speech. Or the listener has an earache, affecting reception. Many such physical factors can block our attempts to communicate.

Or perhaps the communicator is not skilled or is dull, indifferent, seemingly uninterested, or arrogant. The receiver, of course, would rather blame the communicator for poor communication. Maybe it's justified. But the receiver is also responsible for communication. Both (or all) communicants should accept responsibility for the success of a message. You may encode (formulate) a fascinating message, well-worded and well-organized, and you may deliver it in a clear and stimulating manner, but if no one is listening or if no one has any real interest in it, then the communication will be frustrated. On the other hand, a listener who has an interest in the subject and who is making an attempt to understand can overcome the obstacles of a poor speaker, and the communication situation can be made successful.

Monological Communication. Suppose you have just finished a communication. You think you have presented your message clearly, and, therefore, that everyone has understood it. You might be very wrong! Another serious barrier to effective communication is a *monological* approach—the misconception that communication is accomplished by simply saying something, telling people what they ought to know. Reuel Howe (1963) says this **"monological illusion"** is widely prevalent. Delivering a monologue, the communicator loses touch with the receivers because he or she is so self-occupied. The sender of the message concentrates too much on the message itself, on encoding the message and the style of the message, and is blind to the nature and needs of the audience. Most of us have been on the receiving end of a face-to-face monological communication—our eyes glass over, our minds wander, we may listen to a nearby conversation, and we wonder why the communicator hasn't picked up our lack of interest. To be effective, communicators should always seek *dialogue,* not monological communication. In dialogical communication, there is interaction between persons, a flow of meaning that transcends obstacles that stand in the way.

Ideological-Political Barriers. Many communication problems stem from the fact that communicants have differing basic ideologies or political orientations. For instance, suppose you have a close friend who is basically an individualist, with a strong bias against any and all collectivist or group-oriented activities. This ideological individualist will find it hard to communicate with another of your close friends who is of a collectivist orientation. These are basic ideological differences, and they are potent barriers to effective and harmonious communication.

Connected with such ideological differences (as between so-called conservatives and so-called liberals) are *political* differences. For example, in the United States there is a tendency for the individualist (conservative) to gravitate toward the Republican Party and for the collectivist (liberal) to gravitate toward the Democratic Party. It is usually much easier for two Republicans or two Democrats to have harmonious communication about ideological issues than to have very effective interparty dialogue.

Language Differences as Barriers. Suppose this paragraph were written in German or in Russian. If you understand only English or Spanish, you would miss its meaning, even if the meaning were well-encoded and the words were printed distinctly. Communicants will always have trouble communicating if they are not using the same language. This is an obvious barrier. But another version of language difference, perhaps not so obvious, occurs when a speaker or writer uses a version of English that you don't understand. Specialized jargon of various professions and academic disciplines is an example. "Street language" and regional dialect are other examples.

In these cases, you understand the words but you don't understand their special meanings. So, in effect, the writer or speaker might as well be using a foreign language. A language barrier is a type of *semantic noise,* a lack of shared meaning between (or among) the communicants. There are times, of course, when we are communicating with a specialized audience that we will *want* to employ the specialized language or jargon of the audience. But too often we do not even realize that we go around in our own little language worlds. We therefore make no attempt to break out of them and to use language that will be more universally or commonly understood.

Sociocultural Barriers. It is hard to communicate well across social and cultural chasms. This is almost a truism. You have your values, your traditions, your background, your religion, your economic status, and so on. You may meet someone today who comes from a somewhat different sociocultural background. To a greater or lesser degree, you will have communication problems based on these differences. The daughter of a wealthy California lawyer may well have trouble communicating effectively (except about very simple things) with the son of a poor Georgia trash collector. A number of factors (race, economics, education, religion, heritage and occupation, for example) are related to these sociocultural barriers.

It's difficult enough for Americans to communicate with each other, considering these sociocultural barriers. Think of the mounting difficulties that exist among people of different nations. It is no surprise that our international attempts at communication so often get bogged down. Ideology, politics, economics, religion, semantics and differing languages all get mixed up with widely varying cultural values and traditions. Before you know it, almost insurmountable obstacles stand in the way of effective communication.

Other Barriers. There are, of course, many other barriers besides those we have already mentioned. Differences in intelligence among people can damage communication. So can differing levels of education or specialization. A lack of concern for achieving success in communication is also a barrier. And then there is *propaganda,* by which the communicator tries to persuade or manipulate opinion through the use of some kind of deceptive device. Communication is also difficult among communicants who have little or no *experiential overlap* (experiences in common) or who are ignorant about the other communicants (this is especially true of mass communication). All of these barriers do their bit to frustrate or even stop communication or to bring about a kind of pseudocommunication that is based on misunderstanding and dysfunctional responses or consequences.

A Look at Message Entropy

We have summarized many of the barriers to communication. The significance of these barriers is that they can cause a message to *lose information.* And this loss of information is related to what is referred to as **message entropy.** Students of communication have borrowed from the Second Law of Thermodynamics the concept of *entropy*—the tendency of a system to become disordered or chaotic. For communication, entropy means that a message tends to dissipate, to lose energy, to break down, to become weaker. In short, message entropy is the tendency of a message to lose information during the process of transmission.

Harold D. Lasswell (1948) proposed a verbal model for communication that is helpful in studying the various aspects of the communication process. Lasswell's simple formula looks like this:

Who
Says What
In Which Channel
To Whom
With What Effect?

We can relate this model to the concept of a message losing information during transmission. The "who" is the communicator. The "what" is the message. The "which channel" is the mode of transmission. The "whom" is the communicatee (or audience member). And the "what effect" is the consequence of the communication. Researchers and students use the model to shape their various studies and concerns—content analyses (the "what" or message), audience studies (the "to whom"), and finally, the emphasis on the consequences (the "what effect"). Besides the practical, descriptive value of Lasswell's formula, it summarizes the process (without intending to do so) of message entropy in that it presents the steps of the communication process through which a message can (and does) lose "energy" or information.

The process begins with Lasswell's "who"—the communicator. Let's use the example of a reporter in a journalistic situation (we could just as easily use a novelist working on a book or a TV scriptwriter planning a story for a network series). The reporter goes to the scene of a news event—a two-car automobile accident, for example, in which several injuries were sustained. The event (the actual accident) is composed of millions of bits of information, facts, phenomena, or whatever you want to call them. The reporter comes into this environment of phenomena and immediately begins to select some of them for a story. The process of entropy has begun.

"What" will be said in the story is primarily dependent on the selection of facts made at this point by the reporter. The reporter observes certain things, talks to people, makes notes or tape records some comments. Lasswell's "channel" for the message—the reporter's newspaper—comes into play. Back in the newsroom, the reporter selects from his or her notes or tapes and dredges up on-the-scene perceptions. Some of these notes and perceptions are entered into the computer story or typed on copy paper. But what the reporter has left out of the story, even at the beginning of the process, exceeds what is put in. The *loss of information* from the message continues (see Figure 1.4).

An editor or copyreader enters the scene. Often he or she will alter the story, updating it, shortening it to fit a certain allotted space, omitting or changing sentences, and even eliminating whole portions. Next, the story is set in type and laid out on the page, and during this step some of the information may be cut or lost. For example, a "jump" (a continued part of the story from one page to another page) may be misplaced on the wrong page or not printed at all). The message goes on to Lasswell's "whom" (the audience) as the finished newspaper copy is delivered to homes or sold at newstands. Even at this distribution point there can be information loss: a newspaper thrown in a puddle and parts of the story ruined or obscured.

Even if the story of the accident is presented in its entirety in the paper that gets to the reader and is "read," a selective process is at work. The reader, through selective attention, may skip parts of the story or not read it at all. Through selective perception, the reader may miss points or misread

Figure 1.4
Message Entropy in Reporting

Stages:

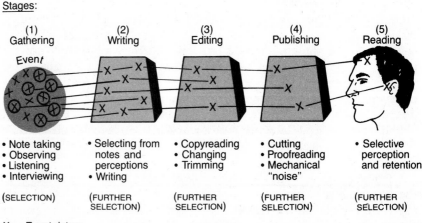

(1) Gathering	(2) Writing	(3) Editing	(4) Publishing	(5) Reading
• Note taking • Observing • Listening • Interviewing	• Selecting from notes and perceptions • Writing	• Copyreading • Changing • Trimming	• Cutting • Proofreading • Mechanical "noise"	• Selective perception and retention
(SELECTION)	(FURTHER SELECTION)	(FURTHER SELECTION)	(FURTHER SELECTION)	(FURTHER SELECTION)

X = Event datum

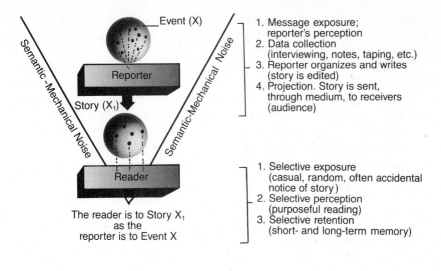

Event (X)

Reporter

Story (X₁)

Reader

Semantic-Mechanical Noise

Semantic-Mechanical Noise

The reader is to Story X₁
as the
reporter is to Event X

1. Message exposure;
   reporter's perception
2. Data collection
   (interviewing, notes, taping, etc.)
3. Reporter organizes and writes
   (story is edited)
4. Projection. Story is sent,
   through medium, to receivers
   (audience)

1. Selective exposure
   (casual, random, often accidental
   notice of story)
2. Selective perception
   (purposeful reading)
3. Selective retention
   (short- and long-term memory)

**Figure 1.5
The Sender-
Message-
Receiver
Symbiosis**

points in the story. And through selective retention, the reader will retain or remember only portions of what is read. Entropy is still at work. So, right up to and including the *decoding* of the story by the reader, information is being lost from the message (see Figure 1.5).

We can't really eliminate entropy from journalism and mass communication. As communicators (of any type) and as communicatees (of any type), about all we can do, as Norbert Wiener suggests in *The Human Use of Human Beings* (1954), is to try to create "islands of decreasing entropy," where messages retain or gain, rather than lose, data. We *know* this will never be fully successful, but the effort will go a long way toward making our messages better represent reality.

An Optimistic
Ending Note

So far in this introductory chapter we have painted a pretty bleak picture. Communication is a difficult process. Barriers impose themselves at every turn. People live in their own little communication worlds. Mechanical and semantic noises are ever-present. Each of us is isolated by thickets of ideology, economics, and politics, and finding our way through such differences is often impossible.

But the story doesn't end here. There is a brighter side to this business of communication. In spite of the obstacles, we can—and do—communicate. We establish common understandings with others. Maybe not completely, and maybe not with everybody, but *generally* we are successful communicators—especially in the practical, everyday business of living. Personal, familial, social and national progress is an empirical sign of communication success. We normally can give directions, get what we want, impart and receive information, deal with complex matters and participate in analysis and interpretation. Our methods may be flawed and inadequate on occasion. Our skills may be wanting. Our minds may encode and decode fuzzily at times. And our messages may be dysfunctional or even lost. But generally, we *do* establish a commonness of understanding. We *do* communicate.

To be sure, we often misunderstand, as well. Our symbols clash and are distorted, or they never trigger any meaning at all. But even in mass communication, we normally do quite well. We understand most messages we receive from television, newspapers, books, radio and magazines. From time to time we hear messages that we don't really understand, but we *think* we understand, and that's understanding enough for us. The fact that several of us may hear the same television speech and then proceed to argue about what was said and what was "meant" indicates that *somebody* has misunderstood the speaker's message. It could be that we *all* have.

So we are really never sure that we communicate *perfectly*. But we muddle through pretty well. Since what is in one person's mind is supposed to be reproduced in another person's mind, we can never be certain that pure communication has taken place. Why not? Because of the uncertainty. No

Mass communication works, despite obstacles.

method currently exists for comparing a message in Mind *A* with a message in Mind *B*. The messages aren't in the two minds at the same moment, so by the time Mind *A* gets feedback from Mind *B* and hears what message it has received, Mind *A* has forgotten its precise complete original message and therefore cannot compare the two messages—and certainly *nobody else* can. (And if you can understand the last sentence, it lends proof to the fact that communication is not really as difficult as it is often reputed to be.)

Communicators and audiences are constantly playing the social game of "communication." It's a lot of fun, but it can be very serious business. In the next chapter, we will look more closely at communicators and audiences, primarily as they relate to mass communication. The so-called mass media are the institutionalized "persons" (communicators) that project their megamessages into the midst of mass audiences with the intention of achieving specific ends.

What is communication? Have we answered the question? Probably not to the satisfaction of everyone. We do know that communication is a "process" or an "event" that takes place between or among communicants when symbols and signs (such as words, gestures, flags) are consciously used to stimulate meaning. The actual mechanism—what takes place, how, and why—of communication is extremely vague, even mystical. So let's now become more prosaic and turn our attention in the next chapter to the communicants (the senders and receivers of messages) and also to the messages themselves.

Retrospective

Communication, whether one-on-one, small-group or mass, is complex and difficult. Its purpose is to establish a commonness or community of understanding between or among persons. One can study the communication process by considering this question: Who says what to whom through what channel with what effect? The process takes place in a context consisting of these basic aspects: an encoder (formulator), a communicator (sender), a channel (means of transmission), a message, a communicatee (receiver) and a decoder (final interpreter or receptor of message). Acting on the message are various distractions or barriers (noises). The response to a message is called feedback, which is very important to the success of communication.

Mass communication is most difficult because the communicator is sending messages to a large, scattered, anonymous, heterogeneous audience from which feedback is difficult to obtain. Messages are always stronger in the sender's mind than they are by the time they get to the receiver. Information is lost along the way; this process of loss is called message entropy. So as we have seen in this chapter, communication is not simple; there is always something omitted, something not clearly understood.

Questions

1. What is mass communication, and how does it differ from other types of communication?
2. What is the difference between interpersonal communication and intrapersonal communication? How are they related (mutually necessary)?
3. What would be an "ideal" interpersonal communication situation—one in which there would be the best chance for a common understanding to be established?
4. What are the main characteristics of a mass audience?
5. What are the main elements (for example, the channel) of a communication situation?
6. Describe the main noises that tend to frustrate communication. What are some other impediments to effective communication?

Suggested Readings

Berlo, D. K. *The Process of Communication.* New York: Holt, Rinehart and Winston, 1960.

Birdwhistle, R. L. *Kinesics and Context: Essays in Body Motion Communication.* Philadelphia: University of Pennsylvania Press, 1970.

DeFleur, M. L., and Ball-Rokeach, Sandra. *Theories of Mass Communication.* New York: McKay, 1975.

Gall, John. *Systemantics: How Systems Work and Especially How They Fail.* New York: Pocket Books, 1975.

Gerbner, George. "Toward a General Model of Communication," *AV Communication Review* 4 (1956): 175.

Harms, L. S. *Human Communication: The New Fundamentals.* New York: Harper & Row, 1974.

Howe, Reuel L. *The Miracle of Dialogue.* New York: Seabury Press, 1963.

Korzybski, Alfred. *Science and Sanity.* Lakeville, Conn.: Institute of General Semantics, 1962.

Lasswell, Harold D. "The Structure and Function of Communication in Society." In *The Communication of Ideas,* edited by Lyman Bryson. New York: Harper & Row, 1948.

McLuhan, Marshall. *Understanding Media: The Extensions of Man.* New York: McGraw-Hill, 1965.

McQuail, D., and Windahl, S. *Communication Models.* New York: Longman, 1980.

Merton, Robert K. *Social Theory and Social Structure.* Glencoe, Ill.: Free Press, 1957.

Schramm, Wilbur. "How Communication Works." In *The Process and Effects of Mass Communication,* edited by W. Schramm. Urbana: University of Illinois Press, 1954.

Severin, W. J., and Tankard, J. W., Jr. *Communication Theories.* New York: Longman, 1988.

Westley, B. H., and MacLean, M. "A Conceptual Model for Communication Research," *Journalism Quarterly* 34 (1957): 32–35.

Wiener, Norbert. *The Human Use of Human Beings.* New York: Avon Books, 1954.

Communicators and Audiences

You're sitting in a Las Vegas nightclub, waiting for the comedian to come on stage. You should be feeling mellow, ready for an evening's entertainment. But you're miffed because your date has done nothing but argue all evening. Or you're distracted because dinner cost more than you expected and you aren't sure you have enough money to get home. Or you're disturbed because the people at the table behind you are talking too loudly. The drums roll and the comedian bounds onto the stage. You listen for a few minutes, but the comedian's routines don't seem funny. Why aren't the jokes funny? Maybe the comedian isn't any good. Maybe you're in no mood to listen. Either way, the communication situation is a failure.

Or you're sitting in a classroom, waiting for a professor to begin the day's studies. You open your notebook and prepare to take notes on new ideas. The professor begins to mumble, or perhaps she speaks brilliantly, but you're just not in the mood to listen. The only notations you put in your notebook are doodles. Another communication opportunity is lost.

Communicators and audiences are symbiotic; they need each other. But often they don't seem to recognize this fact. Communicators gush forth their messages as if there were no audience. And, for their part, audiences pay little or no attention to the communicators, encoding instead their own ideas or their own messages, which they will gush forth as soon as they have the chance. Thus, all too frequently, the message gets lost in a battle for domination between the communicants. Look at TV shows such as "Crossfire" for extreme examples of this situation. Nobody wants to listen; everybody wants to talk. Words tend to dominate communication, and there is little concern for the message itself.

In focusing on communicators and audiences, it is also necessary to say something about the message itself. Encoding and decoding messages is extremely difficult, largely because of propaganda and semantic noise, which attack truth and meaning and compromise message success. So, when we discuss the message later in this chapter, we will concentrate on truth, objectivity, propaganda, and general semantics. Then we'll conclude with a closer look at the receivers of the messages, the audience.

Communicators: The Senders

All communication begins with the communicator, who has something to impart, encodes it, and transmits it. Communicators are not communicators because they encode; we all do a great deal of encoding, but we keep most of it to ourselves. Communicators are communicators because they *send* their encoded messages to somebody else. Sending, of course, is one thing; encoding the message well so as to improve its chance of being received and understood is another.

What the communicator *can* do, of course, to improve communication is to make sure he or she is thinking clearly about the content of the message; encode or formulate the message with as little semantic noise as possible; and know all that can be known about the intended audience. On the other end, the communicatee (receiver) is not a passive vessel; he or she must make an effort to "milk" the content data of the message as thoroughly as possible for the proper *meaning*.

In addition, it often is helpful for the receiver to know as much about the sender as possible. If we know Dan Rather's politics and ideology—something of his background, interests, and values—then we can better understand his network news presentation and commentary. We can even make allowances for certain emphases and omissions, smiles, and gestures that we observe in his telecast. So it is, perhaps, almost as important for the receiver to know about the communicator as the other way around.

Communicators as Institutional Persons

The mass communicator, unlike small-group communicators, is *institutionalized*, as sociologists say. In other words, he or she is part of an organized system of communication, one intended to serve both the medium and society. Every mass medium is a social institution; all mass media taken together form a social institution ("the media"). The communicators (reporters and editors working for a newspaper, for example) are part of this institution; they make up (with other personnel, facilities and equipment) the institutional *structure*. Here we have a big operation, and the mass communicator is a cog in the system, playing a part in the collection, production and distribution of mass-oriented messages.

Functionaries: Institutional Instruments

Mass communicators are often called *functionaries*—instruments through which the media as institutions achieve their purposes, fulfill their reason for being, and serve their own and social objectives. These communicators may find it necessary to blend their own personal objectives into those of their medium; they may have to compromise their values here and there. In short, the communicators must facilitate the objectives of the medium—which are, in the United States, the policies determined by the owners and directors of that medium.

Being a functionary doesn't mean that communicators are devoid of some freedom or that they are mere puppets in the hands of media bosses. Actually, they exercise considerable freedom in determining many message matters: *what* and *how much* will be communicated; *how* the message will be formulated; and often *when* it will be sent. But they are constrained by other institutional considerations, such as management biases, beliefs and decisions; economic considerations; peer pressure and the tendency to mimic what other media are doing; the pressure of wanting promotions or salary increases; and the desire not to stray too far outside the medium's public image or the public's expectations.

Communicator Diversity and Loyalties

Communicators of many kinds can and do manage to work together very well. Within one television station, for instance, you might find some newspeople with either a neutralist (reflective) demeanor or a leadership (directive) tendency. In other words, communicators who are rather passive exist alongside more forceful ones. Introverts work with extroverts, fact reporters with interpretative reporters, objectivists with subjectivists, idealists with realists, conservatives with liberals, specialists with generalists.

Mass communicators, however, tend to gravitate to media that are compatible with their personal values. For example, few writers who work for the *Washington Post* would want to work for the *National Enquirer,* and few writers for *The Nation* (liberal) would want to write for *National Review* (conservative). So we can say that, generally, a mass communicator has a loyalty to his or her own personal value. In addition, communicators may feel a loyalty to one or more of the following:

1. the medium itself—concern for the reputation, good name, and quality of the medium;
2. the "truth"—concern for story integrity and the concept of "objectivity";
3. the audience—concern for the receivers of their messages and concern for the "people's right to know."

In addition to these three loyalties, the communicator may be inclined to support one of the following: the political or general ideological position of the medium; his or her own political position; his or her general religious or moral affinities; or his or her concern with personal security and economic gain. Of course, several of these interests can operate simultaneously. Although they are not mutually exclusive, generally one of them will dominate during a particular period of the communicator's life. However, except perhaps in the case of an *ideologue* (a fanatical devotee to an ideology), these positions and loyalties usually blend. Whatever the communicator's inclinations, they may well influence the messages formulated and sent.

Communicator Concerns

Institutional or mass communicators are concerned people. They have to be. Their messages must be planned and focused for a specific objective. They do not carelessly toss around unstructured messages. They want big audiences, and they want to have an impact. Most of them want to make society better. They see themselves as producing a product that the public either wants or needs. And they see themselves as social facilitators—guardians and persuaders—helping to hold society together while moving it forward.

Self-Image. Mass communicators also see themselves as gatekeepers, agenda-setters, watchdogs for the public, and power-brokers. And, indeed, they are all of these. They provide reality (and much unreality) to the public, determining what to let through the gate of their media and what to stop. They are the basic shapers of the public concern; they set the social agenda, telling us what to consider important by the very fact of selecting which events and issues to expose. They are, at least to some degree, guardians of the public interest, keeping an eye on the excesses of government and the wrongdoings of other social institutions. And, certainly, they are powerful; they can bestow fame and fortune through focusing attention on certain people, and to some extent they can make "nonpersons" of others by ignoring them. In a real sense, they have both the first and the last word in public discourse.

Functions. Communicators are concerned about their functions, too, and we will elaborate on that concern in the next chapter. Here we will merely note that they see themselves as important in many areas, especially in three main areas: (1) disseminating factual information, (2) assisting the public in understanding this information, and (3) entertaining the public. Often these three are referred to as the *news,* the *analysis,* and the *entertainment* functions of the media. It is in fulfilling these three functions that the communicators also serve as gatekeepers, agenda-setters, watchdogs, and power-brokers.

Journalistic communicators are mainly concerned with the first two areas; their messages center on the *news* and *analysis of* this news. Other media communicators (motion picture directors, for example, or the editors and writers of romance magazines) are primarily concerned with *entertaining* their audiences. Information and entertainment often overlap, of course; there are many audience members who find information or news entertaining, and there are many communicators who are adept at infusing their entertainment messages with substantial informational content. The line between news and entertainment is blurring rapidly.

Persuaders and Guardians. Then there are communicators such as editors and writers for political, ideological, or issue-oriented journals (publications such as *Christian Century, Human Events,* and *Commentary*) who are largely in the business of *persuasion.* Advertising communicators and public relations practitioners are also basically persuaders. And ever-increasing in popularity and impact are the televangelists (the TV preachers) who are also in the business of persuasion. Other persuaders include columnists and editorial writers, although, like televangelists, they also inform, interpret and entertain. These days persuasive communication is a big part of the mass media.

Many mass communicators will tell you that they also serve as guardians of the public interest, watching out for public officials and others who might be corrupt and who might damage the public polity. But to quote an old Roman sage: "Quis custodiet ipsos custodes?" Communicators may see themselves as public guardians, but many citizens would indeed like to know "who is guarding us against these guardians?"

Some Communicator Characteristics

Communicators seem to have one common trait: concern. Let's take a closer look at some of these concerned, institutional communicators who work through the media.

Who are the mass communicators? Where do they come from? What are their political orientations? Where were they educated? We really don't have many answers to our questions. Mass communicators tell us everything they can dig up about others, their backgrounds, beliefs and values, but the communicators remain mystery people. We see them constantly on the television screen and in the movies, and we know many of them from their bylines and pictures in newspapers and magazines. We hear their voices on radio, on tape and on recordings. The fact is that we have only a vague notion about the makeup of these mass communicators who are constantly competing for our attention.

We can infer certain things about them from their use of language, their appearance, their voices, and their ideas and emphases. A popular conception of mass communicators is that they have a facility with words, that they are usually forceful, dynamic personalities, that they manifest a certain social interest, that they often seem to have some bias that is hard to keep hidden, that they are often ideologues or true believers, that they are somewhat self-possessed if not outright cocky and arrogant, and that they seem to want to be in the public eye and to expose others to their information, ideas, and opinions. We can also see (at least through television) that they are mainly Anglo-Saxon, male, middle to upper class, confident and eager to be heard.

The Rothman-Lichter Study. From time to time, some academic or formal studies purport to give us a profile of mass communicators. For instance, in the 1980s, two professors—Robert Lichter of George Washington University and Stanley Rothman of Smith College—provided us a look at 240 "media elites" (leading mass communicators). The researchers interviewed these elite communicators at ten prestigious media outlets such as CBS, NBC, the *Washington Post, The Wall Street Journal, Time* and *Newsweek.* What Lichter and Rothman found in their hour-long interviews was interesting.

Some of the results: Only 8 percent attended church or synagogue weekly; 86 percent never or seldom attended any form of religious service; at least 80 percent supported Democratic candidates; they were considered "on the left" ideologically (by 7 to 1) by their co-workers; 80 percent favored abortion on demand; 95 percent believed that homosexuality is not wrong; 55 percent thought extramarital affairs are not immoral; and the overwhelming majority said they were endeavoring to change society—not simply to inform and entertain.

Rothman and Lichter (1986) present a generalized picture of the mass communicators that is not too flattering: antagonistic toward business, the military, fundamentalist preachers, the police, and working-class Americans who are not cosmopolitan. The two researchers also maintain that the elite mass communicators in their study are self-absorbed, generally ill-informed as to foreign affairs, know few or no foreign languages, are lacking in geographical and historical knowledge, are very defensive and have what might be called Machiavellian (ends-justifying-means) ethics.

As you might imagine, not everybody is satisfied with the Rothman-Lichter image of mass communicators. Typical of those who think the study has great weaknesses and little credibility is Herbert Gans, a Columbia University sociologist, who has been critical of the Rothman-Lichter research. He questions their data analysis and reporting procedures and maintains that they hid their political bias behind "a seemingly objective study," highlighting data that supported their position. Professor Gans also says that, even if all the information about personal backgrounds and alleged political opinions were true, no evidence was shown that this was relevant to the way the journalists *actually* present the news.

Other Studies of Mass Communications. Edith Efron, in the 1960s, made a controversial effort to uncover communicator traits. In two books on the subject, *The News Twisters* and *The Left-Leaning Antenna,* she found journalists to be generally biased in favor of liberal positions. Other studies have also concluded that mass communicators are mainly liberal, but the case is far from settled. There are many researchers, especially in the academic world, who see this conclusion as too simplistic, citing the vast numbers of small-town journalists in America who are conservatives.

A decade earlier than Rothman and Lichter, Gay Talese wrote a popular book, *The Kingdom and the Power,* about the *New York Times.* In it, he contributed some insights into the makeup of American journalists—at least those in metropolitan areas. According to Talese, communicators in journalism, like most people in the creative arts, tend to be more sensitive to social ills than is the average person. It is not really surprising, says Talese, that those who enter journalism are by and large liberals and not conservatives. He says that this is a widely held view and that it is probably correct.

Writing about news staffs of American newspapers, Talese contends that they come largely from the lower middle class. He thinks that this class instills a "drive, patience, and persistence to succeed" that serves reporters well in their work. He admits that blacks and minorities from many immigrant populations are underrepresented among mass communicators, but he attributes this mainly to the fact that these groups have traditionally been poor in English-language skills. Since the beginning of the 1970s when Talese was writing, the situation has undoubtedly changed, as more minorities (including women) have come into journalistic media. But there is no doubt but that most mass communicators still are middle-class white men who have a facility with language.

Although studies about the nature of communicators have been sparse in the past, there is hope that much-needed information will begin to accumulate in the next few years. For example, in mid-1988, Professor Charles Self of the University of Alabama did a study of American and British journalists and suggested that they could be classified in five main ways: as the *confident type* with a dedication to social responsibility, as the *independent type* who is largely skeptical, as the *critical type* who wants to reform journalists' behavior, as the *service-oriented type* who wants news to be audience-oriented, and as the *new news-definition type* who feels news is too negative and needs changing. Dr. Self also provided considerable data on journalists—years of education, membership in organizations, and so forth.

Media "Stars." At least a few mass communicators have gone beyond the study profiles and have become more prominent in the public eye. Television people like Barbara Walters, Mary Alice Williams, Bryant Gumbel, Dan Rather, Ted Koppel, Connie Chung, Sam Donaldson, Tom Brokaw, Diane Sawyer, Bernard Shaw, and Mike Wallace have become better known (seen and heard by far more Americans) than are leading government officials—including the president.

Syndicated columnists such as Nicholas von Hoffman, Russell Baker, Roland Evans and Robert Novak, George Will, Erma Bombeck, William F. Buckley, Ellen Goodman, Mike Royko and Lewis Grizzard have given substantial voice to personal print reporters and commentators. In addition to their columns, these people, among many other print reporters and commentators, have become familiar faces through appearances on television, where they regularly appear on such shows as CNN's "Crossfire" and PBS's "Firing Line" and "The McLaughlin Group."

Dr. Ralph L. Lowenstein writes about these "stars" in *Media, Messages, and Men*. He comments:

> It is the *reporter-personality* that draws the premium salary, especially if he is syndicated or in network television. Novelists abandon fiction for subjective news assignments by magazines. Reporters, rather than editors or publishers, run for elective office. And television anchormen on "location" at political rallies are apt to draw larger crowds than major political candidates (1971, p. 97).

It may well be that as mass communication has developed over the years and has become ever more flashy in its grab for larger audiences, it has also become more prone to persuade and less prone to deal in straight news. We watch much "controversy" reporting on TV these days—explosions set by terrorists throughout the world, congressional investigations of various persons, political and social unrest in Eastern Europe, fighting and rumors of further fighting in the Middle East and Central America.

And we watch as news reporters and commentators, as well as "specialists" from academia and elsewhere, tell us what the president said and what he meant (and what he should have said, but didn't say), what the Serbians of the former Yugoslavia are "really like," and what is likely to happen to the U.S. naval bases in foreign countries. Perceptive American TV viewers (and readers of the press) find it easier and easier to recognize, in this interpretative news and analysis, certain biases and persuasive agenda of the communicators.

So here we are—at the place where we can look more closely at language as it infects messages with propaganda and as it tends to obscure meaning with semantic disorders. First, propaganda.

Communicators seldom or never speak of themselves as "propagandists." The term has a negative connotation, largely brought about by its popularization during wars—especially those since World War I. Harold Lasswell focused much attention on the subject by writing about propaganda in the 1920s, and his 1934 definition of propaganda is still a popular one: "Propaganda in the broadest sense is the technique of influencing human action by the manipulation of representations. These representations may take spoken, written, pictorial or musical form."

Propaganda: Playing with the Truth

Propaganda is normally thought of in the context of war. In World War II, propaganda was used on both sides—Goebbels' Nazi posters and "planted" news stories, Hitler's massive Nuremberg rallies, Leni Riefenstahl's powerful Nazi documentary films, the radio broadcasts of Tokyo Rose, Hollywood's patriotic war movies, and Kate Smith's songs. Yet the term itself comes from the Roman Catholic Church. In the 1600s with the setting up of the "Congregatio de Propaganda Fide" (Congregation for the Propagation of the Faith), the term entered common usage. But, of course, propaganda itself (not the term) has undoubtedly been used since the beginning of social discourse. Some would say that it was even present in the Garden of Eden, and certainly wartime propaganda was talked about, studied, and used by the Chinese well before the birth of Christ.

Serious concern for the study of propaganda did not begin in the United States until just prior to World War II, when social scientists such as Hadley Cantril, Leonard Doob, Edward L. Bernays and Harold Lasswell played a significant part. In 1937, the Institute for Propaganda Analysis was established, with Cantril as president. The Institute hoped to educate the American people on the detection of propaganda, so that Hitler's propaganda minister Josef Goebbels would find it more difficult to influence them. (The Institute ceased functioning soon after the United States entered World War II.)

The Institute was privately funded (by the Twentieth Century Fund), and its leadership was composed of outstanding social scientists and other intellectuals concerned about propaganda. Of the various books, pamphlets and other material turned out by the Institute, the most popular was *The Fine Art of Propaganda* (1939), edited by Alfred McClung Lee and Elizabeth Briant Lee, which presented seven propaganda devices with examples of each. These devices proved to be useful ways of describing propaganda and made their way into textbooks and public school curricula —where they are often still found. We'll look at them after we establish a working definition of propaganda.

Toward a Definition of Propaganda

So what? you may ask. So what, indeed! Propaganda is all around us, luring us to accept ideas, causes, candidates, products, ideologies and positions. Out there somewhere is a communicator who wants you to accept his or her position and take a certain action as a result. Of course, not only *mass* communicators are involved in propaganda; your friends and neighbors are, too. Persuaders are all around us, some of them quite unskilled and haphazard in their efforts, but persuaders nevertheless.

In this section, however, we are focusing on propagandists who are working through the mass media. These mass communicators who deal in propaganda may include journalists and nonjournalists alike. What they have in common is this: a will to *persuade* us and to *get us to take a certain action*. These two characteristics are crucial to a definition of propaganda: changing (or causing) beliefs and precipitating action.

The propagandist is *intentionally* persuasive. And he or she usually has a *selfish* motivation, wanting others to accept something he or she personally values. The propagandist is frequently also *devious*. His or her messages are seldom "open" (forthright and full), but are "closed" (unbalanced, biased, carefully selective in content). The propagandist does not want to enlighten or inform us, but, rather, *persuade* us. If tampering with the facts and indulging in emotional appeals is necessary, so be it. You can see signs of this characteristic in the political ads of almost every election campaign.

Perhaps an acronym might help summarize the basic characteristics of propaganda. We call it the "P-A-S-I-D" formula, and it goes like this:

Propaganda is—

P   ersuasive

A   ction-oriented

S   elfish

I   ntentional

D   evious

The Seven Basic Devices

Earlier we mentioned the Institute for Propaganda Analysis and its popular list of seven propaganda devices (see Figure 2.1). Here they are in abbreviated form:

1. *Name-calling.* The propagandist gives good or bad names to products, projects, programs or candidates, without providing any substantive data or evidence to support use of the name. The idea is to rely on a simple "ad hominem" appeal—appealing to one's prejudices by calling names, presenting superficial labels. After all, if we call someone a "pinko" or a "Communist," some people will believe that there "must be something to it."

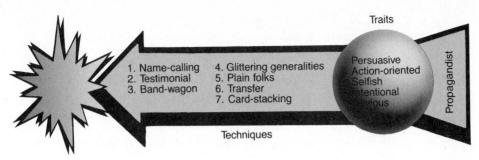

Figure 2.1
Propaganda Traits and Techniques

2. *Testimonial.* The propagandist gets someone to testify to the worth of what he or she is "pushing." A professional basketball player tells us how good a breakfast cereal is; a well-known Hollywood star touts the "great taste" of beef. Use of this technique asks the audience member to like a certain thing *because* someone well-known says he or she likes it.

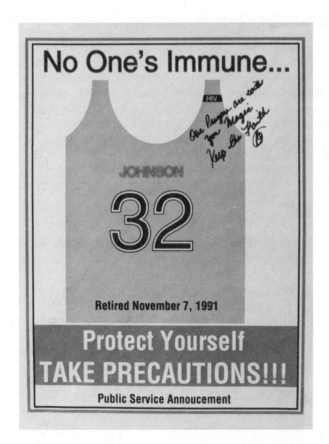

Advertisements often use celebrity testimonials, such as this campaign promoting "safe sex" that features the Los Angeles Lakers' "Magic" Johnson.

3. *Bandwagon.* "Everyone's doing it; you should do it, too." Here the propagandist is appealing to our social instinct, our desire to belong and not to be left out. It is a rather crude device, but it is effective. After all, implies the propagandist, we should not "throw away our vote" by voting for a loser; we need to get on the "bandwagon" that is rolling to victory.

4. *Glittering generalities.* The propagandist uses vague generalizations and "virtue words" (*progressive, loyal, red-blooded Americans, patriotic*) to create a positive image in the minds of audience members. Of course, such generalities can be of the type to create negative images, also. The idea is to plant emotional images devoid of fact or evidence.

5. *Plain folks.* This device is an associational appeal, an attempt by the propagandist to convince the audience that he or she is "one of them." The candidate throws a little hay in Iowa, walks among the chickens and corn, maybe even kisses a baby or two, shakes hands, slaps people on the back. "I understand your problems, people," he or she says in effect. "I am not aloof from you; I know your needs, and I want to help."

6. *Transfer.* The propagandist, by this device, attempts to *transfer* the respect that people of the audience have for some symbol over to a project, product or candidate. The politician "wraps himself in the flag" (especially in certain parts of the country) or perhaps has a Bible on the podium; the professor always comes to class with a stack of books. An image is being created by this simple device, and its associational impact is extremely effective.

7. *Card-stacking.* In this most important device, the "cards" are stacked against the truth. Only the propagandist (the dealer) knows how the cards will come up. This technique is most difficult to detect, because it uses the most devious tricks: for example, lying, biasing, telling half-truths, exaggerations, outright censorship and general distortion. Candidate A says, "My opponent's position is such-and-such"; Candidate B says, "My position is *not* such-and-such." The voter doesn't know which candidate to believe.

Propaganda devices constantly change and new ones are invented. Many of the seven devices listed above can be merged and hybrid devices spawned almost at will. The most successful propagandists are amateur or professional psychologists, always keeping ahead of their audiences and skillfully blending their propaganda potions, taking the sophistication of their audiences into consideration.

Journalistic Propaganda

All right, you say, but is journalism propagandistic? Yes. Certainly not all of it, but much of it is. We don't like to think so, of course. After all, is not journalism to be believed, respected, trusted? Isn't journalism in the "truth" business, not the propaganda business? Although opinion and editorializing have always been a part of journalism, the basic image or stereotype of journalism (news, at least) has traditionally been one of factualness, reliability, and trust.

Advertisements also use the "transfer" technique to suggest glitter by association.

We are considering journalists as propagandists in the sense that they "propagate" or spread their own biases and opinions—attempting (intentionally) to affect the attitudes and actions of their audiences. Large numbers of journalists, including so-called "straight news" reporters, indulge in propaganda if they intend to lead, influence or sway their audiences in certain predetermined ways.

Following are a few propaganda techniques specifically used in journalism:

- *Creation of stereotypes:* The simplification of reality; the presentation of people and events as one-dimensional and static.
- *Presentation of opinion as fact:* Giving opinion disguised as fact (e.g., "President X was unorganized and rambling in his speech yesterday").
- *Speaking through sources:* Getting others to give opinions that are carefully selected to agree with the reporter's own position.
- *Biased attribution:* Using loaded verbs and adverbs to present a negative or positive aura to quotations, direct or indirect. For example, some speakers "snap"; some "snarl"; others "observe"; and still others simply "say."
- *Information selection:* Biasing by decision to use certain facts and to ignore or play down others. If there is a pattern to this choice, and if it is intentially done, then it is propaganda.
- *News management:* Not "censorship" (a term that is reserved for the government), but a mass communicator's decision to omit a story completely—or to leave certain information out of a story, often in spite of a stated belief in the "people's right to know."
- *Use of labels:* Using terms that have "opinion content" rather than "factual content." For example, one story's "terrorists" or "guerillas" might be represented as "democratic rebels" or "freedom fighters"

Jacques Ellul:
Propaganda Can
Be Truthful

We normally think of propaganda as "tall stories," or a program containing lies, but as the French sociologist Jacques Ellul (1965) points out, this is not necessarily the case. Perhaps it was Hitler who popularized this belief with his idea that the bigger the lie, the greater the chance of its being believed. The concept of propaganda as lies is a dangerous one: When we deem something to be true, we are likely to be convinced that it is not propaganda. It may well be. A skeptical or cynical attitude may also be harmful. We believe nothing our opponent says because *everything* he has told us must necessarily be untrue. Then when this opponent or enemy demonstrates that what has been said is true, we are put at a disadvantage in the propaganda war.

For a long time, Ellul says, the effectiveness of truth has been recognized by propagandists. What he means is this: The truth that is effective—that "pays off"—is in the realm of facts. And as Ellul says, facts can be manipulated; facts do not equal truth. It is the whole message that must be considered, not just the recognition of certain facts. A message can be accurate without being truthful, and certainly a message can be accurate and still be propaganda.

We must remember, reminds Ellul, that propaganda in essence is an enterprise "for perverting the significance of events and for insinuating false intentions." And such propaganda can be accomplished with truthful statements. It is not so much what is in the message, but how its "truth" is presented and how much of the truth is left out.

In his seminal book *Propaganda* (1965) Ellul analyzes the many traits of propaganda and shows its broad scope and wide use in the world today (and throughout history). And he gives us a definition that deviates considerably from most which have been given by American students of propaganda. Here it is: "Propaganda is a set of methods employed by an organized group that wants to bring about the active or passive participation in its actions of a mass of individuals, psychologically unified through psychological manipulations and incorporated in an organization."

elsewhere. Question: What is the journalist's intent—to present them favorably or unfavorably?

- *Vague authority:* The use of such introductory portions of interview questions as "Many people are saying that you were not honest in your remarks yesterday. How would you answer them?" ("Which" people? Name them, please. Are you, Mr./Ms. Reporter, simply fabricating that lead-in question?)

- *Selective factuality:* Using specific, untampered-with information and quotes in regard to some persons and "sanitized" or doctored material from others, depending on the intention to give negative or positive image. (Example: "The governor said, 'I ain't going to put up with this damned business any longer'" *as opposed to* "The governor said that he was determined not to have the Senate practice continue.")

- *One-person cross-section:* Projecting to a whole group the opinions of one or two persons. (Example: "New York City residents are rallying around the mayor. Cab driver Pedro Martinez expressed their sentiments when he said. . . .")

- *The "not available" ploy:* Putting into a story, usually at the very end, the statement that a certain person did not respond to some criticism (e.g., "Sheriff Hogan was not available for comment"). This device makes one wonder, at the least, *why* he was unavailable, and how many times the reporter tried to reach him. Was the sheriff in the men's room when called? Was he on vacation in Hawaii? Was he "hiding out" or what? The impact, in any case, is negative.

Journalists have many other propaganda devices at hand, several of which are examples of the seven devices of the Institute for Propaganda Analysis. The journalist can appeal to authority (testimonial), can deal in half-truths and distortions (card-stacking), and can slip into "ad hominem" (name-calling). Journalists can also bias photographs (a very subtle device) and mislead the reader through headlines.

So just what does all this mean? It means, for one thing, that audience members should be skeptical of journalistic messages; they should know that journalists (like everyone else) have axes to grind. Although good journalists grind very few, it is probably safe to say that mass communicators do originate propaganda (not much) and spread the propaganda of others (quite a lot) to a greater degree than most of us believe.

The Search for Truth

Propaganda often makes it difficult for audiences to know the truth. Of course, if there were no propaganda, the audience would still not know *all* the truth. To do so is impossible. The whole business of journalistic communication is to provide *some* of the truth, and this it does. The audience member who insists on the "whole truth and nothing but the truth" is unrealistic. But a conscientious reporter should *try* to provide as much truth as possible.

Journalists must select. They must be subjective, in the sense of deciding

Future Focus Propaganda: The Promise for the Future

Propaganda throughout the world is a potent force—just how potent we don't really know. Billions of dollars are being spent on it each year (many more billions if we count advertising), and the investment in changing minds and enhancing images continues to grow.

Each year it seems that the trend toward using news channels for propaganda increases. Hiding propaganda in what purports to be impartial news is, of course, very effective, and this trend can be expected to continue into the future. The amount of propaganda—of all kinds—is being transmitted with increasing frequency by the world news media. As Ben Bagdikian, in his *The Information Machines* (1971), has said, "There are growing numbers of men who understand how news is generated, organized, and transmitted, and it would be unintelligent of them if they did not use it to their own advantage."

In coming years, propaganda will be more pervasive for several reasons: (1) more channels will be available for reaching more people, (2) nations and private enterprises will provide more resources to persuasive communication, (3) communicators are becoming more skilled in the use of propaganda, (4) stakes are becoming increasingly high in world markets and in international relations generally, and (5) mass communicators are more culturally sensitive and sophisticated in their appeals across national borders and across cultures.

what to put in a story and what to leave out. So really, journalism is a *subjective* enterprise in spite of the loyalty many journalists have to *objectivity*. Journalists, therefore, cannot get at the total or complete truth.

Levels of Truth. Let us look briefly at five "levels" of truth, three of them in the province of the journalistic communicator and two of them beyond the scope of journalistic control (see Figure 2.2).

1. *Transcendental truth:* Truth with a capital "T." The journalist cannot know this; it is beyond all of us. It is the complete, overshadowing Truth, the Truth that goes beyond the potential of a human being to grasp.

2. *Potential truth:* The aspects of the Truth that are in the grasp of human perception and rationality. The journalist can, if diligent enough, obtain potential truth for inclusion in a story. This level, though it is never really reached by the journalist, can serve as an ideal or goal.

3. *Selected truth:* The part of the potential truth that is abstracted or selected from reality by the reporter. It is the selected truth that is found in the notes, tapes and mental perceptions of the reporter.

4. *Reported truth:* The part of the selected truth that actually gets into the reporter's story and is conveyed to the audience.

5. *Audience-perceived truth:* The lowest level of truth, that part of the reported truth that gets into the mind of the audience member.

The journalist has little to say about the first and fifth levels of truth. Transcendental Truth eludes the journalist, and just how an audience member perceives what truth there is in the story is outside the purview of the reporter. So, in concluding this brief section, we must say that truth is always limited, and that the care and thoroughness of a reporter at the third

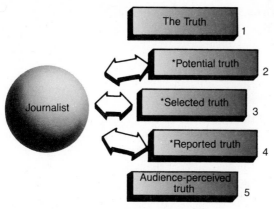

Levels
1. <u>The Truth</u> (transcendental)—Journalist can't reach.
2. <u>Potential</u>—Possibility exists for the journalist to reach.
3. <u>Selected</u>—Part of the potential truth that journalist selects.
4. <u>Reported</u>—Part of the selected truth (notes, perceptions, etc.) that the journalist actually puts in the story.
5. <u>Audience-perceived</u>—Part of the reported truth that actually is received by audience; journalist has no control over it.
*"Journalistic" levels of truth: Levels 2, 3, and 4

Figure 2.2
Levels of Truth as They Relate to the Journalist

level has much to do with the truth at the fourth level. And, of course, ultimately the thoroughness of truth in the fourth level will have some impact on the final perceptions of the audience member at the fifth level.

Now we turn from a search for truth (by both the communicator *and* the audience member) to a search for meaning—a concern with semantics, which is the study of meaning. **General semantics** is the study of the way we are affected by language, how it causes us to think and act. General semantics is important to both the encoder and the decoder of messages, for language can easily be misused and misunderstood at both ends of the communication process.

The founder of general semantics was Alfred Korzybski, a Polish count who came to the United States in 1915. He was a broadly educated man, but was trained as an engineer. Long interested in language and the impact it had on people's lives, he began seminars in the 1930s just off the University of Chicago campus in what he called "general semantics." But he was never a member of the academic community, for his cross-discipline approach was suspect in the minds of establishment scholars.

Korzybski's primary work was *Science and Sanity: An Introduction to Non-Aristotelian Systems and General Semantics* (1933). This difficult book, is the real basis for all general semantics writing and lecturing. In it,

Semantics: Searching for Meaning

Korzybski argued for a scientific approach to the study of language and maintained that much mental illness results from misusing language. Language, he said, affects the way we think, and thought affects the way we act.

Basic Principles of General Semantics

When you read the following principles espoused by general semanticists, you may think they are nothing more than common-sense concepts. But, as Korzybski was fond of saying, common sense is not as common as we normally think. An awareness of these principles in our everyday communication activities should help us avoid many common mistakes with language. Mass communicators, especially, should find them of value.

The "Etc." Concept. It is impossible to say everything about anything. When asked who a person is, we may respond: "He is a reporter for *The Christian Science Monitor.*" So he "is"; but he may also be very much more (e.g., graduate of certain schools, resident of a city and state, husband, father and son). In using language, we must leave out much significant information; there is always more to say, so in essence we can figuratively put "etc." at the end of every message.

Static Language Versus Dynamic Reality. Reality is constantly changing; our language largely stays the same. The University of Michigan today is not what it was in 1940 although it retains the same label. Richard Nixon today is not the same Nixon that was involved in the Watergate affair. China today is not the China of May–June 1989, when democracy fever was rising and falling. General semanticists derived this principle of constant flux from the pre-Socratic philosopher Heraclitus, who said something like, "No man can step into the same river twice," the river never being *the* river that it was. One might even say, as a follower of Heraclitus once observed, that nobody can step into the same river *once,* since the person who is doing the stepping is constantly changing, even as he or she steps. In one sense, if one takes this notion too far, the conclusion would be that "nothing is ever anything" since it is always "in process."

Arab A Is Not Arab B. Members of the same group, race, religion, and so forth are discrete individuals; they are not the same. Thinking in stereotypes should be avoided.

Multivalued Orientation. It is unsophisticated, say general semanticists, to think in terms of either-or; we must eschew such a two-valued orientation. Short and tall. Good and bad. Beautiful and ugly. Conservative and liberal. Instead, we should think on a spectrum. We should try to be as discriminating as possible, making allowances for gradations of quality and quantity. Our language is basically "antonymic" (opposite-oriented), so we naturally think this way, say the general semanticists. But there is an overlap

in reality that is not present in language. How tall must a "short" person be before he is considered "tall"? Such questions indicate a basic weakness in our language usage.

The Map Is Not the Territory. The point here is that language does not equal reality. The word *cow* is not the cow, just as the map of Spain is not Spain. But we often confuse words (language) with things and react to them as if they are things. The implication here is also that our language usage is inadequate to depict reality, forcing us to distort and simplify reality.

Problems with Abstract Words. We should stay as low on the abstraction ladder as possible when communicating. We must avoid abstract words whenever possible, but when we do use them we should try to clarify the meanings we are giving to them. Such terms as *loyalty, profession, patriot, progressive, education* and *intelligence* are abstract, filled with *semantic noise.* Many terms that we use in this book are also abstract (e.g., *communication, journalism, propaganda, truth* and *responsibility*) and must be elaborated upon when they are mentioned. It is through examples and discussion that we give meaning for such terms.

It is not difficult to see that these principles of general semantics are indeed valuable for mass communicators, who can do much to improve their language usage by eliminating semantic noise and clarifying concepts. But what about the audience member? It is more difficult for this person who must deal with the message as it exists, especially if there is little or no chance for feedback. The audience member must live with the message that is received, never really certain about the intended meaning. However, a knowledge of general semantics will give audience members some understanding of the nature of language and the way communicators are apt to use it, thereby increasing the chance that the message will be understood. With this concern for understanding, we come to the audience.

Audiences: The Receivers

Messages are designed and destined for audiences—or at least *individuals* "out there" who can be called audience members. When we want to study or describe persons in a classroom or auditorium listening to a lecture, we can do so with some degree of success. We can, at least, count them and note their behavior during the lecture. And, if we desire, we can get their names and learn other information about them.

Knowing a mass audience is much more complex and difficult. Since such audiences are scattered, fluid, anonymous, unseen and diverse (heterogeneous), we cannot know much about their makeup. So we see that the very nature of a mass audience precludes careful analysis, although many scholars attempt to do it. Intuition plays a big part in giving us a feeling about audiences, how they are composed, who they are, where they are and what interests them, although empirical studies also are helpful in getting insights about them.

Two Main Audience Types

Although mass audiences are difficult to discuss because of their ever-changing and anonymous nature, one type of classification might be helpful in studying them. It is a binary typology based on complexity. One type of audience is the **general public audience;** it is very broad and extremely complex, a kind of all-encompassing, anonymous, massively heterogeneous and scattered mass of individuals. The other type of mass audience is smaller, more specialized, more homogeneous, and usually less anonymous. It is often called a **specialized audience.**

The General Public Audience. Some writers consider the general public audience mythical and unrealistic. Robert O'Hara (1961), for example, in his *Media for the Millions* calls such a mass audience "one of the great fallacies of mass communication." In several of her books, Ayn Rand contends that individual audience members are real, but that mass audiences are unreal. In spite of such skepticism, it does seem that the concept of the general public is meaningful to many and perhaps is the type of audience most think about when they talk of mass audiences.

Members of this general, amorphous audience have no sense of relationship with other members and feel little or nothing in common. They expose themselves to the mass media in an atomized and personal way and have no sense of camaraderie with others in the audience or general public. In this sense, at least, these audience members are more *independent* or *individualistic* in their exposure and response to the mass media than are members of the second main type of mass audience.

The Specialized Audience. The specialized audience, although scattered and to some degree anonymous and heterogeneous, is composed of persons who do have some common interest, political orientation or ideology that causes them to seek after similar messages—to be members of the same audience. They may even be related in certain psychological ways—wanting freedom from authority, for instance. Gustave LeBon (1969) labeled such groups "psychological crowds," not necessarily located in one place, but having a similar motivation.

Readers with specialized interests in economics, for instance, might well subscribe to *The Wall Street Journal*. They form a kind of mass audience, but at the same time a specialized one. The same should be said for those who watch opera on the Public Broadcasting System; without personally knowing each other, they can achieve a kind of cultural or intellectual cohesion with other like-minded audience members.

Audience members or segments of the "mass-mass" audience, as Ralph L. Lowenstein (1971) calls this general public audience, can also be classified in a useful trinary (three-part) way that focuses on the attitudes of the various audience segments. Let us, in conclusion, mention these three basic subgroups.

A Trinary Classification of Audiences

Another way to classify audiences and audience members is to look at their basic attitudes, their values, their interests, their philosophy of life. Since mass media must aim as much as possible at persons with similar interests and attitudes, journalists and other mass communicators want to isolate the basic segments of the general public audience, or Lowenstein's mass-mass audience. In this way, media can aim at specific cluster-types of persons representing sizable segments of the audience. (See Figure 2.3.) Such basic segments, of course, can be classified variously, but here is one fairly simple and useful *attitudinal* typology.

Attitudinal Illiterates. Many members of the attitudinal illiterate audience segment—probably the largest—can, indeed, read and write. Others cannot. But all of them have a negative attitude toward *words,* toward reading and writing and toward serious forms of broadcasting. These audience members adhere to the mass media in a very surface way, exposing themselves to the most superficial and action-oriented media messages. They seek entertainment and excitement in their media exposure. They are superficial message consumers, reading light material that gratifies emotional appetites and gravitating toward picture-oriented messages. They may read some headlines and certain action stories in newspapers, but basically they *do not like to read*.

These "illiterates" are not idea-oriented; they eschew analysis and in-depth stories. They are basically lookers and not readers, emotionalists rather than rationalists. Their communication world is turned inward—toward self-gratification. They are not message-sharers, except in a very narrow sense, for example, with their spouses or children.

Their native intelligence (IQ) and their formal education are related, but peripheral, factors in classifying them in this attitudinal illiterate class. They may have great mental capacities, even a formal education, but do not have the motivation, the interest or the energy to grapple with thoughtful and challenging media and messages. Again, it is their *attitude* that counts, not their capability.

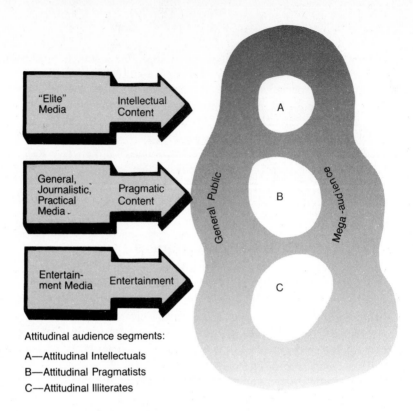

Figure 2.3
The Media and Their Audiences

Attitudinal audience segments:

A—Attitudinal Intellectuals

B—Attitudinal Pragmatists

C—Attitudinal Illiterates

Attitudinal Pragmatists. The attitudinal pragmatist is the one that mainstream American journalism and mass communication pays most attention to. These audience members are social beings, involving themselves in social affairs and being interested, therefore, in knowing what is going on in their communities and in the world. They are *social participators;* they give their time and energies to community activities, they run for office and vote. They have hobbies, travel, converse, argue, buy automobiles and build homes. They watch television; they read newspapers and magazines; they buy compact discs and other recordings; they listen to radio.

The Spanish philosopher Ortega y Gasset (1932) and more recently the American sociologist William H. Whyte (1956) have given us valuable insights into this pragmatic audience. Not lazy in their communication activities, these audience members make an effort to expose themselves to a wide variety of mass media messages—especially those that might be of practical help to them. They want to keep up with the Joneses, or get ahead of them. They want to make money; they want promotions. In short, they are success-oriented.

Since they are basically concerned with status, their ambitions cause them to be great consumers of mass messages, especially those that will give them useful information and helpful analysis. They are the main consumers of advertising. They want to be informed about world-affairs—if for no other reason than to *impress* others with their knowledge. They want to know how to build their own patios, repair their cars, sustain or gain good health, impress their bosses and live more satisfying lives.

Unlike the "illiterates," pragmatic audience members seek messages that will help them advance and live more usefully and happily in their communities. They are in some ways "snobs" but not the kind that isolate themselves from society. They are involved snobs with a kind of arrogant demeanor because they are *accomplishing something,* acquiring physical possessions, getting highly respected titles and associating with elite (highly respected in the community) friends and associates. They appear interested in news, ideas, and issues, perhaps not because they really are, but because it is practical for them to appear to be.

Attitudinal Intellectuals. Attitudinal intellectuals comprise the smallest segment of the mass audience. They are not necessarily the most "intelligent" members of the mass audience, but they have an intellectual attitude. They are concerned with issues, aesthetic matters, philosophy and problems. They are concept-oriented. They ask "Why?"—not simply "What?" They take serious things seriously. They are not drawn to frivolous, entertainment-oriented messages. The intellectual audience member is concerned with the broad strokes of human existence and not with practical, mundane and material aspects of life.

The intellectual is a thinker, an enjoyer of aesthetic quality, and is opposed to the whole *mass* concept. No wonder he or she disdains the mass messages of the mega-media, which are seen as pandering to the lowest common denominator. The intellectuals seek specialized and serious publications, recordings, and radio and television programs; whereas the pragmatic audience members seek serious material because they think it will help them progress in the practical world, the intellectual members embrace serious material for its own sake. And they like to be stimulated mentally. They enjoy thinking; and they want media messages that will stimulate them to thought.

Concluding Observations

We have seen that audience members can be classified in several useful ways. We can suggest several other ways: There are the cynics, the skeptics, the loners, the social adapters, the social misfits, the ideologues, the activists, the passivists. And, of course, we could mention audience types by age, sex, religion, politics, economic class, education and profession.

Perhaps we should make a few observations on the reasons, other than those mentioned in the above section, that certain types of audiences make certain message selections. Among the most important, of course, are these two: (1) the availability of the message, and (2) the potential for personal gain or satisfaction from it. And then there are such factors as state of health, political orientation, amount of leisure time, special interests and finances.

Let us consider a trio of motivational factors that turn people toward the media and their messages in the first place. First, there is *loneliness.* Many people are lonely and want to ease this sense of social estrangement, frustration, anxiety and even fear. So they turn to media messages. Second, there is *curiosity*. People are curious creatures; they want to know what is going on—what others are doing, saying and thinking. It may well be that curiosity is the main factor in a person's exposure to mass media messages. And, thirdly and finally, there is *self-aggrandizement*. They want to be informed and entertained. They want to be helped, and they desire information and other media material that will make them happy, wealthy, healthy and wise. In short, they want messages to help them practically, philosophically, psychologically and religiously.

In conclusion, we reiterate what was said earlier: It is very difficult to discuss audiences because of their amorphous character. But audiences are important, and we should know more about them. In a discussion of mass communication, the focus is usually on the *sender* and not on the *receiver* of messages. Perhaps the reason is that the sender's work is formalized and rewarded with money, whereas the receiver's job is informal, not in the public eye and basically anonymous.

About the only aspect of mass communication more difficult to deal with than audiences is something closely related: the impact that messages have on these audiences (or audience members). We will deal with that topic in Chapter 4, after we have considered the various functions of the mass media in Chapter 3.

Retrospective

There are many kinds of communicators and many kinds of audiences, which makes mass communication extremely difficult. Mass communicators are *institutionalized* people aiming their messages at broad general audiences or large specialized segments of the public. Communicators have various loyalties (such as to their medium or to their audiences) that impinge on personal orientation and ethics.

Propaganda is present in mass communication, sometimes conscious and negative (harmful) and sometimes positive (helpful). Mass media are not primarily propagandistic but do sometimes originate and more often channel propaganda to audiences. Communicators and communicatees should be able to recognize propaganda; journalists should try to get as close to truth as possible in their messages. Therefore, a knowledge of the principles of *general semantics,* which deals with meaning, and how language affects thought and action is helpful.

Audiences can be typed in many ways. One popular typology is *general public* audience and *specialized* audience. Another typology suggests three categories: *illiterate* audience, *pragmatic* audience and *intellectual* audience.

Questions

1. Specify at least six functions or purposes that mass communicators have set for themselves. Are the functions being fulfilled?
2. Communicators may feel major loyalty or commitment to several constituencies such as their medium. Name other areas in which such loyalties may be placed.

3. Give the major findings of the Rothman-Lichter study of media elites. How would you make a case that the findings are not really helpful in describing American journalists?

4. Discuss the main characteristics of propaganda, listing the seven main devices. Describe some of the ways propaganda is used in journalistic situations.

5. Name the primary general semantics principles, and explain how they can be useful in encoding better messages.

6. What are the three types or segments of the general public? Which one is most important to the mainstream communicator seeking a mass-mass audience?

7. What are the three basic "motivational factors" that have an impact on audience members and make them expose themselves to messages?

Suggested Readings

Chase, Stuart, *The Power of Words*. New York: Harcourt, Brace and World, 1958.

Doob, Leonard. *Public Opinion and Propaganda*. New York: Henry Holt, 1948.

Efron, Edith. *The News Twisters*. Los Angeles: Nash, 1971.

Ellul, Jacques. *Propaganda*. New York: Knopf, 1965.

Gans, Herbert. "Are U.S. Journalists Dangerously Liberal?" *Columbia Journalism Review* (November/December 1985): 29–33.

Hayakawa, S. I. *Language in Thought and Action*. New York: Harcourt, Brace and World, 1964.

Hoffer, Eric. *The True Believer*. New York: Harper & Row, 1951.

Johnson, Wendell. *People in Quandaries*. New York: Harper & Row, 1946.

Korzybski, Alfred. *Science and Sanity*. Lancaster, Pa.: The Science Publishing Co., 1933.

LeBon, Gustave. *The Crowd*. New York: Ballantine Books, 1969.

Lee, A. M., and Lee, Elizabeth B. *The Fine Art of Propaganda*. New York: Institute for Propaganda Analysis, 1939.

Lee, John, ed. *The Diplomatic Persuaders,* New York: John Wiley, 1968.

Lichter, L. Robert, Rothman, Stanley and Lichter, Linda S. *The Media Elite*. Bethesda, Md.: Adler & Adler, 1986.

Lippmann, Walter. *Public Opinion*. New York: Harcourt, Brace, 1922.

Martin, L. John. *International Propaganda*. Minneapolis: University of Minnesota Press, 1952.

Merrill, John C. *The Dialectic in Journalism: Toward a Responsible Use of Press Freedom*. Baton Rouge: LSU Press, 1989.

Merrill, John C. and Lowenstein, Ralph L. *Media, Messages, and Men*. New York: Longman, 1979.

O'Hara, Robert. *Media for the Millions*. New York: Random House, 1961.

Ortega y Gasset, José. *The Revolt of the Masses*. New York: Norton, 1932.

Rand, Ayn. *For the New Intellectual*. New York: Random House, 1961.

Riesman, David. *The Lonely Crowd*. New Haven: Yale University Press, 1950.

Talese, Gay. *The Kingdom and the Power*. New York: World Publishing Co., 1969.

Whyte, William H. *The Organization Man*. New York: Simon & Schuster, 1956.

Wiener, Norbert. *The Human Use of Human Beings*. New York: Avon Books, 1954.

CHAPTER 3

Media Functions

London. Think about London for a moment. Picture the city in your mind. What do you see? Westminster Abbey? Bright red double-decker buses? Piccadilly Circus? Perhaps the statue on Nelson's Column, gazing down at quiet Londoners sitting on benches at Trafalgar Square. Are the scenes clear? Sure, it's easy to visualize London.

Now think back. Imagine London a hundred years ago. The picture changes. Corner gaslights. A thick fog rolling through dark streets. Steady clop-clop of horse-drawn carriages. Then, through the heavy fog, a woman walks alone. She seems nervous, in a hurry. She passes quickly and disappears into the night. Silence, then suddenly, from the distance, a high-pitched scream. Police whistles tweet. You hear running feet. Jack the Ripper has struck again.

Big Ben conjures up mass media-produced images of London for most people.

The images are vivid, aren't they? Now ask yourself, how do you know so much about London? Have you been there? Even if you have, how does that help you picture 19th-century London? The answer is quite simple. You get your images from the media. Mass media messages about London have bombarded you for years. You know all about Sherlock Holmes and James Bond and Oliver Twist and Rumpole of the Old Bailey. You've seen London on television dozens of times, on network news as a backdrop behind the commentators, in documentaries and as a locale for popular dramatic programs. You've watched scores of movies set in London. You've read books about London. You've scanned magazine articles about London. Even if you've never been out of the continental United States, you know London's look, London's sounds, London's past, London's present and, in some respects, London's future.

And you learned it all over the years—slowly, almost by osmosis—from a rich brocade of media offerings.

Media Functions: A Variety of Viewpoints

It would be difficult to imagine life without mass media. Media inform us. Media entertain us. Media invade our lives. And yet media, the instruments of mass communication, are a relatively new development in the long thread of civilization. Ancient cave dwellers had no mass media. Nor did the farmers of ancient Mesopotamia or the pharaohs of Egypt or the wandering tribes of Israel. No one picked up a newspaper to read about the sack of Troy or the coming of the Black Plague. Vikings sailed the frigid seas and vassals tilled their crops in feudal European fiefdoms without ever seeing a book or checking the grocery store ads or scanning a weather report. What little they knew about the world around them they knew from firsthand experience, observation or word of mouth.

So why do we need media? Why can't we get along without the media just as easily as did Aristotle or the Aztecs? Perhaps it will help us to understand the importance of modern media if we take a look at some of the different functions they are expected to perform.

Individuals Versus Society as a Whole

We should realize first that there are differences between the roles media play for each of us as individuals and the roles they play for society as a collective whole. As individuals, we all have special needs. You may be drawn to literature and music while your best friend is attracted to science and numbers. You may have grown up in a politically conservative environment while your friend comes from a more liberal background. Your family may be affluent, with plenty of money to spend on advertised products, while your friend's family may have trouble making ends meet. You might even be a Dallas Cowboys fan while your friend prefers the Philadelphia Eagles. You will each have specific interests, personal goals, separate curiosities to satisfy. Media attempt, not always successfully, to answer all those individual needs for both you and your friend.

At the same time, media must also serve the collective cultural, political and economic needs of society. It isn't as easy as it may sound. Media that work well in one system, our own for example, could be quite disruptive in another system, such as Iraq. Not only can media societal roles vary from culture to culture, but also they can often vary within the culture. Media may be used to maintain social equilibrium, to facilitate change or to seek radical alternatives. Media may work within a political system or against it. Media can serve to provide information or to withhold it. Media can grease the economic wheels of a country and keep them turning or bring them to a halt.

These two particular functions—service to the individual and service to society—are very important, and we will examine them in more detail.

Media Form Versus Messages

As students of communication, we should realize that mass media messages may be affected by media form. For example, you are reading newspaper coverage of new tax proposals that will profoundly affect your next year's income. The doorbell rings. You interrupt your reading, answer the door, conduct your conversation and return to your newspaper. You finish the message and understand it. In a different situation, that same message is coming to you on a network news program. This time when you answer the door the message continues without you and is lost forever. You will not be alerted to changes in your taxes unless you find the same information elsewhere.

There are distinct differences within the various media that can affect message content. The message and the medium may well join together in a symbiotic relationship and reach you with clarity, or they may operate in a completely independent and contradictory manner, even to the point of canceling the primary message out. As an example, the narrator in a TV documentary may be describing how tornadoes are formed. Meanwhile, the screen is showing, in gory color, the injuries suffered after a tornado has struck a church filled with worshipers. You're so horrified by the film that you miss what the voice is saying.

Under some conditions the content of a message is more relevant. At other times the physical environment of the medium will be more important. Each can affect the other. How? There are many ways, some obvious, some subtle. Some media, for example, are used as shared instruments. We usually watch television in the company of others. We go to movies together and listen to music together. Or we divide up a morning newspaper and take turns reading sections. Books and magazines, on the other hand, are most often read privately, perhaps even as a barrier against unwanted conversation.

Movies are watched in darkened settings. Television is normally viewed in a lighted room. Newspapers, books and magazines are portable. You can carry them on a plane or in a briefcase. Television, movies and, to some extent, music and radio usually stay in theaters, at home or in the car. Like newspapers, magazines and books can be put aside, the message interrupted without loss. A mind that wanders to a personal worry can cause a movie or television message to disappear forever.

Some media affect us by their insinuation into family routines. Television entertains us and informs us, but it can also act as a babysitter, a family hearth, and a guarantor against loneliness. The TV set is often a welcome extension of the family—a member of the family, if you will. Television viewing becomes almost ritualized. Warmth and family companionship become more important than the message. Movies play another unique role in our society as a part of the mating ritual. When one takes a date to see a movie, the movie's message often becomes secondary.

Immediate Versus Long Range

Media function may be affected by a message that apparently has little immediate consequence but may fester subconsciously and become important over a period of time. For example, a media consumer may hear something unfavorable about a favorite political candidate and be willing to ignore it. But as time passes, the negative report sticks in the consumer's mind, nagging and bothering until, by election day, the consumer decides to vote for someone else. Function can also be affected by the accumulation of minor media messages that gain weight simply through repetition. Perhaps the consumer has truly ignored the first report about the candidate. If the story is repeated and additional facts are revealed, keeping the story in the news day after day, week after week, the consumer's perceptions may thereby be irrevocably altered.

Repetition and accumulation of media messages can be a powerful tool in the hands of a skilled media practitioner. The device is often used by advertisers, propagandists and political leaders. The blackest case in modern history is that of Hitler and his Nazi propagandists. When Hitler came to power after World War I, Germany was still in the throes of deep economic depression. The populace was demoralized. There were numerous different political camps, most of which spent their time warring with each other and ignoring the plight of the people. Hitler, in an effort to consolidate his own position and bring Germans together, sought a common enemy. He and his henchmen took advantage of latent anti-Semitism and chose Jews as the enemy. Jews were assailed at every turn by Nazi officials, party newspapers and even the primers used by young schoolchildren. This was the "Big Lie," the constantly repeated fiction that there existed an international Jewish conspiracy, the goal of which was world conquest. The concept was repeated so often that even sensible Germans began to believe it. In time, Jews were removed from positions in schools and government, deprived of citizenship and forced into concentration camps. The horrors of the Holocaust had begun.

The same techniques of repetition and accumulation of media messages can be used less malevolently to sell toothpaste or a candidate. How often have you encountered television commercials that you hear over and over and find irritating because of their seeming inanity and repetition yet found yourself buying that exact same product at your local supermarket? Probably

University of Pennsylvania researcher George Gerbner.

more times than you'd like to admit. Repetition leads to product identification, and that's half the game in impulse buying, vote gathering and cause reinforcement.

Repetition can affect us even when it's accidental and not being purposely used by media manipulators. George Gerbner, a respected media researcher at the University of Pennsylvania, has studied the cumulative effects of television messages for years. One of his findings is that repetitious (and often distorted) television themes have a decided impact on heavy viewers. Heavy viewers tend to be persuaded by what they see on the television screen and accept it more readily than they accept reality. A heavy diet of televised crime dramas, for example, with their incessant violence and frequent physical confrontations, can lead to what Gerbner calls a "Mean World Syndrome." Heavy viewers of such shows develop an unhealthy fear of victimization and often grossly overestimate their statistical chances of becoming victims of crime.

Some media messages will have no long-range impact, whether they are repeated or not. A message may shock us, amuse us or scare us half to death at the moment we watch it or hear it, but have no lasting effect whatsoever. Consider Jason and his homicidal tendencies in the "Friday the 13th" films. We may scream at every move as we watch him hack, stab and chainsaw his way through a dozen young people in the course of a bloodthirsty two-hour movie, but we walk out at the end without flinching at shadows. And if a wealthy recluse offered us a chance to spend a gorgeous summer lazing for free at some magnificent lakeside camp, it wouldn't matter if we had seen every Jason film from the original through "Friday the 13th—Part 23," we'd probably still go.

Expected Versus Unexpected

Communicators usually have a function in mind when they use the media to send mass messages—to bring an audience up-to-date on the news or to provide an hour of light entertainment, for example. But the results can often be negative and completely unexpected, even startling. You'll get a look at one of the classic cases of *dysfunction* (the negative consequences of media function) when you begin to read in Chapter 8 about Orson Welles' radio broadcast of "War of the Worlds," a fictional invasion from Mars that sent people streaming into the streets in panic.

We know that these dysfunctional disorders can lead to some strange results. People who are made nervous by a heavy dose of unsettling news may, instead of being stirred to action by the news as was intended, end up withdrawing from news entirely (a reaction called **privatization**), or may grow apathetic and lazy (called **narcotization**), or may even fall prey to a **contagion factor,** such as buying a Cabbage Patch doll because there are daily stories about them on the television news. Gerbner's studies provide us with more common examples of dysfunction. The script writers who fashion television crime dramas are trying to entertain us, not turn us into prefabricated victims. And if they *do* entertain us, at least often enough to keep their shows on the air, that's a functional, or expected, consequence. The fact that their programs also have unexpected, negative long-range results for at least a segment of our society is a dysfunctional consequence.

The consequences of media messages are extremely important to the mass communicator. They can mean the difference between success and failure in communication. You'll read more about messages and their effects in the next chapter.

We've already talked briefly about media functions for the individual as opposed to media functions for society as a whole. In a sense, one might say that societal functions are mainly a compilation of all the individual functions strung together to make a whole. But there's more to it than that. The individual turns to media for satisfaction and the fulfillment of private needs. A society properly served by media has more complex needs. Let's take a closer look at both, beginning with the functions for society.

Media Functions for Society

Lasswell's Three Functions

The classic communal media functions were outlined in 1948 by Harold Lasswell, the political scientist who gave us the verbal model for communication that you encountered in Chapter 1. Lasswell's functions, later refined

Journalists often engage in *surveillance of the environment.*

by sociologist Charles Wright in 1959, were identified as *surveillance, correlation,* and *transmission of culture.* According to Lasswell, these functions are basic and exist in all societies. Let's look at each in turn.

Surveillance of the Environment. The first function is the most obvious of the three. It refers to the journalistic service of media—collecting and disseminating information. Lasswell calls it a **surveillance role,** in which media specialists survey the environment, interpret the signs and report their findings to society. In effect, media fill the role of sentries, standing guard to warn of imminent danger to the community. It's a traditional role that has come down to us from the ages. In Spain, you'll find the numerous ruins of towers scattered along the southern coast like crumbling stone silos. They were used centuries ago as watchtowers, where lonely Spanish sentinels scanned the Mediterranean for signs of marauding Moors. If the sentinel caught sight of sails, he lit a fire in the top of the tower to warn the inhabitants of the countryside. In effect, that's what Lasswell says media do today. They watch for signs of danger (natural disasters, rising crime rates, economic indicators, impending war) and light a fire to warn the community. If the warning comes in time, the community may respond by changing the environment to negate the danger. If there's no time for change, the community can still prepare itself to meet the danger.

However, there's more to the surveillance role than spotting danger and relaying warnings. Media also have an obligation to perform a kind of domestic surveillance, gathering and supplying a summary of simple information that will help the community to operate on a day-to-day basis: medical advice, stock market quotations, grocery ads, television listings— anything that provides a more rewarding life for the constituents of the community. And, of course, in a democratic society where government is answerable to the people, the people must be kept informed on political and governmental matters so that they can make rational decisions.

Correlation of the Parts of Society. More than just reporting dangers and providing useful day-to-day news, Lasswell says media must also offer explanations, interpreting the news to help members of the community understand the sense of what is being said. Reporting offers only information. The interpretation, or **correlation,** function provides knowledge, which is essential if a society is to function smoothly. The various parts of society can form opinions on the basis of information if that's all that is available to them, but opinions based on information and *knowledge* are usually closer to truth.

The opinion and interpretation functions of modern media come to us in a number of forms and are performed by a variety of media specialists. Editorial writers, opinion columnists and television commentators offer their interpretations of domestic and world news on a daily basis. Reporters occasionally write interpretative news stories to provide background for us on the meaning of complex news events. Op-ed pages and call-in radio programs provide space for alternative viewpoints. Editorial cartoonists (and comic strips such as *Shoe* or *Doonesbury*) frequently present barbed comments on social questions. In a way, even the normal daily process of editorial selection is a form of correlation. There isn't room in the average newspaper or TV program to report every worthwhile occurrence of the day, so the very selection itself of what is to appear confers status and signifies importance.

Transmission of the Social Heritage. Lasswell's final function— **transmission of culture**—is basically educational. It refers to the passage of social and cultural heritage from one generation to the next. Media not only report the news to the community and interpret the meaning of the news, but they also transmit information about the society itself—its history as a social unit, its mistakes and successes, its norms and values. By providing cultural guidelines, media can help teach the citizens of a society how to live, how to act and what is expected of them. The basic teaching process has traditionally been in the hands of parents, schools and churches, but media augment the traditional teachers and at times even supplant them. Nor is the teaching role as stuffy as it may sound. Cultural information can range from scholarly books to the newest action film. Almost everything we read, see or hear has the potential of instructing us about ourselves. However, not all this instructional material is valid or rewarding. It's often up to the individual to sift through it and determine which values are worth retaining.

Editorial cartoonists frequently assist in *correlation of the parts of society.*

Functions for Society Simplified

Lasswell's three functions may impress you as unnecessary jargon. Surveillance of the environment? Correlation of the parts? Why not just say information and interpretation? As a matter of fact, most media professionals tend to use such simpler terms as *information, entertainment, persuasion, service to the economic system* and (yes, they've clung to one bit of Lasswell terminology) *transmission of culture*.

These five simple functions are quite distinct from each other, but they are not mutually exclusive. Functions frequently overlap. For example, we usually think of nonfiction as "information" and fiction as "entertainment." Actually much nonfiction is entertaining and much fiction is instructional. Fiction gives insight into the human condition. *War and Peace* isn't considered a great novel simply because it is entertaining; no one has ever called it a fast read. Fiction, even in a TV sitcom, can process information and exercise influence on an audience. Any media message can inform or entertain or persuade or sell a product. And just about any conceivable media message will add to the total experience that facilitates culture transmission.

Information. Transmitting information is the journalistic function of media. When you flip through the pages of a newspaper or turn on the network news to watch Tom Brokaw, you are seeking information. And information can come to you in other forms, as well. Every nonfiction magazine and book (including this one) is designed to give you information. The same is true of radio talk shows or Phil Donahue or Oprah Winfrey or "Nova" or any other informational television series. Very little that appears in media fails to inform us in some way.

Entertainment. The entertainment function is also basic. Modern media consumers have more leisure time than their ancestors did, and they apparently prefer to fill it with various forms of entertainment. At least that's the indication we get from television ratings. With the exception of an anomalous program like "60 Minutes," the top-rated television shows are consistently entertainment oriented. They may be light-hearted sitcoms, game shows, or mystery dramas, but they almost always draw more viewers than serious attempts to inform or educate.

Television is today the major media source of mass entertainment, but the entertainment function permeates other media as well. Radio gives us music for all tastes. Movies, books and short magazine fiction offer comedy, tragedy, sex and explosive action for our diversion. Even newspapers offer entertainment in the form of feature stories, crossword puzzles, comics, horoscopes, and humorists like Art Buchwald, Erma Bombeck and Lewis Grizzard.

Persuasion. Media are used to form public opinion, influence votes, change attitudes, moderate behavior, debunk myths and sell products. The persuasive function is most effective, however, when it is performed in a subtle manner. People have long assumed that mass media have incredible power when it comes to changing people's minds. Actually, when it comes to direct, recognizable attempts at persuasion, the media have never proved all that successful. People don't like having their opinions manipulated and they usually resist it. A single, blatantly obvious persuasive message will often create a backlash effect. On the other hand, a well-structured media campaign with a series of subtle, persuasive messages offered over a period of time can have a demonstrable effect on attitudes, especially if the messages are cloaked as entertainment or basic journalistic information. Skilled propagandists, opinion columnists, politicians, public relations practitioners and advertising executives, aware of the public response to blatant persuasion, have learned to adjust their persuasive techniques.

What kind of people are most susceptible to persuasion? Propaganda theorists have told us for years that the most likely victims are irrational people, nonthinkers who may be unable to reason their way through false arguments. But Baruch Gitlis, director of the Israeli Institute for

Propaganda Analysis, believes intellectuals are better targets. He says, "The most intelligent, the most widely read, best educated, are those most easily swayed by propaganda." He suggests they are people whose minds are alert and inquiring and therefore receptive to new information.

Serve the Economic System. In capitalistic societies, media are also involved in service to the economic system (including the economy of the media themselves, since most media exist to make a profit). They promote commercial enterprise through business news, coverage of economic trends, tax information and product identification. The most obvious economic service of the media, however, is the advertising function. Media bring buyers and sellers together by generating audiences and selling them to advertisers, and the advertisers then sell their products to the audiences.

The economic involvement of media can fluctuate from medium to medium and from culture to culture. Some media units are devoted almost entirely to the economic environment (*The Wall Street Journal,* for example, and *Forbes, Fortune,* and *Business Week*). Other specific media units (such as Great Britain's BBC) are financed through government subsidy, operate on a nonprofit basis and carry no advertising at all. On a national level, media involvement can depend on the efficiency of a country's manufacturers, the buying power of its citizens or the fundamental politics of its ruling class. The media of developing countries attract only a fragment of the advertising found in the media of the United States. Former Soviet media, as instruments of the government and ideological enemies of capitalism, all but ignored advertising before the disruption of the Soviet Union.

Transmission of Culture. Although media may not deliberately set out to transmit culture, education is an inevitable result of the other functions. Every media message, if it finds an audience, will have a socializing effect, no matter how slight. Individuals assimilate information and learn from it, adding to their knowledge, their values and their total experience. Media messages, for good or bad, can thus lead to the homogenization of society. Subcultures, learning standardized norms, become more alike. That's how a melting-pot country like the United States manages so easily to accommodate the many cultures that immigrate to its shores. Standardization can go beyond norms and values, even to language. Since the advent of electronic media, many of the regional dialects and accents of this country have softened. We're all beginning to sound more and more like radio and television announcers.

The Fission Factor— Informational Chain Reaction

When physicists first began probing the secrets of the atom in the early 20th century, trying to determine its structure, they had no idea that their studies would lead to a destructive weapon. In time, physicists reasoned that when powerful radioactive materials were brought to critical mass, neutron bombardment would produce a chain reaction, unleashing extraordinary power and energy in the wink of an eye. The atomic bomb became a theoretical possibility. America and Great Britain, worrying that Germany might unravel the secrets of the bomb, enlisted physicists and theoreticians in a scramble to do so first. Many scientists entered the race with ambivalent feelings. They could see both good and evil coming from their labors. They knew they were working on a terrible weapon, but they hoped its awesome power in the right hands might act as a deterrent to future wars.

In a way, media functions have reached that same critical mass. Modern media reporters frequently find themselves either initiating or being swept up in informational chain reactions that can change the world and make it better or do serious damage. At times, the chain reaction takes place within the media themselves, affecting the way they swarm to a story and report it. At other times, the runaway explosion is in the audience, leading to an outburst of unexpected emotion. Either way, good chain reaction or bad, once fission begins, media personnel are often powerless to stop it.

Dogfight—A Small Chain Reaction

Let's follow a mild case and see if we can determine how stories sometimes reach the fission point. In Austin, Texas, in the late 1980s, a pit-bull terrier bitch, brought unleashed to a public lakeside recreation area by her owner, suddenly plunged into the water and attacked a five-month-old Doberman puppy that was playing in the lake with her owner and two friends. In the resulting melee, all three people accompanying the puppy were bitten, and the pup was bitten in the throat so badly that the trachea was crushed. Emergency veterinary surgery failed to save it. The three people were treated for their less serious bites in a hospital emergency room. The pit bull was corralled by an animal-control officer and, because she had not been vaccinated for rabies, was held for ten days for observation. The owner than washed his hands of the dog, and she was euthanized.

The people's dog bites were promptly and routinely reported by the hospital to the county health department and became a matter of public record available to the local news media. No news stories on TV or in the press appeared. Critical mass had not been reached. The people's injuries weren't serious. A dog fight isn't news. Both media reporters and consumers quite properly didn't give a hoot.

Had the pit bull attacked and killed a person, the event would have been considered news and would have been covered. Had another pit bull in another nearby city, San Antonio for example, attacked and killed a person the previous week, the Austin attack would have received even wider coverage. After that, wire-service reports of any attack by a pit bull anywhere in the nation would have been singled out by the wire editors of local newspapers and TV stations and given at least brief mention in local media. Even the attack by the pit bull at the lake would have been covered, despite the fact that the only fatality was another dog. Here is the beginning of the chain reaction, a small-scale fission effect, that can and does lead to media mania (or, as some media critics like to call it, a media "feeding frenzy"). We'll come back to it later to see how far it develops.

For the media consumer, the snowballing coverage that results from informational chain reactions may create a significant awareness of some social problem, or it may cause a kind of dysfunctional hysteria that does more damage than good (see Figure 3.1). The media are also frequently affected. All too often, the growing coverage casts a shadow as huge as a mushroom cloud, hiding the original purpose of the reports and contributing to the consistent outcry that news media are negative, unfair, biased, hysterical, given to crisis reporting, prone to exaggeration and out to get people—or, in this case, pit-bull terriers.

Prevalent though it can be, the fission effect of information is seldom considered in basic news-writing texts when they list the story elements that rookie reporters will use throughout their professional writing lives. These elements come under a variety of names, but all are readily understandable. They are sometimes called *timeliness* (what happened yesterday, today or an hour ago); *prominence* (the names that make the news); *proximity* (what's happening in your own city or nearby); *consequence* (the effect a story will have on an individual or a community); *progress* (triumphs and achievements of persons and communities); *conflict* (war, acts of terrorism, arguments, even surprise and tension); *novelty* (the unusual); *human interest* (that which piques mild interest or tugs at the emotions) and *disaster* (floods, tornadoes, earthquakes, plane crashes, deaths and crises of all types). These news elements are the radioactive isotopes that can lead to media fission, and they are often intermingled in one story. Some are hotter than others when it comes to creating chain reactions. Their relative importance can be argued. What can't be argued is that American news media are highly sensitive to disaster and conflict stories and are often criticized by representatives of foreign media for their preoccupation with death, crime and calamity—crisis reporting.

Do American media lean too heavily on crisis reporting? One Danish official recently complained to the authors of this book that the only time American media ever mention Denmark is when something terrible happens. He claims, for example, that in the last 50 years the only two times Denmark has appeared on the front pages of American newspapers were during World War II when Germany invaded and later when vandals attacked the famous Little Mermaid statue in Copenhagen. His statement is exaggerated, but he has a point. Disasters are a major ingredient of American news stories. To find a press system in which nothing but good news is reported, one must dig back into the recent past. Consider the Soviet Union, prior to its dissolution. In the Soviet press, where dull, boring, good news was the name of the game, plane crashes and train wrecks were seldom mentioned. As a former editor of *Pravda* once said, "This is news which we think the Soviet citizen can live without." The primary function of the Soviet press was to perpetuate the socialist system, not, the former *Pravda* editor declared, to peep through keyholes or report calamities. Consider: When the U.S. space shuttle *Challenger* blew up, the tragedy happened on live television before a horrified audience of millions. When the Soviets suffered a space disaster, it was usually blanketed by secrecy. The only way

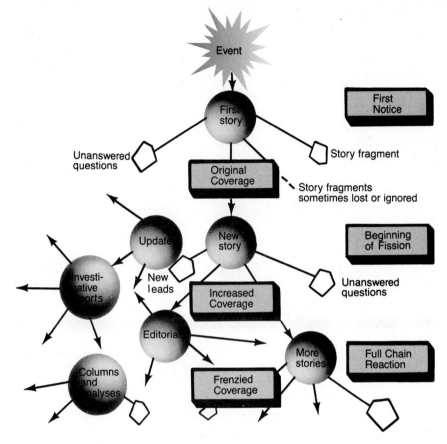

Figure 3.1
Media Fission

American audiences were likely to hear of it was when word filtered through Western intelligence services, often years later.

The one-time Soviet press system has changed drastically. Newspapers and television news programs in Russia and other former Soviet republics are far more likely these days to reflect a Western style of journalism. Did former Soviet citizens sleep more soundly at night for not having been informed of various disasters? Probably. Should Western media similarly self-censor disaster reports? Surely not. And yet the fission factor may be a natural result of such reporting, and can lead to both media mania and consumer mania. And when mania occurs, people get upset.

Sleaze, Bimbos and Politics

An unfortunate example of media fission is the recent obsession with sex and sleaze in political stories. Sex and politics aren't new bedfellows. Numerous national political figures have found themselves the targets of philandering rumors, from Ben Franklin, Thomas Jefferson and Andrew Jackson to Franklin Roosevelt, John F. Kennedy and Lyndon Johnson. But most of those early whisperings stayed in the rumor stage The bald, open obsession with "character" issues didn't hit the front pages until the Gary Hart case, an event that crystallized a lamentable reporting trend during the presidential campaign of 1988. Hart was a presidential hopeful, but was hampered by rumors of womanizing. He challenged reporters in 1987 to follow him and prove to themselves that there was no truth to the reports. The *Miami Herald* took up the challenge. Reporters saw Hart enter a Washington house at night with a young, attractive woman. Neither Hart nor the woman reappeared until the next day. The *Miami Herald* reported it, and a media flap was underway.

The chain reaction was all but instantaneous, like frontier justice at the end of a rope. Other newspapers checked out the young woman and ran their own stories. Syndicated columnists hinted at other unnamed Hart playmates. Television audiences observed a sad-faced Mrs. Hart as she told reporters that if she didn't have a quarrel with her husband over his behavior, she couldn't see that it was anybody else's business. And yet more and more media made Hart's personal behavior their business. Bitterly blaming the media (he didn't blame himself until months later), Hart dropped out of the race. Meanwhile, a new kind of negative political coverage had been unleashed. Microphones were stuck in the faces of other would-be candidates, and they were solemnly asked, before national television audiences, if they had ever committed adultery.

This trend toward gossip and bedroom reporting continued with several new political targets, including members of the Kennedy family (questioned about their sexual activities during a widely publicized rape case), Supreme Court Justice appointee Clarence Thomas (charged with sexual harassment by a former employee) and even presidential candidate Bill Clinton (questioned over and over about a supposed affair with a woman named Gennifer Flowers).

Were these stories the business of future voters? Or were they media fission, one media unit after another jumping on the headline bandwagon, all of them rushing headlong into media mania? At least in political cases, the answers must be "yes" and "yes." Ill-considered behavior, whether sexual or not, on the part of would-be world leaders certainly concerns those whom they would lead. But the stories were also ugly examples of media mania. Tawdry news often becomes big news, and all the news media want in on it while it is still hot. Heated to supercritical mass, media develop a kind of tunnel vision, lending new credence to criticism that American media too frequently indulge in keyhole-peeping and character assassination.

Tunnel Vision—Fact Filter or Blindness?

Tunnel vision can work for or against a reporter, of course. It can be used to cut through extraneous sleight of hand to get to the central facts of a story, or it can blind one to equally important elements in a story. Or, for that matter, it can be used to block out facts that a reporter would rather not pursue. Gary Hart was not the first presidential-minded individual to show a fondness for women, nor will he be the last. At least three modern presidential candidates who preceded him—John F. Kennedy, Lyndon Johnson and Franklin Roosevelt—were suspected by members of the White House press corps of indulging in extramarital affairs. Reporters may have chuckled and traded rumors, but no one ever chased the stories down. (Or if they did, they didn't print them.) In all three of these earlier presidential cases, tunnel vision seems to have dictated that sexual misconduct had little to do with the way the country was being run. The information was made public only after the men died.

Examples of tunnel vision are common, but they don't all deal with sexual feeding frenzies on the part of the press. When recession paralyzed the American economy in the early 1990s, President George Bush, a popular leader when judged on the strength of his foreign policy, found his popularity sagging on domestic issues. Bush's first reaction was to belittle the importance, or even the existence, of a recession. But reporters wouldn't let the story go. In another example of media fission, nightly network news stories spoke of sagging sales. The growing number of jobless workers came up again and again. Democrats condemned the Bush administration for a lack of leadership. Ordinary people were interviewed about their economic fears. Bush talked with reporters on numerous occasions, eager to discuss cataclysmic world events (the Soviet Union was falling apart at the time), but media representatives were far more eager to hear his plans to meet the economic crises at home. Bush, unable to focus on international events as he might have preferred, was forced to admit the recession was real and to channel his energies in new directions. Economics became the major issue in the 1992 presidential election (Clinton's campaign headquarters even sported a sign that read, "It's the economy, stupid," to remind staffers to stay on target). Bush backers complained that the media were partially responsible for the recession, since keeping the story in the public eye reinforced the public lack of confidence. Eventually, his unwillingness or inability to deal with the recession cost Bush the election.

Were the Bush supporters right? Were the media right? Again, the hedged answers must be "yes" and "yes." President Bush would rather have talked to his constituents about his international triumphs, important world events with sound news values—conflict, timeliness and consequence. Voters wanted to hear his views on problems at home: education, rising medical costs, the sagging economy, events with different sound news values—proximity, progress (or lack of it) and consequence. Tunnel vision led both media and media consumers to focus on what they regarded as Bush's relationship to the more important domestic story. To their credit, most news media also reported fully on the international issues that were changing the face of the world map, but the politically embarrassing lack of economic motion got equally big headlines and top-of-the-news airtime.

Media practitioners occasionally get their teeth into a story that rises to prominence and stays in the headlines for weeks, even months. And because it dominates the headlines, the story often remains important. Then stalemate occurs or something comes along to distract media attention and the top-running story drifts lower on the page and finally disappears. Recent examples abound. Economic recessions, starving children in Ethiopia, hostages in Beirut, attempts to oust Noriega from Panama (and a lightning invasion to bring him out), deadly confrontations in Israel or South Africa, problems in the Philippines. Each of these stories got full coverage for a time with daily, even hourly updates, but then a vacuum developed. Had the problems gone away? No, not always. Children still starved. South Africa still seethed. Hostages languished in Beirut (though the release of the American hostages in 1991 brought a fresh spate of stories). Noriega loitered in a Miami jail, then went on trial with minimal public attention. The Filipino government continued its struggle for equilibrium. But the reactor pile had gone dead. Interest had waned.

Going to the Dogs Again

Politics and armed confrontation are subjects usually surrounded with heated opinion, so let's return to the more neutral subject of dogs and see how the chain reaction is doing. While we're at it, we'll consider whether the fission factor is good, bad or somewhere in between.

First, be aware that at least since the years of sensationalism and yellow journalism the bulk of American news media practitioners have responded with enthusiasm to crisis reporting. The assistant city editor of a middle-sized local newspaper, lounging at the city desk and watching the clock creep toward the midnight deadline for the second morning edition, is not sad when the phone rings and she hears a breathless police reporter tell her that a prominent businessman has just shot his wife and her female lover in a posh downtown hotel. The "cop-shop" reporter and the assistant editor are both elated. They have a dramatic news story. It might not be the most important news in next morning's paper, but it will have a big, black headline. The two newspeople aren't ghouls; they aren't glad two people have been shot. They're not jubilant that a prominent businessman, maybe one who has been aloof and condescending to the paper, has committed a crime. At the moment the editor calls to the one staffer still holding down the rewrite bank to take the police reporter's story, no one is thinking of news elements such as prominence and conflict. The story is *news*, and they're happy to have a meaty news story. That's enough.

The fall from grace of a politician such as Gary Hart is news. The failure of the Defense Department to see that tax money was spent properly is news. Pit-bull attacks are news. News reporters and editors know news and act upon it, and then chain reaction can set in, as it did with the pit bulls.

By the time pit-bull terriers got into the news in the 1980s, they had already become a fad. Bred originally from English bulldogs that were used (in a darker era) literally to fight bulls in pits, the dogs had fighting in their genes. "Pit bull" is actually a broad category, covering four different kinds of dogs—the Bull Terrier (the amiable "Spuds McKenzie" breed once used by Budweiser to advertise beer), the small Staffordshire Bull Terrier, the bigger American Staffordshire Bull Terrier and the American Pit-Bull Terrier. All share some characteristics: heavy, broad heads; medium-sized, muscular bodies and a willingness to fight. They were the tough dogs that tough guys wanted.

The stage was set. Macho dog masters turned to money-minded backyard breeders in droves. Small-time drug dealers purchased pit bulls to use as guard dogs. Tough-guy carpenters bought pit bulls and left them for their wives to bring up with the new baby. Gentle grocery-store bag boys who had once wished for a Collie had pit bulls at home, chained in backyards. Tragedy resulted; and pit-bull attacks began to accumulate in the headlines. An elderly woman killed by her neighbor's two pit bulls in California . . . a child mauled in New Mexico . . . more children mauled in Tennessee . . . more kids killed in Florida. News stories led to columns and features. Television teams videotaped pit bulls snarling at animal control officers and spoke gravely of the "pit-bull problem." After a wave of pit-bull headlines and TV spots, audience chain reaction set in, spawning a wave of city ordinances that attempted to restrict the ownership of pit bulls. Responsible dog owners reacted by attempting to quash what they called "breed-specific" laws, hoping to replace them with ordinances outlawing any dog that behaved viciously. Media continued to report the attacks and most of the would-be pit-bull laws. And, as a side result of the fission factor, the media got blamed for creating hysteria.

Nor was it strictly an American phenomenon. In 1991, the British government, provoked by British press reports about the mauling of two children, suddenly decreed that such dogs had no place in British homes and ordered an estimated 10,000 such dogs put to death. The Royal Society for the Prevention of Cruelty to Animals promptly took issue with the decision and announced they would not be used as "state executioners."

Perhaps the ultimate in this media chain reaction is a story that appeared in Texas in 1991 about a small-town district attorney who planned to prosecute two men for using a 60-pound pit bull as a deadly weapon in assaulting two Texas highway patrol officers.

Were American and British mass media wrong to report the maulings of children by pit bulls? Of course not. Were communities wrong in trying to restrict the ownership of dangerous dogs within their boundaries? Certainly not. A dangerous situation came into being, it was reported and the public reacted by trying to control it. Lasswell's "alarm" system was working, just as he said it would. However, the alarm system doesn't always work the way it's supposed to.

Media tumble over each other to zero in on a major story, often letting other stories go unnoticed. Audiences get caught up in the mania, soaking up each and every word, even while they condemn media for reporting them. It's a bit like detecting a fire in a crowded theater. There are really only three things media surveillance units can do. They can shout, "Fire" and risk a panic. They can say nothing and risk a tragedy. Or they can try to lead an orderly evacuation. The problem is that even if media could be contained

Were news organizations wrong in reporting deaths caused by pit-bull terriers?

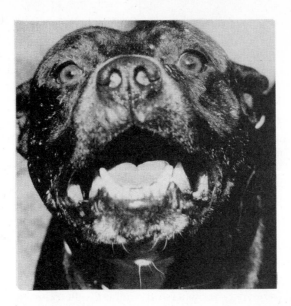

to the sensible approach, the audience fission factor can wreck the best of intentions. In some cases, even a quietly whispered "I smell smoke" can lead to a stampede.

We've been talking primarily about the news, or information, function. Bear in mind that any of the other media functions can also reach critical mass and produce fission and chain reactions. Entertainment functions frequently superheat and give us fads (hula hoops, Rambo movies, Care Bears, Cabbage Patch dolls, Nintendo video games). Propaganda efforts can blow things out of proportion (Hitler's anti-Semitism led inexorably to the Holocaust; the American "Red Scare" of the 1950s gave us bomb shelters and McCarthyism). Economic indicators and media warnings can cause recessions or speed inflation. Cultural heritage, once the product of centuries, can evolve in a twinkling.

And what are the alternatives? More restraint by individual media units? (Not likely in the existing competitive atmosphere.) More sophistication on the part of media consumers? (Without wholesale changes in education and cultural upbringing, this alternative is apt to occur only among isolated individuals.) A single all-powerful industry or government controller who can call a halt at any moment in the fission process? (Hardly an acceptable solution in a democratic society.)

There's no fault here. Like the ambivalent World War II physicists who worked on the atom bomb, news media professionals are aware that informational chain reactions can have both positive and negative results. And, like the physicists, media practitioners are convinced that their positive achievements outweigh the bad things that can happen. Even with an occasional breakdown of the information pile and a damaging runaway reaction among readers and viewers, the steady production of critical information serves the democratic process. And if that's so, the fission factor serves a useful function.

How do media serve each of us as individuals? What selective needs attract us to media? What personal gratifications do we seek? And do we get what we're looking for? Researchers say we do. They say individual audience members turn to media for a number of reasons—for personal improvement, for relaxation, for social intercourse and even as a hiding place.

Cognition—Learning

Cognition means the process of learning. Individuals frequently turn to media to better themselves. They watch the news to see what's happening in the world. They read books that make them think. They look for new ideas in magazines. They turn hungrily to movies, newspapers, radio and television. They want to learn. Sometimes they're looking for specific knowledge—how to repair a leaking faucet, build a tool shed or care for a cat. Or maybe they're looking for general knowledge, willing to sample almost anything to satisfy a craving curiosity.

Consider one very powerful medium—television. Today's children grow up with "the tube." Television has become the basic storyteller in their lives. They learn how the world works from television. They discover aggression and sex. They develop spending habits based on what is advertised on television. By the time the average child graduates from high school, he or she will have spent 15,000 hours in front of the TV set and will have witnessed as many as 30,000 electronic stories and 350,000 commercial advertisements.

Media offer so much information about so many things. When is the last time you were in a hospital operating room? Or on a big-game safari in Africa? Or sitting in the cockpit of a jet fighter, trying to elude an enemy plane? If you're like most of us, the answer is probably never. And yet we all have a pretty good idea of how hospitals work, and what it's like to face a charging rhino, or how to wrench a plane into a quick roll to escape a deadly missile streaking toward the tailpipe. And where do we get such arcane images? You know the answer. We get the information from medical dramas on television, from writers like H. Rider Haggard and Ernest Hemingway, and from movies like "Top Gun." We get many of our images and much of our knowledge from media.

Diversion—Playing

Except for chronic workaholics, most individuals want a bit of rest and relaxation to even out the day. Even when we're looking for knowledge, we like to be entertained. A book has to be challenging or at least interesting to keep us reading. Newspapers and magazines have to grab our attention with good writing and valuable information, or we'll keep flipping pages. If movies don't offer us strong visuals and credible plots, our minds will wander. Television programs have to involve us in the plot, or we'll flip channels. No one wants to be bored.

People need diversion, and mass media provide it. Diversion comes in many forms. If you're bored, media can offer excitement. You'll find

"Playing" a Prime
Media Function

Although such media functions as providing information and entertainment, interpretation and analysis, and guidance and persuasion are normally considered the most important, there are others. One is pleasure-providing, which is detailed in communication psychologist William Stephenson's *ludenic* (or play) theory.

Stephenson draws a distinction between public and private communication behavior. This refinement helps account for research findings that people's media usage only occasionally leads to them taking any purposive action. Thus, Stephenson says, most of the time people are content within their private reading, listening and viewing, even when they disagree with what is being seen or heard. The key, Stephenson says, is understanding that media content are seen mostly as simply "fun," in the sense that they may lead nowhere beyond one's own pleasure. Therefore, even political conflict or disasters can become "pleasurable" merely because they are interesting. All this means that fun or pleasure to the audience is an overriding media function.

It may be, says Stephenson, that media do not *intend* to be playthings for the audiences; the fact is that audiences, if given the chance, "use" the media to fulfill their needs. As audience members expose themselves to media, they "play" with the messages; they manipulate them in a way that is satisfying and self-serving.

Inherent in such "playing" with the media is freedom of choice; so ludenic (play) communication is found where there is considerable pluralism and freedom and a minimum of social control. The important thing in Stephenson's theory is not the information per se, but rather what an audience member does with the information in his or her mind.

So, for Stephenson, there are two basic purposes or functions of mass communication in democratic states: (1) to provide a maximum of communication pleasure (play) in society, and (2) to minimize social control by providing the kind of messages that permit a great degree of audience autonomy in the selective perception process.

Light, even superficial, media messages are important in Stephenson's theory. So-called escapist material is considered not bad, but good, for society. Fads and fancies, gossip and humor are very important. The anxiety or tension in a society is naturally great; mass communication must serve to lessen—not to exacerbate—the many anxiety-producing elements of modern life.

Those media critics who want to reform the media, to provide more serious news and less "fluff," do not agree with Stephenson's theory; they see him as a media apologist or status-quo theorist. Stephenson would answer such critics by reminding them that media are generally giving people what they want, what gratifies their self-interest, and their psychological needs. And, of course, we would point out that it is more democratic to give audiences what they basically want than to tell them what is good for them, what they *should* have.

Source: William Stephenson, *The Play Theory of Mass Communication.* Chicago: University of Chicago Press, 1967.

adventures, new discoveries, puzzles and competition to stimulate you. If you're overstimulated, media may promise soothing calm with quiet stories, soft music and relaxing scenery. If you're tied up in knots from another day in the fast lane, media can also provide emotional release—horror stories to exorcise your fear, television soap operas and romantic movies to put you in touch with romance, love and sex (and not necessarily in that order), or even Charles Bronson gunning down muggers in a dark park to help rid you of latent feelings of violence.

Social Utility—Networking

Media also facilitate our social interaction with family, friends and acquaintances. Consciously or unconsciously, we learn what is acceptable behavior and what is not. We learn how to mix with others, how to act, how to talk. We explore and reinforce our values. We learn how to get along on the job and perhaps even how to get ahead. We learn how to make friends and how to avoid hurting feelings. We keep tabs on current fashions, eat the newest fad foods, and read the latest popular books. It's all part of what propagandists call the *herd instinct*—the need of individuals to belong, to be a part of the mainstream majority. Media help us fit in. Media even give us things to talk about in normal social discourse. Have you ever asked a friend what he or she thought of a certain movie or quoted something you read in a book or magazine? Sure you have. We all do.

Withdrawal—Raising Barriers

Media not only facilitate interaction with society, they also make it easier to withdraw from society. People get tired of being on center stage all the time, smiling and behaving like proper ladies and gentlemen. There are times when we feel crabby, and we just want to be left alone, even if only for a couple of hours. Media give us an excuse to get away from it all. You tell a friend you'll try to come by, but you sit in the dark instead and watch some television program (even a rerun) that has suddenly become fascinating. A relative asks you to dinner, and you say, "Gee, I've got so much reading to do." A neighbor invites you over to play bridge, and you say, "I can't. I've got to tape a movie for my brother." You get on a plane to Los Angeles and the man in the next seat starts talking even before you fasten your seatbelt, so you pick up a magazine or a paperback book and bury your nose in it. Nor are all media barriers directed at other people. Sometimes we use media to delay things we don't want to do. You know you have class assignments or professional job projects hanging over you, but you put them off to finish a book or a television program. The lawn needs mowing, but you'd rather read a magazine. A parent or a spouse asks you to perform a kitchen chore, and you say, "In a minute. I want to see the end of this movie." Media become paper and electronic walls, sheltering us from unwanted intrusion.

To sum it up, media function in a variety of ways—some intended and some unintentional, some with immediate impact and some with long-range, cumulative impact, some through the content of messages and some through the specific format of particular media units—in order to provide a wide range of necessary services for a broad spectrum of general audiences as well as for individual audience members.

But once media perform these diverse functions, once messages have been formulated by communicators and delivered to mass audiences (and to individual members of mass audiences), what is done with the information? Consider this: Queen Elizabeth I, daughter of Henry VIII, was crammed with learning by childhood tutors, but she could learn only the knowledge that was available to her world. Compared to our world, that knowledge was limited. But when she succeeded to the crown, she was motivated and applied herself. Not all college undergraduates apply themselves these days, but they have infinite access to vast amounts of information and knowledge, far more than the regal Elizabeth could ever have imagined. *Today, your exposure to modern mass media has already made you a better-educated person than Elizabeth and nearly all the other people (philosophers and scientists included) who ever lived.* The rest is up to you. How will you use that education?

Retrospective

A variety of media functions affect our daily lives. Media play different roles for individuals and for society as a whole. Messages may be affected by the forms of the media themselves. Some messages will have immediate impact, while others may provide long-range consequences. These consequences may be predictable, or they may be unexpected.

Lasswell says media have three functions for society as a whole: (1) a *surveillance* role, surveying the environment, interpreting signs and reporting findings to society; (2) a *correlation* role, offering knowledge and explanation as a basis for opinion formation; (3) as *transmitters* of social heritage, providing cultural guidelines. In simpler terms, media are used to disseminate *information, entertainment, persuasion, service to the economic system* and *transmission of culture.*

In the process of providing information, media occasionally find themselves losing control of stories—through a surfeit of enthusiasm, through tunnel vision or through the excitability of media audiences.

Media also serve individuals: (1) through *cognition* (the learning process), (2) through *diversion* (rest and relaxation), (3) through *social utility* (interaction with family and friends) and (4) through *withdrawal* (shelter from unwanted intrusion).

Questions

1. How do individual audience members differ from the audience as a whole? Why do we say individual audience members make different demands on media than those made by the collective audience?

2. Name at least five ways in which the format of individual media can affect the messages they relay. Can you think of a specific example in which media form has altered a message directed to you?

3. Suggest some of the ways in which media may function to have long-range effects, even though individual messages may have no serious short-term impact.

4. How can repetition work favorably as a tool of media function? How can repetition work unfavorably?

5. Lasswell claims "transmission of the social heritage" is a necessary function of mass media. Do you think media set out purposely to fulfil this function? If yes, which? All or some? Name them. If no, why not? And how is the function performed?

6. What is the difference between cognition and diversion?

7. How can media help us to network with family and friends? How can media help us to withdraw from family or friends?

Altheide, David. *Media Power.* Beverly Hills: Sage Publications, 1985.

Bandura, Albert. *Social Learning Theory.* Englewood Cliffs, N.J.: Prentice-Hall, 1977.

Blumler, Jay, and Katz, Elihu, eds. *The Uses of Mass Communication: Current Perspectives on Gratifications Research.* Beverly Hills: Sage Publications, 1974.

Klapper, Joseph. *The Effects of Mass Communication.* New York: The Free Press, 1960.

McLuhan, Marshall. *Understanding Media.* New York: McGraw-Hill, 1964.

Monaco, James. *Media Culture.* New York: Dell, 1978.

Real, Michael. *Mass-Mediated Culture.* Englewood Cliffs, N.J.: Prentice-Hall, 1977.

Schramm, Wilbur. *Men, Messages, and Media: A Look at Human Communication.* New York: Harper & Row, 1973.

Tan, Alexis. *Mass Communication Theories and Research.* Columbus, Ohio: Grid Publishing, 1981.

Wright, Charles. *Mass Communication: A Sociological Perspective.* New York: Random House, 1986.

Suggested Readings

Messages and Effects

uppose you're watching a television drama about the Los Angeles police department. The former football star/hunk who plays the lead role goes through the prerequisite number of brawls, car chases and sudden leaps of intuition, then catches a woman who has burned her sleeping husband to death. But it isn't the usual murder motivated by greed, passion or hatred. This woman killed her husband out of fear. He was a rotten person, a spouse-abuser, and she killed him because she seriously believed she wouldn't survive another beating. The LAPD detective/hero arrests her as he must to satisfy the ends of justice, but he does it gently, showing great sympathy for her ordeal.

When you sat down to watch the program, you did so expecting to be entertained for an hour or so. When you come away from the program, you may spend a few moments contemplating a deplorable situation you had never bothered to think about before. Your thoughts may be fleeting, and you may switch to the next program without another thought. Or perhaps the program affects you more deeply, and it has a lasting effect on the kind of husband or wife you become. Or perhaps you're one of those people who think dark thoughts, then look with suspicion at a wife or fiancée and begin planning how to get her before she gets you.

When we talk about *functions,* by and large we are referring to the media and the reasons for the messages they transmit. When we talk about *effects,* one of the topics of this chapter, we are dealing with audiences and how they react to those messages. One side of the "message coin," then, is functional (media intent or purpose), and the other side of the coin is affective (audience response). You've already read a bit about effects in Chapter 3, but it's time to look more closely at the effects of media messages.

Media effects are more amorphous than media functions. What the media see as their functions (what they set out to do) can be ascertained fairly easily. What they *actually* do is more difficult to capture. But the two sides are closely related, since what media try to do they normally succeed in doing—to some degree. For example, if the program about the Los Angeles police has entertainment as one of its functions, then quite likely it will entertain. Usually, then, the function determines the effect, except when there is *dysfunctionalism* (a negative or unexpected result).

Elusive Media Effects

Many media effects seem clear and obvious to us, especially those related to specific cases that are observed soon after the message stimulus. Stimulus—response. The message urges you to buy a brand-new product; you go out and buy it. In this instance we feel we have found a definite effect. But often even such "obvious" effects are elusive and inconclusive. For example, there is the possibility that you will buy the product simply because you come to it first on the shelf or because your cousin asked you to get that particular brand—any number of possibilities quite apart from the message you received.

Usually, however, what the media intend with their messages is effective. For instance, the media see entertainment as one of their functions. They provide it, and we receive it. We are entertained. Therefore, we have been

A successful advertisement like this one has at least three kinds of effects.

affected by the medium and the message. There has been a result intentionally brought about by the medium. In a sense, then, the effect is the result of one of the functions of the media.

For example, television advertising tries to sell Beam toothpaste. One of your family members sees the commercial and learns about the product, then goes out and buys Beam. So TV has had its effect; it has been effective in its advertising message. One of TV's functions (to provide advertising and to make money) has been fulfilled. In this particular case, there have been at least three kinds of effects: (1) profit for the TV station or network that sold the ad time, (2) inducement for people to buy and use Beam toothpaste, and (3) profit for the Beam Toothpaste Company. The television message has been effective in three ways.

A rather serious problem arises at this point. You may already have thought of it. The advertisement was *effective* in the case of your family member, but what about all the other viewers who did not buy Beam? Where was the effect on them? If the ad didn't offer them entertainment or diversion (subsidiary effects), then it didn't have an effect on them.

But who said media were expected to affect *everyone?* The commercial had an effect—even if your aunt or uncle or brother was the *only person* affected. So when we consider media effects, we need not insist on total or 100 percent effectiveness. Thus it is perfectly logical to say that TV violence has an effect on children. Even if only a few children are affected in some way by such violence on the screen, the effect is there.

We do know beyond a doubt that mass messages can have definite effects. We note the vast sums of money raised by various "telethons" for worthy causes throughout the world, to alleviate starvation in parts of Africa or to help farmers who have been squeezed by economic disaster. We see millions of dollars raised regularly by TV evangelists whose pleas for money are "effective" (have the desired effects). The classic example occurred during

Mass media messages can have definite effects. For example, Jerry Lewis' many Muscular Dystrophy telethons have raised tens of millions of dollars.

World War II when singer Kate Smith, broadcasting over CBS radio every few minutes for 18 hours, got pledges for nearly $40 million worth of U.S. War Bonds. Message effectiveness? Of course. Even without a lot of research substantiation, there are certain effects that we know about intuitively.

Commonsense Media Effects

Before getting to the more esoteric matters surrounding media effects and looking at some of the positions taken by researchers, let us consider effects that would seem to be a matter of common sense. We'll deal briefly with only 15 of them here, but you could add many more to the list.

How are you affected by messages that come to you from the mass media? They help you to do the following:

1. *Receive ideas and viewpoints.* Even if you don't act on the basis of the ideas and viewpoints, they will have an impact on you.
2. *Have ideas and viewpoints reinforced.* You receive messages that agree with your own ideas and substantiate and reinforce them.
3. *Have ideas and viewpoints changed.* Some messages conflict with your own viewpoints and convince you to change.
4. *Have ideas and viewpoints moderated.* Perhaps you don't change your ideas completely, but you moderate them to some degree.
5. *Feel a sense of belonging.* Agreeable or psychologically compatible messages cause you to realize that others feel as you do and that you are not alone.

6. *Feel antagonism.* Some messages obviously antagonize you, causing you to become agitated and angry.

7. *Feel security and contentment.* Some messages give you a sense of well-being, happiness, contentment and security.

8. *Feel endangered and insecure.* Some messages create psychic harm, causing you to be anxious and to worry.

9. *Take trips and vacations (or want to).* Some messages cause you to desire to see other places, to become more mobile and adventurous.

10. *Buy generic and specific products (or want to).* Some messages cause you to desire things you don't have.

11. *Feel anger and frustration.* Some messages cause you to snarl at the TV set or throw down the newspaper.

12. *Vote for a particular person.* The message may contain something that will trigger your political support.

13. *Feel embarrassment.* Some messages may be inappropriate for you and cause some degree of embarrassment.

14. *Feel pride.* Some messages instill—or reinforce—in you a pride in hometown, nation or particular activity viewed.

15. *Become inactive.* The mere fact of reading the paper or watching TV keeps you from more active pursuits.

The problem with these commonsense effects is that they are often not intended by the message-senders. We react in unpredictable ways to messages, and what will enrage one person, for instance, will simply amuse another. When communication researchers talk of effects, they want to be scientific and to understand the effects well enough to predict them prior to the message. This goal, of course, is difficult since so many variables enter into every communication situation.

Theoretical Considerations

Actually no unified theory of effects exists today, although scholars in many countries have for years been concerned with media effects. We know that there are effects. But just how great they are and how many are specifically caused by media messages are virtually unanswered questions. Researchers are plagued by such questions as these: Was the reason the person responded to the message in a certain way due to the *form* of the message or due to the mental and psychological *inclination* already present? Was a certain action taken by a person due to the message or due to any number of other physical factors, such as a talk with a friend or a sudden impulse? Such difficult theoretical questions could be extended at length, but we're more interested in other aspects of mass communication for the moment, and much theorizing must be set aside. We cannot escape some theoretical consideration, however, since theory and practice are really symbiotic and natural.

Even though we have said there is no unified or grand theory of media effects, a number of micro-theories have emerged purporting to explain various aspects of media impact. (We'll look at some of these in the next section.) Effects always seem to be dependent on non-media–induced variables, but empirical data and pure speculation continue to spin out conclusions and opinions about media impact and effects. Everyone seems to be certain that media cause some kinds of effects, in some situations, with some people.

After all, mass communicators keep on sending messages, based on the assumption that they are getting through and are accomplishing the purposes intended. Advertisers, for example, continue to funnel billions of dollars into their efforts; they must know (or believe) that advertising is working, that it is having an *effect*. But, in spite of bits and pieces of empirical "proof" found here and there, theory is not solid enough at present to do much predicting as to which media and which messages will be able to have specific, or widespread, effects.

Taking a global or international perspective, we recognize that functions (purposes) of media vary around the world. Since functions differ, effects differ. Advertising may be an important media function in the United States, but in the former Soviet Union it was an insignificant function. Therefore, we would assume that advertising has had an impact on American society that it did not have on Soviet society. And we would be right. (However, advertising has become more prevalent in Russia since the dissolution of the Soviet Union and may well prove to be an important function in the future.)

In every society, however, there are many purposes for the mass media. In Chapter 3 we mentioned some of them for the United States; these are appropriate for a country embracing what is normally called a *libertarian* press system. The media in other ideological systems assume different functions.

J. Herbert Altschull (1984) suggests a simple typology of politico-media "theories" around the world. He distinguishes three types of societies (Marxist, market, and Third World) and emphasizes that different *purposes* for the media are found in each one. The nature of the media in each will affect the messages, which, in turn, have different kinds of impact on society. In a Third World ("developing") country, for instance, low media intensity and rather crude message strategies will not be as effective in bringing about change as media are in a highly developed market (advanced capitalist) society. In addition, the Third World country will stress "development" information (helpful, socially solidifying), whereas a market (capitalist) society might well be able to afford to go further and stress more escapist or entertainment messages. And in Marxist (socialist) societies, the emphasis might be on socially directive and harmonic messages designed for social stability rather than social unrest. This function contrasts with U.S. press theory, which stresses contention, debate, dissatisfaction and criticism.

Some Scholarly Observations on Media Effects

As noted earlier, a number of scholars interested in the effects of communication have formulated micro-theories to explain media impact. Because communication is important in many human activities, scholars interested in communication effects come from a variety of different fields—communication, sociology, psychology, psychiatry and the arts. The micro-

Table 4.1
Some Micro-Theories on the Effects of Media

Researcher(s)	Important Points
	POSITIVE EFFECTS
White (1950)	Media messages keep people in touch with the popular values of society; they have "massifying" (socializing) effects.
Klapper (1960)	Media messages reinforce social values. The media serve as a control mechanism to keep us in relationship to society's mainstream.
Berkowitz/ Klapper (1962)	Media have a cathartic effect, helping to purge unfulfilled desires, hopes, frustrations and negative feelings.
Wright (1986)	Mass media help socialize by teaching, either deliberately or inadvertently, social norms and expectations.
Cooley (1909, 1964)	Media messages enlarge belief-systems and produce value clarification (in which values are developed, reinforced or changed).
	NEGATIVE EFFECTS
van den Haag (1973)	Media messages are often demeaning, manipulative, depersonalizing, hedonistic, shallow or sensational; they "pull down" audience members.
Lazarsfeld/ Merton (1948)	Media cause "narcotizing dysfunction," making audience members mentally and psychologically sleepy and inert.
Wertham (1954)	The media corrupt society by valuing and teaching materialism, brutality, insensitivity and other antisocial behavior.
Allport/ Postman (1947)	Media messages create stereotypes by cataloguing people, actions, institutions and ideas in superficial ways.
	NEUTRAL/MIXED EFFECTS
Huxley (1965)	Most of what the media teach is trivial, superficial and devoid of real substance and value. We could well do without most of what we learn, although we may consider it important at the time.
O'Hara (1961)	Media messages cause social conformity, especially in the area of commercialism in which people come to think of themselves as consumers. Commercial conformity may help explain political conservatism in the United States.
DeFleur/ Ball-Rokeach (1988)	Media messages have little or no effect on people whose social realities are adequate; however, they can alter the behavior of those audience members who need or are dependent on mass messages.
McLuhan (1964)	Media cause effects that relate to the nature of the medium, not to the messages they send.
Ellul (1973)	Media messages create objectives for people, organize personality traits, standardize thought patterns and harden stereotypes (a negative effect).

theories formulated by various scholars can be divided into three types of effects: positive, negative and neutral/mixed. Table 4.1 notes the important points of each theory.

In the days between World War I and the end of World War II, communication scholars generally ascribed powerful effects to the mass media. Researchers in those days attributed great power to the media, seeing media messages as having direct impact on audience members. This belief was called the "magic bullet" model.

Powerful Effects/ Minimal Effects

A Japanese officer threatens a captured American aviator in the 1944 movie, "The Purple Heart." Propaganda-laden movies of this kind, aimed at creating anti-Japanese sentiment, reflect the "magic bullet" theory.

"Magic Bullet" Days

World War II was the heyday of the idea of powerful media and substantial message effects. Perhaps the idea had something to do with the emphasis given to propaganda (discussed in Chapter 2). The assumption was that people are greatly influenced by the mass media, assuming the message is on target and encoded skillfully. Messages were seen as bullets that, if aimed and fired properly, would reach their targets and accomplish their purposes. A simple stimulus-response communication model was dominant. Although the pure "magic bullet" theory was short-lived, it still retains its basic appeal and perhaps has considerable validity.

The **"magic bullet" theory** rears its head from time to time. For instance, it manifested itself in the 1970s in the works of French sociologist Jacques Ellul. He argues (1973) that propaganda is more effective than many Americans believe. The reason: It is so pervasive that we may not even realize it is around—yet it almost totally controls our thoughts and actions, according to Ellul.

Lazarsfeld: Minimal Effects

After World War II, the belief in powerful media effects began to change. Sociologist Paul Lazarsfeld and others began to stress the two-step flow (*personal influence*) model, which tended to moderate or negate the powerful impact of mass communication. Other scholars came up with complex multiflow models. One such was that of Everett Rogers in his many *diffusion-of-information* studies. For Rogers, the two-step flow does not adequately describe the composition of networks of people; what we most often have, according to Rogers, are many steps in the diffusion of information—not just two.

In both the two-step flow model and the diffusion (multiflow) model, opinion leaders were seen as important. The direct media-message stimulus resulting in an individual response was set aside. Instead, scholars traced media messages reaching certain opinion leaders (among others) who used these messages by passing them on to others, thereby diffusing throughout a network of message relayers any effect that the messages might have. Many scholars even thought that the opinion leaders themselves were more important than the media messages in bringing about an effect.

In concert with this two-step/multistep flow was the idea that media messages were only one of many forces acting on people's thoughts and actions. Innumerable factors intruded into the complex process of audience members' thought and action, although media messages did, indeed, have some effect. For at least twenty years following World War II, the "minimal effects" scholarship dominated.

In the 1950s and 1960s, attention turned to television and its effects. One important study by a Stanford University group (Schramm, Lyle, and Parker, 1961) identified three findings about TV and children: (1) low IQs of children correlate positively to heavy TV-watching, (2) children with poor social relationships watch more TV than children with better social relationships, and (3) there is no evidence that TV watching causes delinquency or violent behavior in normal children. Really only the third finding deals with television's effects on children, and the key word here is "normal." The study did not address what effect TV-watching has on "abnormal" children.

Concern about the effects of TV violence on children caught the attention of many American communication students. From 1969–1971, the U.S. Surgeon General sponsored a major study of TV violence and its impact. The results, however, were inconclusive; some kinds of violence will have an effect on some children.

So what about violent and erotic messages on TV? What is their impact on

The Annenberg Effects Studies

Professor George Gerbner and his associates of the Annenberg School of Communications (University of Pennsylvania) have done much research since 1970 on television effects on audiences. They have developed a model that says, in part, that heavy TV-viewing, both among adults and children, is associated with a television-biased view of their society and the world.

The Annenberg researchers have taken an approach combining detailed *content* analysis with an explanation of effects—the latter being determined by *meanings viewers absorb from the screen*. In addition to the content and the meaning factors, the researchers have been concerned also with the amount of *time* viewers spend watching television.

A few of the important aspects of the Annenberg research findings follow:

- Research on TV impact must go beyond studies of single programs viewed in isolation; such impact must be viewed as a powerful cultural force—a part of the social order that maintains the status quo rather than threatening or weakening it.

- The chief aspect of TV is *inculturation*—cultivating stability, social harmony, and acceptance of the status quo.

- Because of its pervasiveness and blend of eye-ear impact, TV has a credibility and power unmatched by any other medium.

- TV has taken the place of religion, of tribal elders and even of formal education. It functions as a socialization agent and control authority, showing how society works and promoting its value system.

- The more people view television, the more fearful they become, the more they sense danger around them, and the more they mistrust other people and authorities.

There are those who have challenged the Gerbner findings. For example, British researchers Mallory Wober and Barrie Gunter suggest that "a model is required which takes into account not simply how much television people watch but also the types of programmes they watch and the different interpretations viewers place on the content they see" (1988, pp. 51–52). In sum, Wober and Gunter seem to come down on the side of those who are ultra-careful about imputing broad impact to TV. They conclude: "Eventually . . . a limited version of the theory [that TV violence, for example, breeds violent behavior] can probably be said to be widely accepted— that some violence instigates violent actions among some viewers, on some occasions" (p. 17).

Sources: George Gerbner and L. P. Gross, "Living with Television: The Violence Profile," *Journal of Communication* 2 (1976), and Mallory Wober and Barrie Gunter, *Television and Social Control* (Aldershot, England: Avebury, 1988).

audiences? Public opinion polls show a great division on such a question among the population generally. Experts also disagree. Some scholars say that such messages might actually be a deterrent to delinquency by permitting youth to work off their aggressions and fantasies vicariously. Others, although they find harmful effects from violence and sex hard to prove, say that such effects are so obvious as to really need no proof.

Interest in the effects of message violence on youth has not disappeared. In 1988, for example, with the release of a violent movie about teen gangs ("Colors") the issue of effects was brought up again. Neil Malamuth, a

Experts disagree about the effects of television—particularly TV violence—on children.

psychologist at UCLA, was questioned by a reporter for *USA Today* about such effects; his main points were these: (1) such movies do cause a certain desensitization to violent images, (2) they affect teenagers in different ways, (3) they portray women negatively, (4) they make gang members seem to be heroes, (5) they are likely to cause short-term violence in youth and (6) more than any other country, the U.S. glorifies violence (*USA Today,* April 20, 1988).

Studies and expert opinions do not really indicate that media messages produce powerful effects. They tend to enhance the minimal effects conclusions of the post–World War II researchers and scholars. Thus we can see that studies and opinions (even among top scholars) are not conclusive and, in some cases, are actually contradictory.

Rebirth of Powerful Effects

In spite of tentative findings and contradictions supporting minimal effects, by the mid-1960s researchers had begun to believe that perhaps, after all, media messages had great effects. A number of scholars, such as Wilbur Schramm and Melvin DeFleur in the United States and Elisabeth Noelle-Neumann of Germany, reemphasized the powerful mass media. Many researchers, like Gerald Kline and Peter Clarke, focused on the messages (on content), believing that *what* people learn from the media gives clues to what is having an effect on them. Sociologist Todd Gitlin (1978) challenged the Lazarsfeld minimal-effects tradition and urged more attention to long-term effects rather than the prevalent research emphasis on short-term effects.

In Germany, Dr. Elisabeth Noelle-Neumann, perhaps Europe's premier audience surveyor, was stressing the media's **powerful effects.** She noted three important factors: (1) the ubiquity of the media (they are everywhere and it is impossible to escape them); (2) the cumulative effects of the media (messages are not individual and fragmented but are repetitive and cumulative and reinforce one another); and (3) there is communicator *consonance* (a great agreement among communicators—leading to a sameness of media messages).

The Spiral of Silence. Noelle-Neumann (1981) introduced her **spiral of silence** concept to support a powerful-media thesis. She contends that people who feel they are of a minority opinion remain silent, thereby reinforcing or enlarging the majority position. These people take a silent stance on an issue.

Their silence results in a kind of contagion of silence among others who share the minority view; and this ever-spiralling or enlarging silence plays into the hands of the vocal majority. The mass media exert great influence and have powerful effects, says the German researcher, because they publicize which opinions they consider important and give cues to the public about which opinions people can talk about or advocate without becoming isolated.

Not an Either-Or Choice

But in spite of an upsurge in powerful-effects scholarship, the **minimal-effects** perspective has not disappeared by any means. It is certainly not a matter of either-or. Some effects are powerful and some are not, just as some messages are more powerful than others (meaning that some are better encoded than others). Many scholars are still stressing that media only contribute to social effects and are not necessarily successful in causing them.

We still don't know, they say, if media are *themselves* powerful or if they are simply secondary factors or triggering mechanisms that have various impacts on society under certain conditions (see Figure 4.1). Candidates run for office and get elected. Did the media put them in? "No," we hear, "but the media probably played a part." But the losing candidates also used the media, some more extensively than the winners, and they still lost. Winners and losers alike knocked on doors, handed out cards, called people on the telephone and talked at the Kiwanis Club and the county fair. They were all very much individuals and not just media events. (Of course there's also the perennial question that resurfaced during the 1992 Bill Clinton/ George Bush race for the presidency—who makes the *better use* of the media?)

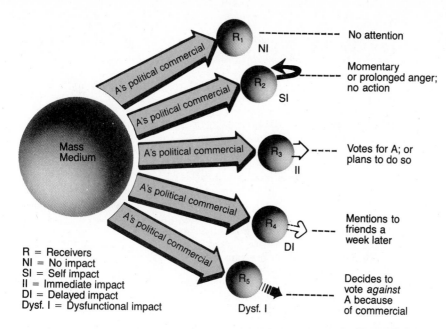

Figure 4.1
Possible Media Effects

R₁ — — — — — — — — No attention
NI

R₂ — — — — — Momentary or prolonged anger; no action
SI

R₃ — — — — Votes for A; or plans to do so
II

R₄ — — — — Mentions to friends a week later
DI

R₅ — — — — — Decides to vote *against* A because of commercial
Dysf. I

R = Receivers
NI = No impact
SI = Self impact
II = Immediate impact
DI = Delayed impact
Dysf. I = Dysfunctional impact

Agenda-Setting

One effect that *is* powerful, according to communication researchers Maxwell McCombs and Donald Shaw (1977) is **agenda-setting.** People learn what to think and talk about from the messages they receive. The media, in effect, largely structure our world of concern and largely dictate our daily interests. For example, many people learned from media reports about the growing need to recycle glass, paper and plastic trash—and some even began to do so voluntarily—long before state and local authorities enacted recycling legislation. The media are powerful instruments of guidance; they help determine the very things we think about and sometimes the things we do. That's real power.

While not denying the importance of agenda-setting, we might stop to wonder about the nature of the effect brought about on us by having our interests largely determined by the media. If they were not set by the media, agendas would nevertheless be set for us—by our contacts, our travels, our conversations, our direct involvement with the environment, our needs and our interests born of nonmedia activities. Naturally we think more about those ideas presented in the media than about ideas not in the media. But *what impact does such consciousness have on us?* The jury is still out on this question, although the natural inference is that what we think most about has the greatest impact on our values and actions.

A television station we know of has the motto "What concerns you concerns us." This motto sounds good and promotes the image that the station is sensitive and "people-oriented." The assumption is that the station finds out what people are concerned about and gives it to them. If that were the case, the *people,* not the media, would be the agenda-setters.

Recent challenges to Western communication efforts (coming largely from the Third World) would certainly indicate that international media effects are real and perhaps dangerous to indigenous cultures. The term *communication imperialism* is used frequently to symbolize the dangerous effects of global communication coming from nations with highly developed media systems.

Propaganda has more obvious effects, and the results usually can be ascertained more easily than can general media message intrusion into another country or culture. Propaganda programs can have measurable and limited effects. General messages of a nonpropagandistic nature are harder to analyze as to discrete results. New ideas and innovations, most research has shown, are spread through international communication. People do respond to, act upon, and modify for their own purposes many messages received from other countries.

Cultural habits and traditions are indeed changed by the intrusion of foreign messages. Rising expectations are generated by external communication. New sensitivities are planted, new wants are created, new aspirations are developed, and new hopes are implanted by messages coming into a country. There is no doubt that global communication has effects of some kind, with some people, in some situations, at some times. But, as with communication effects research within a single country, the verdict is still out as to the extent of such effects.

But most of us don't believe that; we believe that the correct media motto should be "What concerns us, concerns you." That's media agenda-setting.

Certainly we realize that our view of reality can be biased by the media's agenda-setting. Certain political positions, religious views, opinions and ideas can be repeated and given prominence in the media; others can be neglected or minimized. Few people would say that the media realistically reflect, with the proper emphases, the concerns and opinions of society. Media messages correspond only in a rough way to the reality to which they refer. So how are the media agendas formed? In some cases by pressure groups, by media imitating one another, by a tendency to stress atypical and sensational events, by favoring a colorful quote over a more prosaic one, by selectively reporting according to media biases and by "falling for" pseudoevents (manufactured "newsworthy" events).

Defenders of the Status Quo or Agents of Change?

Many scholars see media messages as defending the status quo, sustaining a social equilibrium, and reinforcing already-existing values. This view suggests a kind of *antichange effect,* a passive result of rather predictable messages. Or to use an even more inflated term, such an effect has been described as *media hegemony*—meaning that media views are controlled by a dominant group in society. Some researchers refer to media as "instruments of the dominant view." What this means is that the media (in whatever country) are no more than instruments in the hands of the most powerful group in society, reflecting the dominant ideology.

For example, media content in the United States reflects the capitalist ideology. And the content of the media in the former Soviet Union reflected the ideology of the powerful or dominant entity—the Communist Party elite. In short, defending the status quo is a *powerful-effects* view which says that the effects are inescapable because they are in tune with the basic spirit of the country. In this view, messages in an overall, long-term sense are potent because they have the society's prestige reflected onto them and through them. They serve to stabilize the populace by defending the ideological turf.

However, persuaders and propagandists of all types do not stress the macro-theory above. They may know that it is basically true, but they place their faith in the power of messages to change opinions and affect actions. Advertisers, especially, see messages as agents of change, instruments to get people to make some kind of change—to buy a different car, move into a different neighborhood, purchase a certain brand of soap or take a vacation in Florida.

Actually, the change-agent concept is not contradictory to the defenders-of-the-status-quo theory. It exists right along with it. For example, in the United States the dominant view *is perfectly in line with the concept of free-market competition and persuasive messages.* One has an overall ideological or political effect, while the other (the change-agent view) is easily subsumed under it and has a more localized (economic and pragmatic) effect.

Problems with Effects Studies

We have looked at the commonsense inferences and the scholarship dealing with message effects. Perhaps we should note, before concluding this chapter, some of the difficulties facing effects study generally. Innumerable obstacles exist, but let us briefly look at five.

1. *Messages cannot be separated from the personality of the audience member.*
   Personal variables (such as sex, age, health, economic status, race

and past experiences) will cause a message to have different effects on different receivers. Your "good" news may well be someone else's "bad" news. However, most mass communication researchers are interested in reactions of the total audience (or a majority, at least) rather than those of one individual in the audience.

2. *One medium cannot easily be isolated from others.* A variety of media bombard us every day; one person may hear different versions of a message from newspapers, radio, television, magazines and books. It is impossible for the audience member (or the researcher) to know precisely where the message came from. In fact, he or she may well have gotten the message from a family member or friend directly, rather than from a mass medium. Individuals often not only do not know where they get messages, but cannot even say how much time they give to the various media messages.

3. *Mass messages cannot be isolated from the receiver's physical context.* A message is affected by characteristics of the medium itself. A newspaper or magazine can easily be put aside before the reader finishes reading a message and then picked up later, but a TV or radio message can't be interrupted and resumed (unless it's taped). A TV message is a social experience (interaction between viewers), whereas movie-watching is more solitary. TV permits withdrawal or flexibility by the viewer (leaving the room temporarily or changing channels); movies hold the viewer more closely to the total message.

Such factors, relating to reading, listening and viewing, all play roles in media impact. How then can the researcher set up artificial conditions and hope to obtain real-life results? The dilemma: the lab conditions are unreal and may seriously flaw the results, yet the results are virtually inaccessible to the researcher under normal conditions.

4. *The problem of representative control groups impedes research.* A communication researcher seeking data about the effects of a specific advertisement can expose one group to the ad and isolate another group (the control group) from it. But what about more complex situations? How does the researcher find control groups for investigating problems of vital social concern, such as the impact of obscenity, racial slurs, violence, political bias, religious preaching? Mass media messages penetrate the total American society, and a person not exposed to them in these areas will likely not be representative at all.

If we are attempting to list effects of violence, for example, how will we find a control group of "normal" children who have not been exposed to regular TV fare? If we attempt to select a control group of normal children and expose them to even more TV violence, they then are placed under "abnormal" lab conditions and also run the additional risk of having their psyches harmed for the sake of science.

5. *Elusive long-range effects are often ignored.* In a laboratory situation, a radio listener may evidence an obvious, even startling, reaction to a message. An hour later, the message may be forgotten. Other listeners may not react so strongly at the time, but the message may have a cumulative force that, over time, will affect them intensely. It is virtually impossible to determine cumulative effects. The researcher cannot stay with the receiver except for a limited period, nor can the receiver be

isolated from hundreds of other factors that impinge on him or her over time.

It is easy to maintain (as we often hear) that Mr. X tried to assassinate the president because, since childhood, Mr. X was exposed almost every day to violent TV dramas, movies and reading material. Here a cumulative effect has been postulated as the cause of the attempted assassination. But it is really little more than unsupported speculation.

Conclusion

So what do we *know* from the body of effects research and speculation? Not very much. We do know that under certain conditions mass messages have effects on some people. We know that, but not too much more. We also know that being exposed to a message is not "getting the message" (understanding it). Nor is getting the message the same as being affected by it. And we know that psychological effects are different from overt, action-oriented effects, although often they are somehow related.

That people often receive messages and disregard them is obvious. For example, a majority of American newspapers opposed the presidential candidacies of Thomas Jefferson, Andrew Jackson, Abraham Lincoln, Woodrow Wilson, Franklin Roosevelt, Harry Truman and John F. Kennedy, but they all won anyway.

Research shows that the average American is exposed to nearly 2,000 advertising messages each day but is moved (pro or con) by no more than 15 of them. Other studies show that the individual exposure rate for advertising is considerably less (down to some 300 messages from the mass media), but that the effectiveness rate (what action is taken) is still small—about five "successes" out of the 300.

In spite of these findings, human beings *are* affected by mass media messages. Researchers have shown (at least in some cases) that mass media do, indeed, narcotize their audiences, produce conformity, retard participatory democracy, inculcate habits of violence and delinquency, play into the hands of terrorists and so forth. But it is really impossible for researchers to prove or disprove every such finding because of the innumerable variables involved. And, therefore, it is impossible to *predict* what kind of effect (if any) a certain kind of message will have on an audience.

As we have seen, much attention has been given to powerful and minimal effects, but the definition of these terms is impossible to determine. Just how powerful (by any definition) would the media have to be to be considered powerful or effective? And are there not different types of power or effectiveness? For instance, the mere providing (or withholding) of *information* is one kind of power—regardless of impact. Another kind of power might be the effect of the message on the mind—or the psycho-emotional system. And still another kind of power might be the effect of the message on the *actions* of people. So, taking into account the research and also commonsense conclusions, we present on the next page a three-part postulate, with which we end this chapter:

Research suggests that Americans see 2,000 advertising messages a day, but they are moved by only about 15 of them.

- Media are most powerful in furnishing information and setting agendas for members of a public.
- Media are next most powerful in affecting the thoughts, opinions and attitudes of members of a public.
- Media are least powerful in affecting the actions of members of a public.

Retrospective

Effects of mass communication are hard to appraise. There are so many factors impinging on a particular situation (other than the media messages) that one never is quite sure just what impact the media have. However, there are many indications that media messages have significant impact; we can see this, for example, in the effect advertising has on our buying habits. We also know of the contagious power of news stories about such things as skyjackings and terrorist activities. And we certainly know that mass media set *agenda*—giving us items to think and talk about and possibly to act upon.

Many effects are rather obvious (commonsense) effects. We also know from researchers that there are more complex effects and that these vary in different societies. Some scholarly researchers suggest that media have *powerful* effects; others contend that the effects are *minimal.* The jury is still out on this important problem of mass communication. We still don't know precisely how powerful media and their messages can be in our daily lives.

1. How would you differentiate *functions* of the media from *effects* of the media messages? Do you think that effects are dependent on media functions?

2. What is meant by *commonsense effects*? Name several of the 15 given in the chapter and explain why they are (or are not) obvious effects with no real need for substantiation by research.

3. Would you expect to find the same kind of message effects in developing countries, the Marxist world, and the capitalist (market) world? In what ways would effects be similar, and in what ways would they be different?

4. Marshall McLuhan talks of the medium as being the message. What do you think he means by that? Would it imply that the media have no messages other than themselves?

5. If the mass media were eliminated in the United States, what do you think would be the effect on society? Name at least three important changes that would occur almost overnight in the basic functioning of the society.

6. Explain why Noelle-Neumann's *spiral of silence* might help explain the conformist behavior of a rigid, authoritarian society. What do you think would be the result of people speaking up—even when they feel they are in the minority?

Altschull, J. Herbert. *Agents of Power: The Role of the News Media in Human Affairs.* New York: Longman, 1984.

Ball-Rokeach, S. J., and DeFleur, M. L. "A Dependency Model of Mass-Media Effects." *Communication Research* 3 (1976).

Blumler, Jay G., and Katz, Elihu, eds. *The Uses of Mass Communications: Current Perspectives on Gratifications Research.* Beverly Hills: Sage, 1974.

Chaffee, S. H., ed. *Political Communication: Issues and Strategies for Research.* Beverly Hills: Sage, 1975.

DeFleur, Melvin, and Ball-Rokeach, Sandra. *Theories of Mass Communication,* 2nd ed. New York: Longman, 1988.

Gerbner, George, and Gross, L. P. "Living with Television: The Violence Profile." *Journal of Communication* 2 (1976).

Ellul, Jacques. *Propaganda: The Formation of Men's Attitudes.* New York: Vintage Books, 1973.

Fesbach, S., and Singer, R. D. *Television and Aggression.* San Francisco: Jossey-Bass Publishers, 1971.

Gitlin, Todd. "Media Sociology: The Dominant Paradigm." *Theory's Society* 6 (November 1978).

Klapper, Joseph T. *The Effects of Mass Communication.* New York: Free Press, 1960.

Lemert, James B. *Does Mass Communication Change Public Opinion After All?* Chicago: Nelson-Hall, 1981.

McCombs, Maxwell, and Shaw, Donald. "The Agenda-Setting Function of Mass Media." *Public Opinion Quarterly* 36 (1972).

————. *The Emergence of American Political Issues: The Agenda-Setting Function of the Press.* St. Paul, Minn.: West, 1977.

McLuhan, Marshall. *Understanding Media.* New York: McGraw-Hill, 1964.

Merrill, J. C., and Lowenstein, Ralph. *Media, Messages, and Men.* New York: Longman, 1979.

Noelle-Neumann, Elisabeth. *The Spiral of Silence.* Chicago: University of Chicago Press, 1981.

————. "Return to the Concept of Powerful Media," *Studies of Broadcasting* 9 (1973).

O'Hara, Robert. *Media for the Millions.* New York: Random House, 1961.

Roberts, D. F., and Bachen, Christine. "Mass Communication Effects." *Annual Review of Psychology* (February 1981).

Rogers, Everett. *Diffusion of Innovations.* New York: Free Press, 1983.

Severin, Werner J., and Tankard, J. W. *Communication Theories.* New York: Longman, 1988.

Stephenson, William. *The Play Theory of Mass Communication.* Chicago: University of Chicago Press, 1967.

Wertham, F. *Seduction of the Innocent.* New York: Rinehart, 1954.

Wober, Mallory, and Gunter, Barrie. *Television and Social Control.* Aldershot, England: Avebury, 1988.

Wright, Charles. *Mass Communication: A Sociological Perspective.* New York: Random House, 1986.

Practice & Support

Mass media are our windows on the world, and they come in many forms. The early print media—books, newspapers and magazines—all evolved in special ways over the years. With the taming of electricity, new media developed. Radio gave us sound over long distances. The recording industry preserved words and music for future masses. Early movies offered flickering, silent visuals, then learned to speak. A late arrival on the mass media scene was television, which rapidly became the most powerful of them all.

Where did these major mass media come from? How did they develop? What makes them function? How do they differ from country to country? Who are the people that keep them humming? What economic factors determine their survival? And where are they going in the future? In this section, we will study the media in turn, examining their rich histories, their unique operating procedures, their basic economics and their possible roles in coming years.

We will also examine media corollaries. Advertising and public relations are an integral part of our media system. American mass media depend heavily on advertising for support. Public relations specialists provide a voice for industry and government through the supply of information to communicators. Once the intricate and often unpredictable workings of the media and media corollaries become clear, we can move on to a careful examination of developing issues and concepts that have become increasingly important to us.

CHAPTER 5

Newspapers

Ed Quillen was a journalism major at the University of Northern Colorado not long ago. He was a senior when he took the big chance: He quit college.

He didn't abandon the university because he was bored. He quit because he couldn't wait another year to become a professional journalist.

He applied for a reporter's job at the prestigious *Denver Post.* "Sorry," said a *Post* editor, "you need more experience. Try a smaller paper." Ed talked to other editors and soon decided that if he were going to find a challenging newspaper opportunity in Colorado's hotly competitive journalism market, he would have to hire himself. So Ed took another chance: He borrowed money and purchased the *Middle Park Times,* a weekly in Kremmling, Colo., with a circulation of 1,200.

As editor and publisher of the *Times,* Ed often worked 14-hour days four days a week. Sure, the hours were long, but running the paper was exciting. Ed learned about important events before most people in Kremmling did—accidents, murders, divorces, bankruptcies. He learned how organizations such as city hall really operated. He performed a critical public service: The people of Kremmling depended on him for news about government, who was visiting whom and even what the high school was serving for lunch. All of that information and responsibility was invigorating for Ed.

Ed may not have known it at the time, but when he became a newspaper journalist he joined an exclusive club. There are fewer than 10,000 newspapers in the United States—about 17 percent of the world's total—and they employ only about 75,000 reporters and editors. To put it another way, university professors are six times more prevalent than newspaper reporters.

Newspapers Yesterday

In addition to laboring in an unusual profession, Ed, as a weekly publisher and editor, also worked in a vocation with proud, old traditions that in some ways haven't changed much in centuries. For example, like a 17th-, 18th- or 19th-century weekly newspaper editor, Ed did almost all of the work. He wrote editorials, reported events based on information from business and government sources, sold advertising, designed the newspaper, distributed it, hustled non-newspaper or "job" printing and balanced the books.

Besides laboring like past editors, Ed used much of the same equipment found in newspaper offices of earlier ages, particularly the 19th century. There were pencils and pens, paper for note-taking, typewriters for pecking out stories and machines that created type. Newspapers of the past usually reflected the personality of the owner. Ed's did, too.

In short, Ed's job and tools and even the *Middle Park Times* would have been familiar to the European printers who began the world's first newspapers in the early 1600s. To be sure, Ed would have preferred to have had more employees and better equipment, but the money never seemed to be available. The European printers of yesteryear would have been familiar with that problem, too.

1450	Johann Guttenberg fashions movable metal type to create the first effective printing techniques in Europe.
1605–1610	The first regular newspapers appear in Europe.
1621	The first primitive English *corantos,* reporting foreign news, are sold on the streets of London.
1628	Domestic reports, called *diurnalls,* issue news of Parliamentary proceedings in England.
1690	Benjamin Harris prints the first newspaper in America, *Publick Occurrences.* It is quickly suppressed.
1702	The first daily newspaper in the English language, the *Daily Courant,* appears in London. It lasts only a few days.
1704	John Campbell establishes the first continuing newspaper in America, the *Boston News-Letter.*
1735	John Peter Zenger stands trial for seditious libel.
1783	The first daily American newspaper, the *Pennsylvania Evening Post and Daily Advertiser,* appears in Philadelphia.
1833	Benjamin Day publishes the *New York Sun,* the first of the penny newspapers. James Gordon Bennett's *New York Herald* (1835)

	and Horace Greeley's *New York Tribune* (1841) follow.
1848	Six New York newspapers join forces to form the Associated Press in an attempt to cut telegraph costs.
1851	Henry J. Raymond begins publication of *The New York Times.*
1878	Joseph Pulitzer buys the *St. Louis Post-Dispatch.* He will purchase the *New York World* in 1883.
1887	William Randolph Hearst takes over the *San Francisco Examiner;* he will buy the *New York Journal* in 1895 and begin famed head-to-head competition with Pulitzer.
1923	American Society of Newspaper Editors adopts Canons of Journalism.
1950	Offset printing becomes feasible for newspapers.
1958	United Press (est. 1907) and International News Service (est. 1909) combine to form a single wire service, United Press International.
1963	Major dailies begin setting type by computer.
1972	*Washington Post* begins Watergate coverage, for which it will win a Pulitzer Prize.
1982	Gannett launches *USA Today.*

The Newspaper Emerges

Newspapers began between 400 and 500 years ago in Europe as political tracts, pamphlets and, later, newsletters and news sheets, commonly called *corantos.* To be sure, there were examples of news sheets predating even these materials, such as the *Acta Diurna* (or the "day's actions") published by the Roman government about 100 B.C. and the block-printed "palace report" of the Tang dynasty in China, circa 618–907. Unlike these earlier publications, however, the European newsletters and sheets of the 1500s were *not* published by governments. The little news sheets also were not issued regularly and seldom bore a title or any authorship, undercutting their reliability and disqualifying them as true newspapers. All things considered, in the late 1500s the most regular and reliable news (or "intelligence," as it was often called) came from the local tavern.

The European news sheets evolved into regularly published newspapers between 1605 and 1610 in Belgium, the Netherlands and Germany. *Nieuwe Tidingen,* first published in Antwerp, Belgium, about 1605, is an example of one such early newspaper. Newspapers such as *Nieuwe Tidingen* carried information about business, war and peace and, more rarely, the actions of government.

As the press developed, press law developed. American colonial press law, of course, had its roots in England. For that reason, it's important to understand the environment in which English newspapers operated. King Henry VIII issued a proclamation in 1534 licensing all printers. The theory was that a printer could pursue his commercial interests—and keep his license—so long as those interests did not undermine the government. The printer (and *printer* is the correct word because most people who began news sheets in this era were printers who selectively reprinted information rather than gathered it) also agreed to submit to prior censorship. Thus, printed criticism could be headed off several ways. Prepublication censorship and threats of license removal would eliminate most problems. If all else failed, there was the charge of *seditious libel,* or criticism of the state.

Thus, English printers and their descendants—publishers, editors, and later, *journalists,* an inclusive word for those who gather and publish information—were tamed by the whips of censorship, licensing and libel. Nonetheless, newspapering did prosper in England. For example, by 1621 there was a weekly coranto in England, and by 1665, the twice-a-week *Oxford Gazette* was available. A daily paper, the *Daily Courant,* appeared in 1702, and by 1750 England had five prosperous dailies and numerous nondaily newspapers.

American Colonial Newspapers

Prior to 1690, America had little need for newspapers because English weekly newspapers were readily available. In addition, the local business climate was not particularly favorable for newspapers because the colonial population was small and largely illiterate, barter was favored over cash (which discouraged advertising), and transportation was dreadful. Philadelphians, for example, had to wait two to six weeks to receive mail from Boston, a city only 300 miles distant.

But perhaps the real reason for the slow development of newspapers in the American Colonies was the philosophy of political leaders such as the governor of Virginia, who in 1671 supposedly said, "I thank God we have no free schools or printing; and I hope that we shall not have them these hundred years. For learning has brought disobedience and heresy and sects into the world; and printing has divulged them and libels against the government. God keep us from them both."

The good governor's attitude was apparently in vogue in Boston in 1690 when the first American newspaper, *Publick Occurrences, Both Foreign and*

Domestick, made its debut. The newspaper, published and edited by Benjamin Harris, lasted one issue. American journalists such as Harris still had to seek permission to publish their periodicals, even though licensing in England wasn't required after 1694. When they received permission, they usually displayed it on the front page of the newspaper with words such as "Published by Authority." Harris not only did not have permission but, to his credit and misfortune, published a story about the King of France who, in an apparent lapse of judgment, seduced his son's wife. Authorities promptly closed the newspaper.

John Campbell, the Boston postmaster, was next to try his hand at publishing a newspaper. Campbell's *Boston News-Letter,* a handwritten sheet published with approval, appeared in 1704. Campbell got his news from merchants, sea captains, politicians and soldiers. The paper was dull but prosperous.

Other journalists tried other approaches. Beginning in 1721, James Franklin, who was Benjamin Franklin's older and perhaps more hot-tempered brother, published a politically lively newspaper called the *New England Courant.* The paper was published without authority. After a jail sentence for contempt and a grand jury investigation, the elder Franklin succeeded in accomplishing one truly significant political goal: He broke the back of the Massachusetts licensing law in that it remained on the books but was no longer enforced.

Besides licensing, colonial publishers also suffered under what today seems to be a strange libel law. *Libel* means defamation. For example, accusing a government official of incompetence—in the 1690s or in the 1990s—is defamation. Under modern libel law, if the official is indeed incompetent and it can be proved, you can escape an expensive libel judgment. However, under English and colonial American libel law, the greater the truth the greater the libel. Thus, if you called attention to an official who was incompetent, and you were correct in your assertion, you would be guilty of libel because you would be eroding the authority of the state.

A New York publisher named John Peter Zenger ran afoul of libel laws in 1734 when he deliberately criticized the governor of New York, a political enemy, for incompetence. The governor, who apparently felt he was guilty as charged, ordered Zenger jailed. Zenger hired Alexander Hamilton, an elderly if first-class lawyer; together they eventually prevailed in allowing a jury to decide both *the truth of the statement* and *whether the statement was punishable,* both normally the job of the judge. Zenger was freed, but unfortunately the decision was a legal aberration. Other publishers had to continue to battle the tradition of English libel law and later American seditious libel law until 1800.

Despite Zenger's New York trial, it was clear by the 1750s that Boston, with a population of about 15,000 and at least six of the Colonies' dozen weekly newspapers, was the capital of American journalism. Even so, the Boston newspapers followed the general pattern in the Colonies: Newspapers, a little like meteors on a summer night, would appear, burn bright for

N. E.   Numb. 1.

The Boston News-Letter.

Published by Authority.

From **Monday** April 17. to **Monday** April 24. 1704.

London Flying-Post from Decemb 2d to 4th. 1703.

Etters from *Scotland* bring us the Copy of a Sheet lately Printed there, Intituled, *A Seasonable Alarm for Scotland. In a Letter from a Gentleman in the City, to his Friend in the Country, concerning the present Danger of the Kingdom and of the Protestant Religion.*

This Letter takes Notice, That Papists swarm in that Nation, that they traffick more avowedly than formerly, & that of late many Scores of Priests and Jesuites are come thither from *France*, and gone to the North, to the Highlands & other places of the Country. That the Ministers of the Highlands and North gave in large Lists of them to the Committee of the General Assembly, to be laid before the Privy-Council.

It likewise observes, that a great Number of other ill-affected persons are come over from *France*, under pretence of accepting her Majesty's Gracious Indemnity; but, in reality, to increase Divisions in the Nation, and to entertain a Correspondence with *France*. That their ill Intentions are evident from their talking big, their owning the Interest of the pretended King *James* VIII. their secret Cabals, and their buying up of Arms and Ammunition, wherever they can find them.

To this he adds the late Writings and Actings of some disaffected persons, many of whom are for that Pretender, that several of them have declar'd they had rather embrace Popery than conform to the present Government, that they refuse to pray for the Queen, but use the ambiguous word Sovereign, and some of them pray in express Words for the King and Royal Family; and the charitable and generous Prince who has shew'd them so much Kindness. He likewise takes notice of Letters not long ago found in Cypher, and directed to a Person lately come thither from St. *Germains*.

He says that the greatest Jacobites, who will not qualifie themselves by taking the Oaths to Her Majesty, do now with the Papists and their Companions from St. *Germains* set up for the Liberty of the Subject, contrary to their own Principles, but meerly to keep up a Division in the Nation. He adds, that they aggravate those things which the People complain of, as to *England's* refusing to allow them a freedom of Trade, &c. and do all they can to foment Divisions betwixt the Nations, and to obstruct a Redress of those things complain'd of.

The Jacobites, he says, do all they can to perswade the Nation that their pretended King is a Protestant in his Heart, tho' he dares not declare it while under the Power of *France*, that he is acquainted with the Mistakes of his Father's Government, will govern us more according to Law, and endear himself to his Subjects.

They magnifie the Strength of their own Party, and the Weakness and, Divisions of the other, in order to facilitate and hasten their Undertaking; they argue themselves out of their Fears, and into the highest assurance of accomplishing their purpose.

From all this he infers, That they have hopes of Assistance from *France*, otherwise they would never be so impudent, and he gives Reasons for his Apprehensions that the *French* King may send Troops thither this Winter, 1. Because the *English* & *Dutch* will not then be at Sea to oppose them. 2. He can then best spare them, the Season of Action beyond Sea being over. 3. The Expectation given him of a considerable number to joyn them, may incourage him to the undertaking with fewer Men if he can but send over a sufficient number of Officers with Arms and Ammunition.

He endeavours in the rest of his Letters to answer the foolish Pretences of the Pretender's being a Protestant, and that he will govern us according to Law. He says, that being bred up in the Religion and Politicks of *France*, he is by Education a stated Enemy to our Liberty and Religion. That the Obligations which he and his Family owe to the *French* King, must necessarily make him to be wholly at his Devotion, and to follow his Example; that if he sit upon the Throne, the three Nations, must be oblig'd to pay the Debt which he owes the *French* King for the Education of himself, and for Entertaining his supposed Father and his Family. And since the King must restore him by his Troops, if ever he be restored, he will see to secure his own Debt before those Troops leave *Britain*, The Pretender being a good Proficient in the *French* and *Romish* Schools, he will never think himself sufficiently aveng'd; but by the utter Ruine of his Protestant Subjects, both as Hereticks and Traitors. The late Queen, his pretended Mother, who in cold Blood when she was *Queen* of *Britain*, advised to turn the West of *Scotland* into a hunting Field will be then for doing so by the greatest part of the Nation, and, no doubt, is at Pains to have her pretended Son educated to her own Mind. Therefore, he says, it were a great Madness in the Nation to take a Prince bred up in the horrid School of Ingratitude, Persecution and Cruelty, and filled with Rage and Envy. The Jacobites, he says, both in *Scotland* and at St. *Germains*, are impatient under their present Straits, and knowing their Circumstances cannot be much worse than they are at present, are the more inclinable to the Undertaking. He adds, That the *French* King knows there cannot be a more effectual way for himself to arrive at an Universal Monarchy, and to ruine the Protestant Interest, than by setting up the Pretender upon the Throne of Great *Britain*, he will in all probability attempt it, and tho' he should be perswaded that the Design would miscarry in the close, yet he cannot but reap some Advantage by imbroiling the three Nations.

From all this the Author concludes it to be the Interest of the Nation, to provide for Self defense; and says, that as many have already taken the Alarm, and are furnishing themselves with Arms and Ammunition, he hopes the Government will not only allow it, but encourage it, since the Nation ought all to appear as one Man in the Defence

of

FIRST ISSUE OF *THE BOSTON NEWS-LETTER*
(Reduced)

The *Boston News-Letter:* America's first successful newspaper.

awhile, then disappear because of too few subscribers or too little advertising.

Press of the New Nation

By the period of the American Revolution, there were about four dozen newspapers in the Colonies, with circulations ranging from a few hundred to a few thousand. Philadelphia had nine newspapers, including the nation's first daily, and, in fact, rivaled Boston as a center of journalistic activity. This bustle may have occurred because Philadelphia equaled Boston in population or perhaps because the city was the nation's birthplace and a news center much like Washington, D.C., is today. Another explanation is that Philadelphia was the home of the indefatigable Benjamin Franklin, who in 1729 took over publication there of the soon-to-be famous and profitable *Pennsylvania Gazette.*

Franklin had started his newspaper career in Boston but moved to Philadelphia to avoid an apprenticeship with his brother, James, who, as you recall, owned the *New England Courant.* Beginning a newspaper at this time wasn't a particularly difficult financial hurdle for Franklin or anyone else in the new nation. A printer could save enough money in two or three years to buy the used equipment necessary to open his own shop. And with that, the printer immediately could become a journalist—or more accurately, a newspaper editor, advertising salesman and circulation manager.

These 18th-century American newspapers were usually small. They were often fewer than four pages printed on both sides, with each page a little wider and longer than this book. Circulation was equally small. Less than a thousand subscribers was common; several thousand was unusual. Editorial copy included some news stories (such as obituary, government, crime, court, and weather articles) but more typically consisted of politically related letters and essays. The typical 18th-century American journalist considered himself or herself to be a printer first, an editor second and a reporter—someone who actually gathered news—last, if at all.

Most American newspapers supported the Revolutionary cause, and after the war was won, they lobbied for a clause in the nation's new Constitution guaranteeing freedom of expression. When the First Amendment to the Constitution was finally approved 15 years after the signing of the Declaration of Independence, it permitted a degree of press freedom for United States' newspapers that was unsurpassed then—and now—anywhere else in the world.

American journalists, who by the end of the 18th century were more likely to consider themselves editors first and printers second, took their newly won press freedom to heart; thus, as the new nation's press matured, it became even more outspoken than it was during the pre-Revolutionary period. In fact, this era in American journalism came to be called the "partisan press" period because the most outspoken papers were affiliated with and often supported by political parties—notably the Federalists and the Anti-Federalists. These two parties disagreed over the powers of the new government. The Federalists supported numerous newspapers, including the New York-based *Gazette of the United States* and the *Porcupine's Gazette and Daily Advertiser* in Philadelphia. Anti-Federalist publications included the *National Gazette* and, later, the *Philadelphia General Advertiser,* edited by the grandson of Benjamin Franklin.

Personal attacks (sometimes later followed by physical ones) were the order of the day for these newspapers. For example, here's what Franklin's grandson, Benjamin Bache, had to say about former President George Washington in a 1797 issue of the paper, popularly known as the *Aurora:*

> If ever a nation was debauched by a man, the American nation was debauched by Washington.
>
> If ever a nation has suffered from the improper influence of a man, the American nation has suffered from the influence of Washington.
>
> If ever a nation was deceived by a man, the American nation has been deceived by Washington. . . .

Even politically unaligned newspapers often wandered far from modern standards of neutral or objective reporting. This type of journalism prevailed until the mid-19th century, when it began to be replaced by a new kind of newspaper, a paper for the unaligned and barely political reader.

The Penny Press

American journalism changed significantly when a new kind of newspaper, called the penny press, was created in New York City. If you mention the penny press to a modern journalist such as Ed Quillen, one name and several ideas come to mind. The name is Benjamin Day, who founded the New York *Sun*. The then-new ideas were popular news reports—such as police news and human interest stories about ordinary people—all marketed in an easy-to-read, three-column format targeted to the middle and lower class at an affordable price.

Day's ideas were new because prior to the 1830s most newspapers were intended for special or elite audiences. Mercantile papers, the *Wall Street Journals* of their day, were aimed at businessmen, for example. Party newspapers were for the party faithful. There were many general newspapers, of course, but they tended to concentrate on the political events of the time, running ponderous essays by affected parties. In all, it wasn't particularly exciting reading for the literate bricklayer or teamster.

In addition, most of New York City's 11 other newspapers sold for 6 cents a copy, a price that would also buy a pint of cheap liquor. For readers who, at best, earned a dollar a day, the 6-cent newspaper cost too much. On the other hand, Day's paper, introduced in 1833, was priced at an affordable penny—perhaps the price of a shot of whiskey.

Day executed his plan by borrowing money to purchase the nearly defunct New York *Sun* and announcing in it that "the object of this paper is to lay before the public at a price within the means of everyone all the news of the day." The project was a success. The average circulation of a New York daily in the early 1830s was 4,000 copies a day; by 1839, Day's *Sun* was selling 50,000 copies a day.

Aside from the formula of popular news at a penny a paper, the penny press was sold on the street (rather than by subscription, as was customary) and featured extensive classified advertising. In addition, Day hired *reporters,* which was unusual. Earlier papers had grown large enough so that the publisher could no longer spare the time to write the entire paper, but the editor usually solved that problem by hiring an assistant editor rather than a reporter. Day not only hired reporters, he hired specialists: police reporters, court reporters, political reporters, all theoretically writing without a political ax to grind.

The *Sun* soon attracted imitators, such as James Gordon Bennett's *New York Herald,* started in 1835. The clones appeared because the nation was ready for a popular press for a variety of reasons. By the late 1830s, cities such as Philadelphia, New York and Boston were populated with relatively large numbers of people who could read and who wanted to buy newspapers for information and entertainment. And these papers attracted advertisers because readers had money to spend for manufactured goods. Finally, large, relatively inexpensive press runs were possible because of steam-powered rotary presses, unheard of in the 1700s. It all added up to the dawn of a new day for American journalism, a day of newspapers about the people and for the people.

The U.S. Media Barons and Their Newspapers

The 19th century was a time of growth for American newspapers. In 1830, there were 65 dailies and 500 weeklies in the country. By the end of the century, there were more than 2,000 dailies and 12,000 weeklies.

Newspaper circulations grew, too. In the early 1800s, New York newspapers—the nation's biggest—seldom boasted circulations beyond a few thousand a day. By the end of the century, some New York newspapers sold a million copies a day. These huge press runs were possible because the one-page-at-a-time press of the early 1800s gave way to the steam-driven presses, one of which could print 48,000 12-page newspapers per hour.

The hub of American journalism also changed. Boston, which was the media center of the country during much of the 1700s, lost that position to Philadelphia when that city became the nation's capital and news center in 1790. In the early 1800s, however, New York began to assume the proportions of the nation's media center, an honor it still enjoys. Why New York? It was the nation's biggest city by the early 1800s—by 1850, it was four times as large as Baltimore, then the nation's second largest city—and as such, could support many newspapers. City schools produced large numbers of potential readers, and contributed to a literacy rate of 80 percent of the U.S. population by the time of the American Civil War.

This situation eventually led to the creation of newspapers of great

Media baron William Randolph Hearst.

enterprise and readership. Examples include *The New York Herald,* edited by Bennett who, for example, used horses, ships, trains, carrier pigeons and, after 1844, the telegraph to retrieve reports from places where news was breaking. When James Gordon Bennett, Jr., became editor, he continued the tradition, for example, sending journalist Henry Stanley to Africa in 1871 to "find" missionary David Livingstone, who wasn't really lost. There was the thoughtful, socialist and often utopian *New York Tribune,* founded in 1841 and edited by Horace Greeley. And, of course, there was *The New York Times,* started in 1851 for $100,000 by Henry J. Raymond as a newspaper of record where important speeches, for example, would be printed in full. Other American cities had great newspapers, too, but few papers could match those in New York for scale, whether the measurement was circulation size or publisher involvement.

Regarding publisher involvement, no history of 19th-century American newspapers would be complete without mentioning Joseph Pulitzer and William Randolph Hearst. They are monumental if controversial figures in American journalism.

Pulitzer was a Hungarian immigrant born in 1847, who, at age 20 and after service in the American Civil War, got a job as a reporter for a German language daily in St. Louis. He was successful and by the time he was 31, he purchased the *St. Louis Post-Dispatch,* the city's leading afternoon daily. With popular, colorful, enterprising and often sensational reporting, he pushed the soon-to-be prestigious *Post-Dispatch* and later the slightly

Rival media baron Joseph Pulitzer.

sleazier New York *World,* which he bought in 1883, to national prominence. In his final years, he endowed the school of journalism at New York's Columbia University as well as annual awards for outstanding work in journalism and the arts.

Hearst was born in California in 1863 with "a silver spoon in his mouth"—almost an apropos saying in his case because he inherited much of his wealth from family silver mines. He learned the newspaper business courtesy of the family-owned *San Francisco Examiner.* Hearst bought the *New York Journal* in 1895 and began a massive circulation battle with Pulitzer. The struggle spawned what is now known as yellow journalism— the use of sensational stories and presentation to attract readers. The term originated as a reference to a popular *World* comic strip called the "Yellow Kid," which was printed with yellow ink in order to attract reader attention. But discounting excesses, Pulitzer and Hearst also published newspapers that championed ordinary citizens' struggles and featured investigative reporting—in short, newspapers of influence.

Press Associations and the Evolution of the News Story

While American newspapers in New York and beyond were changing, the methods of gathering and writing news were also changing. Few newspapers have the resources to cover news beyond their circulation area. The solution to that dilemma is to purchase news from another source: from a news organization in the distant city where events are occurring or, more typically, from an organization that specializes in collecting news from a variety of far-flung places. Organizations that specialize in collecting and writing news for other news organizations are called **press associations** or **wire services.** Charles Havas began a press association in France in 1833 that in the 20th century became one of the world's most important news services, Agence France Presse. Many other important world press associations, such as London-based Reuters and Berlin's Wolff, also appeared during the mid-1800s.

In the United States, six New York newspapers created the New York Associated Press in 1848. That organization, now known as the Associated Press, was and is a cooperative. Newspapers are members, rather than subscribers, and news organizations are assessed fees for the operation of the nonprofit AP.

These press associations, particularly the AP and its ancestors, contributed to the evolution of the news story content and structure. For example, 19th-century news stories, even those in the penny press, often lacked modern objectivity. Press association reporters had to create neutral accounts of events because the press association served newspapers of varying views. Eventually, this concept of neutral or objective reporting became the ideal for all U.S. newspapers.

In addition, wire service reporters—and the telegraph, which they used to transmit many stories—changed the very structure of the news story. Before the American Civil War, the typical news story was often wordy and written chronologically. The **inverted pyramid** style of newswriting soon emerged as war correspondents filed stories over battlefield telegraph lines where wordiness meant extra expense and chronological order meant a story's critical ending was never received if the line was cut during transmission. The inverted pyramid required the story's first paragraph to sum up what happened in one sentence, while answering the questions *who, what, when, where* and perhaps *why* and *how*. Subsequent paragraphs explained the story in a declining order of importance. Today, most news stories are written using this approach.

The Modern U.S. Newspaper Emerges

By 1900, the American newspaper had much in common with the paper of today. For the most part, reporting was neutral and stories were written using the inverted pyramid structure. In addition, the sharp personal journalism that once pervaded all aspects of journalism was more the exception than the rule, except on the editorial page, where personal opinion belonged. In short, by the turn of the century, most American editors were producing newspapers that were reliable and objective.

However, if the typical daily newspaper was philosophically mature by the early 1900s, it was only an adolescent technologically and economically, with plenty of changes just around the corner. For instance, technology quickly changed the way stories were reported, written, set into type and printed. By about 1900, typewriters, invented 30 years earlier, started appearing in newsrooms, and reporters soon found themselves abandoning their longhand in favor of pecking at keys. About the same time, reporters also began using the telephone to relay stories to other writers who specialized in transforming field reporting into finished articles. Ottmar Mergenthaler's automatic typesetter—the Linotype—speeded up the process of getting stories into print, but still required an operator to retype a

The *National Enquirer,* which sells 4.5 million copies a week and boasts that it has ''the largest circulation of any paper in America,'' is a contradiction. For example, even though the colorful tabloid with huge screaming headlines looks like a newspaper, it's considered a magazine by the Audit Bureau of Circulations. And although the *Enquirer* made its reputation in the 1960s and 1970s with lurid and often doubtful stories about bizarre crimes, two-headed babies and alien landings in Iowa, the *Enquirer* of the 1990s is pedestrian when compared to its supermarket competitors. And finally, though the *Enquirer* is hardly *The New York Times* or *The Washington Post,* it pays its reporters and writers more than many *Times* and *Post* staffers make. Reporters, who ferret out information, make up to $100,000 a year; writers make even more.

The *New York Enquirer* was born in 1926 and purchased by Generoso Pope Jr. in 1952 for $75,000. By 1960, Pope had turned the paper into the *National Enquirer,* featuring a formula of blood and guts and, some say, inaccuracies.

The blood and guts, two-headed babies and aliens are mostly gone now. What happened to the *Enquirer* of the 1950s and 1960s that we knew and loved? Television actress Carol Burnett sued the paper in 1976 because of an inaccurate story, settled for $800,000 in 1981, and in her wake created a calmer—and, some say, more accurate—publication. Today's *Enquirer,* which is aimed at married, working mothers under 35, deals in celebrity gossip, matrimonial and medical tips and human interest stories that would be acceptable in many if not most American newspapers and magazines.

Well, what about accuracy? Are *National Enquirer* stories true? Yes, the publication's editors say. Here's why. Story ideas are checked against *Enquirer* files, fleshed out by reporters, checked again by a team of researchers and finally approved by the publisher. If the publisher—that was Gene Pope's role until his death in late 1988—approves the story idea, a writer goes to work. The writer's completed story is checked and edited and finally checked again by the publisher—and by company attorneys if necessary.

But critics smirk. The *Enquirer's* sources for stories are often unidentified (''An insider told the *Enquirer . . .''), critics point out. Thus, only *Enquirer* reporters, researchers, writers and editors can judge the credibility of a source. Too, the *Enquirer* frequently pays sources, which is considered sleazy journalistic practice.

The question of the quality of the *National Enquirer* is an interesting and ongoing debate, but for *Enquirer* editors, it's a moot point because the jury's verdict is in on the new and improved *Enquirer:* Circulation is growing.

---

reporter's story, as did the photocomposition typesetter, introduced in the late 1940s and early 1950s. By the 1970s, computers that produced type had marched out of the newspaper's production department and replaced the reporters' typewriters, allowing them to typeset their own stories.

In addition, photojournalism, which was technologically possible in the 1800s, found its way into the newsroom in the early 1900s and forever changed the appearance of newspapers. Since the 1600s, newspapers had used *woodcuts* or printed drawings to illustrate some stories, but by World War I, photographs were prevalent. Eventually "picture" newspapers were born. One such picture newspaper, the New York *Daily News,* was established in 1919 and is now America's sixth largest circulation paper.

Newspapers also used new technology to print color advertisements and, later, color photographs. Occasional color was used by some papers beginning in the 19th century, but high-quality color as a routine part of news coverage dates from the birth of *USA Today* in 1982. *USA Today's* color is the product of extremely sophisticated computer-based, satellite-transmitted technology, only recently available.

Economic forces also brought about major changes in 20th-century daily newspapers. One such change was the growth of afternoon or "PM" papers, a trend sometimes attributed to the growing prevalence of the electric light bulb and the gradual shortening of the typical work day, which together encouraged evening reading.

In the mid-1960s, however, the number of PMs began to decline. Much of their circulation shifted to morning or "AM" newspapers. This decline may have happened because of competition from television or perhaps because of the changing lifestyles of readers. In any case, the dwindling numbers of PMs reduced the number of newspapers in most communities so that by the 1990s, only about 80 American cities had two newspapers. In those cities, both papers were often owned by the same company because economic forces during this period had dramatically increased the number of daily newspapers owned by chains. For example, fewer than 40 American cities in the 1990s were served by two or more papers under *different* ownership. (And in many cases, that competition occurred under a joint operating agreement, a federally approved merger of all but the editorial departments of the competing newspapers.) In summary, by the 1990s, the typical American city was no longer home to a large number of fiercely competitive family-owned newspapers, as was the case in the early 1900s. It was served by one or perhaps two dailies owned by the same chain.

Newspapers Today

Let's come back to Ed Quillen's little country weekly. In some ways—in its basic informational role, sole ownership and profit orientation, for example —Ed's paper is quite like its ancestors. In other ways—in its philosophy of public service, its writing style, and, lately, its technology—it's very much a product of the late 20th century.

Overview of the U.S. Newspaper Industry

Of the world's 60,000 newspapers, about 8,000, or one in eight, are dailies. America has about 9,000 newspapers, of which about 1,500, or approximately one in six, are dailies. Clearly, most of the world's and America's papers are other than dailies—that is, they are published once, twice or even three times a week. Of America's dailies, most—about 1,000 in the 1990s—are afternoon newspapers, although, as you've read, that number decreases each year.

Circulation of U.S. dailies stands at about 60 million copies a day for morning and evening papers (see Table 5.1). Sunday circulation totals another 62 million copies. Each paper, of course, is read by more than one

DAILY ● NEWS **EXTRA EDITION**

NEW YORK'S PICTURE NEWSPAPER

Average net paid circulation of THE NEWS, Dec., 1927:
Sunday, 1,357,556
Daily, 1,193,297

Vol. 9. No. 173 56 Pages   New York, Friday, January 13, 1928   2 Cents IN CITY LIMITS 3 CENTS ELSEWHERE

DEAD!

Story on page **3**

(Copyright; 1928: by Pacific and Atlantic photos)

RUTH SNYDER'S DEATH PICTURED!—This is perhaps the most remarkable exclusive picture in the history of criminology. It shows the actual scene in the Sing Sing death house as the lethal current surged through Ruth Snyder's body at 11:06 last night. Her helmeted head is stiffened in death, her face masked and an electrode strapped to her bare right leg. The autopsy table on which her body was removed is beside her. Judd Gray, mumbling a prayer, followed her down the narrow corridor at 11:14. "Father, forgive them, for they don't know what they are doing?" were Ruth's last words. The picture is the first Sing Sing execution picture and the first of a woman's electrocution.—*Story p. 3; other pics. p. 28 and back page.*

This secretly taken *Daily News* photograph of convicted killer Ruth Snyder being executed in 1928 is typical of aggressive word and picture reporting found in the United States during the 1920s and 1930s.

Table 5.1
Twenty Largest U.S. Daily Newspapers

Average Daily Circulation[1]

The Wall Street Journal	1,795,206	(m)	Chicago Sun-Times	528,324	(m)
USA Today	1,506,708	(m)	The Boston Globe	508,867	(m)
Los Angeles Times	1,146,631	(m)	The Philadelphia Inquirer	502,149	(m)
The New York Times	1,145,890	(m)	The Star-Ledger, Newark	481,027	(m)
The Washington Post	802,057	(m)	The Dallas Morning News	479,215	(m)
Daily News, New York	777,129	(m)	New York Post	437,918	(m)
Newsday	758,358	(all day)	Houston Chronicle	419,725	(all day)
Chicago Tribune	724,257	(m)	Star Tribune, Minneapolis	410,920	(m)
Detroit Free Press	580,372	(m)	The Plain Dealer, Cleveland	410,237	(m)
San Francisco Chronicle	556,765	(m)	The Detroit News	398,630	(e)

[1]ABC FAS-FAX, Sept. 30, 1992

Source: Audit Bureau of Circulations. Reprinted with permission.

person—typically, between 2.2 and 2.7 people per issue, depending upon the characteristics of the newspaper and its readers. Weekly circulation, by the way, accounts for another 55 million copies.

Newspapers, which are usually 60 percent or more ads, lead all American media in advertising revenue, with 23 percent of the total in 1992. Television, for example, logged about 22 percent of all advertising dollars that year and was followed by direct mail, yellow pages, radio, magazines and other assorted media (see Figure 5.1).

Newspapers, especially the dailies, are largely owned by more than 100 chains, the 20 biggest of which control nearly 600 papers (see Table 5.2). As you've read, America's locally owned daily newspapers have been quietly succumbing to chain ownership for decades. But the mortality rate has quickened of late. Loren Ghiglione, author of *The Buying and Selling of America's Newspapers* (1984), says: "Almost 90 percent of the daily U.S.

Figure 5.1
Newspapers' Share of Advertising: 1992

Source: McCann-Erickson, Inc., Newspaper Association of America. Courtesy of McCann-Erickson, Inc. Reprinted by permission.

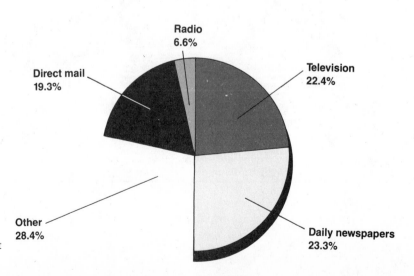

Radio 6.6%

Television 22.4%

Direct mail 19.3%

Other 28.4%

Daily newspapers 23.3%

Table 5.2
Twenty Largest U.S. Newspaper Companies (ranked by daily circulation)

	Daily Circulation[1]	Number of Dailies	Sunday Circulation	Number of Sunday Editions
Gannett Co. Inc.	5,882,595	81	6,070,256	66
Knight-Ridder Inc.	3,701,479	28	5,193,557	24
Newhouse Newspapers	3,038,360	26	3,889,713	21
Times Mirror Co.	2,760,334	9	3,468,786	8
Dow Jones & Co. Inc.	2,360,256	23	531,547	14
Thomson Newspapers Inc.	2,148,136	120	1,930,561	78
The New York Times Co.	1,964,681	24	2,557,634	16
Tribune Co.	1,425,359	7	2,029,971	7
Scripps Howard	1,330,367	21	1,314,351	13
Cox Enterprises Inc.	1,322,207	18	1,761,092	16
Hearst Hewspapers	1,209,644	12	1,795,829	10
MediaNews Group	1,138,761	18	1,349,964	15
Freedom Newspapers Inc.	932,883	27	985,979	19
The Washington Post Co.	854,346	2	1,205,014	2
Central Newspapers	818,845	9	999,577	4
McClatchy Newspapers	803,938	12	946,970	9
Donrey Media Group	790,235	55	810,372	48
Capital Cities/ABC Inc.	749,331	8	991,169	6
Copley Newspapers	746,957	11	811,005	7
The Chronicle Publishing Co.	734,854	6	903,560	3

[1]Average for six months ended Sept. 30, 1992

Source: Thomas Vander Poel, Lynch, Jones & Ryan; Audit Bureau of Circulations. Courtesy Audit Bureau of Circulations. Reprinted with permission.

newspapers sold since 1975 have been purchased by newspaper chains. At the current rate, there will be no single, family-owned dailies by the year 2000."

Why all of this selling and buying? From the chains' perspective, good newspapers make good profits. Publishers who had sold out say that their decision was based on an economic survival of the fittest. They cite the attractively high purchase prices paid by chains along with the desire to escape heavy government inheritance taxes.

Newspaper industry statistics clearly confirm the selling trend. In 1910, only about 3 percent of the nation's 2,200 daily newspapers were operated by chains (or "groups," the term preferred by multiple-media owners and their public relations departments). By 1974, chain ownership had increased to 55 percent of the nation's daily papers. By the 1990s, chain ownership of the country's dailies had grown to a whopping 74 percent. Circulation is another measure of group influence. About 20 years ago, groups controlled 58 percent of the country's daily circulation. Now they control more than 80 percent.

Why do groups insist on getting bigger? If a company is profitable, it has

GLOBAL GLANCE
Newspapers: A Quick World Survey

Some 60,000 newspapers are published worldwide, with an approximate circulation of at least 500 million. Readership, however, is probably three times the circulation figure because copies are passed from person to person, placed in libraries and schools and posted in public places.

About one-third of all newspapers are published in North America, another third in Europe, and the remaining third in all other parts of the world. Countries with the highest newspaper readership are Sweden, Britain, Norway, Denmark, Japan and the United States.

At least half of the world's newspaper circulation is in Europe. North America accounts for about another 25 percent of the circulation, and the rest of the world for 25 percent. Many areas of the world—about 40 countries, mainly in Asia and Africa—are virtually without newspapers, and those that exist are very small and crude sheets of about four pages. Fewer than 50 countries have daily papers with as many as 12 pages.

Of all the world's dailies, about 25 percent are in the English language. Following English, the greatest number of dailies are Chinese, followed by German and Spanish.

Most of the international prestige newspapers are found in Europe and North America. These are the papers that are taken seriously by serious people such as scholars, librarians, government officials and writers around the world. Representative of such papers are Europe's *Neue Zuercher Zeitung* (Zurich), *Sueddeutsche Zeitung* (Munich). *Le Monde* and *Le Figaro* (Paris), *El Pais* (Madrid), *Corriere della Sera* (Milan), *The Times* and *The Telegraph* (London), *Svenska Dagbladet* (Stockholm) and *Berlingske Tidende* (Copenhagen).

Papers of similar prestige in the United States would be *The New York Times, The Washington Post, The Christian Science Monitor* and the *Los Angeles Times.* Other such papers around the world include *Izvestia* of Moscow, *Asahi Shimbun* (Tokyo), *Renmin Ribao* (Beijing), *Globe & Mail* (Toronto), *O Estado de S. Paulo* (Sao Paulo), *Excelsior* (Mexico City) and *The Statesman* (New Delhi).

Circulation leaders among the world's newspapers are found in Japan, Russia, Britain and the United States, where dailies such as *Yomiuri Shimbun, Daily Express* and *The Wall Street Journal* typify the big circulation papers. A circulation of a million copies daily is a very large one in the global context. No more than 30 daily newspapers have such large circulations.

Le Figaro of Paris is one of a small number of international newspapers of great prestige.

three options under America's economic system: first, plow profits back into new businesses or new equipment for businesses it already owns; second, declare dividends and pay that cash out to the stockholders; or third, pay taxes on the profits. The usual approach is to do a lot of the first, a little of the second and, if possible, none of the third.

Group ownership of the news media, and newspapers in particular, is bad news, say critics who believe concentration of ownership leads to mischief or mediocrity. What's wrong, anyway, with an out-of-town or out-of-state newspaper owner? Nothing, in many cases. For example, group owners are quick to point out that some locally owned newspapers are dreadful and actually improve when purchased by a group.

Nonetheless, national studies of group newspaper ownership suggest several potential problems. Critics charge that editors and writers who work for group papers often come from other parts of the country, don't know enough to adequately report about local problems and are transferred about as soon as they learn what makes a community tick. Critics also charge that some group-owned newspapers avoid editorializing on controversial local matters and turn to "canned" editorials from headquarters that appear in a number of newspapers at the same time.

A factor difficult to measure but even more significant is the degree of financial commitment an out-of-town owner will provide. For example, will an out-of-town owner put as much money back into a newspaper as one who lives in the community? Critics say no, charging that some group owners see their newspapers only as profit centers, leaving the publications with emaciated budgets and little local news.

In sum, the statistics suggest a question: Will the locally owned U.S. daily newspaper in 2000 be—like a 25-cent vending machine cola—fondly remembered, but as extinct as a woolly mammoth?

Newspaper Operation

Daily newspaper organization varies some with the size of the paper. Let's look at the organizational structure of a medium-sized newspaper—one with circulation of, say, 45,000 (see Figure 5.2). The newspaper is managed but probably not owned by its publisher. The publisher (who also may be the paper's editor) supervises all operations of the newspaper, which has five departments or divisions: *advertising,* which sells ads; *editorial,* which produces the news; *production,* which prints the paper; *circulation,* which distributes it and *business,* which handles administrative tasks.

- The advertising department is headed by an advertising manager who supervises sales representatives, although the titles may vary from paper to paper. Some sales representatives sell local retail or **display advertising.** Others sell national advertising. Still others sell **classified advertising,** ads arranged or classified according to subject. Space that isn't filled with ads is called the **news hole** and is the responsibility of the editorial department.

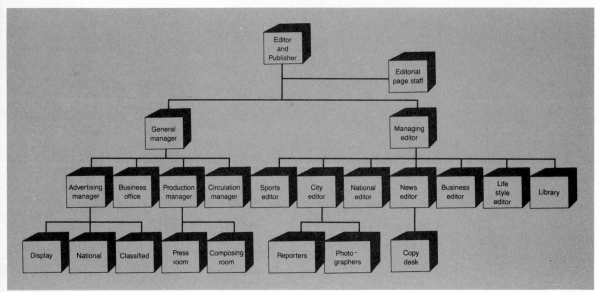

Figure 5.2
Organization of a Medium-Sized Daily Newspaper

- The editorial or news department is directed by a managing editor. The ME, as he or she is frequently called, supervises numerous other editors, including those for the newspaper's sports, national and local news, business and lifestyle sections. The ME also may oversee the newspaper's editorial writers. You'll read more about this department later in this chapter.

- The production manager heads a team of compositors and printers who reproduce the newspaper, after ads have been sold and news stories written.

- The circulation department, headed by a circulation manager, is responsible for getting the newspaper delivered, both to customers' homes and to street racks or boxes. Most customers who have contact with their daily newspaper deal with someone in this department.

- The business department oversees administrative functions such as accounting. The head of the business department is the business manager or the general manager or even the publisher.

Newspaper Dollars and Cents

Some of the daily newspaper's revenues come from subscriptions. However, most revenues—80 to 90 percent—come from local, national and classified advertising.

Ad rates are based on circulation, which is measured by a not-for-profit, self-regulating association called the Audit Bureau of Circulations. About 1,200 daily newspapers are ABC members. ABC publishers are required to maintain records of their circulation and make those records available to the

ABC auditor when requested. For paid publications, those records verify payment for a single copy or a subscription. Then the auditor, who is nobody's fool, uses a sampling procedure to determine whether the information the publisher has provided ABC is true.

How does the newspaper spend its money? Production costs the newspaper the most—from 25 to 30 percent of total expenses—followed by administration, advertising, news and circulation. Note, however, that percentages and ranks can be misleading. Even though news ranks next to the last in costs, *The New York Times* reportedly spent between $80 and $100 million each year of the late 1980s for news coverage.

Now that you have the numbers, here's the story behind the figures. The American newspaper is clearly a medium in transition. Most U.S. cities, which once had numerous newspapers, are served by only one paper or by two newspapers under common ownership. In America's smaller towns, that paper usually is a PM. In metropolitan areas and locales where television is a serious competitor, it's almost always an AM. Those papers typically make lots of money, Wall Street investment analysts say. For example, a medium-circulation daily paper with good management and no substantial print competition can produce a 10 to 20 percent profit on advertising and subscription revenues before paying taxes, a ratio considerably higher than many other businesses, including banks. Newspapers that operate under less-than-desirable competitive conditions—that is, with serious print and broadcast competition in the same market—have pretax profits of about half that amount.

But profits depend upon readers, and there's some evidence to suggest there may be a reader shortage down the road. In the 1920s, newspapers began to deal with reader defections for the first time. Initially, the competitor was radio, which offered local news as early as 1920 and network news beginning in 1924. By the late 1950s, television news also began to

---

The Top 10 Daily Newspapers

Every so often, journalists ask other journalists or experts to produce a list of the country's best daily newspapers. For example, *Time* magazine made such a list in 1974 and again in 1984. This list is from *Adweek,* an advertising industry publication that polled 13 experts in the late 1980s. Note that all but four of the 11 newspapers are based in the northeastern United States.

1. *The New York Times*
2. *Los Angeles Times*
3. *The Washington Post*
4. *The Wall Street Journal*
5. *The Philadelphia Inquirer*
6. *Newsday*
7. *The Christian Science Monitor*
8. *Chicago Tribune*
9. *The Boston Globe*
10. *The Miami Herald* and *San Jose Mercury News* (tie)

Source: *Adweek.*

threaten the newspaper's audience, and, according to the Roper Organization's public opinion poll for the television industry, by 1963 television had replaced newspapers as the medium Americans most consulted for news. By the 1970s, the newspaper industry circulation numbers didn't look good at all. In fact, daily newspaper circulation essentially stopped growing in 1985. In 1986, combined circulation of morning and evening newspapers actually declined more than 250,000 copies from 1985 figures while the population grew by more than 2 million persons. Here's another way to look at these figures. In the late 1940s, most American households bought more than one newspaper every day. As a result, the total number of newspapers sold relative to all households was 130 percent, or 1.3 papers per home daily, according to the Newspaper Association of America. By the 1990s, the number of newspapers sold each day relative to all households was less than 67 percent.

The trend is clear: While overall readership is still increasing slightly, particularly on Sunday, per capita newspaper readership—the formal name is **market penetration**—is declining. It is dwindling, in fact, to a point where it is far below that of many European nations.

The U.S. Newspaper Reader: A Profile

If part of the newspaper industry's problem is the disappearing reader, publishers need to know who is—and isn't—reading their product. Recent newspaper-financed studies suggest that about two-thirds of all Americans over age 18 read a daily paper and that men and women read in about equal numbers. Surveys suggest that regular readers of daily newspapers tend to be upper-income, older (that is, over 45), college-educated, married homeowners who are long-time residents of their communities. In other words, readers are people who can and do buy goods—an advertiser's dream.

On the other hand, nonreaders are often relatively poor, young (under 30), high-school-educated, unmarried apartment-dwellers who are short-term residents of large cities. These nonreaders say they don't buy newspapers because they don't have the time to read and because papers cost too much. Some add that newspapers are dull and that television, which is where they get their information, isn't.

If a disproportionate number of readers are an advertiser's dream, why bother with nonreaders? Newspaper owners want to reach the poor, young nonreaders because they may eventually become middle-class consumers, and if they haven't developed the newspaper reading habit in their 20s or early 30s, they may not ever develop it. "News 2000," a project of the giant Gannett group, is an example of an attempt to attract nonreaders (and better serve current readers). The "News 2000" plan calls for each Gannett newspaper to survey people from various community cultural, economic, lifestyle, racial, religious and social groups. Editors then use this market research to tailor the newspaper's content to the community's needs. Typical changes include more color, graphics, short *USA Today*-type stories and less "spinach journalism," which is news that editors think is important despite its lack of appeal.

Some 125 daily newspapers yielding nearly 65 million copies each day indicate the massive readership and importance of the print media in Japan.

One newspaper—*Yomiuri Shimbun*—claims a circulation of at least 8 million copies a day nationwide. Most Japanese readers spend at least 30 minutes a day with their newspapers because reading is an important and enjoyable experience for the average Japanese. As a matter of fact, it has been said that Japanese don't just read their newspapers: They are drawn into them as they are drawn into their baths.

Five national papers are found in Japan. The most prestigious perhaps is *Asahi Shimbun* (*shimbun* is the word for newspaper). The other four national papers are the *Mainichi Shimbun,* the *Yomiuri* (which is the largest), and the *Nihon Keizai* and the *Sankei* (which are similar to *The Wall Street Journal* in the United States).

In addition to the top dailies, there are dozens of small regional and city-based dailies. All of them flourish and provide large amounts of local news. Many households read both a national paper and a regional or local paper.

Editorial staffs are huge in Japan. For example, *Asahi* ("Rising Sun") has some 3,000 reporters and editors. Staffers must be from prestigious universities and go through a series of tough mental and psychological exams. Once employed, they will likely remain with that paper for their entire careers.

How people read the newspaper is mostly what you might expect. Papers are usually read close to the time of purchase or delivery—seven out of 10 papers are delivered. One study suggests that a majority of newspaper readers browse through the newspaper page by page rather than zero in on specific items. Readers are often attracted by items because of positioning—the front page has high readership, for example—or because the item has accompanying pictures or is large, as in the case of an advertisement. In addition, one study suggests that readers spend about 30 minutes with a small daily paper and up to 50 minutes with a fat metropolitan paper, although other surveys suggest a more typical reading time is about 20 minutes.

In general, all kinds of people read all kinds of content, but when grouped by sex or age, readers do show preferences. For example, men usually read local, national and international news, followed closely by sports. Women read local, national and international news, too, but follow that with strong preferences for advice columns and food pages. And, statistically speaking, practically no one tackles the crossword puzzle, although editors who inadvertently leave it out of the paper for a day will tell you otherwise.

The U.S. Newspaper Reporter: Quite Another Profile

Who are reporters? In the early 1980s, *Time* magazine published a cover story about the press and used this description, distilled from commonly heard complaints about reporters, to lead the article:

Although black-owned and black-oriented newspapers have served readers in the United States for nearly 200 years, the integration of general circulation daily newspaper staffs by blacks and other minorities has been a relatively recent and not completely successful experience.

Serious, organized integration of U.S. newspapers by publishers and trade groups began in the 1960s. Minority employment goals varied from one news organization to another but are best exemplified today by the efforts of the American Society of Newspaper Editors to increase minority newsroom staffing to reflect the proportion of minorities in the population. Despite the ASNE goal, recruitment and retention of black and other minority journalists has fallen short of expectations. By the 1990s, for example, minorities made up about 22 percent of the U.S. work force but constituted only about 18 percent of the overall staffs of America's daily newspapers. Worse still, minorities accounted for only about 10 percent or reporters and copy editors (African Americans held most of the jobs) and a dismal 6 percent of newsroom supervisors.

Why haven't the goals of ASNE and others been met? The most prominent minority journalism groups—the National Association of Black Journalists, the National Association of Hispanic Journalists, the Asian American Journalists Association and the Native American Journalists Association—suggest that the reasons include too few minority students studying in university journalism programs and too few minority faculty members teaching in those programs. In addition, too few newspapers are owned by minorities, the groups explain. Finally, some groups say that minority journalists who work for nonminority-owned newspapers often see their careers stalled below management level, which results in their leaving the field. For example, 40 percent of the minority journalists surveyed in a 1985 study by the Institute for Journalism Education said they planned to leave journalism within five years.

White women, unlike African Americans, played a prominent part in the newspaper business from its earliest days—as publishers, editors, reporters, photojournalists, and typesetters. However prominent their roles, they have been and are to some degree still severely under-represented on the staffs of American daily newspapers. In the 1990s, for example, women made up 48 percent of the U.S. work force and 39 percent of daily newspaper and newsroom staffs. However, only about 29 percent of the top newsroom manager jobs were held by women and only 7 percent of America's daily newspapers were published by women.

In short, America's daily newspapers are controlled by white males. Even so, many reporters and mid-level editors are women, and women are beginning to take their places as newsroom managers. For blacks and other minorities, progress is less evident.

Women have been employed as reporters by U.S. newspapers for many years. They are now beginning to become newsroom managers.

They are rude and accusatory, cynical and almost unpatriotic. They twist facts to suit their not-so-hidden liberal agenda. They meddle in politics, harass business, invade people's privacy, and then walk off without regard to the pain and chaos they leave behind. . . .

The statement is a teaser, of course, but the question raised is legitimate: Do reporters and readers share similar viewpoints? In 1986, David H. Weaver and G. Cleveland Wilhoit of Indiana University published a landmark study, "The American Journalist: A Portrait of U.S. News People and Their Work," of U.S. journalists that updated an earlier study and provided a hint at an answer. Subsequent studies filled in even more gaps.

According to the studies, there are more than 75,000 daily and weekly newspaper reporters and editors in the United States (and another 35,000 broadcast reporters). The typical newspaper reporter is a 32-year-old white Protestant male—although more than 40 percent of reporters and editors are women—who has a bachelor's degree, most likely in journalism or communication. He is middle-class, married with children and is politically middle-of-the-road, although he may identify with liberal positions and call himself an independent. In any case, he denies his opinions affect his stories. He's not as religious as the typical American. He probably reads one or more of these publications—*Time, Newsweek, The New York Times, The Washington Post, The Wall Street Journal*—and avoids joining community or professional organizations. Finally, the typical reporter will leave journalism in his 40s for a job with more money and benefits and better working conditions. Of course, some reporters land management positions in the news business: The Weaver and Wilhoit study suggests that managing editors are about six years older and a little more conservative than their reporters but otherwise share many of the reporter's characteristics.

The picture that emerges from Weaver and Wilhoit and from other studies is that newspaper readers are older, more conservative and more religious than reporters. So what? The answer is that as a result, reporters sometimes cover events in ways that alienate or offend readers. For example, one mid-1980s study asked reporters and readers if a story based on secret government documents involving national security should be published. Seven out of 10 of the journalists answered "sometimes" whereas almost seven out of 10 of the readers said "never." This discrepancy results in criticism of the press, which you'll read more about later in Chapters 13, 14 and 15.

All newsgathering, whether for print or broadcast, begins with a question: Is this event newsworthy? Reporters and editors answer that question by asking additional questions about the event. The exact queries will vary from time to time and place to place, but there's a consensus among American editors and reporters that an event under consideration for coverage should be examined for *timeliness,* and then for *conflict, consequence* (or importance), *human interest, novelty* (or unusualness), *prominence* and *proximity*.

The U.S. Newsgathering Process

The Elements of News

Let's assume you're the editor of the daily newspaper in San Marcos, Texas. You learn that the county medical association will sponsor a series of public discussions about AIDS, Acquired Immune Deficiency Syndrome, at nearby Southwest Texas State University. The first speaker in the series, a local physician who heads the medical society, will talk about how AIDS is spread. Should you assign a reporter to cover the talk? Perhaps. First, you ask yourself, "Is the story *timely?*" The more recent an event is, the more news value it has. Daily newspapers operate on 24-hour cycles; weeklies, of course, operate on seven-day cycles. If something happens within the cycle, it's timely. In this case, the event hasn't happened yet, so timeliness isn't a problem.

Conflict, which is next on your list, means that a story about a physical or psychological clash is more newsworthy than a story about a harmonious relationship. A crime story has conflict, for example. The AIDS story has the potential for some conflict because the doctor will probably debunk some commonly held notions about how the deadly disease may be spread.

Consequence, or importance, refers to the impact of an event. If a large number of people are affected, the story has great importance. If few are affected, the story has less importance and, consequently, less news value. A major winter storm that paralyzes San Marcos has great importance. A routine meeting of a local club has little importance and might merit one paragraph at best. The AIDS lecture has importance because it deals with a disease that may touch the lives of a number of San Marcos residents in the 1990s.

What about *human interest?* Many editors define human interest as any topic that interests people, but they also consider a story about a child, an animal or sexuality to be especially intriguing. (Some editors include health and money as well.) The AIDS story qualifies because it touches on most of the human interest elements.

Next, you must wrestle with the question of *novelty* or unusualness. Every day nearly 20,000 U.S. commercial airline flights land safely. That's to be expected and isn't news. However, when an airliner crashes, that's unusual and is big news. Is the AIDS meeting unusual? No, you learn, because meetings like it are to be held all over Texas.

Prominence means names make news. If the president has the flu, it's news. If you have the flu, it's not. Because the doctor leading the AIDS discussion has little prominence, the story has little prominence. On the other hand, the story does have *proximity,* or nearness to the reader. To put it another way, a meeting in San Marcos is more newsworthy to you and your readers than a similar meeting in Chihuahua, Mexico.

You add up the newsworthiness score: The story is timely, probably will have conflict, and does have consequence, human interest and proximity. It lacks only novelty and prominence. Clearly, it's worth covering.

Editors usually don't add up the pluses and minuses of stories in a formal way such as this, but they do subject each story and even part of a story to a mental checklist to determine news value.

Other Characteristics

To be of service, newspaper stories must have many qualities besides newsworthiness. Two somewhat contradictory requirements are *speed* and *accuracy.* Newspaper reporters often work under gut-wrenching deadline pressure. Two hours to attend and write about a session such as the AIDS meeting in which many items were discussed is not unusual. At the same time, the story must be absolutely accurate. Names, numbers and quotations all must be correct. In short, because newspapers are primarily concerned about events that occur within their publication cycle, the late story has little value, but the inaccurate story has even less value.

In the midst of struggling for precision and speed, the reporter also tries to achieve *objectivity* or neutrality. Like doctors and lawyers who sometimes must deal with patients and clients they dislike, journalists often cover individuals for whom they have little sympathy or empathy. That's acceptable. What is not acceptable is when the subject of the story or the reader of the story can detect the reporter's attitude.

Good stories are also *fair* stories. Fairness, for example, means that when a charge is made by a news source, the person who is attacked should be contacted for his or her side of the story. Stories also must be sufficiently *complete* to allow the reader to understand the context of an event. Completeness in the AIDS meeting story, for example, means including the fact that the San Marcos AIDS meeting was only one of many in Texas. Without that information, the casual reader might assume the town was being singled out for some reason.

Reporters at Work

Gathering, writing, editing and packaging the news is a collaborative act at daily and larger weekly newspapers. No one person is responsible for the final appearance and placement of a news story. For example, let's assume you're a reporter for the *Daily Times-Call,* a 20,000-circulation daily in Longmont, Colo., about 30 miles north of Denver. If you're a beat reporter—someone who covers the same offices every day, such as city hall, police or education—you create your own assignments. If you're a beginner, you're more likely to be a general assignment reporter: You take your orders from the city editor.

The *Times-Call* is an afternoon newspaper, which means most of the reporters work between 7 a.m. and 4 p.m. and face their major news deadline at about noon. From 7 until 8:45 a.m., you rewrite five news releases provided by individuals or organizations seeking publicity. Then the city editor, who supervises the reporters who cover the metropolitan Longmont area, assigns you to a 9 a.m. meeting. You cover it, return to the office at 10:15 and write the story by 11 a.m. When you're finished, the city editor checks the story and asks you to include a couple of items you've forgotten.

Your story then goes to the news editor. The news editor decides where the story will be placed in the paper. Unfortunately, she picks a spot—page three—where a big advertisement has been positioned, which requires your story to be shortened by two paragraphs. She passes the story along to the copy editor and her assistants, who shorten it, then check it for accuracy, sense, spelling and grammar, and write a headline for it.

Still other editors may decide whether a photograph or a chart of some kind will be used. At some point in the process, the managing editor may see the story, particularly if it is important. Otherwise, the managing editor confines herself to overseeing the entire news operation rather than individual stories.

Interviewing sources is an important part of reporting.

USA Today, the nation's second largest circulation newspaper and one of a handful of papers considered to be national in coverage and distribution, begins its life at 6:30 each morning with the arrival of the paper's wire and national editors. As other editors arrive for work at the paper's 31-story headquarters building in Rosslyn, Va., a preliminary "budget" or page-by-page plan for the paper's contents is created.

By mid-morning most of the publication's 300 news staffers are at work. Editors assign stories, order pictures and charts—a typical issue will use more than 20 charts and as many pictures—and make a tentative selection of stories for *USA Today*'s four section fronts. By late afternoon, the mix of stories, charts and pictures and their placement has been largely decided, with the exception of sports stories, which can be changed as late as early morning.

The first editorial material is electronically sent to the composing room about 5 p.m., where headlines, stories, pictures, charts and other materials are assembled into complete pages. A photograph is made of the completed page and the results scanned by laser and beamed to a satellite, which relays the material to about three dozen printing plants at various U.S. locations. Sports and weather pages go to composition last and by 11:25 p.m., everything has been sent to the leased satellite 22,300 miles above the Pacific Ocean.

The first pages of the first of two *USA Today* editions roll off the presses at 11:45 p.m., and at a little after midnight trucks haul early papers to post offices for same-day delivery. Some news, such as late-breaking stories or sports scores, is routinely inserted as late as 1 a.m., although the possibility exists for some copies to be modified as late as about 4 a.m.

In the early hours of the new day, still more trucks—about 400 in all—pick up papers for delivery primarily to the paper's 119,000 television set-shaped news boxes (which, by the way, cost $250 each). In all, more than 1.5 million copies are delivered by early morning. Half go to vending machines or newsstands. Fifteen percent is home delivered, 15 percent goes to hotels and airlines for free distribution, and another 15 percent is mailed. Three percent goes to schools. About 35,000 customers in Europe and Asia also receive the paper.

In short, *USA Today* is a technological and numerical wonder: Eighteen hundred employees in all. Seventy-seven meetings and 4,700 cups of coffee and tea a week. Fifteen thousand outgoing telephone calls a day and 6,000 incoming calls. Twenty-eight million bytes of computer memory. More than 121,000 tons of paper from 2.5 million trees and nearly a million gallons of ink a year.

Sure, *USA Today* stories are short and superficial. And it's true, the paper does seem to put a happy face on even the most dreadful news, a formula founder Al Neuharth of the Gannett company called the "journalism of hope." But in 1987, after five years of operation, *USA Today* made a profit, after revolutionizing the way American newspapers look. Cathie Black, then the paper's publisher, put it this way, "We've proved that when the news product is right, the readers and advertisers will follow."

Source: *USA Today*, Sept. 15, 1987, p. 4E.

By the way, you're not off the hook at 11 a.m., which is when you've finished the meeting story. From 11 until deadline, you complete a telephone interview with a city official about a new municipal policy and write the story. After lunch, you work on two stories for the next day.

Future Focus The Newspaper of the Future

The newspaper of the future will probably be either a customized product or a paper for an elite audience, experts say.

The customized or tailored newspaper, described by Clark Hoyt and Trueman Farris for the Associated Press Managing Editors association in the early 1980s, would allow editors to deliver different newspapers to different readers. Hoyt, managing editor of the *Wichita* (Kan.) *Eagle-Beacon* and Farris, managing editor of the *Milwaukee Sentinel*, wrote: "As a managing editor, how would you like to produce pages or sections in your newspaper that vary from copy to copy? How about being able to give a reader who is a nut about automobiles a full section of auto news while his next door neighbor, who is a fishing fool, would get no auto news but a lot of fishing news in the same space?"

Hoyt and Farris predicted that the technology to produce customized papers economically will be available by the 1990s. That technology includes:

- newspaper pages that can be assembled on a computer screen, a process called *pagination,* which is already in use at many newspapers;
- cameras that use no film and can electronically transmit computerized pictures back to the newsroom, a process now possible;
- satellite delivery of ad copy to speed page creation, a process now used; and

- ink-jet presses and sophisticated inserting and sorting machines to allow printing to stop, change modes, restart and send the correct paper off to the correct subscriber, equipment that is now being developed or refined.

The alternative to the customized newspaper for a general audience is a paper for an audience of "elites," somewhat like the business, government, political and military readers who heavily patronized many American Colonial papers.

The study by Hoyt and Farris was supplemented in 1989 by another APME report called "Newspapers in the Year 2000." The observations made in that report were somewhat similar to those made by Hoyt and Farris.

For the next few years, however, newspapers will probably be much as they are today, albeit with better writing, more color and graphics and perhaps even "teletext" or "videotext" supplements. **Teletext** is a one-way flow of televised information, such as the text of a stock market report or an abbreviated wire service report, for which a fee is charged. **Videotext** is a fee-based two-way system—"interactive" is the buzz word for the technology—that allows the subscriber watching the service to select highly specific reports or services at the push of a button.

The Workplace: The Electronic Newsroom of the 1990s

You write your stories on a video display terminal (or VDT), which looks like a personal computer except for a slightly more complex keyboard. Your notes from telephone interviews also may be written on the VDT. When you need to see your notes, you call them up in a split-screen format, with your story occupying one portion of the screen and the notes in the other part. In addition, if you report from the field—say, from the county seat 20 miles away—you may write your story on a laptop computer and send it to the newspaper office using a modem and a telephone.

The newspaper library is computerized as well. If you need to look at a story published last year or you want to search old files for previous mentions of a name, you ask the computer for help. Finally, you may have access to a data base in a distant city. A data base is a specialized electronic encyclopedia, which is kept constantly up-to-date. Most big dailies and a few small ones use them. For example, if the Longmont city council is contemplating passing a law requiring cats to be leashed when outdoors, you can probably find an appropriate data base to search for all other instances of cities with similar ordinances.

All of this computerization means there's precious little paper in the newspaper office because your stories are electronically sent to other editors, who merely call them up on their computer screens and edit as necessary.

Photojournalism: 1890s to the 1990s

Story readership improves with pictures, research shows. And computers are changing photojournalism as much as they have changed the way words are processed.

Photojournalism, of course, is based on photography, which is an old technology. The camera dates from the 1400s, and perhaps earlier. It was originally called a *camera obscura* and was used by painters such as Leonardo Da Vinci to correctly render perspective. The camera improved in the 1500s when lenses were fitted to it. Photo chemistry dates to at least the 1600s, and by the late 1700s, numerous scientists had observed that silver would darken when exposed to light. Joseph Nicephore Niepce and his son, and later Louis Daguerre, merged the camera obscura and chemistry to produce early photographs, which he described in 1839. By the early 1840s, photography—at least, daguerreotyping, which used a metal film that produced a mirrorlike metal print—was common in Europe and the United States. The metal daguerreotypes gave way to glass-based film and paper prints in the mid-19th century and to flexible film printed onto paper in the 1880s.

From the 1830s until the 1880s, photography was occasionally used to record news events, but printing technology generally didn't permit the photographs to be published. Instead, artists sketched drawings at the scene or made drawings from photographs, and the drawings were reproduced as woodcuts. In 1880, as a result of experiments in the 1870s, Stephen Horgan, using a special press, pioneered a method for reproducing photographs in a publication. By the late 1890s, photographs, also known as **halftones** because continuous tones ranging from black to gray to white are reduced to a series of dots, began to appear occasionally in newspapers using traditional presses.

Woodcuts and halftones lived side by side for many years, but by about the time of World War I, the halftone emerged victorious. Picture wire services, such as United Press's Acme Newspictures and the AP picture service, appeared in the mid-1920s, legitimizing photojournalism as an accepted way of reporting the news.

Although cameras became smaller and film better, photojournalism in American newspapers changed little until color and computers found their way into the darkroom in the 1980s. Today, assignments are routinely shot in color. The precise procedure will vary with the sophistication of the newspaper's technology, but at many dailies, color film is scanned into a

Sketch artists of the 19th century gave way to photojournalists in the 20th.

computer after it is developed. Using the computer, the photojournalist can enlarge or enhance portions of the picture and even transform it into a black-and-white image if necessary. The wire services also use computers to receive, edit and if necessary enhance photos before sending them by land lines and satellite to local newspapers.

Photojournalism's basic technology—silver-based film—still reigns, but photojournalists predict that the 1990s will be the final decade of silver photography. The successor will be an electronic camera that uses a disk to record color images. Several brands are already available and as picture quality improves, the electronic cameras will find their way into the newsrooms of the world.

Wire Services and Syndicates

As you've read, few newspapers cover events beyond their circulation area. Instead, they depend on press associations, commonly called *wire services.* The heavyweight U.S. wire services are the Associated Press and United Press International. The latter was created by a series of mergers of early press associations, the last being in 1958. Reuters and Agence France Press are also used by major papers. Many newspapers also subscribe to supplemental services, such as those run by *The New York Times,* the Copley,

Izvestia (News) of Moscow announced in late 1992 that the 18 main newspapers of the Commonwealth of Independent States (successor to the USSR) had lost at least 18 million subscribers. One reason is that newspapers are now several times more expensive than they were even in 1991, and the people of the CIS are in a far more uncertain financial situation. There are more publications now, but their readership is down.

In 1992, only 40 percent of the nearly 2 million readers of *Pravda* had renewed their subscriptions over the previous year. The labor union daily *Trud* did better, keeping about 70 percent of its 12 million readers of a year before. *Argumenty i Fakty* (begun only in 1988), the C.I.S.'s largest newspaper, managed to reach a fantastic 22 million readers by 1993.

Most newspapers were struggling in 1993, and circulations were changing, some radically, from month to month. The general slump in most subscriptions led to self-promotion campaigns. Television commercials and contests were used to entice readers.

The government gave subsidies to some newspapers to keep them going. All in all, the newspaper picture was mixed—with interesting publications enjoying a period of increased freedom and other publications struggling beneath mounting economic problems.

Newhouse, Scripps Howard, Knight-Ridder and Tribune Company newspaper groups, and by the *Los Angeles Times* and *The Washington Post.*

By any definition, wire service material is a bargain. For example, the two Phoenix, Ariz., daily newspapers in the 1980s devoted about 4 percent of their newsroom budget toward AP bills, but AP provided 37 percent of the news published—a deal for the papers but perhaps not for the readers.

The AP is a nonprofit cooperative, governed by a board made up of directors selected from among its more than 1,500 U.S. daily newspaper and 6,000 broadcast members. It serves 95 percent of the nation's daily papers, representing 99 percent of circulation. The AP also serves 10,000 news outlets in 114 other countries.

By contrast, UPI and the supplemental services are profit-seeking enterprises and have far fewer clients. UPI, which was recently restructured as a so-called "super-supplemental" service, had fewer than 700 newspaper subscribers in the late 1980s. Reuters, which does most of its business outside the United States, reportedly had fewer than 100 U.S. newspaper clients and AFP even fewer. The other major supplemental services' newspaper client lists are numerically sandwiched between those of AFP and UPI. *The New York Times* service has about 300 U.S. clients, with the *Los Angeles Times/Washington Post,* Scripps Howard and Copley services averaging between 200 and 300 clients. The Gannett news service, available only to papers owned by the giant Gannett company, the nation's largest owner of newspapers, reaches perhaps 100 newspapers. The Knight/Tribune and Newhouse services each reach about 50 client papers.

AP's 2,000 journalists around the world turn out several million words a day, in addition to hundreds of photographs. The actual "wires" vary from satellite transmissions to telephone lines to other leased communication systems. Some stories and pictures are intended for in-state use only—the AP has a bureau in most states, with each bureau operating like a small newsroom—while the best and most important materials find their way to the prestigious national wire.

On the other hand, the major supplemental services distribute perhaps two dozen stories a day. In the case of *The New York Times, The Los Angeles Times/The Washington Post,* and Knight/Tribune services, stories are primarily written by reporters employed by client papers. The Newhouse, Scripps Howard and Copley services have their own extensive staffs and bureaus, in addition to using stories from client papers.

In addition to the true wire services, newspapers also utilize **syndicates** to buy materials ranging from editorial cartoons and opinion columns to comic strips and features such as Ann Landers and the daily horoscope. The average medium-sized newspaper may subscribe to three or four dozen such features. Behind all of this business are a dozen major syndicates—United Features Syndicate, which handles comic strips, including *Peanuts,* is perhaps the largest. It is 10 times the size of many smaller services.

Yet whatever their size and however many members or clients they have, the wire services and syndicates serve one purpose: to supplement locally produced news packages.

Retrospective

With the invention of movable type and the appearance of mass-produced books, crude newspapers were born.

In England and in the American Colonies, newspapers thrived, although initially they suffered from stifling censorship and libel laws. In time, the American press grew from an elite media to one that served the masses as well.

By the mid-20th century, the American newspaper industry had undergone great change. Technology changed the look of American newsrooms and newspapers. At the same time, economic forces encouraged groups to gobble up family-owned newspapers. Television and the changing needs of readers weakened many newspapers—particularly PMs—leaving scores of cities with only one paper or with two owned by the same corporation. In addition, circulation failed to keep up with population growth in the United States, setting the scene for newspapers of the elite once again.

Questions

1. Do you think the presence of weekly newspapers in England helped or hurt the development of weeklies in the American Colonies?

2. What was the "partisan press" period? Do we have a partisan press today?

3. Is *USA Today* a modern version of the penny press? If not, why not?

4. What does "yellow journalism" mean to you?

5. How has the technological explosion of the last quarter century changed the way newspapers gather and report news?

6. Do you think nonlocal ownership of a community's only daily newspaper is helpful or harmful? Why?

7. Based upon what you have read, do newspaper reporters and editors seem to be like your friends and family? If not, how do reporters and editors differ?

8. The Associated Press is now the main source of national and international news for most newspapers. Is this a dangerous trend?

9. Who or what is responsible for the disappearing newspaper reader? Television news? Is it a combination of broadcast news, a deterioration of reading for information and enjoyment, and growing semi-illiteracy? Or is it mainly the increasing price of a newspaper, now a quarter on average?

10. Do you read a newspaper every day? If not, why not?

11. Do you think that publishers and editors such as Ed Quillen and his metropolitan counterparts will be able to produce the kinds of newspapers needed to hold readers' attention in an electronic age? If not, which papers will survive: rural weeklies such as the *Middle Park Times* or metropolitan papers?

Suggested Readings

Brooks, Brian S., et al. *News Reporting and Writing.* New York: St. Martin's Press, 1992.

Emery, Edwin, and Emery, Michael. *The Press and America.* Englewood Cliffs, N. J.: Prentice-Hall, 1992.

Fink, Conrad C. *Media Ethics.* New York: McGraw-Hill, 1988.

Friedlander, Edward Jay, and Lee, John. *Feature Writing for Newspapers and Magazines.* New York: HarperCollins, 1993.

Friedlander, Edward Jay, Marsh, Harry, and Masterson, Mike. *Excellence in Reporting.* St. Paul, Minn.: West, 1987.

Ghiglione, Loren. *The Buying and Selling of America's Newspapers.* Indianapolis, Ind.: R.J. Berg & Co., 1984.

Harrigan, Jane R. *Read All About It: A Day in the Life of a Metropolitan Newspaper.* Chester, Conn.: the Globe Pequot Press, 1987.

Hulteng, John L. *The News Media: What Makes Them Tick?* Englewood Cliffs, N. J.: Prentice-Hall, 1979.

Kobre, Kenneth. *Photojournalism: The Professionals' Approach.* Stoneham, Mass.: Butterworth-Heinemann, 1991.

Mencher, Melvin. *News Reporting and Writing.* Dubuque, Iowa: Wm. C. Brown, 1991.

Merrill, John C., and Fisher, Harold. *The World's Great Dailies: Profiles of 50 Newspapers.* New York: Hastings House, 1980.

Schramm, Wilbur. *The Story of Human Communication.* New York: HarperCollins, 1988.

Wolseley, Roland E. *The Black Press, U.S.A.* Ames: Iowa State University Press, 1990.

CHAPTER 6

Books

When lawyer John Grisham walked into court to try his first case, he, was petrified. It was not a pleasant experience. Pleading his cause with dry voice and sweaty palms, he decided there must be a better way to make a living. So he turned to writing. The result was a runaway best seller about a young lawyer who is hired by a crooked Memphis law firm.

Books with law as a background aren't new. Lawyers have been around as heroes for years. Just watch old "Perry Mason" reruns if you don't believe it. But lawyers had pretty much faded from literary view until Scott Turow (author of *Presumed Innocent* and *The Burden of Proof*) and Grisham (author of *The Firm, A Time to Kill* and *The Pelican Brief*) came along. Their hot-selling novels spawned a flood of legal-beagle imitators. Publishers and literary agents have been inundated by tons of unsolicited manuscripts about criminal trials and legal heroes, most of them written by lawyers who wanted to cash in on the craze.

And some of them will get printed. Over 50,000 new books are published every year in the United States alone, most of them conceived and crafted by writers working at home, pursuing their own artistic or commercial interests. First-time writers may range from 16-year-old French schoolgirls and successful lawyers to 80-year-old club women from Dubuque. The printed results can be anything from fine art to pure schlock.

Our Print Heritage: Books Yesterday

Books are our oldest mass medium. They have been around since the invention of written language, though they could hardly have been considered a mass medium back in the early days. Very few people could read or write. Even if there had been a literate audience, there were no printing presses available for mass production. Hand-copied books were very expensive. In the time of the Caesars, when a Roman scholar finished a new book, all he had to show for it was a parchment scroll, meticulously hand-lettered, perhaps with a few illustrations running along the margins. If he was proud of it and had the financial resources, he might then hire 15 or 16 scribes to sit around for a month or so and copy the original. When the copies were done, he bundled them up and sent them to a small circle of literate, wealthy friends, with perhaps a special copy on the finest parchment for the emperor. That's about as close as early books came to making the best-seller list.

In the beginning, only religious orders, the ruling elite and the occasional wealthy merchant ever saw a book, much less possessed one. But a worldwide thirst for permanent knowledge sparked a slow and stumbling search for means to reproduce the wisdom of the ages. The oldest published extant book, printed from woodblocks in China, dates back to A.D. 868. It took longer for the craft to reach Europe. Early 15th-century European printers experimented with woodblock carvings, which were stained and pressed against parchment, linen and ragstock papers. A few of these early woodblock prints, bound together in sheets, were used in an attempt to reach the masses. They were largely picture books, since few people could read. Most of them contained crudely carved religious scenes of the saints. They were never printed in huge numbers, but even the few that were printed were extremely popular.

Then, in the middle of the 15th century, Johann Gutenberg developed a press and movable type that could be set in complete sentences, printed and then broken down and used again and again. Movable type had existed in the Orient for centuries, where prayer charms and money were already being printed. But Chinese, Korean and Japanese movable types consisted of thousands of complicated ideographs, whole words carved in blocks. Gutenberg gave us an efficient method of printing with only the 23 simple characters (three of our modern letters hadn't yet been invented) in the Roman alphabet. It was one of civilization's most important inventions.

And it spread rapidly. Printers across the face of Europe carved their own type and constructed their own presses. Within 60 years, books were being published on some 1,700 presses in almost 300 European towns. Most of the early printed books were either religious in nature—bibles, prayer books, hymnals—or dealt with legal subjects. They were still expensive, but they were more accessible.

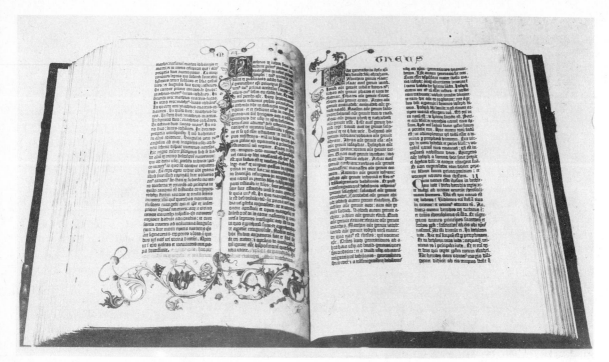

This richly illustrated Gutenberg Bible, opened to the beginning of the New Testament, is one of the world's most valuable books.

Print Comes to the United States

The first printing press to reach the Colonies landed in Massachusetts in 1638, just 18 years after the Pilgrims landed at Plymouth Rock. It was installed at the new Harvard College, where it was needed to print the various religious texts for school and college classes. The first book to come off the press was the *Bay Psalm Book,* in 1640. But books weren't a popular form of printed information in those early days. The land was too raw, too new, and most early settlers were too busy surviving to have much time for books. Nor did they have much time for newspapers, like those that had been growing in Europe. The first newspaper, Benjamin Harris's ill-fated *Publick Occurrences,* didn't appear until 1690. The first magazine didn't come along until 1741.

Dime Novels and Paperbacks

In the 19th century, cheaply produced paperback books discovered mass audiences in America. A man named E. F. Beadle started a line of inexpensive songbooks and sold them for ten cents each. They were so popular that Beadle decided to branch out with adventure novels about the American frontier. Beginning in the 1870s and spreading over the years, Beadle's firm cranked out 2,200 titles, selling for either a nickel or a dime under the imprints "Beadle's Dime Library" and "Beadle's Half Dime Library." These "dime novels" were the forerunners of modern paperback books, and they were smash sellers.

They were short novels, usually about 75 pages long. And none of them was great literature. One story, *The James Boys and the 49ers,* began like this:

Crack!

Crack!

Crack!

Unluckily for old Jack Farley, his aim was not equal to his courage.

His shots were both bad misses.

A shower of cold lead came in answer.

Other publishers quickly jumped on the money wagon. Frank Tousey offered "The Five Cent Wide Awake Library," featuring a writer called "Noname" and titles like *Denver Dan and his Band of Dead Shots.* An obscure Iowan named William F. Cody turned himself into a national hero by changing his name to "Buffalo Bill," and a writer who called himself Colonel Prentiss Ingraham scribbled a total of 121 wildly glamorized dime novels supposedly based on Cody's life. Horatio Alger wrote 120 books eulogizing hard work and the American experience under such series umbrellas as the "Luck & Pluck Books," "Tattered Tom Books," and the "Brave & Bold Series."

There was also rich profit in pirating European books. Publishers would send rowboats out to meet sailing ships from Europe to grab early copies of, for example, the latest installment of Charles Dickens' *Martin Chuzzlewit*. They would then race back to shore to be the first to serialize the story in a newspaper or to put out a hastily composed paperback copy, all without paying a single cent to the original writer. The international copyright law of 1891, which finally granted royalties to writers whose work was being used, ended this practice. Dime novels also played out. Three decades of cutthroat competition had driven most paperback prices down to a nickel. Yet production costs were still climbing. By 1900, the dime novel had all but disappeared. Pulp adventure fiction sought a new home in paperback magazine form.

Corporate Consolidation

Just as the newspaper industry has been affected by the growth of newspaper chains in this century, many publishers in the book business have also been touched by a trend toward consolidation under one conglomerate roof. Traditionally independent book houses, like surviving independent newspapers, often provide an irresistible lure for giant, profit-oriented media companies, not only in America but worldwide. If a publishing house is temporarily on shaky financial ground, it may find itself quickly swallowed by a media giant. Nor are the results always unfavorable. A merged publishing house may lose some of its creative independence when it falls under a conglomerate umbrella, but the new corporate structure may also provide a fresh injection of creative talent and financial security.

These international media mixes come in all shapes. Book publishing houses can find themselves aligned with strings of newspapers, magazines, movie studios, cable-TV companies and even other book publishing companies from all over the globe. America's MCA Inc., for example, owns G.P. Putnam's Sons, as well as Universal Studios. Rupert Murdoch's News Corp. Ltd. of Australia owns *The Times of London, TV Guide* and several other American magazines, a stable of Australian and American newspapers, Fox Television and Fox movie studio, as well as a British publishing firm and HarperCollins in New York. One of the biggest media conglomerates in the world, Bertelsmann AG of West Germany (which numbers British, French and Spanish magazines as well as the Literary Guild book club among its many international media holdings) bought Doubleday and Dell publishing houses in 1986 and merged them with Bantam Books. Hachette S.A. of France operates magazines like *Elle* and *Paris Match,* as well as a Spanish publishing house and the Encyclopedia Americana. British-based Pearson PLC runs *The Financial Times,* Penguin Books and *The Economist* magazine.

This feverish trend toward consolidation led to what may be the world's largest media conglomerate when two media giants, Time, Inc. and Warner, merged in 1990. Warner entered the media marriage with a trousseau that included a publishing house (Warner Books), a movie studio, several hot television programs, a home video operation and Warner Bros. Records. Time, Inc. countered with some of the most successful magazines in America (*Time, Sports Illustrated, Fortune* and *People,* among others), as well as Home Box Office (HBO), its own publishing house (Time-Life Books), a cable-TV company, shares in other media corporations, such as Whittle Communications of Tennessee and Turner Broadcasting Company, plus a couple of other book publishing companies. But bigness may be a problem. Though the huge conglomerate enjoyed revenues of $12.02 billion in 1991, the corporate image suffered through a variety of controversial decisions, including the release of Oliver Stone's "JFK" (a movie touting a discredited conspiracy theory), Ice-T's "Body Count" album (featuring a single called "Cop Killer," which drew howls of protest and led to a boycott of Time Warner products and services) and Madonna's erotic picture-book "Sex" (which many critics dismissed as soft-core pornography).

Books Today: Structure of the Industry

Book publishers like to say of their world that publishing is a blend of idealism and commercialism. True. On the general scale of things, the weight tips more to the side of commercialism. But American publishers know they are dealing with American literature, and most would rather publish an important book by a new F. Scott Fitzgerald than another sudsy best seller by a Danielle Steele.

A second popular saying in the world of publishing is that there are no great undiscovered manuscripts. This statement is more dubious. Book editors are not known for patience, and they frequently stop reading manuscripts by unknown authors after the first paragraph or at most five pages, feeling capable of judging a book-length work on such a short sampling. Usually, the editor is right. If the opening paragraph is bad or the first five pages indifferent, the aspiring writer has not done his or her job properly. Yet, such hasty judgments can lead to long repentance. Pity the 27 publishers who turned down Herman Wouk's highly successful *Caine Mutiny,* the 20 who rejected the zany best seller *Jonathon Livingston Seagull* and the 121 who said "no" to the off-beat *Zen and the Art of Motorcycle Maintenance,* which, after it was finally published, went on for years selling 100,000 copies annually.

Mistakes in publishing are made because publishing is by no means a predictable business. As an industry, it's fairly profitable, grossing $10 billion from the sales of reprints and some 50,000 new titles annually. But the MBA-types who rushed into publishing during its conglomerate phase found it hard to punch the value of a capable editor's gut feelings into a computer. Like the writers whose works they deal with, editors are creative, intuitive, sometimes haphazard and occasionally temperamental. Outbursts can be part of the publishing process. When softback publishing wizard Ian Ballantine, founder of Ballantine Books, used to trot down the hall from his art department shouting loudly, "I hate you all," the other editorial workers would barely turn their heads, even though such diversions could be welcome. Like reading a book or, for that matter, writing one, editing a book is a quiet, lonely operation, and publishing offices tend to be quiet, humdrum places.

A Typical Publishing House

The typical publishing house is a perhaps surprisingly small suite of offices, usually in New York, with Boston and Philadelphia trailing as established publishing centers. Four or five editors can be responsible for a smaller house's entire output. Working under them in the larger houses you'll find editorial assistants who do the actual work of corresponding with, say, a mystery novelist about changes suggested by a senior editor to tighten up a slow chapter. A copy writer may be cranking out the copy for the book jacket or the editorial assistant or the editor may take on the job. A few offices away, a copy editor is combing the rest of the manuscript for factual errors or for misused semicolons. The head of the art department, off in the best-lighted corner of the building, has assigned the jacket art to one of several artists. And the managing editor, whose responsibility is not acquisition, not content and not commas, but rather the actual manufacture of the book, is keeping an anxious eye on everyone's deadlines and dozens of other details. Few houses have their own printing and binding facilities. These tasks are jobbed out, as may be typesetting and rendering of any illustrations. Typesetting might be done in New Jersey, or Japan or the Netherlands, depending on which firm makes the low bid, promises the best schedule and does the best work. And that's just part of the publishing process.

Books can be slapped together and printed within a week or 10 days and distributed within two weeks, under extraordinary circumstances. In the 1970s, "instant" books enjoyed the brief attention of publishers, who gave magazines competition by getting out quick book-length treatments of such timely major topics as Watergate, the Pentagon Papers and, later, the Israeli commando raid on the airport at Entebbe. The capability is there. Oliver North's testimony on the Iran arms-for-hostages scandal was similarly rushed into print in the late 1980s. But such instant books are rare. For most books, a minimum of nine months to a year elapses between the time a manuscript is accepted by a publisher and its appearance in book stores.

How Books Are Put Together—From Manuscripts to Galleys

To examine the publishing process, let's follow one book. A Texas veterinarian with a busy practice and a wry sense of humor decides to write about some of his more humorous animal encounters. It takes over a year to put the book together. He's lucky in that among his clients are a married couple who both write novels, and they like the manuscript and recommend it to their New York literary agent. The agent likes it too and sends it to one of the publishing giants, Random House. It's turned down, but with a regretful note saying that the editor fears the no-vote might come back to haunt him. The agent sends several copies simultaneously to several other publishers (a practice not recommended for newcomers submitting their own books). The agent, of course, tells the publishers of the simultaneous submission. The publisher of one aggressive new house likes the book and phones with an offer of a $2,500 advance against royalties. This advance is very modest when compared to the $5 million that William Morrow & Company advanced James Clavell for *Whirlwind* or the $4.94 million that Warner Books offered novelist Alexandra Ripley for the sequel to *Gone With the Wind,* but it's not unheard of for a new writer.

The agent won't accept the $2,500 offer anyway; the editorial board of another publishing house has notified him earlier that it is on the verge of making a decision on the book, and that house is talking a bigger advance. The agent informs the aggressive house that he must wait for the decision. A short time later, the second house phones the agent with its decision: negative. The aggressive publisher, meanwhile, has gotten even more enthusiastic about the book, and she phones again, raising her offer to $5,000 as an advance against royalties, but only if the agent will close the deal within the hour (an attempt to block the other house out). The agent, pleased at the turn of events, accepts. His fee is a mere 10 percent, but $500 beats $250, and he'll get 10 percent of future royalties once the book has earned back the advance in the bookstores.

The contract is signed. The manuscript is edited. Changes are suggested and made. The happy author is asked if he can be available to promote the book on TV talk shows. You bet he can. This is a publisher in a hurry. The

Autograph sessions by authors—here, Gloria Steinem signs copies of her new book—are a common way of marketing books.

copy-edited manuscript is sent straight through the typesetting process, rather than, as usual, back to the author to look over the minor changes made by copy editors. Galleys arrive—a pile of long sheets, each containing the equivalent of three printed book pages. Oops. Several lines have been dropped here. A copy-editing change doesn't make sense there. Author and editor hash out the small problems and make revisions. A fall publication date is assigned for the book. It heads out to the printer, and the public relations and advertising staffs—sometimes only one person in a very small house—get busy trying to set up those talk shows, design ads for newspaper book sections and select names of appropriate book review editors who will receive review copies when they're available. The agent orders a couple of early sets of bound galleys; he will send them to literary agents with whom he works in the United Kingdom and elsewhere to start exploring foreign sales.

The Next Step: Sales Reps and Bookstores

One last vital step remains for the enthusiastic publisher: to inspire the sales force. The weak link in the publishing chain is getting a book into the hands of a reader who will enjoy it, and the shelf life of many would-be works of literature, whether mass-marketed in a grocery store or ordered by an elite bookstore, is often literally less than that of a box of crackers. If a book doesn't sell fast, back it goes to the publisher. In the case of paperbacks, the front cover is ripped off and sent back and the book itself is junked. Edwin McDowell, who writes knowledgeably on publishing for *The New York Times,* has summed up the situation: "The average bookstore lacks the shelf space to hold anywhere near the 50,000 new titles published each year, much less than the 700,000 other titles in print. And books that cannot get into the stores usually disappear with hardly a trace."

To meet the challenge of convincing bookstores to stock their books, publishers first try hard to sell their own sales representatives on a new title. They regularly whisk an entire sales force, plus editors and marketing staffers, off to Florida or the Bahamas for intensive conferences designed to pump up the sales reps' enthusiasm, which then is expected to rub off on booksellers. Reps are so important that their opinions can lead to major changes in jackets or publishing schedules. Long after the writer's work is done, the fate of his or her book is profoundly affected by the traveling salespeople who must actually market it and by buyers for large bookstore chains.

Economics of the Book Industry

The veterinarian's book falls into the large catch-all category called trade hardback books. Aimed at the general public, a **trade book** can be fiction or nonfiction, although the latter are surer sellers and therefore predominate. Trade books are the novels, biographies, diet books, exercise books and other miscellany that you buy in a bookstore or through a book club or read in a library. A special category, **children's literature,** is classed with trade books by the Association of American Publishers (AAP). The other major categories are **mass-market paperback** books and **educational** books— professional and technical books, college texts and primary- and secondary-school texts.

Trade books get nearly all of the publicity—book reviews, talk shows, advertising, prominent space in bookstores—but educational books get more of the sales. For example, the book industry brings in somewhat over $10 billion in sales each year. Educational books usually account for a whopping 40 to 50 percent share of the total (the figure varies from year to year). Trade books earn some 25 to 30 percent of the total. Mass-market paperbacks account for about 10 percent. The remainder of the industry money pie goes to smaller categories such as religious books, mail-order books, subscription reference publications and the output of the small but highly select university presses.

Trade books would be less profitable if publishers could not participate in subsidiary rights to paperback resale, book club sales and, in some cases, movie sales and foreign sales. The new author usually gets no more than half of the amount of a resale to a mass-market paperback house. The hardback publisher gets the rest. Once an author becomes established, he or she may be in a position to negotiate a more favorable 60/40 split, and a well-known author represented by a savvy agent can often retain all movie, TV and foreign-sale rights for the author's own bank account.

Apart from subsidiary-right sales, authors are paid on the basis of royalties. Most trade hardback book contracts provide a 10 percent royalty rate (that's 10 percent of the selling price) for the first 5,000 copies. The royalty normally rises to 12.5 percent for the next 5,000 or so copies and then hits a plateau of 15 percent.

Both publisher and author must make their living on the sale of books and any subsidiary rights. Unlike the other print media, books contain no advertising. Although efforts have been made, particularly by soft-back publishers, to include the occasional odd page of advertising, readers tended to find the advertisements irritating and promptly ripped them out.

Too, there is inherently little opportunity for consumer-product loyalty. When a customer buys a Betty Crocker cake mix, he or she often does so because Betty Crocker mixes have worked in the past. When a media consumer picks up a *Washington Post* or a *Time* magazine, he or she knows the publication and trusts it. But when a book buyer picks up a new novel, it's rarely on the basis of who published it. In fact, the consumer probably won't even notice the publisher's name. He or she will buy a book because Stephen King wrote it. If Stephen King changes publishers, the reader goes right with him. It isn't the imprint of the publishing house that sells a book. It's the author, a catchy title, a flashy book jacket, word of mouth, literary merit or pure hype that sells it.

Superman dead? You better believe it. It happened in the fall of 1992. The Man of Steel, once faster than a speeding bullet, able to leap tall buildings, avenging angel of the helpless and oppressed, was brought to his knees and killed by Doomsday, an escapee from a cosmic insane asylum. DC Comics, the creative home of the Superman saga, would only guarantee that the superhero would stay dead until March of 1993, but comic lovers lined up to buy the death issue, convinced it would someday be worth more than the $1.25 purchase price.

Maybe he deserved to die. After all. Superman was already more than 50 years old, graying at the temples and growing a pot belly. And the rest of comic society's flashy four-color superheroes are aging right along with him. *Plastic Man* on Geritol? *Wonder Woman* using Oil of Olay? *Captain Marvel* wearing a truss?

When comic books began (you can trace them back to a Procter and Gamble giveaway in 1933, but it was the first issue of *Action Comics* in 1938, starring Superman, that really sent adventure comics into orbit), they were as predictable as the alphabet—52 pages between gaudy paper covers, selling for 10 cents each. Heroes wore tights and bright long johns, usually with a flowing cape, and they clobbered evildoers with balloons that said "Biff!" "Bam!" and "Socko!" The bad guys were easy to recognize, too. They had funny names like Penguin, Riddler, Toyman and Mr. Mxyzlptlk, and they wore masks and had outlandish plans, like sinking the eastern seaboard into the Atlantic or freeze-drying the entire population of Salt Lake City. Comic heroes and their villainous foes didn't waste time on relevance. Comic books were for kids.

Comic books matured slowly over the years. First it was a touch of class in illustrated classics like *The Count of Monte Cristo* and *Tale of Two Cities;* then it was a touch of horror in titles like *Crypt of Terror, The Werewolf Legend* and *The Haunt of Fear. Mad* magazine came along to poke fun not only at the comic industry, but at American life in general. Underground comics reached for a counterculture audience and greater freedom of expression, including pornography and scatology, during the mid-1960s in comic books like *XYZ, Zap* and *Despair.* Even the adventure comics changed. Superheroes like *Thor* and the *Fantastic Four* developed problems. *Spiderman,* zapped by a radioactive spider, can perform super feats, but he spent his early days moping because he couldn't tell anyone who he was. Now he's (shudder) married.

Today a comic book can cost $2 and be anything but comic. *RAW,* which calls itself "The Comics Magazine for Damned Intellectuals," regularly deals in plot lines featuring restlessness, anxiety, despair, and outright paranoia. The stories are urban, complex, discontented and drenched with metaphor. The old adventure heroes are still leaping and cavorting through their paces, but many of them have changed. *Superman*'s death proved that. Shazam! Is nothing sacred?

Media Interrelationships

Books are a particularly interesting example of the peculiar manner in which modern mass media interrelate. Consider:

- A *Los Angeles Times* reporter named Lynn Lilliston writes a series on megavitamin therapy, which is reprinted around the country in such papers as the *Miami Herald* and the *Long Island Press*. Letters pour in from people who hope they can be helped by the therapy—and from a Fawcett Gold Medal editor who wants Lilliston to enlarge the information into a book.

- A New York adventure-magazine editor, Phil Hirsch, reads a curious story in *The New York Times* about a well-off philanthropist who is

Peter Benchley's *Jaws* quickly hits the best-seller lists, then spawns three movies. Here, Benchley's gigantic shark circles its prey. Books such as *Jaws* often have many media lives.

trying to track down important human artifacts missing since World War II. Hirsch asks a pair of writers for a freelance article on "The Search for Peking Man" for his magazine, then likes it well enough that he contacts them for a book on related topics for his publishing chain.

- A Doubleday senior editor, Tom Congdon, asks a magazine writer named Peter Benchley to lunch. Congdon really likes the work of this writer, who is an expert on sharks. Has Benchley ever thought of writing fiction? The final result of their luncheon was *Jaws,* which hit the best-seller list in hardback, went to Bantam Books for a $575,000 advance, was sold to filmmakers Richard Zanuck and David Brown for the Stephen Spielberg movie, and eventually went on to spawn "Jaws II" and "Jaws III."

- A young reporter named Nicholas Profitt, fresh out of journalism school, is sent by a newsmagazine to cover the Vietnam war. Years later, as Profitt matures and continues his climb up the rungs of journalism, the final result of his experience in Vietnam is an acclaimed work of literature, the best-selling novel *Gardens of Stone.* Like *Jaws,* it too is made into a movie.

And so it goes. Magazine and newspaper articles can lead to big books or little books. Books can lead to movies or TV miniseries and documentaries. Movies and TV miniseries can lead to increased book sales. As information circulates within the media system and one medium feeds another, a lot of garbage can pass through the system, but both interesting fact and meaningful literature can become available for the reader. And that's what keeps readers coming back.

Future Focus *Where Next?*

Computers may play a vital role in the future of books. The time has come when publishers expect authors to deliver manuscripts on floppy disks, allowing the editing, rewriting and typesetting processes to be done on a computer screen. The biggest barrier so far is the incompatibility of many home computer systems. This book, for example, was written by three authors in three locations, all using different computers. In order to exchange editorial ideas and suggestions, each of the three had to send hard copy on paper to his two co-writers. Floppies would have simplified editing, but they would also have required hunting down compatible machines in order to tinker with changes. Floppies in a book publisher's hands will represent a huge reduction in typesetting costs. When publishers solve the compatibility problem, submission on floppies may become mandatory.

Computers may also serve the book industry in the future in the form of an electronic bookstore. Distribution has always been the weak link in the book publishing chain. Authors do their work, editors edit, production people produce, and then copies of the book may languish in a warehouse somewhere, without ever finding their way to major bookstore shelves. But a Florida database company introduced BookMart in 1988, with 1,000 book titles for electronic browsing. The system carried only five pages of text and a book-jacket description, at a cost to the author or publisher of $250 a year for each computer listing. It was only a small beginning by one small company, but it may well be a hint of things to come.

Retrospective

Books are the storehouses of our history and culture. They are also, along with magazines, the last stronghold of the freelance writer. Unlike other media that rely on salaried personnel for stories and messages, books and magazines still depend on outside writers for the bulk of their material.

Books have been with us longer than any other mass medium, though they were originally available only to the wealthy and literate. With the development of the printing press, books eventually became more accessible. The process of publication—from manuscript to finished book—is slower than for other media. Modern publishing houses usually produce books in three major categories: *trade, educational* and *paperback.*

Questions

1. Why are books so suited to cultural and informational storage? What makes them different? Do any other media fit this select classification?
2. Since the Chinese had been printing for 600 years before Gutenberg's invention of movable type, why did his new development have such an important impact on printing?
3. If books are a blend of idealism and commercialism, which do you think is usually most important? Why? Should it be that way?
4. How many people do you know who have written books? Could you write one? If so, what would you write about?
5. Suppose you have finished writing your first book. What are the steps you must take to get it accepted by a publisher? What are the steps after it has been accepted?

Berg, A. Scott. *Max Perkins: Editor of Genius.* New York: E. P. Dutton, 1978.

Block, Lawrence. *Writing the Novel: From Plot to Print.* Cincinnati, Ohio: Writer's Digest Books, 1985.

Davis, Kenneth. *Two-Bit Culture: The Paperbacking of America.* Boston: Houghton Mifflin, 1984.

Dessauer, John. *Book Publishing: What It Is, What It Does.* New York: Bowker, 1981.

Hollick, R. *Book Manufacturing.* Cambridge, Eng.: Cambridge University Press, 1986.

Tebbel, John. *Between Covers.* New York: Bowker, 1986.

Tebbel, John. *A History of Book Publishing in the United States* (in four volumes). New York: Bowker, 1972–1981.

Suggested Readings

CHAPTER 7

Magazines

When freelance writer Howard Morland was given an assignment by a small political magazine to write an article on how to make a hydrogen bomb, he did what any intelligent writer would do—he did his homework.

Morland took a guided tour of an atomic-power plant and conducted interviews with experts, but most of all he delved deeply into printed materials at the library, researching unclassified sources such as highly technical books, specialized magazines and articles in scientific journals. The resulting piece for *The Progressive,* "The H-Bomb Secret: How We Got It and Why We Are Telling It," became famous when the United States government, for only the second time in its history, asked the courts to apply the principle of prior restraint to block publication of the article (you'll hear more about both prior restraint cases in Chapter 14).

That was in 1979. The article was eventually published, and no one triggered a nuclear holocaust with a do-it-yourself H-bomb, as the government had feared. Were it not for all-but-unprecedented government resort to prior restraint, Morland's thorough job of researching books, magazines and journals would be long forgotten. It's not unusual for writers to apply themselves to such rich resources. From their beginnings, magazines and journals have been repositories of more (and more varied) knowledge than any of the other media.

Not only have magazines become our historical, cultural and informational storehouses, they are one of the last bastions of the independent writer. Anyone with an idea worth presenting and the writing ability to make it palatable can still find an open market in magazines. Some 11,000 magazines and periodicals publish regularly in this country, and the bulk of their printed material comes from hard-working freelance writers. The field is wide open.

Magazines Yesterday

Magazines were slow to join the field of mass-media giants. Books came off European presses for 150 years before newspapers got their start. And newspapers held center stage for almost another hundred years before magazines finally put in an appearance. Then, in 1704, a young British radical named Daniel Defoe (who later wrote the classic adventure tale *Robinson Crusoe*) put together some big ideas and a small amount of money and began to edit a four-page publication called *Review.* It came out three times a week, and it looked a lot like the newspapers of the time. But the content was different enough to be successful, and five years later, it had an imitator, the *Tatler.* The *Tatler* was the brainchild of another young man, Richard Steele, who soon joined forces with Joseph Addison to produce a third magazine, the *Spectator.* Addison and Steele turned the essay into an art form.

The first two American magazines came out in 1741, only three days apart—thanks to a minor feud between a pair of Philadelphia printers. Ben

Franklin, publisher of the Philadelphia newspaper, the *Pennsylvania Gazette,* had planned for a year to bring out the first colonial magazine, which he intended to call the *General Magazine and Historical Chronicle, for All the British Plantations in America.* But Franklin's crosstown rival, Andrew Bradford, publisher of the *American Weekly Mercury,* swiped Franklin's idea and beat him to the streets by three days with his *American Magazine, or a Monthly View of the Political State of the British Colonies.* (Early magazine publishers had a fondness for long titles, as you can see.) Bradford's *American Magazine* lasted only three months; Franklin's *General Magazine* lasted six months.

Impermanence was the norm for early American magazines. Over the next 60 years, only four of the many new American magazines managed to survive for longer than 14 months. They were essentially leisure reading material for an audience that had little time for leisure. Circulations were low, usually under 1,000. Advertising was scarce. Government control by the Crown was harsh. But with the American Revolution and the turn of the new century, audiences began to grow. Illiteracy diminished. Printing techniques improved. A burgeoning middle class clamored for knowledge, literature and entertainment. By 1825, magazines were entering a great new era, equal to—if not briefly surpassing—newspapers as a national force. Many of the magazines launched during this period lasted 150 years. Some are still with us.

THE
GENERAL MAGAZINE,
AND
Hiſtorical Chronicle,
For all the *Britiſh* Plantations in *America.*
[To be Continued Monthly.]

JANUARY, 1741.

ICH   DIEN

VOL. I.

PHILADELPHIA:
Printed and Sold by B. FRANKLIN.

The Rise and Fall of the Magazine Giants

As the 19th century came to a close, magazines were in full stride. The Civil War brought maturity to the magazine industry; the completion of the transcontinental railroad in 1869 provided easier distribution; a new law in

When S. S. McClure, founder of a 19th-century newspaper syndicate, decided to enter the magazine field in 1893, he did it right. He gathered about him a solid staff, including talented associate editor John Phillips, crusading reporter Lincoln Steffens, Chicago writer Ray Stannard Baker, and a researcher/biographer named Ida M. Tarbell.

The magazine was called *McClure's,* and for its first nine years it was a modest publication filled with timely articles and entertaining fiction. Shortly after the turn of the century, however, *McClure's* stepped boldly into the annals of magazine history by launching a series of investigative reports on fraudulent business practices, government corruption and social inequities.

The first lengthy, hard-hitting report, written by Ida Tarbell, ran in serial form from 1902 through 1904. Tarbell, a careful researcher who had already written excellent studies on the lives of Napoleon and Abraham Lincoln, spent two years meticulously gathering her material before she wrote the first installment. The ensuing series was called "History of the Standard Oil Company," and it exposed the manipulations of oil baron John D. Rockefeller and the devious business practices that had crushed so many competitors and led to his giant oil trust.

The steady stream of investigative articles was immensely successful and the circulation of *McClure's* soon topped the half-million mark. By the time it was over, Rockefeller's personal reputation had suffered so badly that he hired the first public relations expert, a man named Ivy Ledbetter Lee, to help him revitalize his public image.

Tarbell's co-worker, Lincoln Steffens, followed the Standard Oil series with "The Shame of the Cities," detailing corruption in city governments across the country. The Tarbell and Steffens articles delighted the public and scandalized gov-

ernment leaders. Other publications quickly followed suit. Magazines like *Cosmopolitan, Collier's,* and *Ladies' Home Journal* quickly joined the fray, offering their own scathing exposés.

Theodore Roosevelt, president at the time, was so disturbed by the increasing criticisms of the magazine press that he referred to the writers angrily as "muckrakers," comparing them to a man in *Pilgrim's Progress* who was so busy raking straws, sticks and dust from the floor that he refused to look up, even though a heavenly crown awaited him. Roosevelt meant the term derisively, but the public and most of the investigative writers accepted it cheerfully and used it as a badge of honor. Yes, they were *muckrakers,* and proud of it.

All but one. Ida Tarbell, the first lady of muckrakers, always insisted that Roosevelt had misread *Pilgrim's Progress* and that the odious title should have been applied to the subjects of the articles, as in the "muckrakers of great wealth." She preferred to think of herself as a balanced, objective historian, and she wrote these words in her 1939 autobiography, *All in the Day's Work:*

This classification of muckraker, which I did not like, helped fix my resolution to have done for good and all with the subject which had brought it on me. But events were stronger than I. All the radical reforming element, and I numbered many friends among them, were begging me to join their movements. I soon found that most of them wanted attacks. They had little interest in balanced findings. Now I was convinced that in the long run the public they were trying to stir would weary of vituperation, that if you were to secure permanent results the mind must be convinced.

1879 lowered mailing costs; and Ottmar Mergenthaler's 1884 invention of the automatic typesetting machine improved production methods. It was time for a dramatic rise in magazine numbers. Starting from a post–Civil War total of about 700, the American magazine population grew to nearly 3,500 by the turn of the century. And some big-name magazines blazed across the late 1800s. *McClure's Magazine* and *Munsey's Magazine* were popular reformers, along with the original *Cosmopolitan,* exposing corporate corruption, fraud and monopoly. E. L. Godkin argued eloquently on behalf of democratic principles in his magazine, *The Nation.* Cyrus H. K. Curtis founded *Ladies' Home Journal,* which reached over a million subscribers. Curtis also bought a foundering magazine called *The Saturday Evening Post* for $1,000 and turned it into a national giant. Magazines became massive national media, aimed at general-interest audiences, with mounting circulations and spiraling influence.

The new century brought increasing success to general-interest magazines, but it also brought new challenges. The automobile and a new media toy, motion pictures, fought doggedly for a share of the public's leisure time. Big general-interest magazines survived and continued to grow. Then came radio, with free news and commentary and free dramatic plays. Movies got better and added sound. General-interest magazines survived again. By the outbreak of World War II, the field was dominated by four mass-circulation magazines—*The Saturday Evening Post, Collier's, Life* and *Look.* *Life,* a brainchild of Henry Luce, publisher of *Time* magazine, was perhaps the greatest picture magazine ever published and a special favorite of advertisers. Life (forgive the pun) and the future looked rosy.

But then came one challenge too many. Television. Advertisers abruptly found a dazzling new medium that could reach far more potential customers at a cheaper cost. It may seem strange to say a magazine died because it was too successful in attracting readers, but that's what happened. The giant general-interest magazines, incredibly expensive to produce, found themselves with bloated subscription lists and millions of magazines that had to be printed and delivered on schedule, but without enough advertising to pay the freight. Their success with subscribers, no longer matched in the advertising arena, dealt them all a death blow. *Collier's* was the first to go, in 1956. *The Saturday Evening Post* hung on until 1969. Then *Look* and *Life* wallowed in red ink and also succumbed. Some of the old favorites, like *Life* and *The Saturday Evening Post,* have been revived as monthlies for nostalgia lovers, but general-interest magazines have never been the same since.

Magazines Today: Structure of the Industry

Magazines did not, however, disappear like dinosaurs. They evolved. Today, whatever your interests, there are probably several magazines designed to meet your needs—and on a number of levels within each broad topic. Take women's magazines. In the early days, such pioneers as *Godey's Lady's Book* thought it was enough to offer a few fashion stories, some household hints, and a helping of romantic, feminine fiction. No more. To attract an audience today, a women's magazine must match the complex, individual interests of its readers. Fashions are covered in *Vogue* and *Harper's Bazaar.* Young single women with urban backgrounds often turn to *Cosmopolitan.* African-American women read *Essence.* Women committed to the ongoing struggle for women's rights may find what they seek in *Ms.* Young women planning a June wedding can pick up *Modern Bride* or *Bride's Magazine.* At some period after the wedding, they may need *Expecting* or *Baby Care.* Women with older children are apt to read *Parent's Magazine* or *Today's*

Family. The list goes on. Wherever a publisher can isolate a potential audience with well-defined interests, plenty of time to read and the income to support a modest but profitable circulation—and can convince advertisers that this audience exists and can be delivered—a new magazine will spring up.

Concept

Magazines, whether specialized or general in scope, are a necessary medium. If Daniel Defoe and Benjamin Franklin hadn't decided to launch magazines, the idea would still have formed somewhere in someone's mind. Magazines, neither as fleeting as newspapers nor as permanent as books, fill an important print void. Newspapers are rapid, temporary publications. Except for the occasional multipart series or thoroughly researched "think pieces," they give us hastily gathered information with only as much depth as deadlines allow, and they are usually discarded within 24 hours of publication. Books are more permanent and can delve into ideas and events with great intensity, but the lead time for preparing a book can take years in the writing and another year in the production process. Magazines can deal with important issues far more quickly than a book and in much greater depth than newspapers. And when a magazine chooses to stick with an issue over a period of time, it can have a powerful, cumulative impact.

Further, while newspapers began as local instruments in this country and have remained essentially local in nature, magazines and books developed over the years as truly national print media. There are some excellent city, regional and state magazines, to be sure, as well as local and regional book publishers, many of them flourishing, but most magazines and books are directed to national audiences. Magazines however, unlike books, can deliver those national audiences to advertisers. That's why magazines with good ad revenues continue to thrive, at a relatively low cost to the consumer, while book prices continue to climb.

Types of Magazines

Of the 11,000 magazines publishing regularly in this country, a huge majority, perhaps 80 to 90 percent, are business, agricultural, and professional magazines—magazines like *Cotton Farming, Candy Industry* and *Quill*. These publications, called **trade magazines,** are not written for general consumers but are targeted to manufacturers, production experts, dealers, retailers, technical specialists and skilled professionals. These are magazines you'll seldom see on a news rack.

There are also **little magazines,** literary publications like *Antioch Review* and *Southern Folklore Quarterly,* and **academic journals,** scientific and scholarly publications, like *Journal of Clinical Psychology* and *Journalism Quarterly*. Both types are usually *refereed;* that is, submissions are reviewed and judged by an editorial panel prior to acceptance for publication. Thus it is something of an honor to have one's work included. Finally, both the

GLOBAL GLANCE
Japan's Amazing Maze of Magazines

Japanese readers have some 2,600 different magazines from which to choose. This is an amazingly large variety for any country, much less a compact island nation like Japan. Japan, with a population of about 120 million, supports magazine circulations that exceed 2 billion copies, monthlies and weeklies sharing about equally in the readership. And the overall number of magazines is growing; for every one that ceases publication, two more spring up.

Some of the biggest Japanese magazines are:

Ie No Hikari (Light of the House), a monthly family magazine with nearly 1.5 million circulation;

Shukan Pureiboi (Weekly Playboy), a male-youth-oriented version of Hugh Hefner's American publication, with more than a million circulation;

Shukan Posuto (Weekly Post), a general-interest magazine but somewhat scandal-and-sex-oriented, with nearly a million circulation;

Riidaazu Daijesto (Reader's Digest), the Japanese version of the American monthly but including some new material, with about 800,000 circulation;

Josei Jishin (Women's Own), a heavy dose of fashion and romance, with about 700,000 circulation; and

Bungei Shunju (Chronicles of Art and Literature), a very serious magazine with think-pieces on almost everything.

---

literary magazines and the journals are usually edited and published by universities.

That still leaves a healthy number, close to a thousand, of **consumer magazines,** magazines that appear regularly at newsstands, in drugstores and at your local supermarkets. Today's consumer magazines cover a dazzling variety of specialized topics and interests. With the possible exception of *Reader's Digest,* no legitimate general-interest magazines managed to survive the mid-century trauma of television. In their place is a new breed of magazines, either offering a single subject of broad appeal (like *TV Guide* or *Bon Appetit*) or covering a wide variety of topics but targeted specifically to audiences with demonstrable demographic differences (like *Signature,* the Diners' Club magazine for affluent men and women, or *Esquire,* the hip magazine for upwardly mobile young men).

Consumer magazines break down into several categories—men's magazines, women's magazines, city magazines, gardening, sports, hobbies, science, travel, business, humor, sex, politics. We could go list-happy trying to cover the unlimited array of consumer magazines competing for the attention spans of readers. There's a newsstand in the Pan Am Building in New York, for example, that occupies 1,200 square feet of lobby space. It's thought to be the largest newsstand in the country, selling about $2 million worth of magazines every year. That's 2,500 magazines a day. Walk among the 18 special-interest sections that crowd the store's aisles and you'll find magazines on everything from automobiles to the zodiac. You'll encounter

Magazines, through subscription and single-copy sales, can accumulate enormous paid circulations, which are vigorously verified twice a year by the Audit Bureau of Circulations. These ABC figures, once released, are the lifeline of magazines, since they help to determine advertising rates.

Top Ten Magazines by Total Circulation

1. *Modern Maturity**	22,450,003
2. *Reader's Digest*	16,269,637
3. *TV Guide*	15,053,018
4. *National Geographic**	9,763,406
5. *Better Homes and Gardens*	8,002,794
6. *The Cable Guide*	6,951,677
7. *Good Housekeeping*	5,188,919
8. *McCall's*	5,066,849
9. *Ladies' Home Journal*	5,065,135
10. *Family Circle*	5,065,131

Membership associations, delivery primarily by mail

Source: Folio Special Sourcebook Issue 1992

electronics, environment, erotica and evangelism. You'll see science, sewing, shooting and square dancing. You'll wade through wine, war, woodworking, and wrestling. If you're young and active with an interest in water sports, you'll find magazines called *Boating, Sailor, Surfer, Skin Diver* and *Water Skier.* If you're older, you can browse through *Grandparents, 50 Plus, Dynamic Living* and *Modern Maturity.*

You get the idea. If you have special needs and special interests, someone out there has probably designed a magazine just for you.

Staff Organization

The size of a magazine staff depends on many things—circulation, ad revenues, writing concepts. There are major magazines like *Time, Newsweek, Business Week* and *Forbes* that generate all their own copy, with little interest in freelance submissions. These four magazines (all among the top ten in ad revenues) can afford massive information-gathering crews.

Time magazine, for example, lists a hierarchy of editors in its bulging staff box—from editor-in-chief, editorial director and corporate editor down through a managing editor, three executive editors, a chief of correspondents, an editor at large, an editorial operations director, nine senior editors, a picture editor, 16 associate editors and 13 assistant editors. Writers are also sprinkled through *Time's* organizational chart under a variety of titles. The magazine has 16 senior writers, 4 staff writers, 10 reporters and 19 reporter-researchers in its New York offices, and 81 hard-working correspondents scattered in 27 major cities around the world. Correspondents are layered in as contributing editors, special correspondents, senior correspondents and regular correspondents. There are additional listings for copy desk, art, photography, makeup, technology, imaging, and production crews. And these listings don't include the hundreds of "stringers," local newspaper reporters who pick up occasional extra checks for running down answers to queries from *Time's* home office. *Newsweek's* staff organization is very similar, with as many as 300 editors, writers and photographers working around the globe to produce a weekly record of the world's news.

But most magazines, particularly those that depend on freelance submissions, operate with much smaller staffs. Take a typical trade journal. There are thousands of trade journals scattered across the United States, publishing 40 to 60 pages of copy every month, circulating to 40,000 or 50,000 readers, and doing it with perhaps four or five people at the helm. A typical staff box will show listings for an editor, an associate editor, an art director, an advertising sales manager and a circulation manager. Five people, and three of them have nothing to do with the writing side. That leaves only two people to make decisions on what will appear in the magazine and to write and edit all copy to make sure it conforms to the magazine's style.

Staff salaries aren't bad, but they aren't overpowering either. *Folio* (a magazine catering to magazine management) determined in its 1992 salary survey that the average top management person made $63,436 a year, the average editor pulled down $45,608, senior editors earned $43,314, managing editors averaged $40,814, and art directors were paid $42,485.

Staff Writers and Freelancers

We mentioned freelance writing as one of the characteristics differentiating magazines from other media. Newspapers rely on salaried personnel at wire services, sister newspapers and syndicates for much of their national material, whereas local stories, editorials and features are almost always written by their own staff members, people actually employed by the newspaper. Except for travel sections and Sunday supplements, freelance submissions are seldom encouraged and infrequently used. Radio and television news programming is also usually staff-produced or comes from networks and wire services. Entertainment programming, it's true, is often written by independent freelance members of the Screenwriters' Guild, but they're a very select and professional group, hard for the outsider to crack. Movies are the same. Anyone can sit down and write a movie script, but finding a home for it without the proper credentials takes a great deal of luck and pluck (more than most writers will ever see). And if you think you've written a hit song that the record industry will snap up, forget it. Like film and television scripts, song manuscripts are returned unopened to guard against lawsuits filed by amateurs who claim their ideas have been ripped off. You have to know someone or work with an agent to get through the door.

With books and magazines, it's different. They are the last two great refuges of the self-employed writer. Books are written almost entirely by outside writers, usually working alone or through an agent until a book idea is placed, then with an editor who guides the manuscript to completion and through the production process, as we have already seen. Although there are heavily staffed magazines like *Time* and *Newsweek* that prefer to generate their own story ideas and do their own writing, the overwhelming majority of magazines are lightly staffed and, like books, must depend on independent freelance submissions. Most of them couldn't survive without freelance writers. Nor would they want to. Instead of relying on a small in-house staff of writers and editors to come up with article ideas, they can dip into the bottomless pool of bright, energetic freelancers, all trying to come up with something new enough and interesting enough to be salable.

Competition among freelance writers can be fierce. The bigger consumer magazines, with huge circulations and ad revenues, can offer top dollar and attract some of the best writers in the world. Smaller magazines—the ubiquitous trades, for example—offer more modest rates and must usually depend on writers with less experience or special interests. There isn't as much competition on the trade level, but freelance ideas must still be sound and the writing must be acceptable. A freelance writer, working his or her way up from low-grade markets to the top markets, encounters a tough training process, just as stringent as the training ground through which each salaried newspaper or magazine staffer must advance. The difference is that newspaper and magazine staff writers usually have editors and co-workers to help them through the process, whereas freelancers learn at their own pace and usually alone.

For the accomplished freelance writer, it's a dream world—magazines on every imaginable subject, eager for fresh material. If freelance writing interests you, find yourself a copy of *Writer's Market,* a 1,000-page annual publication that sells for about $25 and lists between 4,000 and 5,000 magazines that buy freelance articles. Or try the *Standard Rate & Data Service Directory* at your library. If, on the other hand, your interests run to magazine staff work, keep the thousands of trade magazines in mind. They are a ripe field for entry-level journalism and writing students.

Design and Production

Magazines also offer a rich field for artistically inclined design people. Published on slick paper with finer reproduction techniques than most newspapers or books, magazines often rely on graphic devices, lively headings and energetic use of color to enhance their pages. An eye-catching cover design can be particularly important, especially for magazines that depend heavily on rack sales. *TV Guide,* for example, which is usually toward the top of the circulation lists for all magazines, distributes a little over half of its 15 million copies (8,600,000) to regular subscribers. The rest (6,500,000) are single sales, copies purchased on impulse. Covers have to be attractive and interesting to spur these impulses. They must also walk a careful line between familiarity and novelty—enough like past covers to identify the publication quickly, yet with sufficient differences to show that the issue is a new one.

The subject of the cover can also sell copies. Magazines like *Time* and *Newsweek* have made an art form of cover-story illustrations. *Time* editors

Magazine covers are an important marketing tool.

once proudly printed a 54-page gallery of 2,810 of their finest cover paintings and photographs for distribution to subscribers. *Vanity Fair* sales shot up phenomenally when actress Demi Moore appeared pregnant and nude on the cover.

Economics of the Magazine Business

Magazine economics are somewhat complex. Most magazines depend on two regular streams of revenue—consumers who buy the magazine product and advertisers who purchase space to reach the consumers. For example, American consumers spend approximately $5 billion a year on magazines. Advertisers spend another $6 billion a year on advertising space. It sounds simple enough, half the revenue from sales and half from advertising. But every magazine tends to have a different economic formula. The 50/50 figure can vary wildly in either direction, all the way from pure subscription publications with no advertising, such as *Consumer Reports, MAD* and *Ms.*

magazines, to so-called "controlled circulation publications," such as *Cotton Farming* or *Rice Farming,* which depend entirely on advertising and either give their products away or sell them at a very low cost to specialized audiences.

Nor can you always judge a magazine's success by how many ad pages may appear in its issues. Not anymore. A magazine's rate card, traditionally a carefully prepared list of prices the magazine will charge for various varieties of advertising, was once considered sacred. If you wanted to advertise in a magazine, you had to pay its rates. But thanks to the recession of the 1990s, the worst recession in magazine publishing in decades, the standard rate card has become no more than a starting point for negotiations. Looking for new ways to entice advertisers, magazines began to experiment with massive discounts and preferential treatment to old customers and big buyers. A huge number of ad pages, once an accurate measure of a magazine's success, may now only show who is cutting prices the fastest. And once the rate card loses its honor, it may be difficult to reinstate it, even when times turn good again.

Whether times are good or bad, starting a new magazine can be a risky venture. Perhaps a targeted audience isn't really out there. If you make a wrong guess and encounter a weak market, the advertisers will shun you. If the market proves much stronger than you expected, competition from other new magazines is sure to follow. Some of them may be better than you, and both readers and advertisers will shift their allegiance. Because the two revenue streams, advertising and circulation, can fluctuate so unpredictably, many new magazines don't last. Nevertheless, for every magazine that dies, a new one springs up. For example, in the three-year period between 1988 and 1991, some 355 consumer magazines disappeared from the listings in *Standard Rate & Data,* while over the same three-year period 558 new magazines took their places. Like frontier prospectors, magazine entrepreneurs have dreams of striking it rich, of finding a motherlode of readers who will turn a magazine into a gold mine. And it happens just often enough to keep them coming.

Future Focus Do-It-Yourself Magazines

Probably the most important new trend in magazine production is **desktop computer publishing.** It's now possible for anyone with a bit of design capability, working on a low budget and using a personal computer like Macintosh and publishing software like *Microsoft Word,* and *PageMaker* and *Adobe Illustrator,* to write copy, typeset it in a variety of fonts, design it onto the page, add excellent illustrations, and shoot it right off to the printer. Newsletter and company publication editors have dived into the new technology with relish. A number of smaller consumer magazines have also joined the desktop publishing revolution. For magazines with bigger budgets, some of the publishing technology giants—like Scitex, Sun and Camex—have jumped into the electronic publishing field with the development of dedicated systems for pagination and color prepress.

The field is so hot that there are now several magazines devoted strictly to desktop publishing (a classic example of specialization), including a monthly "how-to" magazine called *Publish!*—which is itself, of course, produced completely on computers.

Desktop publishing is perhaps the decade's most important development in magazine publishing.

Retrospective

Magazines, once the great national medium for a general-interest readership, are now more specialized. There are magazines to fit almost every fragmented interest and choice audience. And if these specialized audiences attract advertisers, other imitators are sure to follow.

They come to us in four major categories: trade magazines, little magazines, academic journals, and the more popular consumer magazines. And these periodical publications, even more than books, are a ripe field for freelance writers. Unlike other media that rely on staff personnel for stories and messages, magazines depend on outside writers for the bulk of their material. And the wide range of magazines, from lowly trades to top consumer magazines, allow a learning experience.

Questions

1. What really killed the magazine giants? Competition from television? Lack of advertising? Rising production costs? How were these three problems interrelated?
2. What are the major similarities between magazines and books? How do they differ? Which would you rather write for?
3. How does a freelance writer differ from a staff writer? Which do you think works hardest? If you wanted to write for magazines, which would you rather be? Staff writer? Freelance writer?

4. Describe the average magazine office. If you were putting out a small magazine, what are the most likely titles you would list in your staff box?

5. Can you think of a specialized audience that is so far untapped by the magazine industry? If so, how would you go about creating a new magazine to answer the needs of that audience?

Suggested Readings

Click, J. W. and Baird, Russell. *Magazine Editing and Production.* Dubuque, Iowa: William C. Brown (4th edition), 1986.

Ferguson, Rowena. *Editing the Small Magazine.* New York: Columbia University Press, 1976.

Ford, James. *Magazines for Millions: The Story of Specialized Publications.* Carbondale: Southern Illinois University Press, 1970.

Friedlander, Jay and Lee, John. *Feature Writing for Newspapers & Magazines.* New York: HarperCollins (2nd edition), 1993.

Mayes, H. R. *The Magazine Maze.* New York: Doubleday, 1980.

Mogel, Leonard. *The Magazine: Everything You Need to Know to Make It in the Magazine Business.* Chester, Conn.: Globe Pequot Press (2nd edition), 1988.

Taft, William. *American Magazines for the 1980s.* New York: Hastings House, 1982.

Tebbel, John. *The American Magazine: A Compact History.* New York: Hawthorn Books, Inc., 1969.

White, Jan V. *Designing for Magazines.* New York: Bowker, 1982.

Winship, Janice. *Inside Women's Magazines.* Winchester, Ma.: Pandora Press (Unwin Hyman Media Studies), 1987.

Wolseley, Roland. *The Changing Magazine.* New York: Hastings House, 1973.

CHAPTER 8

Radio and the Recording Industry

I magine this: You are studying. You turn on your radio. You hear the following:

Ladies and gentlemen, here is the latest bulletin from the Intercontinental Radio News. Toronto, Canada: Professor Morse of Macmillan University reports observing a total of three explosions on the planet Mars, between the hours of 7:45 P.M. and 9:20 P.M., Eastern Standard Time. This confirms earlier reports received from American observatories. Now, nearer home, comes a special announcement from Trenton, New Jersey. It is reported that at 8:50 P.M. a huge, flaming object, believed to be a meteorite, fell on a farm in the neighborhood of Grovers Mills, New Jersey, 22 miles from Trenton. The flash in the sky was visible within a radius of several hundred miles and the noise of the impact was heard as far north as Elizabeth.

We have dispatched a special mobile unit to the scene. . . .

A newscast, right? Wrong. These lines are from the early minutes of what is perhaps the most famous radio program in the history of the United States, "War of the Worlds." The one-hour show was based on H.G. Wells' 19th-century story of the same name and aired on the Columbia Broadcasting System on Oct. 30, 1938—yes, Halloween eve. The program described a bloody Martian invasion of planet Earth, using a clever storytelling device: an ordinary musical program interrupted by frequent news announcements and "remote" broadcasts from various locations.

Even though "War of the Worlds" used simulated news breaks, star and co-producer Orson Welles didn't believe listeners would take the Halloween spoof seriously. For example, the show was clearly identified several times during the broadcast as a "Mercury Theatre on the Air" entertainment program. In addition, the script obviously compressed days and perhaps weeks of activity into one hour, as Welles' Martians landed in rural New Jersey, appeared, blasted civilian and military forces into eternity, and finally marched on to the Big Apple and other population centers.

But Welles was wrong. Many people took the program seriously— panicked, in fact—particularly in the northeastern part of the United States where the "Martians" first landed. For example, New Yorkers deluged CBS with calls, and the Philadelphia city hall switchboard was swamped with requests for information, according to The Associated Press. The AP also reported that the Providence, R. I., power company received numerous calls urging that the electricity be turned off to save the city from Martians approaching in the darkness. In Birmingham, Ala., people gathered in groups to pray, and in Indianapolis, Ind., according to the AP, a woman interrupted a Methodist church service, screaming, "New York destroyed. It's the end of the world. You might as well go home to die. I just heard it on the radio." In all, hundreds of people fled and thousands telephoned police stations and newspaper offices for more information.

The "War of the Worlds" panic vividly demonstrated the power of a relatively new medium and also raised important questions. For example, why did a portion of the audience panic? The simple explanation is that many people tuned in late and missed cues that the program was entertainment rather than news. But that doesn't explain why longer-term listeners believed that the Martians could land and take over much of the northeastern United States within one hour. And if those long-term listeners believed what they heard, why wasn't a majority of the audience of 6 million affected?

As you have read, the answers to questions about a mass communication medium's effects on an audience are often complex. However, researchers have suggested that those who believed that tentacled Martians were skampering across the New Jersey flatlands were the victims of several

Orson Welles directs a "Mercury Theatre" production in the 1930s.

unusual cultural and historical factors. First, there was great trust in radio in general and radio news in particular, a trust exploited by the broadcast's numerous fake news breaks (a technique the Federal Communications Commission now forbids). Second, the program was broadcast to listeners who were recovering from the traumas of World War I and the Depression and who were psychologically preparing for World War II. Add listeners' individual peculiarities and a riveting, well-done show to those circumstances, and marauding Martians become possible.

Would that kind of program have the same impact today? Apparently not, because when National Public Radio broadcast an updated, $80,000 version of "War of the Worlds" on Oct. 30, 1988, few listeners took the sleek show as anything but entertainment.

Yesterday's "War of the Worlds" and today's music and information-laden radio have common ancestors: dedicated scientists from many periods and places struggling to understand the possibilities of electricity and the electromagnetic spectrum.

The Earliest Days: From Electricity to the Wireless Telegraph

Radio is the result of perhaps 2,500 years of observation, experimentation and invention. Much of that effort dealt with understanding the nature of electricity, first noted by the Greeks in 640 B.C. Radio, of course, depends

---

Past Pointer Media Mileposts: Radio Waves Come Crashing In

1864	Mathematician James Clerk-Maxwell proves electricity can produce a detectable magnetic field.		1934	Mutual Broadcasting System joins growing radio networks. FCC is established by Congress.
1901	Guglielmo Marconi transmits a nonvoice wireless signal across the Atlantic Ocean.		1938	CBS's "Mercury Theatre" panics nation with Orson Welles' adaptation of "War of the Worlds," by H.G. Wells.
1920	Westinghouse radio station KDKA debuts in Pittsburgh.		1940	Edward R. Murrow describes horrors of war, live from London.
1922	AT&T station WEAF sells first commercial air time to real estate firm.		1943	FCC pressures NBC to sell one of two radio networks, which becomes ABC.
1926	RCA and its subsidiary, NBC, form first coast-to-coast radio networks, dubbed the "Red Network" and the "Blue Network."		1952	Television stations proliferate; TV will quickly borrow radio's programming and steal its audience.
1927	New Columbia Phonograph Broadcasting System forms third network to compete with NBC.		1972	All-news formats join deejay and music formats.
			1980	Popularity of FM radio soars.
1933	Edwin Armstrong patents new invention, FM radio.		1994	FCC allows a single company to own as many as 40 AM and FM stations, up from a maximum of 24.

upon electricity: Sound intended for broadcast is converted into electro-magnetic waves that are transmitted at the speed of light, then captured and converted back into sound by the radio receiver.

The modern history of radio probably began with Scottish physicist James Clerk-Maxwell's 1864 mathematical proof that electricity could produce a detectable magnetic field. Maxwell, of course, was building on many earlier theories and in turn, German Heinrich Hertz proved and reported Maxwell's notions in 1888. Hertz's work laid the groundwork for various experiments with the "wireless telegraph" in the 1890s, including those of Russian scientist Alexander Stepanovich Popov and more signifi-cantly, Italian physicist Guglielmo Marconi. By late 1901, Marconi had successfully transmitted a nonvoice signal across the Atlantic Ocean. In 1906, Canadian Reginald Fessenden transmitted voice signals. The vacuum tube, which amplified sound enough so that voice signals could be sent over long distances, also came in 1906, thanks to American Lee De Forest.

Radio pioneer Guglielmo Marconi.

Although there were experimental voice and music broadcasts in many countries during this period, until about 1920 radio was used primarily for maritime and military purposes. For example, when the H.M.S. *Titanic* sank in the North Atlantic in 1912, one-third of her 2,200 passengers were rescued because the Titanic's wireless operator was able to contact a nearby ship, albeit too late for the other passengers. That ship passed along information to a young wireless operator, David Sarnoff, who worked for Marconi's American company. Sarnoff, by the way, would later head the Radio Corporation of America and, of course, its subsidiary, the National Broadcasting Company.

Into America's Living Rooms

At the end of World War I, Marconi's American company sold its U.S. interests to General Electric, which, with Westinghouse and American Telephone and Telegraph, formed RCA in an attempt to capture the radio equipment market. However, equipment couldn't be readily sold until there were regularly scheduled broadcasts, a deficiency that was remedied in the early 1920s.

Radio as we know it today began in 1919 in the Netherlands and a little later in Canada. American radio emerged in the fall of 1920, with the appearance of station KDKA in Pittsburgh, Pa. (although there were earlier experimental stations). KDKA officially debuted with a Nov. 2 broadcast of presidential election returns gathered from newspapers. After KDKA's appearance, the number of radio stations grew tremendously for a few years. In 1921, there were five stations on the air for 50,000 radio sets. In 1922, 30 stations were providing programming for perhaps 600,000 radios. And by 1923, there were 556 stations sending signals to millions of sets. That

GLOBAL GLANCE
Early Radio
Development
Around the World

Radio developed in much of the industrialized world at about the same time. For example, in 1919—one year before KDKA began broadcasting in Pittsburgh—a station in the Netherlands was on the air. And a Canadian station began broadcasting the same year as KDKA. Radio broadcasting also had an early start in Australia—in Melbourne in 1921 and Sydney in 1922.

France and what was then called the Soviet Union started radio broadcasting in 1922, and Belgium, Germany, Spain, and Czechoslovakia began the following year. By 1926, several other countries—including Italy, Finland, Poland, Norway, Mexico, India and Japan—had radio stations on the air.

The British Broadcasting Corporation was founded in 1922. First a private corporation, the BBC was made public in 1925 and was a broadcasting monopoly in Britain until 1954, when the independent Television Authority was begun. The BBC was highly respected, and many countries such as Denmark, Sweden, and India patterned their systems after it. Other countries followed the private enterprise example of the United States, although they often created a public radio system as well.

figure remained more or less stable until the mid-1930s, when the number of stations began growing steadily again.

Who owned all of these stations is as important as how many were on the air. KDKA, for example, was owned by Westinghouse, which made receivers. By 1922, GE, AT&T and RCA also had at least one station on the air. Other station owners included radio set manufacturers, retailers, newspaper publishers, preachers and educational institutions. The set manufacturers and the retailers probably hoped that their stations would stimulate sales. Newspaper publishers saw stations as a way to promote their primary product. Preachers saw a way to reach potential converts. Universities envisioned radio as a way to reach new kinds of students.

A Commercial Enterprise. People initially listened to these early stations with headphones attached to crude radio sets that were difficult to tune. By the mid-1920s, however, sets sprouted speakers, ran on electricity rather than notoriously leaky batteries, and looked almost like a piece of furniture. What people heard, whether they listened on a cheap crystal set or a more expensive Atwater Kent model, was talk, music, and, for a time, absolutely no commercials.

The concept of selling time for a commercial message is credited to AT&T and its New York City flagship station, WEAF. Selling time for use of its facilities was something the telephone company could understand because of long distance calls, and when it was approached in 1922 by a real estate firm that wanted to pay a "toll" to broadcast a message, WEAF happily parted with some air time.

At first, most broadcasters and government officials opposed the use of commercials to generate revenue. Sarnoff, head of RCA, likened broadcasting to a public institution such as a library. Goodwill, he suggested, was sufficient reward. Fat chance. By 1926, WEAF, bought by RCA for $1 million, was making $750,000 a year from advertising, and the message was clear: Ads paid the bills, and then some. By 1929, the National Association of Broadcasters advocated limiting hard-sell commercials to before 6 P.M., but few broadcasters were listening to NAB's pitch. They were too busy selling commercials.

The Networks and Regulation

As the sale of commercial time developed, so did mechanisms for increasing the impact of programs. Why limit distribution of a good, sponsored program to only one station? broadcasters asked. The answer was the creation of "chain" or network broadcasting.

At first, the networks were temporary, such as the 12-station link created in 1924 for the "Eveready Hour," sponsored by Eveready Batteries. The actual linkage consisted of telephone lines, supplied by AT&T, of course. In 1926, RCA and its subsidiary, NBC, formalized a permanent coast-to-coast network when it took over AT&T's station lineup (dubbed the Red

American public radio and its private, not-for-profit network, National Public Radio, had their beginnings in the scores of educational radio stations founded during the turbulent 1920s. Those were tough times: although some 200 stations were licensed to broadcast at educational institutions, only 38 were actually operating by 1937. The 1950s brought a rebirth of educational stations, this time mostly in the somewhat cheaper to operate FM band.

In 1968, the private, not-for-profit Corporation for Public Broadcasting was created—CPB felt the word *public* reflected the stations' work better than the word *educational*. Its purpose was to stimulate and partially fund (from tax dollars) public networks and local public station growth. As a result, CPB created television's Public Broadcasting Service in 1969 and National Public Radio in 1970.

Today NPR serves more than 440 of the country's 1,500 or so public and noncommercial stations. The typical NPR station programs classical music, jazz and/or news and information to an audience a little richer, older and better educated than Americans in general. Most of the stations are licensed to colleges and universities, but a substantial number belong to community organizations and even school districts.

The budget of an FM public radio station in a Southern state provides an example of where the money comes from and where it goes. The station, a 100,000-watt all news and talk operation, is licensed to a state university and takes in about $1 million a year. About 24 percent of that comes from CPB and federal grants. The licensee and the state provide 43 percent of the budget, and the rest (33 percent) comes from earned income from contributions, grants from foundations and other underwriters. The money is spent this way: 58 percent for programming, much of which goes to NPR, 17 percent for engineering and technical support, 15 percent for general administration, and 10 percent for fundraising and promotion.

United States Public Radio and Television Stations' Funding Sources.
Source: Corporation for Public Broadcasting

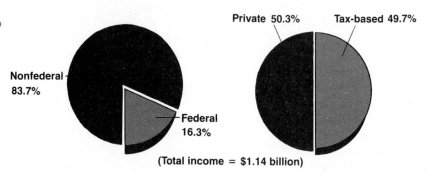

Nonfederal 83.7%
Federal 16.3%

Private 50.3%   Tax-based 49.7%

(Total income = $1.14 billion)

NPR has had a reputation as an award-winning, in-depth news alternative for two decades, but has matured into a primary news source in the 1990s. The addition of hourly news summaries, national daily call-in programs, weekend versions of well-produced weekday news programs such as "Morning Edition" and "All Things Considered," and riveting around-the-clock coverage of the Persian Gulf War pushed NPR to its more prominent role in journalism. The recognition of Cokie Roberts, Nina Totenberg and Linda Wertheimer for their expertise and original reporting also contributed to the ascent of the network. NPR's news programming became so complete in the early 1990s that a few NPR affiliates—such as KQED–FM in San Francisco, Calif., WFSU–FM in Tallahassee, Fla., WHRV–FM in Norfolk, Va., and WUWM–FM in Milwaukee, Wis.,—successfully changed to all news and talk.

Network) and began its own chain (the Blue Network) as well. Some stations were owned and operated by the network and some were merely affiliates.

The network plan was simple. A sponsor created or bought time on a program originating on a network's flagship station, which in turn provided the show to affiliated stations. The sponsor got exposure for its products, the network received a fee for originating the show, and the affiliates received a portion of that fee for carrying the program.

The plan made practically everyone happy, so happy that by 1927 there was even a third network, the Columbia Phonograph Broadcasting System, originally named for the Columbia Phonograph Record Company, which helped finance the operation. By 1928, CPBS was very much the property of a key advertiser, the Paley family, which owned a cigar company. The network was quickly renamed CBS and until the late 1980s was headed by the man who bought it and brought it from obscurity, William S. Paley.

Chaos and Regulation. By 1927, 681 stations were broadcasting to millions of Americans, but all was not well. Radio stations interfered with one another by changing frequency, power and times of operation at will, despite some government regulation, namely the Wireless Ship Act of 1910 and, later, the Radio Act of 1912, the passage of which was influenced by the *Titanic* disaster. Both laws were aimed at maritime radio, and although the 1912 law had more or less established the concept of licensing, a 1926 court ruling made even that power unclear.

The Radio Act of 1927 brought some order to radio broadcasting. The law created an enforcement agency, the Federal Radio Commission, and established the radio spectrum as public property for use in the "public interest, convenience, and necessity." The law decreed that the FRC had the right to fairly distribute licenses and assign frequencies, power and even operating times, as well as the right to refuse licenses to certain applicants or to take away licenses from those not operating in the public interest. In addition, the law provided for both protection of First Amendment rights and appeal of decisions.

With passage of the Communications Act of 1934, the five-member FRC became the seven-member **Federal Communications Commission.** The FCC's duties embraced both wireless and wired communications—including what would come to be called television.

Radio Meets Television

The 1930s and 1940s brought more changes to American radio. Networks became more competitive with the creation of the Mutual Broadcasting System in 1934, but perhaps more important, virtually all network programs became more polished. For example, national and international transmissions, especially newscasts prior to the outbreak of World War II, became both better and more common. Major stars appeared, such as comedian Jack Benny and ventriloquist—a strange act for radio, admittedly—Edgar Bergen. There was high-quality drama, such as the "Mercury Theatre," and big-stakes (for the time) quiz programming. The polish was to be expected: Audiences were huge because during the dollar-scarce 1930s and the commodity-scarce war years of the 1940s, network radio was *the* entertainment and immediate information source. Everything on television today—drama, comedy, variety, music, news and sports—was found on radio yesterday.

The radio listener of the 1930s and 1940s uses his radio to bring a world of information into his living room.

With the arrival of television after World War II, radio's future became unclear because popular radio programs moved over to television, as did national advertising dollars later. In short, television borrowed radio's programming and stole its audience.

By the late 1950s, network radio—except for news and sports—had all but disappeared (although some dramatic programs continued until Thanksgiving Day, 1960, when the networks consigned them to the electronic landfill). Radio, even the networks' owned and operated stations, became a local medium again, as it was in the early 1920s. Recorded music, a cheap and easy way of carving out an audience niche, became radio's primary programming tool, and the musical host, the disc jockey, became king of the mountain (despite occasional charges of *payola,* playing music for cash or drugs provided by recording companies). Radio's great strength, although perhaps not obvious in the 1950s, 1960s or even the early 1970s, became obvious: programming targeted to a specific audience.

In the last two decades, numerous U.S. radio networks—including the American Broadcasting Company, CBS, and Westwood One and its subsidiaries, the NBC Radio Network and Mutual—have again begun to help local radio stations in a meaningful way. This rebirth of the networks

Comedian Jack Benny

Pioneer broadcast journalist Edward R. Murrow begins his career with vivid radio reporting during the darkest days of World War II. He goes on to a distinguished career in television and public service.

may have started in 1968 when ABC—formed more than two decades earlier when litigation forced the sale of NBC's Blue Network—created multiple individualized networks aimed at specific audience types. In any case, networks that you have heard of and ones you haven't (for example, the Satellite Music Network, with more than 1,100 affiliates) now beam targeted programming to thousands of local stations, often by satellite.

The 1970s and 1980s also saw the rapid growth of a special kind of networklike program, the nationally **syndicated show.** The syndicated program is leased to many stations in return for a fee from each. Stations recoup costs plus earn profits by selling commercial time within the program.

Other common variations on the syndication theme include the show that is provided at low cost or free to stations in return for a little or a lot of commercial time within the program. In the **barter-purchase** (or **cash-plus-barter**) deal, for example, the program syndicator finds one or more major advertisers who will buy commercials within the program. The syndicator markets the show—say, one about automobile repair—at a low cost to stations across the country, which sell the remaining commercial time to local advertisers. Theoretically, everyone wins. The producer and syndicator make a profit, the major program advertisers get relatively cheap networklike exposure, and the stations get some revenue from the local advertising generated by the low-cost program. The other variation is the **pure barter** (or **all barter**) show, which also is underwritten by advertisers and marketed by a syndicator but is largely or completely filled with nonlocal commercials and is provided free to stations. All three of these programming approaches are widely used by radio and television stations today.

Radio Today

Radio stations are somewhat like shoes: They come in various types and sizes, but they all function about the same way. In the United States, for example, there are AM (or amplitude modulation) stations, which have been around since 1920, and shorter-range FM (or frequency modulation) stations, which were pioneered by Edwin H. Armstrong and introduced in 1941 as a way to provide better sound. There also are commercial and noncommercial stations and network-affiliated stations and unaffiliated ones. There are even a number of government stations, such as the Voice of America, which is aimed at listeners in other countries. All together, there are more than 11,000 radio stations in the United States today, although that number will have changed by the time you read this because it has been growing steadily since the 1920s.

Structure of the U.S. Radio Industry

About 44 percent of all stations are commercial AMs and the rest are either commercial FM (about 42 percent) or noncommercial FM (14 percent) outlets (see Table 8.1). Even though the number of AM and FM stations is

TABLE 8.1 NUMBER OF U.S. RADIO STATIONS		
AM		4,963
FM		4,742
FM educational		1,570
	Grand Total	11,275

Source: Federal Communications Commission, mid-1992.

about equal, surveys show that nearly eight out of ten listeners prefer FM, which once had few advocates but has been on an equal or better audience footing with AM since 1980. All of these stations—AM and FM, commercial and noncommercial, network-affiliated and unaffiliated—rain signals down on more than 558 million radio sets in the United States. Two-thirds of the sets are in homes and the rest are in workplaces and vehicles.

Like other mass media, most radio stations are very profitable and, as a result, they tend to be acquired by well-paying groups when offered for sale. In fact, a majority of all commercial radio stations are owned by groups— individuals, corporations or networks that hold two or more stations. Capital Cities/ABC, CBS, Park Communications, Westinghouse and Willis Broadcasting are among the companies holding the largest number of stations in the United States. Do the names seem familiar? They should. Two are old, old names in the broadcast business, and all except Willis are companies with extensive media holdings.

The pervasive ownership of radio stations by groups is even more remarkable in light of government restrictions. For example, the FCC limits groups to 20 AMs and 20 FMs. In addition, the FCC prohibits newspapers from owning radio stations in the main market they serve (unless the stations were owned before the rule went into effect). The government also limits common ownership of radio stations—as of 1994 no more than four stations, for example—in the same city.

Station Operation

Radio stations tend to be organized in somewhat similar ways, whether they are AM or FM, affiliated or unaffiliated, owned by conglomerates or by individuals. Typically, a general manager or station manager who operates a radio outlet in a medium-sized market—a city with a population between 50,000 and 250,000, such as Des Moines, Iowa—has his or her station organized into at least five departments: sales, traffic, programming, news and engineering.

Sales. The *sales* department sells advertising, of course, which pays the bills at all commercial stations. A sales manager supervises account executives who call on various clients to sell air time. Network or syndicated shows bring in some money, but most of the sales manager's efforts are concentrat-

Radio signals rain down on more than 558 million receivers in the United States.

ed on selling *national* and *local* commercials, known as "spots." National spots are sold to national advertisers—Chrysler, Ford and General Motors, for instance—who don't want to buy time on a network program but who wish to advertise in a specific market. Local spots, which bring in most of radio's advertising dollars, are those purchased by area businesses or individuals, ranging from the local lumber store to the person running for mayor. Cost for a 30-second spot varies from $1 per airing in small towns to more than $1,000 in major markets.

Traffic. All of the national and local ads are scheduled by the *traffic* department, which attempts to avoid placing similar advertisers in adjacent time periods. In addition, the traffic department must carefully space or deliberately cluster the spots throughout the broadcast hour, depending upon the station's programming format.

The status of minorities and women in radio is similar to that in the newspaper industry, as described in the Special Spot in Chapter 5. Surveys show, for example, that despite the efforts of the National Association of Broadcasters, the Radio-Television News Directors Association, special interest groups and numerous station owners, African-Americans and other racial and ethnic minorities have about the same proportion and type of representation in radio and radio news as in the newspaper business. In other words, with the exception of stations catering to African-American or Hispanic audiences, minorities are underrepresented—particularly in management positions—in comparison to the national work force. These minorities also are underrepresented in the ownership of U.S. radio stations, holding only about two percent of the nation's stations.

Women in radio are somewhat better represented, but still lack management clout, surveys show. Although most stations have at least one female on-air host and news staffs typically are at least one-third female, only about one out of four news directors and few station managers are female.

Programming. The *program* department is headed by a program director or PD. After consulting with the station's general manager, the PD selects network or syndicated programs if appropriate and creates local shows. In creating local programs, the PD determines a programming pattern, oversees the music **playlist,** supervises announcers and disc jockeys, and helps produce commercials and jingles (unless those are created in a separate *production* department).

News. The *news* department, headed by a news director, may have one or perhaps two reporters who cover the community. If news isn't particularly important to the listeners or advertisers, the news director may simply broadcast wire service copy in what is called a "rip and read" operation. In the 1990s, one in four commercial radio stations had no news department at all. A station without a news department may designate an employee such as a disc jockey to read stories from the wire service.

Engineering. The *engineering* department, headed by the chief engineer, is responsible for performing maintenance on the station's equipment and keeping the station on the air.

Engineers, by the way, are survivors with soldering irons. When advertising revenues drop, the sales manager may find the contents of his or her desk in a cardboard box by the station's front door. When audience numbers drop, the PD, the disc jockeys and the news director are often fired. But if the station is to continue to broadcast, an engineer is required. Even fully automated stations, with their whizzing and whirring tape recorders or compact disc players, have engineers.

Now that you have read about the organization of a station in a medium-sized market, please heed a cautionary note: A station in a large market such as New York City or Los Angeles probably will have more departments than the five you've read about. And a small-market station

The disc jockey is king at most U.S. radio stations.

may collapse five departments into three. However, all of these stations function similarly: They acquire or create programming that attracts audiences that in turn attract advertisers.

Let's look at this process in more detail, beginning—where discussions of mass-communication content usually begin—with dollars and cents.

Radio Dollars and Cents

Advertising brings in virtually all of a commercial radio station's revenue but in an order that you might not expect. According to the National Association of Broadcasters, if a typical station received $1 a year in revenue, local advertising would account for about 77 cents of that, national and regional spots would bring in another 21 cents, and network compensation, if any, would amount to perhaps a penny or two.

The typical station's expense dollar breaks down in approximately this way: 43 cents for administration and overhead, 28 cents for promotion, advertising salaries and commissions, 21 cents for program costs (including the salaries of local on-air personnel), 4 cents for news, and 4 cents for engineering and equipment.

If expenses don't exceed revenue, there's a profit. A reasonably well-managed station will make a profit of perhaps 20 percent—for example, a $200,000 profit on $1 million in national and local time sales. Perhaps one-quarter to one-half of all commercial stations do not show a profit, although some industry experts say that this figure is artificially inflated because of the stations' accounting methods.

It's obvious that the key to a profitable station is a highly competitive chunk of the more than $9 billion a year spent on radio advertising in the United States. Because advertising is sold on the basis of both quantity and quality of audience, capturing the correct proportion of the correct audience is absolutely critical. That requires a thorough understanding of both radio listeners and programming possibilities.

Radio Listeners. Figuring out who listens to what programming, as well as when, where, why and how they listen, is the job of the audience measurement company. Several companies analyze radio audiences. Arbitron, however, is the 900-pound gorilla in the group; its figures are taken very seriously by station program directors and by advertisers and their agencies.

In general, Arbitron reports that almost everyone listens to some radio each week, and the average listener devotes about 23 hours a week to radio. Arbitron estimates that listening is highest in the morning hours and lowest after midnight, with a steady decline in between. Typical morning listening occurs at home, whereas afternoon listening is often done at work or on the road. Most people listen to both AM and FM during the week, but one-third of all radio listeners use FM only and about one-fifth use only AM.

Arbitron divides the day into "dayparts," and again into 15-minute segments. Listeners are counted if they tune in for five minutes or more in any 15-minute segment. The dayparts include:

Morning: 6 A.M. to 10 A.M., weekdays

Daytime: 10 A.M. to 3 P.M., weekdays

Afternoon: 3 P.M. to 7 P.M., weekdays

Evening: 7 P.M. to midnight, weekdays

Overnight: midnight to 6 A.M., weekdays

Weekend: 6 A.M. to midnight, Saturday and Sunday

People are usually at home during the morning daypart—although they may be driving to work, which explains why the early hours are called "morning drivetime." Daytime listeners usually are at work. The afternoon daypart is also called "drivetime," because of listener commuting (although students who have returned from school constitute an important audience for many stations). Evening listeners are often students wrestling with

Of all the mass media, radio is dominant throughout the world. It is the one area where the developing nations have made significant progress in the last couple of decades. During the period from about 1970 to 1990, the number of radio receivers globally increased nearly 300 percent. Part of this was due to the transistor revolution of the 1960s and 1970s and the lowering of prices on radio sets.

The largest percentage of growth of radio has been in the so-called Third World, but still the disparity between the developed and developing world is huge—about a 7 to 1 differential. Radio is able to transcend the huge illiteracy of the Third World, is able to span distances easily, is easily portable, is inexpensive, and is widely accessible. However, in a region like Africa, where radio is so important, there are still fewer than 200 radio sets per 1,000 people, according to UNESCO.

Developed nations (the First World) have two-thirds of the some 40,000 radio transmitters. In spite of the penetration of radio programs into the developing world, the fact remains that most of the programming originates in the First World. It is little wonder that the Third World feels their interests and cultures are being neglected globally, even through the air waves.

---

homework. Overnight listeners are traveling, at work or struggling with sleeplessness. Weekend audiences are similar to daytime audiences but are fewer in number and usually listen at home. Of course, all of these very broad generalizations are subject to additional variation as a result of factors such as the age, sex and location of the listeners.

Station Formats. As you've read, radio is marketed as a medium that can deliver a targeted audience. With general listener information, a lot of experience and a little luck, a program director may be able to format a station's sound to deliver, for example, a large proportion of 18-to-34-year-old married women who have jobs outside the home and—perhaps, if it's important to the advertisers—who also drive BMWs and cook highly seasoned meatloaf at least twice a week.

According to Arbitron, five formats drew about two-thirds of all listeners over the age of 12 in the 1990s. The format shares in order of popularity are *adult contemporary, top 40, news-talk, album-oriented rock* and *country*. Other popular formats—again, in Arbitron's order of share of audience based on listeners over 12—include *urban, oldies, Spanish, easy listening, religious* and *classical*.

Let's look at those formats in more detail. But be forewarned: First, what you are about to read about formats is a generalization and may or may not be true in your community. Format popularity varies by time of day, gender and age of listeners and station location. In addition, many stations overlap categories, airing one kind of music or sound at one time of day and a slightly different kind at another time. Finally, one program director's adult contemporary may be another's top 40 radio.

- Adult contemporary or "middle-of-the-road" (MOR) stations play performers such as Barbra Streisand and Barry Manilow. The largest

CHAPTER 8 Radio and the Recording Industry

share of listeners are women between 25 and 54 years of age. A very popular format, more than 17 percent of all radio listeners over 12 listen to this type of station, according to Arbitron studies.

- Top 40 stations play rock and roll, often with a "countdown" format, such as the one pioneered by Casey Kasem in 1970. Kasem's "American Top 40" show, aired by ABC on some 500 stations until Kasem's departure in 1988, moved to the Westwood One Radio Network in 1989. Top 40 artists include Prince, Madonna and Huey Lewis and the News. Most of the top 40 audience is under 24 and is heavily female. This format accounts for 14 percent of all U.S. listeners. Top 40 stations are often FM.

- News-talk stations include two variations: *all news* and *talk.* All-news stations, created in the mid-1960s, are expensive to program because they are labor-intensive. These stations provide frequent updating of news as well as features and usually promote themselves by telling their listeners to "Give us 20 minutes and we'll give you the world." Talk radio features a lineup of strong air personalities and telephone call-ins.

News-talk is one of the most popular radio formats in the United States and Rush Limbaugh is one of the super-stars of the national radio talk shows.

Most news-talk stations are AMs, appeal to audiences over 35 and together capture about 11 percent of all listeners, according to Arbitron.

- Album-oriented rock stations, popular with more than 10 percent of all listeners, play performers such as Van Halen and Bruce Springsteen. AOR stations specializing in classic rock might play Janis Joplin, Led Zepplin, The Grateful Dead and Pink Floyd. Audiences are often under 34, although older audiences typically listen to classic AOR stations. AOR formats are frequently found on FM stations.

- Country or "C and W" stations play country music with all of its variations—from western music to country rock. Listeners are often over 35. Nearly 10 percent of all radio fans listen to country, according to Arbitron, but in the south central United States the audience share is much higher.

Here are other somewhat less popular formats:

- The urban contemporary format may also include soul and rhythm and blues or even jazz programming. Audiences tend to be 12 to 44 years old and account for more than 9 percent of all listeners.

- Oldies, nostalgia and big band music appeal to people over 35 and encompass more than 6 percent of all listeners. Artists range from The Beatles and Buddy Holly to Glenn Miller and Duke Ellington. This format is often on AM stations.

- Spanish formats include many, many variations and take in about 4 percent of listeners, most of them in the 25 to 64 age range. Inexpensively purchased AM stations often program Spanish formats.

- Easy listening or "beautiful music" stations might play Herb Alpert or Henry Mancini. Audience members tend to be over 45 and include more than 4 percent of all listeners. Most of this kind of music is found on FM.

- Religious stations grab slightly more than 2 percent of the audience share, according to Arbitron. Listeners typically are female and are 25

ARLO AND JANIS ® **by Jimmy Johnson**

years and older. The format is used by both AM and FM stations but is more commonly found on AM operations.

- Classical stations, which are often FM public radio stations, appeal to people over 35 and capture nearly 2 percent of the audience.

In summary, the program director uses basic information about listeners as well as experience to format a sound for a potential audience. The audience is then measured, and commercial time is priced accordingly. Because many diverse audience variables are ordinarily measured, it's possible for a station with a relatively small number of listeners to be the market leader because it has the most listeners of a particular type at a particular time.

The Radio Newsgathering Process

Whatever the format, radio stations usually offer some news. True, the news may be occasional and then gleaned only from national wire service reports, but it's news nonetheless.

Radio news is both like and unlike newspaper news. In general, similarities include the elements of news (you remember conflict, consequence, human interest, novelty, prominence, proximity and timeliness) as well as speed, accuracy, objectivity, fairness and completeness. The prime difference between newspaper and radio news is that time rules everything on radio, and stories are usually very, very short. That shortness—covering a story in 30 seconds rather than 30 paragraphs, for example—requires simplification, which reduces the likelihood of completeness and may also affect accuracy, objectivity and even fairness. Radio news also requires repetition, which, with simplification, adds up to a story with information value that only slightly exceeds that provided by a newspaper headline.

Still, radio news is an important and popular service. The Roper Organization's continuing study of Americans' news consumption habits shows radio to be the third most popular source of news, after television and newspapers. An AP Broadcast Services study in the late 1980s of U.S. adults who listen to radio at least 30 minutes a day revealed that most radio listeners—even top 40, AOR and easy listening fans, believed by some not to be avid news consumers—"need and expect news and information" from their favorite station and want at least a newscast an hour.

Reporters at Work. A radio reporter's day will vary with the station's format. A top 40 station with a microscopic news department might require only that its part-time reporters cover a few stories a day by telephone and use the rest of the time to rip and read wire service stories. On the other hand, a major-market news-talk station might have its journalistic troops marshaled like the formations found in a newspaper or television newsroom. In between these examples are stations with two- or three-person news departments. Let's look at one of those.

Assume that you're a reporter at a station with a three-person news department. You are assigned five or six stories a day and typically produce one of two kinds of pieces: "reader" stories or readers with "actualities." The reader is simply a radio version of a newspaper story, explaining who, what, when, where, why and how in perhaps 30 seconds and in a conversational, repetitious style. The reader with an actuality is a story with prerecorded audio such as a reporter's voice and/or one or more taped quotations or "sound bites."

Some of your stories are written as a result of telephone interviews and some are based on personal interviews. For example, if you are assigned to write a reader story about a speech given by the governor, you would tape the speech as you listened to it, then write a story. After you write the reader, you might be asked to produce several additional versions of the story for airing on newscasts later in the day.

An actuality version of this story would require a taped introduction from the place where the speech was given, followed by one or more sound bites of important but short parts of the speech. You also might have to write an introduction to the actuality for the announcer reading and playing your story. Of course, after you write the actuality story, you might be asked to create several additional versions for airing during the day.

You can see from this that radio reporting is significantly less collaborative than newspaper reporting: The reporter who covers the story often writes it, edits it and sometimes airs it as well. In fact, much of radio is noncollaborative. More than any other mass medium, radio means flying solo.

The U.S. Recording Industry: Radio's Older Kissin' Cousin

As you may recall, symbiosis occurs when two or more different creatures live together in a helpful or nonhelpful way. For example, bacteria—tiny animals—live inside people. Some of these organisms help people digest food. Some make people sick. Although the radio and recording industries aren't biologically alive, they do have an economically symbiotic relationship. It works like this: Most U.S. radio stations play records. The records attract listeners who attract advertisers whose dollars permit the stations to make a profit. Of course, this door swings both ways: Radio stations assist recording companies by showcasing new artists with generous portions of free air time.

This relationship is to be expected because the American radio and record industries both became major mass media at about the same time. The recording industry was born in 1877, just a few years before Hertz proved James Clerk Maxwell's theory that radio waves could be sent and received. The record's birthplace was Thomas A. Edison's Menlo Park, N.J., laboratory where Edison recited a nursery rhyme into a crude recording and playback machine built by one of his helpers. As the wizard of Menlo Park spoke, his words ("Mary had a little lamb . . .") were transmitted by a stylus onto a hand-cranked, tinfoil-covered cylinder. Each sound set up a vibration, which caused the stylus to make a tiny dent in the tin. When the tin record was played back, the stylus retrieved the sounds.

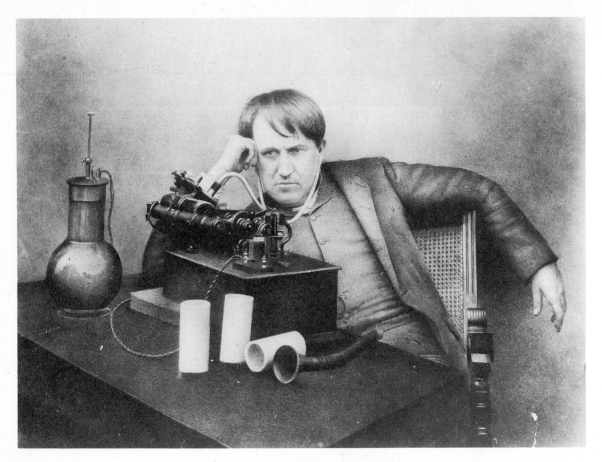

The phonograph, Thomas Edison's favorite invention.

Edison filed a patent application for his phonograph—in Greek, the word means "sound writer"—but faced competition almost immediately. For example, two competitors patented a somewhat similar device that used a longer-lasting wax-covered cylinder. Another competitor swapped Edison's cylinder for a better-sounding, more easily stored disc. By the 1890s, home phonographs, office dictating machines and crude jukeboxes using both cylinders and discs were all available but not ovrwhelmingly popular.

A few years later—as Marconi experimented with sending wireless messages great distances—the fledgling recorded sound business began to favor an Edison competitor, Emile Berliner. Berliner's firm, the Victor Talking Machine Company, introduced the popular disc-playing Victrola in 1906, and the Edison cylinder soon became as popular as outdoor plumbing.

Recording Industry Dollars and Cents

The first two decades of the 20th century saw the emergence of the world's first record superstar, opera singer Enrico Caruso, despite the poor quality of most recordings. Still, record sales climbed until radio emerged in the

1920s, when sales declined because broadcasters offered free music. The record industry countered with electrically powered phonographs and an improved recording process, much as the videocassette recorder industry of the 1980s added bells and whistles to boost sales. But when the Great Depression struck the United States in 1929, not even higher quality recordings could save a leisure-time business from the economic rocks: Retail record sales dropped from $75 million in 1929 to $46 million in 1930 to $5 million in 1933.

By 1938, record sales were back up to a bearable $26 million, thanks to price cuts and an improving economy. Succeeding decades brought even better business, and when sales weren't up to projections, the record industry manufactured new wrinkles. For example, the industry introduced the 12-inch, vinyl, 33⅓ revolutions per minute long play (or LP) record in 1948—the very breakable and brief 78 rpm record was the standard then—and the 45 rpm single in 1949, both of which led to the widespread adoption of the multispeed turntable. Later, magnetic tape, pioneered by the Third Reich's Germans but appropriated and refined by American recording companies, reduced costs and improved sound quality and pumped sales up to $511 million in 1958.

Sales continued to climb until 1979, when receipts suddenly declined from $4.1 billion to $3.6 billion. By 1984, however, the record industry had recovered, with $4.3 billion in sales. What happened? There were numerous reasons for the industry's illness—spiraling costs and too few buyers were key factors—but the paramedics primarily responsible for the resuscitation are of more importance: cable's Music Television channel, created in 1981, and Video Hits One (VH-1), first offered in 1984. Both channels are symbiotic media forms featuring saturation doses of record-plugging "videos."

American record companies now release perhaps 2,000 titles each year worth more than $8 billion, according to the Recording Industry Association of America. Of course, record buyers come in all colors, shapes, and ages, but white males under 25 years of age are the dominant force in the marketplace. As you might guess, rock and roll is the best selling music—its titles account for about one-third of all sales—with urban contemporary, country, pop and classical recordings taking smaller shares of the market.

Volumewise, audiocassettes, which overtook the LP in 1983 as the most purchased type of recording, account for the majority of recordings sold. Compact discs and music videos share the rest of the market (see Figure 8.1). Dollarwise, however, CDs take the lion's share. Two-thirds of all of these recordings are bought in record stores, RIAA says.

Figure 8.1
Estimated Shares of Recorded Music Shipments by Format for 1994

Sources: Veronis, Suhler & Associates, Wilkoesky Gruen Associates. Reprinted by permission.

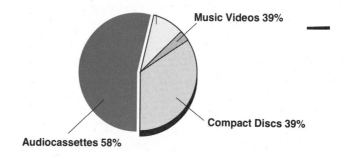

Music Videos 39%

Compact Discs 39%

Audiocassettes 58%

Producing and Marketing a Record

Making a record is a joint venture between a performer and a recording company. The performer is often recruited by a record company "artists and repertoire" (or A&R) agent who seeks out promising acts, contract in hand. With the contract signed, the A&R representative may supervise the recording session, handling everything from budget to song selection or may step out of the picture and leave those tasks to the record's producer.

The session itself involves multiple "takes" of the same song on numerous magnetic tracks. Recording engineers are responsible for the final merging of the best takes of vocal and instrumental work. Their work yields a "master" tape recording.

The manufacturing process varies with the type of recording to be made. Audiocassettes are recorded from the master tape using high-speed duplicators that replicate the original at 64 times normal speed. The original is copied numerous times onto a long tape, which is then cut into lengths appropriate for cassettes and inserted into cassette shells.

Compact discs (CDs) are made using a much more complex and (yes, you guessed it) expensive manufacturing process requiring absolutely dust-free conditions and a laser beam.

Future Focus Compact Discs, Digital Audiotape and Beyond

Just as Edison's sound cylinders gave way to other recording forms, the venerable vinyl disc has given way to an alphabet soup of new sound forms such as compact discs (or CDs) and digital audiotape (or DAT).

The CD, introduced in Japan in 1982 and in Europe and the United States in 1983, now sells significantly better than vinyl LPs, according to the National Association of Recording Merchandisers. While more costly than vinyl LPs, the CD's computer-created, laser-read sound is as good as the original in a medium with no distortion or disc wear, features that make it popular for both consumers and radio stations.

Album-length CDs, CD audio singles and compact disc videos (CDVs) are available now. Interactive compact discs (CD-Is) and even recordable CDs are expected to be widely available in the mid-1990s. CD-Is will understand user commands and recordable CDs will allow home recording of extremely high-quality sound.

DAT is the recordable CD's close cousin. First marketed in Japan in mid-1987, DAT machines, which are somewhat like 8mm videocassette recorders, offer up to two hours of playing time compared to a standard CD's 74 minutes. A DAT recorder is much more expensive than a CD player, however, and a DAT will wear out sooner than a CD.

While the recorded performance is being manufactured, the company's marketing team swings into action. Advertising and merchandising people produce print and broadcast ads, jacket materials and even retail point-of-sale displays. Video producers create or contract for the almost mandatory video. Artists' relations experts coordinate road tours and media exposure, with help from company public relations professionals. Promotion experts track and promote radio station air play. Product managers oversee all of these efforts.

Records get to retail stores in one of three ways. If a firm is large enough—the Camelot Music chain is an example of one such business—record companies directly supply it with recordings. Other retailers are serviced through wholesalers called "one-stops" and "rack-jobbers." One-stops are wholesalers that specialize in supplying smaller chains or even single stores with selections. One-stops also may specialize in specific types of music. Rack-jobbers often handle record departments in chain stores such as Wal-Mart or Kmart. The rack-jobber may lease the record department or just stock it.

Expenses are astronomical or at least stratospheric. According to RIAA, a rock album often costs $200,000 to record, a cost that is charged against a performer's royalties. A video clip adds at least another $50,000. All together, record companies invest $500,000 per album on average. More than eight out of ten popular and nine of ten classical albums lose money for the record company. If the odds for financial success are that long, why bother? The answer is the same one used by movie moguls and their investors: Most albums (and movies) lose money, but when a company has a hit, it's usually blockbuster-big. How big? Take Michael Jackson's "Thriller." It sold almost 40 million copies in the United States and abroad.

Against a few million dollars in development costs, Jackson's album was a runaway success.

These figures may confuse and even distress you. If you want to understand the record business at its simplest, remember this: Radio station air play, which is where we began this part of the chapter, is perhaps the most critical part of the recording industry marketing process.

Retrospective

Radio began as a maritime and military medium in most parts of the world. When commercial possibilities became apparent after World War I, modern radio emerged. In the United States, advertising was quickly recognized as the most efficient way of supporting the new medium, and by the late 1920s, three networks were in operation.

Regulation was necessary from the beginning, but wireless regulation sufficed until 1927, when the Federal Radio Commission was established. By 1934, the FRC had been replaced by the Federal Communications Commission, which had enhanced regulatory responsibilities.

Television changed American radio into a highly targeted medium, aimed at specific demographic groups. Targeted radio is now being assisted by a variety of networks, which, unlike the chains of yesteryear, also offer audience-specific programming—much of it delivered by satellite. At the same time, AM audiences are scurrying in large numbers to FM.

The recording industry also is facing change, but from CDs and perhaps DAT recordings.

Questions

1. When National Public Radio aired an updated version of "War of the Worlds" in 1988, there was virtually no public reaction. Have radio audiences changed that much in 50 years? If so, how? If not, why didn't the 1988 radio audience react more like its 1938 cousin?

2. How did the sale of commercials encourage the expansion of radio networks? Do you think radio networks have outlived their usefulness today?

3. Why did the radio drama die?

4. Do you think that today's radio programming for targeted audiences is a bad trend? If not, why not?

5. Who or what is the culprit for the disappearing AM listener? Should all of the blame be placed on sound quality?

6. Research suggests that radio stations using the "middle-of-the-road" (or MOR) format capture the largest proportion of listeners in each market. Can you name an MOR format station in your community?

7. Explain why radio news is so noncollaborative.

8. If CDs drop in price, as is expected, do you think single discs, LPs, cassettes and DATs will be a factor in the marketplace?

Barnouw, E. *A Tower in Babel*. New York: Oxford University Press, 1966.

———. *The Golden Web*. New York: Oxford University Press, 1968.

———. *The Image Empire*. New York: Oxford University Press, 1970.

Chapple, Steve, and Garofolo, Reebee. *Rock 'n' Roll Is Here to Pay: The History and Politics of the Music Industry*. Chicago: Nelson-Hall, 1977.

Dranov, Paula. *Inside the Music Publishing Industry*. White Plains, N.Y.: Knowledge Industry, 1980.

Eastman, Susan Tyler. *Broadcast/Cable Programming: Strategies and Practices*. Belmont, Calif.: Wadsworth, 1993.

Emery, Edwin, and Emery, Michael. *The Press and America*. Englewood Cliffs, N.J.: Prentice-Hall, 1992.

Fornatale, Peter, and Mills, Joshua. *Radio in the Television Age*. Woodstock, N.Y.: Overlook Press, 1980.

Gelatt, Roland. *The Fabulous Phonograph: 1877–1977*. New York: Macmillan, 1977.

Head, Sydney, and Sterling, Christopher. *Broadcasting in America*. New York: Houghton Mifflin, 1990.

Keith, Michael C, and Krause, Joseph M. *The Radio Station*. Stoneham, Mass: Focal Press, 1989.

MacDonald, J. Fred. *Don't Touch That Dial! Radio Programming in American Life from 1920 to 1960*. Chicago: Nelson-Hall, 1979.

Paley, William S. *As It Happened: A Memoir*. Garden City, N.Y.: Doubleday, 1979.

Sterling, Christopher, and Kittross, John. *Stay Tuned: A Concise History of American Broadcasting*. Belmont, Calif.: Wadsworth, 1990.

Stokes, Geoffrey. *Star-making Machinery: Inside the Business of Rock and Roll*. New York: Random House, 1977.

Suggested Readings

CHAPTER 9

Television

On Jan. 22, 1987, R. Budd Dwyer, Pennsylvania's 47-year-old state treasurer, called a news conference just before noon at his Harrisburg office. Reporters assumed that Dwyer, who was to be sentenced the next day for up to 55 years in prison for fraud, would announce his resignation. Instead, Dwyer made a rambling statement critical of the criminal justice system and then pulled a .357 Magnum pistol from a brown envelope while reporters stared in horror. Television cameras videotaped that 16-second session, which sounded like this:

Dwyer (drawing the gun): When I, and I. . . .
Voice (as some reporters ducked): Budd, don't!
Another voice: Budd, no, Budd, no!
Dwyer: Please leave the room if this will, if this will affect you. . . .
Voice: Budd, don't!
Dwyer's aide: Quiet down.
Dwyer: Don't . . . , don't . . . , don't . . . , this will hurt someone.
Voice (as Dwyer put the gun into his mouth and shot himself to death): Ohhhhhh!
Another voice: Holy—!
Third voice: Oh my God, oh my God!

The carnage was recorded by numerous reporters and photographers. Most U.S. TV stations carried the story during the evening news, using either no videotape of the suicide or cutting away from the video as Dwyer drew the gun or put it into his mouth. Only a few stations—three of them in Pennsylvania—showed the moment of suicide during newscasts. For television viewers, the lesson was clear: Virtually all of the television stations in America had access to an audience-boosting, high-impact story that could have been presented under the guise of public service. However, almost all of the stations discarded what they possessed in favor of a restrained approach.

Still, for some viewers, even the restrained Dwyer suicide coverage was a horrific intrusion. And many, from the blood-splattered reporters who covered the story to the viewers who tried to understand it, wondered if Budd Dwyer would have killed himself if no one had come to his news conference.

Television is clearly a powerful mass communication medium, imprisoning viewers for hours at a time, stimulating fads and changes in the language, helping to elect presidents and, perhaps, providing a stage for acts such as Budd Dwyer's suicide.

Television Yesterday

Televised coverage of a major event such as a presidential campaign or a war often is both extensive and riveting, but the primary fare of American television is entertainment.

Television as an entertainment medium made its debut to some extent in

1928 when the General Electric Company began broadcasting a short but regular schedule on WGY in Schenectady, N.Y. During that initial television "season," WGY aired a television remote broadcast as well as a drama. While WGY beamed out its weak signals, the Federal Radio Commission authorized the Radio Corporation of America to build W2XBS, a New York City television station. Both of these stations were essentially experimental and transmitted extremely crude pictures to very few TVs. Still, reducing an image to an airborne signal that was later reconstituted in a box was a technological marvel.

The Earliest Days

Television, even the crude system in use in the late 1920s, was the product of hundreds of years of observation and discoveries. For example, television's development drew on previous research in electromagnetism, chemistry, and other areas of science and on technology such as the telegraph, the telephone, radio, and even motion pictures. In addition, there were two 19th-century developments that were particularly important for the invention of television: English scientist F.C. Bakewell's 1847 proposal for a "copying telegraph" that—theoretically, at least—could transmit images, and an 1884 patent for a television scanning device by a German scientist named Paul Nipkow.

Past Pointer Media Mileposts: Pictures from the Air

1884	German Paul Nipkow patents television scanning device.
1923	Vladimir Zworykin demonstrates early television system.
1928	Experimental TV station WGY begins sending signals.
1936	Nazi Germany covers Berlin Olympics with primitive television.
1938	Television sets go on sale to public at $600 each (about half the price of a new car).
1941	FCC authorizes first 10 commercial TV stations, only to see wartime freeze on television development.
1948	Following wartime freeze, FCC freezes TV development again, until 1952.
1951	First transcontinental TV hookup connects New York to San Francisco.
1959	Quiz show scandals rock TV industry.
1960	Presidential debates between John Kennedy and Richard Nixon are televised live.
1962	Telstar satellite makes live international telecasts possible.
1969	Moon landing appears on live television around the world.
1975	Sony introduces "Betamax" home-video recording system. The VHS system follows two years later. By 1985, VCRs will be in 40 percent of American homes.
1983	M*A*S*H captures 60.2 rating and 77 share with final episode.
1987	Nielsen switches from diaries to people meters for measuring national television audiences.
1991	French baker pays $6,000 for the first high-definition, wide-screen TV set sold in the west. Japanese HDTV transmissions increase to eight hours a day, but few watch because HDTV sets, available since 1990, cost $35,000.

All of these observations and discoveries began to come together in the 1920s in the form of various early television systems. One of the first systems was demonstrated in 1923 by Vladimir Zworykin, who was employed by Westinghouse and later RCA. Philo Farnsworth, a brilliant American inventor who worked independently of Zworykin, also made significant contributions during this period, as did John L. Baird in England. By 1930, the giants of American broadcasting—RCA, GE and Westinghouse—had merged their television research teams under Zworykin, who with more than 40 engineers eventually solved enough of the medium's technical problems to make it viable.

Television Catches On

The 1930s brought more experimental stations, better pictures (including a demonstration of color TV and large screen projection), and an operating television system in Germany in 1935 and Great Britain in 1936.

Beginning in 1938, TV sets became commercially available in the United States. The American TV sets, priced at more than $600 each (or about half the cost of a new car), didn't sell particularly well because they were expensive and there was little to watch. In addition, there was no guarantee that the electronic standards wouldn't change and render the sets obsolete. As a result, when RCA's New York City station broadcast a program in 1939 featuring its chief, David Sarnoff, extolling the virtues of television from the World's Fair, the transmission went to perhaps 120 sets in greater New York.

David Sarnoff makes television history when he stands before cameras to dedicate RCA's pavilion at the 1939 New York World's Fair.

Even so, stations continued to broadcast and by 1941, the Federal Communications Commission formalized television engineering standards and authorized 10 stations to go on the air. War broke out a few months later, consumer electronics manufacturing was discontinued and what television there was continued to play to a very small house. At the end of the war, only six stations (using channels 2 through 6) served the United States. There were National Broadcasting Company stations in New York City and Philadelphia, Columbia Broadcasting System stations in New York and Chicago, a New York station owned by DuMont (a set manufacturer that would later start a network) and a Los Angeles station owned by showman Don Lee.

As World War II ended, the FCC found itself with more than 100 commercial TV applications on file and regular network television among New York, Philadelphia and Schenectady. Although commercial broadcasting was about to blossom, the FCC continued to tinker with television's technical standards, first reducing **VHF** or Very High Frequency channels from 18 to 13 in 1946, then deleting channel 1 from new sets in 1947.

By 1948, 41 stations in 23 cities were on the air, broadcasting comedy (Milton Berle's "Texaco Star Theater," for example), drama ("Kraft Television Theater"), westerns ("Hopalong Cassidy" and "The Lone Ranger"), variety (Ed Sullivan's "Toast of the Town"), sports (the World Series), network news (the "Camel News Caravan" with John Cameron Swayse) and special events (the national political conventions of 1948).

By the end of 1948, there were 975,000 TV homes in the United States. While these viewers watched their flickering little screens, most were probably unaware of a major technical and political battle brewing that would freeze the number of television stations in the United States at 108 for four years and then introduce a new television service, educational television and color TV.

The Freeze: Interference, the UHF Question and Color

The FCC found itself wrestling with three major technical problems in September 1948, when it froze all TV channel allocations.

There was interference between stations operating on the same channel, particularly in the crowded broadcasting corridor between New York City and Norfolk, Va. That geography, of course, included Washington, D.C., and some very demanding television viewers—the nation's lawmakers.

In addition, 12 VHF channels were deemed to be inadequate for the future needs of the entire United States. More channels were required, and more channels meant that the FCC had to set guidelines for a new television service—**UHF** or Ultra High Frequency.

Finally, the time had come to select a color broadcasting system for the United States. The FCC had two obvious choices: a system created by CBS or one being promoted by RCA. The CBS color system, in development for a decade, was technically superior to the competing RCA system, but initially required two channels to broadcast pictures and even then was not compatible with existing black and white TV sets. Also, color sets using the CBS system would have to utilize huge cellophane filters spinning inside the set at more than 1,400 revolutions per minute.

In 1952, with 16 times more TV sets than there had been in 1948, the FCC announced its decisions in a ruling called the "Sixth Report and Order." Broadcasting licenses would be allocated between the VHF spectrum and a 70-channel UHF service. Educational or noncommercial broadcasters would receive 242 channels—80 VHF and the rest UHF. Finally, the FCC selected CBS's noncompatible color system as the American standard. CBS? Yes, CBS was selected even after a lawsuit by RCA, but a year later the FCC changed its mind and approved RCA's compatible approach, the current standard.

As the FCC's freeze thawed, Americans found themselves watching four networks—the American Broadcasting Company, CBS, NBC, and the DuMont network (which went out of business in 1956)—offering many, many programs. For the most part, viewers watched shows that had been born on radio and transplanted to TV, although the new medium managed to create a few shows of its own. Many of the network programs were live and were repeated for various time zones because videotape did not yet

Lucille Ball and Desi Arnaz become household names with the "I Love Lucy" series in the 1950s.

exist. Later, film became popular, which gave birth to reruns, first shown in the summer of 1952.

Some of the programs of the 1950s still have a familiar ring: "I Love Lucy," "Today," "The Tonight Show," "Face the Nation," "Captain Kangaroo," "Alfred Hitchcock Presents" and, of course, "As the World Turns." Some of these programs, such as "Today" and "Face the Nation," were produced by the networks. Most were made by outside production companies under contract to the networks. A few shows such as "Science Fiction Theater" were made by outside firms and syndicated to stations across the country. Some shows, beginning in 1954, were even made in color.

Television Comes of Age

American television of the 1960s was both similar and dissimilar to its present form. For example, by the mid-1960s, network satellite transmissions somewhat like those of the 1990s were possible, and all three networks were presenting color programs: 90 percent of prime-time programming for NBC, 50 percent for CBS and 33 percent for ABC. A few years later, most commercials also were in color, as were presidential news conferences.

Network news, expanded to 30 minutes nightly by the mid-1960s, began to take its modern form, too. Television covered the assassination of President John F. Kennedy in 1963 and the national mourning that followed. Later, the "tube" gave Americans vivid images of the violent integration of the country and, in 1968, the brutal murders of Martin Luther King and Robert F. Kennedy. And there were the bloody Vietnam War and the massive peace protests, all in living color.

Still, there were significant differences in television viewing then. People watched more network programming because viewing choices were limited. For example, ABC, CBS and NBC captured 92 percent of the nationwide prime-time audience in the 1960s, whereas today the figure is about 60 percent and shrinking. People watched more local programming, too, because there were half as many channels in the mid-1960s as in the 1990s. Cable television with its delivery of signals from faraway stations was rare, and the home videocassette recorder as an alternative to network and local offerings didn't exist.

Television Today

As you have read, some significant changes have come to the television industry since the 1960s. Today, there are about 1,500 full-power TV stations in the United States, about half of them VHF and half UHF (see Table 9.1). There are also 1,300 low-power TV stations serving the United States. U.S. stations represent only a fraction of the world's 35,000 television stations and relay transmitters, but American stations program for longer periods and to bigger audiences than do stations in other parts of the world.

Table 9.1 Number of U.S. Television Stations		
VHF commercial		557
UHF commercial		587
VHF educational		124
UHF educational		237
	Total	1505
VHF low power		466
UHF low power		825
	Grand Total	2796

Source: Federal Communications Commission, mid-1992.

Structure of the U.S. Television Industry

Three-quarters of America's television stations (or about 1,100 stations in all) are commercial in nature. And about 60 percent of those commercial broadcasters are affiliated with ABC, CBS or NBC. In addition, Fox counts more than 150 stations as affiliates. Of the noncommercial stations, most are UHF and almost all are affiliated with the Public Broadcasting Service.

Because television stations, like other mass media, tend to be very profitable, joint ownership of commercial stations by individuals, groups or networks is common. That's surprising in the face of two restrictions.

The first restriction is money: Television stations are very expensive. For example, in 1988 Gannett, owner of the nation's largest newspaper chain and numerous broadcasting stations, paid an estimated $155 million for two VHF network affiliates—WTLV in Jacksonville, Fla., and WFMY in Greensboro, N.C. A little later, Tak Communications, which owns television stations in Wisconsin and Hawaii, bought WGRZ, a UHF Buffalo,

GLOBAL GLANCE
News for the
World: Television

Since the 1980s, television news has made great inroads throughout the world. In particular, the Cable News Network (CNN) has established itself as a prime provider of global news. Beginning in 1985 with its news service to Europe, CNN expanded its coverage to the whole world by 1990. Nearly 150 countries were served by CNN in 1993.

In the late 1980s, both CBS and NBC began sending their American evening news programs to Europe, CBS through a French channel and NBC through an English satellite channel. Visnews, by 1990, was distributed in nearly 90 countries. Rupert Murdoch's News Corp. Ltd. was reaching out from Britain to other countries in the 1980s. By the early 1990s, both Europe's EBU ("Euronews") and Japan's NHK were getting into the global act.

It is obvious that although the TV global coverage is improving, the television news flow between East and West continued to favor the West. A principal reason international TV news broadcasting has not done better in Asia is that most television in that part of the world is government-controlled. To a large degree, this is also true in large portions of Africa.

N.Y., NBC affiliate for more than $85 million—cash. It's true that network-affiliated stations are the Cadillacs of the used television station lot, but even a financially ill non-network-affiliated outlet with a weak signal can be pricey because of too few licenses for too many would-be buyers.

The second restriction comes from the FCC. Under current FCC rules, no owner may hold more than 12 television stations in most cases (14 in the case of owners with at least two stations with significant minority ownership); an owner also may not own stations reaching more than 25 percent of the nation's television homes. In addition, the FCC discourages common ownership of TV and radio stations in the same market and prohibits newspaper owners from buying TV stations in the same market they already serve. Even so, most commercial television stations are group owned. The heavy hitters in terms of both quantity and quality of stations owned include Capital Cities/ABC, CBS, NBC and Fox, along with non-network organizations such as Allbritton Communications, Chris Craft Industries, Gannett, Hearst, Group W and Tribune Broadcasting.

By the way, what the FCC gives it can take away, or at least try. The FCC has yanked the licenses of some broadcasters over the years for flagrant abuses and has fined many more for infractions of rules. A case in point is a two-decade-old battle with RKO General, which once owned more than a dozen radio and TV stations. The FCC, which accused RKO of bilking advertisers and misrepresenting information to the Commission, said the company was unfit to hold its licenses. RKO denied the charges but sold many of its stations nonetheless.

In summary, the "typical" commercial station is a very valuable, group-owned VHF or UHF network affiliate; the "typical" noncommercial station is a publicly owned UHF outlet affiliated with PBS.

Station Operation

The nation is divided into more than 200 television markets. Stations in small markets—such as Alpena, Mich., the nation's smallest television market—often have few employees and assign them duties that bridge several departments. Stations in major markets such as New York City have large staffs, many departments and little employee crossover. Stations in middle-sized markets such as Rochester, N.Y., usually have around 100 employees spread among four or five departments, including *sales, programming* and *production, news,* and *engineering* (see Figure 9.1). A station manager or general manager will oversee each of these departments and may directly supervise a *business* department, which handles accounting and clerical activities. If these departments sound familiar, it's because they have counterparts in radio.

Sales. Billions of dollars are spent on television advertising each year. Some of that money goes to the national networks, which sell commercial time within their programming. The local station sales manager is responsible for

Special Spot

Public
Broadcasting:
America's
Alternative
Television Service

Almost all of America's more than 350 noncommercial VHF and UHF television stations are Public Broadcasting Service affiliates. Public television began a good deal like public radio. It was called "educational" for some time, then came to be known as "public" broadcasting. And like public radio, it's always been commercial broadcasting's poor cousin.

Public television's roots lay in the FCC's "Sixth Report and Order," which reserved 242 television channels for noncommercial use. The first educational station, KUHT at the University of Houston, went on the air in May 1953. Fifteen years later, 146 stations, about half VHF and half UHF, were broadcasting. Nonlocal programming, some good and some very, very bad, was distributed by mail through the National Educational Television "network."

In 1968, as you have read, the nonprofit Corporation for Public Broadcasting was created, which in turn drew the blueprints for PBS in 1969 and began passing along money to the revenue-starved public stations.

Today, more than 94 percent of Americans can receive at least one public television station, and two out of three Americans watch noncommercial TV at least once a month. Although those figures are good news for public stations, the average station's viewer share is only 5 percent.

Some public stations operate independently, whereas others function as part of a state network and retransmit programs from a mother station. State governments and broadcasting authorities are licensees of about 35 percent of the stations; independent community organizations own another 35 percent; and the remainder are licensed to colleges, universities, and local school districts and governments. About half of the money to run these public television stations and networks comes directly or indirectly from local, state and federal taxes, with the rest contributed by individuals, foundations and businesses.

Public television station programs are created primarily by other public television stations, often with the production and satellite-distribution help of PBS. A somewhat smaller portion comes from independent producers not affiliated with public stations. Foreign and international coproductions account for another major chunk of programming, with lesser amounts coming from the originating station and other sources. Major categories include children's, information and skills, cultural, instructional and news and public affairs shows.

capturing as much of the remaining revenue as is possible. He or she accomplishes that by selling commercials or "spots" to national and local advertisers who want to purchase time in a specific market rather than on an entire network. These locally sold spots, which may appear during local or network programs, are scheduled by station traffic personnel.

Advertising charges are based on the length of the commercial, the estimated size of the audience and the total amount of business the advertiser does with the station. A single 30- or 60-second spot, broadcast within the best-rated program in prime time, is most expensive. For a station in a place such as Little Rock, Ark., in 1994, the cost could be as much as $1,800 for a 30-second locally sold spot on a popular network program or as little as $100 for a similar airing within a movie on the least-watched independent channel. **Prime time,** by the way, means what it sounds like: It is the station's most valuable time because audiences are largest. Prime time varies with the time zone in which the station operates. For stations on the East and West Coasts of the United States, prime time is

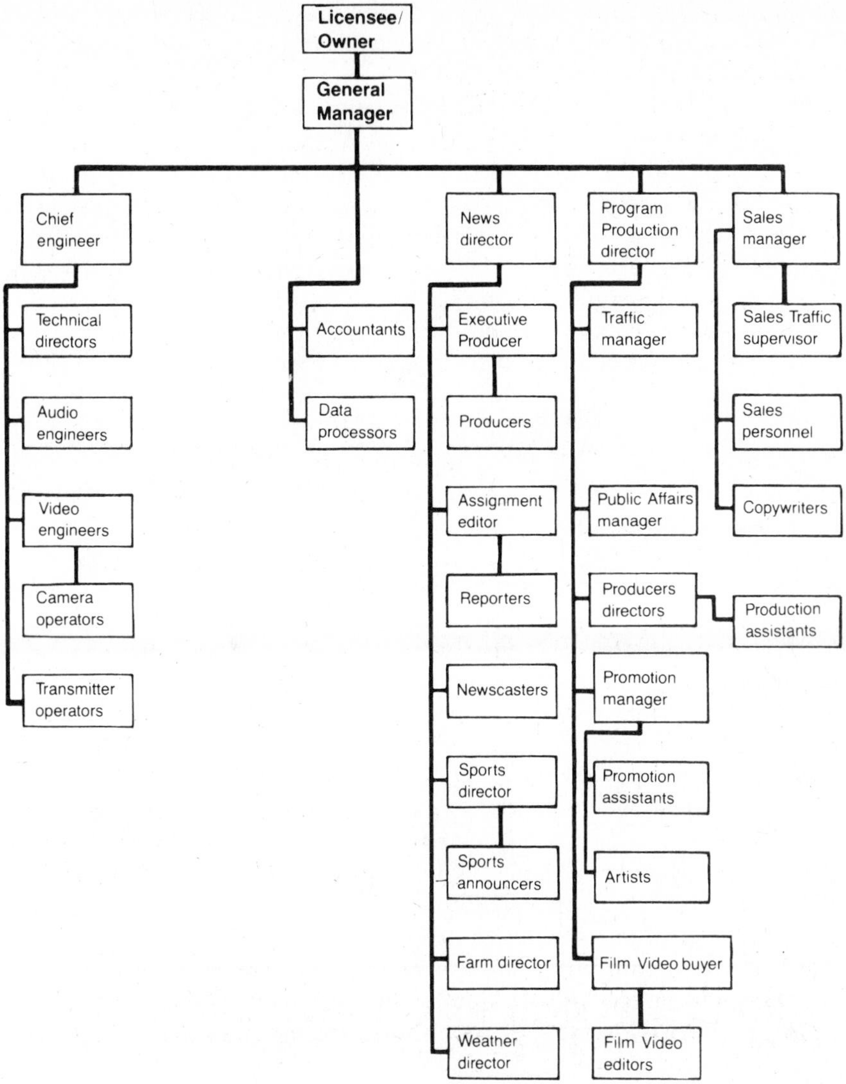

Figure 9.1
Organization of a
Medium-Market Television
Station

Figure 9.1 Organization of a Medium-Market Television Station

Licensee/Owner — General Manager

- Chief engineer
  - Technical directors
  - Audio engineers
  - Video engineers
  - Camera operators
  - Transmitter operators
- Accountants
- Data processors
- News director
  - Executive Producer
  - Producers
  - Assignment editor
  - Reporters
  - Newscasters
  - Sports director
  - Sports announcers
  - Farm director
  - Weather director
- Program Production director
  - Traffic manager
  - Public Affairs manager
  - Producers directors
  - Promotion manager
    - Promotion assistants
    - Artists
  - Film Video buyer
    - Film Video editors
  - Production assistants
- Sales manager
  - Sales Traffic supervisor
  - Sales personnel
  - Copywriters

from 8 p.m. to 11 p.m. every night except Sunday, when it begins at 7 p.m. For Midwestern and Mountain time zone stations, prime time is from 7 p.m. to 10 p.m., except for Sunday, when it extends from 6 p.m. until 10 p.m.

Other time periods (using Eastern Standard Time) are less costly. They include *early morning* (dawn until 9 a.m.) and *daytime* (from 9 a.m. to 4 p.m.), both of which appeal to audiences of women and schoolchildren; *early fringe* (from 4 p.m. to 7 p.m.) for general audiences; *access* (from 7 p.m. to 8 p.m.) for all audiences; and *late news, late fringe* and *late-late* (11 p.m. until dawn), which appeal to singles and youthful adults.

Programming/Production. The television program director has a Herculean task: acquiring and airing audience-attracting programs at a cost that will allow the station to make a profit.

If the station is an ABC, CBS or NBC network affiliate, about two-thirds of the programs will come from that source. The network will compensate the station for its time (generally at between 15 and 30 percent of what time on the station normally would cost an advertiser), and the station can even slip in a few commercials of its own. While network-owned-and-operated stations or "O and O's" usually carry virtually all available network programs, network affiliates don't have to and usually do not. The reason is that the network compensation produces little revenue compared to what the affiliate station could earn from local and national advertisers with a popular locally created or syndicated show in the same time period. As a result, network affiliated stations occasionally refuse to broadcast network programs—"preempt" is the nice word—in order to broadcast locally sponsored shows such as movies. In 1988, for example, ABC affiliates preempted an average of one hour of ABC's 22 hours of programming per week.

Even if the program director accepts virtually all of the network's offerings, he or she still must lease or acquire from syndicators several hours of programming such as "Wheel of Fortune" or "Star Trek: The Next Generation" for certain non-prime-time periods when network programming is not available. As you read in Chapter 8, some of this programming is rented at full price, whereas other programs are acquired under barter-purchase or pure barter terms.

If the program director works for a station unaffiliated with any network, *all* shows must be locally produced or obtained from syndicators. The latter can be expensive. For example, WCIX, a Miami, Fla., station, had to spend $13 million for the rights to 255 episodes of "M*A*S*H." If that figure takes your breath away, consider this: "The Cosby Show," which became available for syndication in 1988, is expected to have earned Viacom, its syndicator, a total of $600 million by the time you read this.

As if all of this responsibility weren't enough, the program manager may also be responsible—through a subordinate, the production manager—for production of several hours of newscasts per day, as well as for production of local commercials for the sales department and promotional announcements for other departments.

News. The typical TV news department, headed by a news director, employs about 18 full- and part-time reporters, photographers and editors. Some stations, particularly independents, have no news department; others such as network-affiliated stations in the largest U.S. markets, have more than 75 full- and part-time employees.

The news director will probably air several hours of newscasts a day. Depending on the size of the market served, these newscasts may include a morning program, a noon news show, one or two newscasts prior to the beginning of prime-time programming, and a final newscast at the end of

The television industry, like the newspaper industry, is committed to increasing the number of minority and women employees. However, like the newspaper industry, minority employment goals have thus far not been achieved.

In the early 1990s, for example, minorities made up about 22 percent of the U.S. work force but held only about 19 percent of the jobs in television. In news, which is a highly visible and important area, minorities accounted for 16 percent of all jobs (a slight increase from a decade earlier) and a dismal 8 percent of the news directorships. Most of those minorities who held the news jobs—about 62 percent—were African American, with Hispanics, Asian Americans and Native Americans accounting for the rest.

At the same time, minorities owned about 2 percent of the country's TV stations. The federal government had some success in improving that situation in the 1980s by providing tax incentives for owners who sold stations to minority broadcasters. For example, television personality Geraldo Rivera, film star Richard "Cheech" Marin and three other Hispanics formed a company in 1989 to purchase television stations under just those circumstances.

In the early 1990s, white women were better off than minorities but were to some degree still severely underrepresented in the television industry. For example, women made up 48 percent of the U.S. work force then and about 38 percent of the television industry work force. In TV news, women held about one-third of the jobs and anchored or coanchored news programs at virtually every network affiliate. However, only 18 percent of the nation's news directors were women.

In short, America's television networks and stations have been and are controlled by white males. Women are frequently clerks and sales representatives and reporters but are only beginning to take positions as managers. For African Americans and other minorities, progress is less evident.

The presence of minorities and women in significant positions on network and television station payrolls is only part of the dimension of the problem. The other equally important aspect is how minorities and women are portrayed on television entertainment programs. It is in this arena that the greatest progress seems to have been made. For example, just three decades ago, African Americans were virtually unseen in network and syndicated entertainment programming, and women were rarely portrayed as anything but homemakers. Programs such as "The Cosby Show," "Oprah Winfrey" and "L.A. Law" illustrate how far producers and audiences have come in a relatively short period.

Even so, there's a lot of work to be done, according to the National Commission on Working Women, which analyzed 80 network series in the early 1990s. The group found that there were as many space creatures depicted on network television as there were Hispanic, Asian and Native American characters. The group also found that male characters outnumbered female characters and that when women were portrayed, they were rarely over 40 years old.

prime-time broadcasting. You'll read more about the news department later in this chapter.

Engineering. The chief engineer, with staff assistance, maintains equipment and supervises overall audio and video quality. In addition, engineers operate cameras and other equipment used to produce programs such as newscasts.

How It All Fits Together. Let's see how all of these departments work together from 7 p.m. until 8 p.m. Eastern Standard Time on a weeknight. During this time period, the station airs two programs: the local 7 o'clock news and a syndicated game show, "Wheel of Fortune."

The news, of course, is a product of the news department, although the "live" parts of it are directed by the production department and photographed by engineers. "Wheel of Fortune" is leased from a syndication company. Both programs have numerous time slots for commercials. Some of the commercials are produced by the station's production department and some are delivered ready to air. All of the commercials, however, have been sold by the station's sales representatives. Engineers, of course, keep the equipment working during the hour. Finally, business department personnel will bill sponsors and their advertising agencies and will pay employees and the syndicator of the game show.

The goal of all of these departments is simple: to broadcast programming that will satisfy the right kind of viewers in sufficient quantities to continue to attract advertisers.

Television Dollars and Cents

More than $100 billion dollars was spent on advertising in the United States in 1991. Television captured more than $27 billion of that as well as a 22 percent share, second only to the newspaper industry's $30 billion a year and 24 percent share.

Like radio, television lives or dies by advertising because sponsors directly or indirectly provide *all* of a station's revenue. Television advertisements are sold much like radio ads: Advertisers are told that particular programs will deliver a specified quantity and quality of audience. The price of the ad, as you've read, is based on the program achieving that audience goal.

To be more precise, about 96 cents of a large-city network-affiliated station's revenue dollar comes from national, regional and local advertisers. The remaining 4 cents in station income comes from network compensation. Network monies, however, may play a decreasing role in affiliate station revenues in the future. For example, ABC, CBS and NBC sharply reduced affiliate compensation in the early 1990s. That economy measure came shortly after ABC advised affiliates that they would no longer be compensated at all for broadcasting some sporting events, such as the Super Bowl, the Olympics and the World Series.

A TV station's budget is spent in much the same way as it is in radio: for administration, promotion, selling costs, entertainment and news programming and engineering. Leftover money is profit, and as in the case of radio, a well-managed television station can make a sobering profit. The National Association of Broadcasters estimates that the typical commercial television station in the early 1990s managed a profit of about 20 percent before taxes. Profits at some stations approach 50 percent, according to industry analysts. Of course, it is possible to lose money with a television station, particularly a UHF independent station in a highly competitive market, but it's not easy to do so.

The bottom line is the same as it is in radio: Networks, local stations and program suppliers must create programs that will attract adequate numbers of the right kind of viewers who, in turn, will attract advertisers. Doing all of that requires sound business sense and, of course, knowledge of the audience.

Television Viewer Measurement. As you have read, figuring out who watches what programming, as well as when, where, why and how they watch, is the job of the audience measurement company. A. C. Nielsen and Arbitron, the two best-known national ratings companies, use somewhat similar methods.

These companies use a statistical *sampling* technique to measure the size of the audience for a particular program as well as the characteristics of the people in the audience. In this case, sampling means that the television preferences of several thousand carefully chosen families are measured to reflect the viewing habits of the whole audience. If that sounds silly to you, have faith. Even the U.S. Census Bureau uses sampling techniques to check the accuracy of census-takers' work.

Let's first look at how the size of the audience is estimated. In the case of Nielsen, about 4,000 homes are hooked up to cigar-box-size gizmos called "people meters." The people meters can tell when the TV set is off or on, and when it's on, what channel is being watched and by whom. The "whom" portion is tricky because viewers (including guests in the house) must identify themselves to the meter periodically. All of the results are automatically reported at least once a day to Nielsen's operations center in Florida. Using that data, Nielsen provides daily and weekly estimates of audiences nationwide and in more than two dozen U.S. cities. In addition, using meters and viewer-completed diaries, Nielsen also surveys audiences up to seven times a year in each of the nation's more than 200 television markets.

The size of the audience is usually expressed as a **rating** or a **share.** A rating is an estimate of the percentage of households viewing (or hearing, in the case of radio) a particular program when compared to all the *potential viewing households* in a market. A share of audience refers to the percentage of viewing households compared to all the viewing households *currently watching television* in the market.

Here's an example. Let's assume that there is a television station serving Poison Spider, a community in central Wyoming. If there are 100 households with televisions in Poison Spider (which is probably a gross overestimate considering Poison Spider's isolation), a ranching-oriented news program with a rating of 12 would capture 12 households. However, that same program could have a share of 90 because 90 percent of all households watching television at that time were tuned to the ranching show.

Now let's look at CBS's "60 Minutes," which during one week in the winter of 1992 had a national Nielsen rating of 21 and a share of 34. On a national level, a rating point is worth 1 percent of the nation's more than 93 million television homes (rather than 1 percent of Poison Spider's 100 homes). As a result, CBS's show was seen in 19.5 million homes (21 percent

× 93 million), by 34 percent of the total viewing audience. By the way, that's a very high rating. Successful prime-time network programs often have a rating in the mid-teens and a share in the 20s. Television's highest rating and share, achieved on Feb. 28, 1983, with a special episode of the CBS series "M*A*S*H," captured a 60.2 rating and a 77 share.

The rating point is important because it is a key component for establishing the charge for a commercial. The loss of a single rating point for a prime-time network program over a year may mean the loss of more than $100 million in revenues for the network and, eventually, loss of compensation for the local station as well. Rating points for local programs such as the evening news are less valuable, but still economically important.

The networks, local stations, advertising agencies and advertisers pay for all of this research to the tune of tens of millions of dollars a year. Major market stations, for example, typically have to fork over as much as $1.3 million a year for each rating service. Until 1994, when Arbitron stopped providing local television ratings because it was unprofitable, some stations took two services, which often provided unsettlingly different results. For example, in one 1988 rating period, "Eye on L.A.," a news program from Los Angeles-based KABC, got an 11.1 rating from Nielsen and an 8.5 from Arbitron. In any case, someone's show is always at the bottom of the viewer preference list. And as one California-based broadcast consultant put it, "That [rating service fee] is a lot of money for someone to come in and say your baby's ugly."

The ratings companies, of course, also measure the *type* of audience for both network and syndicated programs. For example, audience measuring companies found in the 1990s that "Star Trek: The Next Generation," a popular program syndicated in more than 200 television markets, was especially strong with two important types of audiences: men of all ages, and women between 18 and 34 years old. This information is important for advertisers because 18- to 34-year-old viewers buy large quantities of the products most commonly advertised on TV. Viewers 18 to 54 years old are also desirable, which means "Star Trek" reached the upscale audiences advertisers seek.

This numerical wizardry is not accomplished without criticism, of course. Network executives don't particularly like the people-meter technology because the little boxes have shown their prime-time audiences to be somewhat smaller than previously estimated. When an audience is smaller than expected, the networks often rebate prime-time spots to advertisers to keep them happy. By mid-1988, which was the end of the people meters' first television season, those freebies had amounted to more than $40 million, according to one CBS executive.

The people meters show smaller network audiences because the devices are in too many homes with VCRs and cable TV, network executives say. Viewers with cable TV, of course, have access to many programs other than those provided by the networks. Network executives say that inaccurate audience measurement also occurs because people who agree to use the high-technology meters aren't typical viewers. This last charge, however, is a variation on a decades-old criticism of the rating system: Do viewers who represent thousands of other viewers watch the same programs they would watch if they were not being monitored?

In addition to measuring the size and nature of TV-viewing audiences, rating companies also reveal something about why and how people watch television. People watch TV because they enjoy it, and they easily tolerate the commercials in exchange for free entertainment, surveys suggest. According to Nielsen, the typical television household has the set on for about seven hours a day, although that figure varies with household characteristics: For example, children increase the overall viewing time, as do low family income and having pay cable. Age and sex also play a factor in household viewing: Female adults watch more TV than male adults, and among children, teens watch less than kids between 2 and 11 years of age. However, household viewing time notwithstanding, if you're "average," you watch 30 hours of TV a week. To put it another way, between age 2 and 65, you'll spend about 10 years of your life watching TV.

Audience research also shows viewership to be lowest in the morning and to peak between 8 p.m. and 10 p.m. Audiences vary throughout the week, with viewership smallest on Saturday and biggest on Sunday night. And, as you might expect, research shows that audiences are larger in the winter than in the summer. Finally, research identifies the most popular type of program as the situation comedy.

How the Networks Operate

In the face of the Fox television network, the Cable News Network and numerous ad hoc or temporary interconnections of stations for sports, news or special events, the word *network* is becoming increasingly difficult to define. So, in order to simplify matters, let's examine the operation of the traditional networks—ABC, CBS and NBC.

ABC, CBS and NBC operate somewhat like television stations, with a few additional twists. As you might expect, they have sales departments to peddle commercial time and traffic departments to schedule it. They have programming departments that acquire shows from outside producers, and news and sports departments to produce their regularly scheduled newscasts and special news and sports coverage. The networks' engineers maintain the complex equipment needed to acquire and broadcast all of this programming. But in addition, the networks typically have departments to censor commercials and entertainment programming—the industry term is "standards and practices"—and other departments to deal with affiliates and manage network-owned-and-operated stations.

Because entertainment and to a lesser extent news and sports programming are the keys to attracting large and affluent audiences that in turn will attract advertisers who will pay the bills, let's take a detailed look at how prime-time programs are acquired.

The Birth of a Network Movie. In the early 1990s, ABC, CBS and NBC each contracted for three dozen made-for-television movies per year at a cost of nearly $3 million each.

TV movie deals typically begin with an oral sales pitch by a veteran television or movie producer, who presents an idea permitting use of as many well-known television personalities as the movie's budget will permit. The idea may be original or may be based upon a newspaper or magazine article, a short story, a book, a play or even an earlier movie. The producer has assembled or "packaged" this idea by himself or herself or with the help of a talent agency that uses its client list to put together a writer, a director and a cast.

If the network likes the proposal, it contracts for a narrative description or "treatment" of the story. If the treatment is approved, the network authorizes creation of a script. If the network approves the final script (which typically has been taken through at least three drafts) and other elements of the project, it authorizes the production to start. The terms of the typical contract call for a "license" fee to pay for 80 to 90 percent of the production costs of the film in return for one or perhaps two network airings. The producer makes a profit when the movie is licensed for later showings on independent stations, on foreign television or in theaters abroad.

A network series is sold in much the same way. Each of the three networks typically looks at 150 scripts per season, of which perhaps 30 become half-hour, one-hour or two-hour pilots. As you have read, the network funds almost all of the cost of an initial or "pilot" show. Pilot production costs in the 1990s were astronomical: A half-hour series cost $600,000 to $700,000, and an hour-long show required $1 million to $1.5 million. If the pilot is unsuccessful, the producer absorbs any loss above the license fee. If the pilot's ratings are acceptable—and only six or seven at each network are—the network approves the 12 episodes needed for half a season's programming, or, in some cases, the full season's 22 episodes. A successful series might be aired on the network for many years, depending upon ratings, or it might be canceled after one season. The longer the program's run, the better the syndication possibilities are for the producing company: About 100 shows or five years on the network is considered optimum.

Programming Approaches. Much of the success of any program, whether it's a network entertainment show or a local newscast, depends upon the competition the program faces. As a result, networks and local stations engage in a variety of strategies to ensure the success of a program. Two common approaches are the use of *lead-in* programs and *counter-programming* techniques.

The lead-in programming approach assumes that people watch similar kinds of shows. As a result, a network might program situation comedies for an evening, or back-to-back drama programs, or a light drama followed by a light movie. If a network programmer has two strong programs and a weak one, she would insert the weak one in the middle of the two strong shows, hoping that viewers would be too lazy to switch channels in the middle of the evening's lineup.

The other most common approach is counter-programming. In this case, the programmer looks at shows on competing networks and offers alternatives. For example, if two networks were offering comedies during prime time, a competing network might program a change-of-pace blockbuster movie during the same time period.

The results of the network and local programmers' work are constantly measured, but special attention is given to three major annual ratings periods called **sweeps.** They occur in November, February and May because they are presumed to be typical viewing periods. During sweeps, viewers can expect video treats. During the February 1992 national sweeps, for example, the networks used different strategies: CBS aired the winter Olympics, while ABC and NBC used series programming and movies to attract viewers. Fox Broadcasting offered the "Fox Summer Games," specials tied to a beach theme. CBS won the sweeps.

By the way, ratings companies are on the alert for attempts to "hype" ratings during sweeps periods, particularly at the local station level. For example, when the news anchor of Los Angeles' KNBC jokingly asked ratings families to "leave that Nielsen meter on" during a news report that occurred during the 1988 sweeps, the research director of rival KCBS pointed out that the statement violated Nielsen guidelines.

As you can see, even local news is concerned with strategies guaranteed to ensure its success with audiences. For details, read on.

The Television Newsgathering Process

The essential elements of television news—qualities such as conflict, human interest, importance, prominence, proximity, timeliness and unusualness—are shared by print and broadcast journalists. Of course, there are significant differences between the two media. For example, pictures are crucial in television and often supplementary in a newspaper or a magazine. In addition, TV stories are short, traditionally little more than one minute in length, whereas print stories can and do sometimes go on and on and on. For those reasons, complex stories without powerful pictures— intricate economic pieces, for instance—are sometimes given short shrift on TV. Conversely, simple stories with exceptional pictures—petty thieves who have the bad luck to be colorfully shot to death by the police—are sometimes overplayed to the extent that the TV adage "If it bleeds, it leads" is more truth than legend in some newsrooms.

Television News: The Entertainment Factor

These characteristics trouble media critics, who charge that TV journalism is more entertainment than news, more style than substance. In truth, the charge that TV news is superficial entertainment is sometimes difficult to deny, particularly at middle- and small-market stations. Remove the commercials from a 30-minute newscast at one of these stations and perhaps 23

Ethics: A Big Concern for Broadcasters

Electronic Media, a weekly trade paper for radio and television broadcasters, surveyed 144 of its readers in the late 1980s regarding ethical standards in the industry. Many weaknesses were found. There was business pressure on news coverage, one-sided reporting and too much freedom for inexperienced reporters, the survey respondents said. "Plain, old-fashioned deception and lying" also ranked high as an ethical concern among the broadcasters. The greatest concern, however, concerned making a profit without giving so much attention to greed, sex and violence.

Sixty-eight percent of the broadcasters felt that ethical standards were lower in the late 1980s than a decade earlier. More interesting is the fact that 87 percent of the broadcasters said that most of their professional colleagues would be willing to "bend the rules" to achieve their ends.

To whom do these broadcasters turn when facing a tough ethical problem? Most—45 percent—said they turned to a colleague. Nineteen percent said they turned to their spouse, 10 percent said a friend outside broadcasting and another 10 percent said they sought help from God.

minutes remain. Remove the bloated five-minute weather forecast and perhaps 30 news and sports stories remain. These stories, which are presented in perhaps 17 minutes in between cute anchor banter, are often little more than headlines and sound bites.

Media critics also accuse TV journalists (and to a lesser extent, their print brethren) of emphasizing bad news, sensationalizing certain aspects of stories, invading the privacy of newsmakers and reporting with bias, a series of violations that have come to be known in the news business as the "unholy four." TV and print journalists respond by pointing out that controversial and unusual news is often troubling news, that one viewer's sensationalism is another's good journalism, that many newsmakers *seek* media attention and that journalists do their best to balance stories but in the process often offend both opponents and proponents of an issue.

Despite this criticism, news consumers seem to like television news. In fact, consumers seem to prefer TV news over newspaper coverage. Beginning in 1963, Americans began citing TV as the source of most of their news, according to a series of surveys done for the television industry by the Roper public opinion organization. Why? Clearly, TV news has more impact than its print counterpart. In addition, it's easier to consume and absolutely free unless it's on cable. The Roper survey also suggested that a majority of Americans, if faced with conflicting reports of the same story in different media, would believe the television report over the newspaper report.

These attitudes are reflected by the huge audiences television news attracts—60 million each night for the ABC, CBS and NBC newscasts and millions more for the Public Broadcasting System's "MacNeil-Lehrer Newshour" and for local newscasts. These audiences, of course, explain why the networks and local stations spend billions of dollars a year on newsgathering. For a closer look at news at a local level, read on.

Reporters at Work

About 80 percent of the nation's 1,100 or so full-power commercial television stations employ reporters. In the 1990s, those stations' news staffs ranged between a low of one part-time reporter and a high of about 75 full- and part-time employees, depending upon market size and network affiliation. As you might expect, a small-market independent station was least likely to have a news department whereas a major market network affiliate was most likely to have a full staff. Taken as a whole, TV stations averaged about 18 full- and part-time news department employees, less than half that of a comparable daily newspaper.

Reporters and editors at TV stations earned salaries somewhat similar to those earned by reporters and editors at newspapers in the same city. Anchors at stations in the top 50 markets made a great deal of money, often edging into six figures.

The Broadcast Reporter. By contrast, however, the typical television reporter usually works more traditional hours than his or her newspaper

Even though network news audiences are dwindling, more than 60 million people tune in nightly.

counterpart. A television reporter at a medium- or large-market network affiliate typically labors from about 9 a.m. to perhaps 6 p.m.

For a detailed look at a TV reporter's day, let's suppose that you're a reporter at WDAF television, an NBC affiliate in Kansas City, Mo. You are assigned to cover a city council meeting. There are many ways to complete this kind of assignment, but here's a common approach.

You and your photographer—together you comprise an electronic news gathering or "ENG" crew—haul your equipment to city hall. When you arrive, you ask for a meeting agenda or schedule of events. The agenda provides clues about how to cover the story. You zero in on the most important and controversial part of the meeting, a proposal to make the city's main downtown street one-way.

Interested citizens speak for and against the street proposal, and you tell the photographer which segments of the arguments you want to tape. After the speech, you interview the councilwoman who proposed the change. Based on what you've heard, you summarize the story for yourself and then write an introduction. You memorize that introduction, and the photographer videotapes your opening or "standup."

Back at the station, you view the videotape, select the images you want in the final "package" that will be aired and then prepare your story and videotape editing instructions. Working from your instructions, a tape editor assembles the story. After the story is electronically stitched together, you record your scripted narration onto the videotape. Finally, you write a one-paragraph introduction to the story, which the person anchoring the newscast will read.

If you work for a large-market station such as WDAF, you will cover perhaps two more stories during the day. The final story of the day— perhaps assigned at 3 p.m. for a 6 p.m. broadcast—is obviously produced with more nail-biting than stories covered earlier in the day. If the final story of the day occurs quite close to air time and is newsworthy, you may be asked to do a "live" broadcast, perhaps using WDAF's satellite news-gathering (SNG) technology. SNG equipment allows a reporter's story to be sent from a remote location to a satellite, then back to the station.

From this you can see that television reporters' tools are different from those used by newspaper reporters, but the essential principles of reporting are the same: speed, accuracy, objectivity, fairness and completeness.

Other organizational components are the same, too, such as newsroom organization and the role of editors. Newsrooms at stations such as WDAF are usually organized somewhat like those of daily newspapers: In both media, editors control the reporters' destinies.

The principal television newsroom editorial players are the news director, the executive producer and her assistants, the assignment editor and his assistants, and the videotape editors.

A news director usually heads a TV station's news department and has responsibilities like those of a newspaper managing editor, including hiring and firing and the "look" and "sound" of all newscasts. At many stations, the news director supervises an executive producer who oversees other producers who, in turn, are responsible for the content and organization of their specific news program. The producers are similar to a newspaper's associate and assistant managing editors.

Reporters and photographers are sent by the assignment editor to cover stories. He or she is much like a city or state editor at a newspaper, deciding what to cover and, in some cases, how to cover it. The assignment editor may also critique the work of the reporter.

Videotape editors, who assemble a story from bits and pieces of video and audio tape, have no precise parallel to newspaper editors but are closest perhaps to those copy editors who design the appearance of stories and pictures. When the story is assembled on videotape, editorial control passes back to the producer, who is responsible for the day-to-day content of a particular newscast. The producer can order changes—in writing, selection of videotape or length of story, for example—as can the executive producer and the news director.

In summary, television reporting, like newspaper reporting, is a collaborative effort often involving reporters and photographers and many editors: a news director who supervises the station's reporting, an assignment editor who decides what stories will be covered, numerous producers who help shape stories, and videotape editors who assemble the final product.

The Workplace: TV Newsroom of the 1990s

There is strong evidence to suggest that tomorrow's television reporters may have to be significantly more versatile than today's TV reporters: Tube reporters might have to be techno-journalists who will report, shoot, edit and engineer their stories.

Modern ENG crews can include many specialists. For example, national

U.S. television stations typically use two-person news crews.

network news crews often use as many as four people: a camera operator, a sound person, a producer and a reporter. Television stations in the top 10 markets—Los Angeles, for example—often field crews with three people. Stations in smaller cities—such as Kansas City, Mo.—use two persons, a camera operator and a reporter. But the smallest markets already require techno-reporters who shoot, report and edit stories, an approach known in broadcast journalism as the "one-man band." Now, because of a downsizing of equipment and economic restraints, network and local news executives say the small television station's "one-man band" will become the standard of the 1990s. Tomorrow's TV reporter may be required to cover the story, operate the camera and recorder, edit the finished tape in a portable editing room in the back of a van, then transmit it all by satellite to the local station or the national network.

Former NBC News president Larry Grossman put it this way: "It's no longer the era of the 1,000-pound pencil. It has become the two-ounce pencil. And that's going to change things." In fact, most of that Buck Rogers technology is already in place. Heavy, bulky ENG cameras linked by cables to separate, bulky ¾-inch videotape recorders have given way to light, small, one-piece camcorders using ½-inch or 8 mm tape. Editing systems are now suitcase-sized. Satellite transmitters, once the size of a two-story house, have shrunk to the size of a filing cabinet or a van. These "flyaway" or "driveaway" uplinks allow reporters to send stories from anywhere to anywhere.

Network news programs of the 1990s will increasingly use automatically controlled cameras. Here, NBC anchor Ann Rubenstein performs for robotic cameras.

Cable News Network executive vice president Ed Turner describes the brave new world this way: "The arrival of the flyaway uplink will demand a more knowledgeable reporter, and we don't care whether he is young or old—but you'd better be informed. It's going to mean a continuing drift away from the cosmetic, blow-dried reporter of the 1970s."

Cable Television

More than half of all American homes with TV are connected to a **cable television** system, which for a monthly fee provides dozens of wired channels without signal interference. Interference is caused by a variety of technical gremlins, the simplest of which is that television signals (like FM radio signals) are transmitted by line-of-sight, which means that viewers in a valley cannot receive pictures well, if at all.

How Cable TV Works

Cable, also called **CATV** or *community antenna television,* arrived in the 1940s, 1950s, 1960s or 1970s, depending upon location. In Astoria, Ore., CATV's tentacles began spreading in the late 1940s when an entrepreneur erected an antenna on the top of an eight-story building, capturing out-of-reach local television signals for subscribers. At the other end of the country, in Mahanoy City, Pa., cable began in 1948 when a television set salesman erected a mountain-top aerial and fed a signal to demonstration sets in his store window.

More elaborate cable systems were created in other communities, but one built in 1950 in Lansford, a coal-mining community in Pennsylvania's Panther Valley, was typical. Lansford, 75 air miles from the three Philadelphia television stations that provided the region's only signals, couldn't receive TV because the Blue Mountains blocked transmissions. The mountains also thwarted healthy profits that could be made by selling TV sets. As a result, four Lansford radio dealers (and an attorney, of course) raised $12,500 and erected a hilltop antenna tower—today it would be called the system's **head end**—to capture the signals. A **distribution system** amplified the signals and sent them down the hill to **house drops,** where subscribers paid $100 for the cable installation and $3 a month for three-station service.

Cable's growth since the days of the Panther Valley three-channel system has been phenomenal, paralleling that of television. In 1952, there were 14,000 cable subscribers hooked up to 10 cable systems in the United States. By 1960, 650,000 households subscribed to more than 600 systems. A decade later, nearly 2,500 systems served 4.5 million households. Today more than 11,000 cable systems serve more than 57 million households in more than 30,000 communities with an average of 29 channels, in return for a basic service charge of about $18 per month. Pay cable—services such as Home Box Office—is found in more than 32 million TV homes.

Technically, a typical cable system today works like the Panther Valley system did, with a few variations. The head end usually includes one or more satellite earth stations as well as traditional antennas. Other variations include the use of both above-ground or underground wires in the distribution system (at a cost of between $10,000 and $300,000 per mile), as well as two-way capability so that cable subscribers can use the system to send a message *back* to the head end. What kind of message? Perhaps a request to provide a pay cable event in exchange for a fee. (By the way, don't confuse CATV with a SMATV or Satellite Master Antenna Television system. A SMATV system, often found in an apartment complex or a hotel, uses an earth station to reap a satellite signal, then distributes that signal to individual apartments or rooms.)

Economically, however, the CATV business has changed a great deal since the early 1950s. Most systems now operate as a monopoly under authority given by a political subdivision such as a city or county. In addition, service is **tiered.** Basic cable includes local and distant commercial superstations such as Atlanta's WTBS and the Cable News Network, Chicago's WGN and New Jersey's WWOR and commercial cable networks, such as Music Television or MTV, the Cable-Satellite Public Affairs Network or C-SPAN, the Weather Channel, the Entertainment and Sports Programming Network or ESPN and the USA Network. A higher fee brings satellite-delivered pay cable services, such as Home Box Office and The

CNN's news programs now reach around the world, thanks to cable and satellite technology.

Disney Channel. Some of these stations and nonpay cable networks provide service free because they carry lucrative advertising, and others charge the cable operator a small fee per subscriber. The pay services, such as HBO, charge perhaps $10 a month and allow the cable operator to keep a portion of that fee. In addition to this legal but monopolistic tiered service and the commissions from pay services, one of every five cable operators also accepts advertising at $2 to $600 a spot on a **local origination channel,** which may offer diverse local programming ranging from city council meetings to sporting events. Such advertising, however, provides the typical cable system with less than 5 percent of its overall revenues.

There is potential for great profit and because of that, large multiple system operators (MSOs) dominate the industry, buying mom-and-pop cable systems for an average of $1,800 per subscriber. The biggest of the big MSOs is Colorado-based Tele-Communications Inc., with more than 600 cable systems serving nine million subscribers in 44 states. The MSOs tend to own program services as well: Tele-Communications owns part of seven cable channels, and second-ranked American Television & Communica-

Future Focus Big, Sharp and Wide: The TV of the Future?

By world standards, American television is technically inferior. The picture looks fine on a small TV screen, but when it's transmitted to a 26-inch set or, worse, to a 40-inch projection television, the image lacks clarity. The reasons are complex but traceable to America's antiquated color television system, developed in the early 1950s.

Help, however, is definitely on the way. The cavalry riding to Americans' rescue includes dozens of TV set manufacturers and the Federal Communications Commission. Their goal is to offer one of several *high-definition* or "advanced television systems" to Americans by the mid-1990s.

The systems under study, many of them modifications of America's current NTSC (National Television System Committee) standard, will produce a picture twice as good as a current image, be in wide screen to allow movies to be shown as they were filmed and feature stereo sound, of course. And the new system that is eventually selected probably will be able to provide normal-quality pictures to America's more than 140 million existing black and white and color sets. However, because the new picture will be so appealing, TV set makers are expected to manufacture affordable HDTV television sets to cash in on the advance.

In truth, a high-definition *recording* and *transmitting* system already exists that is *four* times better than NTSC—reportedly as detailed as a movie in a theater. That system, developed by NHK of Japan, probably won't be adopted for the United States because broadcasts using it couldn't be viewed on existing TV sets. However, the NHK recording system, which broadcasters around the world can easily use, has already been utilized to videotape programs. The Canadian Broadcasting Corporation, for example, used the system to tape a mini-series in 1987, and CBS used a variation of the system to produce "Innocent Victims," a $2.5 million, two-hour, 1988 "docudrama" about babies with Acquired Immune Deficiency Syndrome. Cable TV movie channel executives are also expected to air many HDTV-made movies in the 1990s.

As for the Japanese, they have married their NHK recording system to a noncompatible high-definition transmitting standard for Japan-wide use. Test HDTV transmissions began in 1989 and regular programming started in 1991.

---

tions, a subsidiary of Time Warner (660 cable companies serving 4.5 million subscribers in 32 states), owns HBO and Cinemax pay channels. Another MSO, Viacom, owns MTV, VH-1, Nickelodeon, Showtime and The Movie Channel.

What's wrong with MSOs owning program services? Perhaps this: In the early 1990s, more than 90 percent of Time Warner's systems carried HBO and 75 percent carried Cinemax. However, only 60 percent of Time Warner's cable systems carried the rival Showtime channel and perhaps 25 percent offered The Movie Channel. Caveat emptor.

"Zipping" and "Zapping": Videocassette Recorders

In addition to cable television, one other device has dramatically changed Americans' TV viewing habits within the last generation. That device is the videocassette recorder or VCR, a machine that most savvy 5 year olds have some working knowledge of.

There were no video recorders in the mid-1950s. By 1995, more than 88 percent of American homes with television sets will have videocassette machines. What happened in those 40 years is a story worth retelling—a tale of angry and then jubilant movie studio executives, horrified television advertisers, and generally wary network executives. For the entire story, read James Lardner's book, *Fast Forward* (1987). For a quick scan, read on.

The videotape recorder or VTR was born because U.S. television networks wanted to provide programming at a convenient time in all time zones without repeating live shows. For example, a live program aired at 8 p.m. Eastern time would be shown at 5 p.m. Pacific time, which was too early. An airing at 8 p.m. Pacific time would require the live show to be repeated, or perhaps filmed and shown using a crude system called kinescope. The VTR, loosely based on the magnetic audio recorder, a device appropriated from the Germans after World War II, could record a program and then play it back at the appropriate Pacific Coast time.

The first VTR, which cost $50,000 and was as big as a room, was introduced by the Ampex Corporation in 1956. That VTR quickly killed live television but soon ushered in the age of home videocassette recording.

By 1960, Ampex had asked a Japanese company, Sony, to design a smaller VTR. Sony agreed, but asked for the rights to sell nonbroadcast machines. Another Japanese company, Toshiba, introduced an engineering change that made even smaller VTRs possible, and by the mid-1960s, Sony and others were selling $1,000 reel-to-reel black-and-white VTRs to businesses and schools.

Market forces soon forced the design of a broadcast-quality color videocassette recorder or VCR, made available in late 1971. In 1975, Sony modified that to make a consumer VCR called the Beta, named for a Japanese calligraphic term. Two years later, a Japanese competitor, Matsushita, and its sister company, JVC, introduced a competitive $1,000 VCR. That system was called VHS or Video Home System, and it now dominates the U.S. VCR market.

Meanwhile, motion picture producers, fearful that they would lose control of copies of their films because people would tape them from broadcasts, sued Sony to prevent home copying. A 1984 U.S. Supreme Court decision settled the dispute with a ruling that recording for home purposes did not violate copyright.

Of course, consumers were taping general programming as well as movies

---

Buying a Videotape: Where the Money Goes

The $29.98 retail price of a typical movie on videotape winds up in a lot of different pockets, according to an analysis by Cambridge Associates, a Stamford, Conn., research firm.

To begin with, the tape, cassette shell and duplicating labor cost $4.50, the company estimates. The program owners take $6.28 for their profit and overhead, and another $4.50 goes to the producing company for royalties (which, in turn, is then subdivided). Marketing and distribution costs $3, and 60 cents is spent on cooperative advertising. The distributor charges $2.10 to get the tape to the retail store. The remaining $9—unless the tape is on sale—is the retailer's profit.

About 60 percent of all tapes are sold at video stores, with department and discount stores grabbing 9 percent of the pie. Mail-order firms and convenience and bookstores sell the rest.

Table 9.2 Channels Taped by Videotape Recorder Households		
Network affiliates	68 percent
Independents	14 percent
Pay services	9 percent
Cable original	5 percent
Public Broadcasting Service	4 percent

Source: Electronic Media.

and playing it all back at their convenience, a procedure called "time-shifting." Broadcasters and advertisers quickly learned that viewers watching time-shifted programs used the VCR's fast forward button to "zip" through commercials or, if they owned an ingenious device called a "commercial killer," they could automatically "zap" the spots while recording. Why, advertisers asked increasingly queasy broadcasters, should they pay high prices for airing commercials that never reached viewers? At the same time that consumers were zipping and zapping spots, they were renting movies in increasing numbers and avoiding broadcast programs, which thrilled studio executives but caused a decline in the overall ratings of some network programs and further worried broadcasters.

Which brings us to the present and a big question: Who uses VCRs and how are they used? AGB Television Research discovered that the average VCR is more likely to be found in homes with children and with pay cable than in homes without children and with basic or no cable. Surprise, surprise.

Even more interesting is the fact that the typical VCR is used more than seven hours a week—2.4 hours for recording and 4.7 hours for playback (see Table 9.2). Prime time is the most common taping time, with daytime in second place. VCR owners spend about 3.5 of the 4.7 playback hours watching rented or purchased tapes and the rest of the time watching home-recorded tapes. In other words, people tape the equivalent of a two-hour movie and another program each week, and play back part of that programming plus perhaps two rental movies a week. The VCR has revolutionized TV viewing habits by giving viewers the ability to be independent of network programming schedules. VCRs fill a need for busy people, who now can attend the school band concert on Monday night and still keep up with the happenings on "Murphy Brown."

Retrospective

Television sprang from telegraphic, telephonic, radio and even motion picture technology, but was nurtured in a more stable environment than radio because the corporations and governments developing television in the 1920s, 1930s and 1940s applied what they had learned about running radio stations and networks to the fledgling medium.

In the United States, television thrived after World War II, despite a temporary governmental freeze on station license allocations. By the early

1950s, the freeze had been lifted and commercial, noncommercial and even color television became part of the American culture. Television news became especially important during the 1960s, and for the first time rivaled newspapers in the public credibility and acceptance.

Recently, with the transformation of cable television from a broadcast support system to a broadcast competitor, and with the appearance of the VCR, viewers have had expanded choices and the network share of the audience has subsequently declined. At the same time, local news has taken on increased importance at the expense of network news. Experts expect the "advanced television systems" of the future to increase overall viewing audiences and contribute even more to the changing share of audience.

Questions

1. The R. Budd Dwyer incident illustrates several problems regarding television news. Explain two of those problems.

2. Television didn't become a popular medium in the United States until after 1945. Why not?

3. What caused the "freeze" that occurred in the early 1950s? How had television changed by the time the "thaw" occurred?

4. Cite some basic differences between television in the 1960s and today.

5. Why are modern television stations traditionally owned by groups or chains? What are the advantages and disadvantages of such ownership?

6. What is syndication? Describe the difference between barter-purchase and pure barter syndication.

7. Describe the operating divisions of a network-affiliated television station.

8. What is the difference between a rating and a share? Under what circumstances might a rating be relatively low but a share fairly high?

9. How do people meters measure audience? Do you think they are accurate?

10. Assume that you program an independent station in your community and that your rivals are airing two hours of political coverage. How might you counter-program your station for that evening? What kind of lead-in might you use?

11. Cite several differences between covering a story for television and for a newspaper.

12. What is the difference between cable and pay-cable? What does tiered service mean?

13. Do you think there will be national television networks in the future? If so, what form might they take? Is cable television primarily responsible for the networks' decline in audience share?

14. Do you think that the growth of local television news into what has been the network's domain is a bad trend? Will local or regional news broadcasts devour the newspaper audiences as well?

15. Will television programming of the year 2,000 be significantly different from what you see today, or will TV be much like that of the 1960s—technologically fancier but essentially the same?

Suggested Readings

Baldwin, Thomas, and McVoy, D. S. *Cable Communication*. Englewood Cliffs, N.J.: Prentice-Hall, 1983.

Barnouw, Erik. *Tube of Plenty*. New York: Oxford University Press, 1990.

Bergreen, Laurence. *Look Now, Pay Later: The Rise of Network Television*. Garden City, N.Y.: Doubleday, 1980.

Bliss, Edward. *Now the News: The Story of Broadcast Journalism*. New York: Columbia University Press, 1991.

Ellerby, Linda. *And So It Goes*. New York: G. P. Putnam's, 1986.

Emery, Edwin, and Emery, Michael. *The Press and America*. Englewood Cliffs, N.J.: Prentice-Hall, 1992.

Fang, Irving R. *Television News, Radio News*. Minneapolis, Minn.: Rada Press, 1985.

Head, Sydney, and Sterling, Christopher. *Broadcasting in America*. New York: Houghton Mifflin, 1990.

Lardner, James. *Fast Forward: Hollywood, the Japanese, and the Onslaught of the VCR*. New York: Norton, 1987.

MacDonald, J. Fred. *Blacks and White TV: African Americans in Television Since 1948*. Chicago: Nelson-Hall, 1992.

MacDonald, J. Fred. *One Nation Under Television: The Rise and Decline of Network T.V.* Chicago: Nelson-Hall, 1993.

Sterling, Christopher, and Kittross, John. *Stay Tuned: A Concise History of American Broadcasting*. Belmont, Calif.: Wadsworth, 1990.

Westin, Av. *Newswatch: How TV Decides the News*. New York: Simon & Schuster, 1982.

Zettl, Herbert. *Television Production Handbook*. Belmont, Calif.: Wadsworth, 1992.

Movies

I t was Dec. 11, 1938, a cold Sunday evening. Forty acres of decaying sets from movies such as "King Kong" dotted a motion picture backlot in Culver City, Calif., just west of downtown Los Angeles. The sets had been superficially redressed to look like an 1860s Atlanta, Ga., street.

On a signal from a bespectacled man named David O. Selznick, the sets were ignited. Seven Technicolor cameras recorded the fire and later, 250 studio employees using 10 fire trucks and 15,000 gallons of water doused the inferno, which was the first scene photographed for "Gone With the Wind."

American Film Institute members recently ranked Selznick's "Gone With the Wind," released in 1939, as the "greatest American film of all time." And *Variety,* the authoritative show business periodical, says the movie is the biggest moneymaker of all time, too, if its revenues are adjusted for inflation.

While GWTW is a sterling example of successful mass communication, it's an even better example of how movies are packaged, financed, produced and distributed—in the 1930s and in the 1990s.

GWTW first saw the light of day as a $3, three-pound, 1,000-page novel written by Georgia homemaker Peggy Marsh (better known by her maiden name, Margaret Mitchell). Mitchell's book was an instant hit when it was published in 1936, selling 176,000 copies in three weeks and 1.7 million copies within one year (and more than 25 million copies by the 1990s).

Selznick, who liked to make movies based on popular books because they offered some guarantee of box office success, bought the film rights to GWTW for $50,000. In many ways, Selznick was the perfect person to bring GWTW to the screen. He owned his own film company, Selznick International, following successful stints in the early and mid-1930s as head of production at RKO Radio Pictures (where he was responsible for hits such as "King Kong") and later at Metro-Goldwyn-Mayer studios. In addition, he was intelligent, shrewd (he added the "O" to his name to make it memorable), a hard worker, lucky (he married the daughter of Louis B. Mayer, head of MGM) and, most importantly, ready—ready to tackle what would turn out to be a $4 million, four-hour film that would earn 10 Academy Awards.

By 1938, Selznick had picked a director, George Cukor, who specialized in love stories, and hoped to sign MGM superstar Clark Gable for the Rhett Butler lead role. However, Gable didn't want the job because he didn't think he could handle the acting demands, especially under Cukor's sensitive rather than action-oriented direction. But Gable soon gave in: He was in love with actress Carole Lombard and needed money to divorce his second wife. In addition, Mayer, for whom Gable worked, wanted his star to do GWTW, and the strong-willed Mayer usually got what he wanted.

The final Gable "loan-out" deal worked to everyone's advantage: MGM agreed to provide a somewhat willing Clark Gable and half of GWTW's budget in exchange for half of the GWTW profits and the right to distribute the film (which is why GWTW videocassettes carry an MGM label on them more than 50 years later). The only problem with the MGM offer was that Selznick had a contract with MGM-rival United Artists to distribute all of his films, which meant that GWTW had to be delayed until the UA contract expired. Selznick wanted Gable, so he agreed—and waited.

After Selznick saw GWTW slip off the best-seller list in March 1938—months before production could begin—he decided to fuel public interest in the movie by launching a fraudulent nationwide search for an amateur actress to play the lead Scarlett O'Hara role. His minions interviewed 1,400 tank-town Scarletts. Scarlett's role, of course, was also sought after by every major actress in Hollywood, including Katharine Hepburn, Bette Davis and even comedienne Lucille ("I Love Lucy") Ball. British actress Vivien Leigh was eventually selected, after 90 actresses were given screen tests.

Clark Gable and Vivien Leigh still stir audiences with their performances in ''Gone With the Wind.''

Selznick also needed a screenplay. By mid-1938, after efforts from more than a dozen writers, including famed novelist F. Scott Fitzgerald, he had one. Unfortunately, the finished script would have yielded an unmarketable six-hour movie, so additional rewriting—much of it by Selznick—was required even after the cameras started to roll.

In December 1938, GWTW filming started with the dramatic backlot burning of Atlanta. Most movies are photographed out of chronological order or "continuity" to allow maximum use of people and materials in a minimum time, and GWTW was no exception. Selznick first shot the fire scene, which appears in the middle of the movie, because he wanted to clear old outdoor sets cheaply to make way for new ones.

On Jan. 26, 1939, director Cukor began filming in earnest. On Feb. 13, Cukor was fired for rewriting dialogue without permission, and action director Victor Fleming was hired. Fleming, fresh from directing MGM's "The Wizard of Oz," was Gable's choice. Shooting began again on March 1 and continued until April, when Fleming, who thought the screenplay was terrible, was replaced by yet another director. The reason for the blood-letting was simple: Selznick insisted on personal supervision of all elements of production, a task two of the three directors thought was their prerogative.

Altogether, shooting—also called "principal photography"—took five months and ate up 240 hours worth of expensive color film. GWTW's numbers are astronomical: 684 scenes, each made up of many shots from different angles; 2,500 actors and actresses; a single scene that required 1,500 nonspeaking players or "extras" and 1,000 dummies; 125 days of filming for Leigh (who was paid $30,000) and 71 days for Gable; 1,475 animals including horses, mules, oxen, cows, pigs and dogs.

On June 27, 1939, filming of GWTW was finished and six months of editing began. The problem: trimming 160,000 feet of film to 20,000 feet. To complicate matters, retakes were ordered in August after Selznick was dissatisfied with several scenes. After final editing and musical scoring, GWTW was finished, but Hollywood's censorship office objected to Gable's last line: "Frankly, my dear, I don't give a damn." Selznick prevailed and GWTW premiered—with the "damn" intact—in Atlanta on Dec. 15, 1939, $1.2 million over budget and a year and four days after the first scene was photographed.

Now, more than 50 years later, GWTW is still being seen, on network television—CBS got rights for a 20-year run beginning in 1976—and on videotape. At last count, the picture had earned MGM and its successors more than $79 million from U.S. movie theaters, plus monies from theaters abroad, the $35 million for television rights and millions of dollars from the sale of more than 500,000 videotapes.

There are two lessons to be learned from GWTW. First, theatrical movie-making is a business; profit rather than art is the name of the game. For example, Selznick selected Mitchell's Pulitzer Prize-winning novel

Movie fans remember 1939 as the release date for both "Gone With the Wind" and another perennially popular American movie: "The Wizard of Oz."

The films were similar in some respects. Both were in Technicolor, then a seldom-used process; both were demanding (GWTW because of its scope and "Oz" because of special effects such as a Kansas tornado, disappearing witches, flying monkeys and Jello-covered horses-of-a-different-color); both had numerous writers (10 for "Oz" and 16 for GWTW); both starred Metro-Goldwyn-Mayer legends (16-year-old Judy Garland in "Oz"); both were released by MGM; and both were mostly but not entirely directed by Victor Fleming, who quit "Oz" to direct GWTW, only to be replaced by a third director. Fleming was also unsure of both films' success and even rejected a chance to share in the profits of GWTW, which he said was a "white elephant."

When they were released, both movies were nominated for the Best Picture Academy Award, although "Oz"—unlike GWTW—received less-than-wonderful reviews ("No trace of imagination, good taste or ingenuity," *The New Yorker* charged) and didn't make any money for nearly two decades, until it was sold to television.

Though "Oz" and GWTW were exceptional movies, they shared theaters with other classic films released that same year: "Mr. Smith Goes to

"The Wizard of Oz" is one of the many famous films released in 1939.

Washington," Frank Capra's story about corruption in the U.S. Senate, starring Jimmy Stewart; John Ford's "Stagecoach," a landmark western starring John Wayne; "Gunga Din," an adventure set in India, starring Cary Grant and Douglas Fairbanks; and the Academy Award-winning production of a dedicated English schoolteacher, "Goodbye, Mr. Chips." In all, if the movies of 1939 were wines, they would be a prize vintage.

because he liked it *and* because any film made from it would have a built-in audience. This dynamic combination of a best-selling book and a superstar such as Gable made the film an attractive package, which helped Selznick get financing. In addition, Selznick made many other decisions with an eye on the bottom line, including conducting the bogus national search for an amateur Scarlett, shooting GWTW in the expensive Technicolor process and reducing it from its initial six-hour length to three hours and 45 minutes.

Second, making movies is a collaborative effort, encompassing the efforts of scores of technicians, craftsmen and artists. When Selznick ordered the burning of "Atlanta," he needed the efforts of more than 100 experts to write the scene, modify the old sets that were to be burned, photograph the fire and record sound, put the blaze out, process the film, project it for evaluation, then edit and musically score it.

1877	E. Muybridge uses 24-camera sequence to prove running horses have all four feet off ground simultaneously.	1963	First "multiplex"—a movie theater with more than one screen—opens in shopping mall in Kansas City, Mo.
1896	Thomas Edison unveils first projecting Kinetoscope.	1967	Soviet film "War and Peace" becomes most expensive movie ever made (estimated cost: $100 million).
1903	Edwin S. Porter film, "The Great Train Robbery," is released.	1968	Rating system is introduced for American movies.
1915	D. W. Griffith produces film masterpiece, "The Birth of a Nation." It is three hours long and will later be considered savagely bigoted.	1972	"Deep Throat" draws national attention as mass release porno film.
1927	Warner Brothers releases first talking movie, "The Jazz Singer," starring Al Jolson.	1975	"Jaws" becomes money-making champ, earning $129 million.
		1977	"Star Wars" surpasses "Jaws," making $193 million.
1939	"Gone With the Wind" premiers in Atlanta, will eventually be named "greatest American film of all time."	1982	"E.T." breaks "Star Wars" record, earns $228 million.
1953	"The Robe" is released in new "wide screen" Cinemascope in an effort to compete with television.	1991	"Terminator 2," at an estimated cost of $94 million, becomes second most expensive movie ever made.

Yesterday's Movies: A Brief History

Selznick's Hollywood, a place awash with powerful studios headed by moguls such as Mayer and contract stars such as Gable, is itself now "gone with the wind." True, the movie-making process is about the same and a deal is still a deal, but the Hollywood of the 1990s is more corporate and restrained.

To understand today's Hollywood, let's look at movie-making's earliest days. In movie terms, let's "flash back" to the beginning of the movies, using, of course, a motion picture screenplay format. For the narrator, imagine the voice of your favorite movie star—perhaps Tom Cruise or Madonna.

The Earliest Days: The Flickers

FADE IN

INTERIOR—MEETING ROOM OF THE ROYAL SOCIETY, LONDON—HIGH ANGLE SHOT

It is 1824. We ZOOM IN on Peter Mark Roget as he prepares to read his paper to members of a British scientific society.

NARRATOR

Motion pictures are based on an optical principle explained by Peter Mark Roget in London in 1824. Roget's "persistence of vision" theory suggested that people see images for a fraction of a second after they have been withdrawn. As a result, a series of sequential, rapidly presented still pictures could be used to create the illusion of motion.

DISSOLVE TO

CLOSE UP—CHILD LOOKING AT ZOETROPE

NARRATOR

Roget's theory was tested and refined as inventors and businessmen around the world made devices that flipped or rotated drawings. One machine, a popular toy called the Zoetrope, used a rotating drum with drawings of animals and people inside.

DISSOLVE TO

INTERIOR—EDISON LABORATORY, NEW JERSEY—WIDE SHOT

It is October 1889. We SEE William K. L. Dickson as he adjusts an early Kinetoscope and demonstrates it for his employer, Thomas Edison.

NARRATOR

After the first practical photographic process was unveiled by Louis Daguerre in France in 1839, photographs replaced drawings in these machines. Photography improved over the years as Daguerre's metal film was replaced by paper and glass and finally celluloid. In 1889, after George Eastman made long strips of flexible film available for experimentation, Thomas Edison and his assistants began work on a camera and the first Kinetoscope, a large, wooden, boxlike peep-show viewer that would present a minute of 35mm motion picture film to a single customer.

DISSOLVE TO

INTERIOR—KOSTER & BIAL'S MUSIC HALL, 34TH STREET AND BROADWAY, NEW YORK—HIGH ANGLE SHOT

It is April 23, 1896. We ZOOM IN on Thomas Edison as he prepares to unveil his new projecting Kinetoscope, which has been in development since the late 1880s.

NARRATOR

Edison's design was widely copied in the early 1890s because it was protected only under U.S. patent law, and peep-show machines—some of which, to be fair, were invented independently of Edison—were soon found in most major U.S. and European cities. Four years later, Edison—increasingly aware of the commercial possibilities of what would soon be called movies—built in West Orange, N.J., the "Black Maria," the first motion picture studio. Later, he modified the Kinetoscope so that it could project pictures on a screen and first demonstrated it at a New York City music hall.

A peek into the Kinetoscope yields a minute-long movie.

Thomas Edison's projecting Kinetoscope makes motion picture theaters possible.

FILM CLIP OF THE "MAY IRWIN—JOHN C. RICE KISS"

NARRATOR

Edison's presentation, which was not the first
projection of a movie—German and French showmen
managed that a year earlier—consisted of anything
that moved. A sneeze, a kiss, a train rounding a
bend—all were considered exciting.

FADE OUT

Movies Learn to Tell a Story

FADE IN

INTERIOR—A FILM STUDIO IN THE PARIS SUBURBS—WIDE SHOT

It is 1899. We SEE George Méliès in his studio, as he prepares to
shoot "Cinderella."

NARRATOR

The next step in the development of movies was the
narrative film, the movie that silently told a story.
Like movies and the equipment to make them,
narrative storytelling developed in Europe and the
United States at about the same time. In France,
magician Georges Méliès filmed "L'Affaire Dreyfus" in
1899 and followed it with "Cinderella," "Red Riding
Hood," and "A Trip to the Moon" in successive years.
Méliès used startling special effects to tell his stories,
including the dissolve to signify a transition from one
scene to another, although the films were stagelike by
modern standards in that the camera did not use
medium shots or closeups.

DISSOLVE TO

EXTERIOR—A RAILROAD STATION IN NORTHERN NEW
JERSEY—WIDE SHOT

The year is 1903. We SEE Edwin S. Porter directing a scene from
"The Great Train Robbery."

NARRATOR

In the United States, Edwin S. Porter completed the
landmark film, "The Great Train Robbery," in 1903
and with it introduced many modern movie
techniques, including closeups, panning the camera
from left to right, tilting it down to follow action,
using rear-screen projection in a studio to simulate
outdoor action, and telling two stories simultaneously
by cutting back and forth from one scene to another.
Because Porter's film was a success, he also set the
standard for movie length at one reel, or about 10
minutes.

DISSOLVE TO

FILM CLIP FROM "THE BIRTH OF A NATION"

NARRATOR

A decade later, films were still one reel, thanks to a
cartel of nine businesses called the Motion Picture
Patents Company, which licensed all cameras and
projectors and included the largest producers and
distributors in the country. Independent filmmakers,
who were to found the studios that dominate
Hollywood today, fled to southern California

D. W. Griffith directs an actor as his camerman films "Death's Marathon" in 1913.
Griffith will go on to make "The Birth of a Nation" in 1915.

beginning in 1910 to escape the restrictions of the
Patents Company. By 1915, what many consider to be
the greatest American silent film, "The Birth of a
Nation," was filmed by D. W. Griffith. Three hours
long and with music provided by an orchestra, it told
the story of the American Civil War and the
Reconstruction that followed.

DISSOLVE TO

FILM CLIP FROM CHAPLIN'S "THE TRAMP"

NARRATOR

By 1917, the Patents Company was outlawed by the
U.S. Supreme Court, Hollywood was established as the
American film capital, one-reelers were outmoded and
the star system was born, with Charlie Chaplin—
million dollar contract in hand—as its king. Prior to
this time, film companies preferred anonymous

Charlie Chaplin, in character, directs a movie.

players. As performers became better known, they demanded better pay, a system still in effect. By the 1920s, American filmmakers, spared the ravages of World War I, became known for comedies such as Chaplin's and action films, and Hollywood became the center of world movie-making. During the 1920s, American movie companies also established another movie tradition: They acquired theaters to guarantee proper display of their products, a process the U.S. government stopped two decades later.

FADE OUT

Talkies: "The Jazz Singer"

FADE IN

EXTERIOR—NEW YORK CITY THEATER, 1925—WIDE SHOT

We SEE a line in front of the theater, as 1920s cars pass.

NARRATOR

In the late 1920s, the silent film died. Movies, of
course, were never truly silent. Theaters had staff
musicians on hand, ranging from piano players in
third-run theaters to full orchestras in first-run
houses. The music set the mood and drowned out the
noise of the patrons. However, sometimes the music
was inappropriate. For example, silent screen star
Mary Pickford recalled that she took friends to a New
York City theater to see her performance in the
somber "Madame Butterfly" only to hear a piano
player bang out "Alexander's Ragtime Band" as
accompaniment. The Warner brothers, who ran a
nearly bankrupt studio of the same name, were the
first to cash in on sound films, with "Don Juan" in
1926 and "The Jazz Singer" in 1927. Both used a
hybrid technology called Vitaphone: 16-inch
synchronized records that easily broke and were good
for only 20 plays.

DISSOLVE TO

EXTERIOR—NEW YORK CITY THEATER, 1930—WIDE SHOT

We SEE a line in front of the theater, as 1930s cars pass.

NARRATOR

By 1930, modern sound-on-film replaced Vitaphone,
and the sound era began in earnest. Initially, sound
movies looked like the static, stagelike productions of
the early 1900s because the audio-recording
technology required a sound-proofed stationary
camera. By the early 1930s, the camera was freed
again, and movies, though they were usually in black
and white, assumed modern proportions.

DISSOLVE TO

EXTERIOR—NEW YORK CITY THEATER, 1940—WIDE SHOT

We SEE a line in front of the theater, as 1940s cars pass.

NARRATOR

The 1940s saw increasingly sophisticated productions,
including Orson Welles' famed "Citizen Kane," judged
by many to be the best American film of all time.

Dealing with Television

FADE IN

INTERIOR—LIVING ROOM OF AMERICAN HOME OF THE
1950S—WIDE SHOT

We SEE a "typical" American family engrossed in a television
program.

NARRATOR

The motion picture industry faced numerous problems
after World War II. The first problems began in the late
1940s and early 1950s when the U.S. Supreme Court,
acting on complaints from independent theaters,
ordered production companies to "divorce" themselves
from some nonproduction activities because they were
restraining trade. The studios elected to get rid of
their theaters. Later, television cut into their
audiences, and the studios responded by reducing the
number of movies made and terminating contracts
stars, such as Clark Gable. The stars then incorporated
themselves, formed production companies, and the
studio system, as David O. Selznick, Louis Mayer and
others knew it, was dead.

FADE OUT

Orson Welles uses
innovative camera angles
and other unusual
techniques in directing
"Citizen Kane," a film
judged by many critics to
be the best American
motion picture of all time.

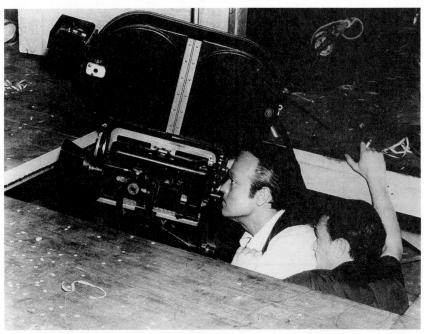

Welles also stars in "Citizen Kane," which is a fictional account of the life of media baron William Randolph Hearst.

Movies Today

Reduced to its simplest, the worldwide motion picture industry has three components: **producers,** who make movies; **distributors,** who market them to theaters and other outlets; and **exhibitors,** typically theater owners, who present films to the public. For a detailed view of this process, let's look at American producing companies, which make fewer than half of the world's feature films but earn more than half of all movie revenues.

Structure of the U.S. Motion Picture Industry

Some movies are produced by old, well-known firms that own large studios. Examples of the "major" companies include Walt Disney Pictures (and its sister companies, Touchstone and Hollywood Pictures), Metro-Goldwyn-Mayer, Paramount Pictures, Sony Pictures (and its subsidiaries, Columbia

Motion pictures have been an international medium since the first crude movies were projected in Germany and France 100 years ago. As you have read, the first international hits were French-made fantasy films. Later, American action and comedy movies, Italian spectacles, and British, Swedish and Danish dramas played on theater screens all over the world.

World War I, however, decimated the production abilities of many countries in Europe and provided the American film industry with a significant head start. Even so, in the 1920s technically excellent but somber German dramas and Soviet films using innovative editing techniques were widely distributed, along with French, British and Scandinavian products.

In the 1930s, economic catastrophe and the introduction of sound again slowed motion picture development in many places, including the United States. But as European film industries were recovering, World War II began. By 1945, the American film industry—virtually untouched by two World Wars—was clearly the dominant box office force in the world.

That is not to say that the U.S. film industry is without world competition. Producers in many countries—Indian filmmakers, for example—make more movies than their Hollywood counterparts. And the top three international buying and selling sessions—the Cannes Film Festival in France, the "Mifed" in Milan, Italy, and the American Film Marketing Association fair in Los Angeles—attract film producers, distributors and exhibitors literally from all over the world.

In 1992, for example, more than 5,000 buyers and sellers attended Mifed, trading good, bad and indifferent films from countries as diverse as Argentina, Iceland and Russia. That Mifed turned out as others in the past had: American films captured the lion's share of the world's box office dollars, while most foreign films did not fare well in the United States.

and TriStar Pictures), 20th Century Fox, Universal Pictures and Warner Bros. These companies account for about 40 percent of each year's films but about 90 percent of movie revenues each year.

Other movies are produced by less well-known "minor" companies that lease studio space as needed. The 21st Century Film Corporation is an example of a prolific organization with virtually no production facilities. In addition, many movies are produced by less permanent "independent" companies created for the purpose of producing a few pictures, which are then provided to major or minor distribution companies for release.

At its simplest, the company that makes the movie distributes it. Consequently, most of the major production companies have distribution arms, though the names may differ. For example, Walt Disney, Touchstone and Hollywood usually release through Buena Vista; Metro-Goldwyn-Mayer through MGM/UA; Paramount through Paramount; Columbia and TriStar through Sony; and Fox, Universal and Warner through distribution companies bearing their names. Minor companies may release under their own name or through a major distributor.

Production and distribution are linked by a popular common denominator: money. The majors and minors often finance their new movies with profits from previous films, stock sales, loans and the most common arrangement—limited partnerships. However, if distribution fuels new production, the small independent producer who makes only a film or two a year could have a difficult time raising money or, for that matter, arranging for distribution of a single movie. There are many ways the independent can solve these money and distribution problems: The three most common approaches are *distributor financing, cofinancing* and a *negative pickup* arrangement.

In a distributor financing arrangement, an independent producer puts together a package that often includes a story, a star and a director and then finds a distributor, which could be a major studio, to provide the money to make the movie and later distribute it. In this instance, the independent producer gets about half of the net proceeds, if there are any.

Cofinancing works similarly, but the distributor provides only part of the money necessary to make the movie. The rest must come from the bank or other backers.

In the negative pickup arrangement, the independent obtains a contract from the distributor guaranteeing that the film will be purchased for an established price upon completion. The contract then allows the independent to raise all of the money from banks or financial backers.

One common source of film financing for independents, minors and even a few majors has been Silver Screen Partners, a partnership made up of more than 85,000 investors across the country who by the early 1990s had put up between $2,000 and $500,000 each to make about $1 billion worth of movies. This borrowed money brings with it oversight. Financial backers often refuse to finance controversial films, and when they do lend money, they also exercise control over preproduction, production and postproduction in order to protect their investment.

According to *Variety,* the show business trade journal, more than 200 American feature films were made and theatrically released by U.S.-based

Biggest
Moneymakers

The amounts indicated below are rental revenues from U.S. and Canadian theaters. In addition, most of these films earned money from foreign theatrical showings, videocassette sales and pay and broadcast television.

Movie	Year Released	Rental Revenues
1. "E.T., the Extra-Terrestrial"	1982	$228 million
2. "Star Wars"	1977	$193 million
3. "Return of the Jedi"	1983	$169 million
4. "Batman"	1989	$150 million
5. "The Empire Strikes Back"	1980	$141 million
6. "Home Alone"	1990	$140 million
7. "Ghostbusters"	1984	$132 million
8. "Jaws"	1975	$129 million
9. "Raiders of the Lost Ark"	1981	$115 million
10. "Indiana Jones and the Last Crusade"	1989	$115 million

Source: Variety, May 16, 1993, p. C-76. Copyright 1993 *Variety.* Reprinted by permission.

companies in 1992. Major movie companies made and distributed about 67 films of their own; they also distributed 60 minor or independently made features either because they bought the movies or agreed to release them for a fee. Minor and independent producers released another 82 American-made movies.

Each year many American movies—309 of them in 1992—fail to reach U.S. theaters. Some are unfinished because of lack of money. Some are eventually distributed through video stores, without theatrical showings anywhere. Some are released for overseas markets only, never to be seen in the United States. And yes, some are so bad that no one anywhere would ever want to see them.

Exhibition is the last step in the movie-making process. Although the exhibitor might be a video rental store, the term usually refers to a movie theater. There are about 5,000 theaters in the United States with more than 22,000 theater screens: California has the largest number and Hawaii the fewest. There also are 1,000 drive-in theaters, a number that drops each year. In all about one billion tickets are sold at an average price of about $4.75, pouring a total of more than $5 billion dollars into the corporate pockets of exhibitors, distributors and producers. Sometimes the pockets all belong to the same pants because movie producers—with the federal government's blessing this time—are furiously buying theaters. For example, Sony owns one chain, Universal's parent company owns half of the huge Cineplex-Odeon theater chain, and Warner Bros.' and Paramount's parent companies own one chain. Financial analysts say that movie producers want theaters because they can keep the portion of the ticket price that now goes to the exhibitor, make profits from concessions and control film release patterns.

Making Movies Today in the United States

Whether they are conceived by a major studio, a minor or an independent production company, movies are made in much the same way. In every instance, films go through a *development, preproduction, production* and *postproduction* process, which usually takes between one and two years (see Figure 10.1).

Let's look at how a movie is made at a big studio. The **development** process starts with an idea and ends with a movie script. Although some movies are based on an original story, most are developed from a newspaper or magazine article, a short story, a novel or a play, which is brought to the attention of the studio by the author's agent. If the story is promising, the studio buys motion picture rights and hires a writer to create a script, also called a "screenplay." A script written by a member of the Screenwriter's Guild costs perhaps $100,000. It usually goes through many versions by many different writers and often has color-coded pages to identify who wrote what. Of every 10 ideas turned into scripts, only one gets made into a movie.

Future Focus The Last Picture Show?

In 1929, 110 million Americans went to the movies each week. That was the highwater mark of movie attendance, which has now declined to about 20 million a week. In fact, surveys show that many Americans—44 percent—don't go to the movies at all. One study in the late 1980s suggested that only 24 percent of Americans go to the movies more than once a month (with 8 percent attending every other month and 24 percent attending once a year). And who are those monthly moviegoers? People under 30, a segment of population that is shrinking. People over 40 account for fewer than 20 percent of all admissions, whereas teenagers account for 25 percent, according to the Motion Picture Association of America.

In addition, theaters are getting a smaller portion of the money that moviegoers spend on entertainment each year, despite climbing ticket prices. For example, in 1981, about half of the money consumers spent on entertainment went to movie theaters. By 1986, that share had dropped 25 percent, according to the National Association of Theatre Owners.

Exhibitors have long known the causes of attendance and money problems; they are the victims of a one-two punch. Television landed the first blow in the late 1940s, and the videocassette recorder, now found in more than 70 percent of American homes, won the second round in the 1980s.

What's the solution? Exhibitors, distributors and producers tried to compete with television in the 1950s by providing movies in color, widescreen and stereophonic sound. They also experimented with three-dimensional movies and even movies that emitted odors. Later, exhibitors reduced the size of theaters and automated them so that they could offer something for everyone without increasing labor costs. In the 1980s and 1990s, exhibitors improved projection and sound systems, and some began to rent and sell videocassettes. They also expanded their concession stands, where they make most of their profits.

Will movie theaters exist in the year 2000? Exhibitors say yes, but agree that they must provide an experience that can't be achieved at home with a rented videocassette.

When the script is finished, **preproduction** begins. A team headed by a *producer* (who manages the production) and a *director* (who is responsible for creative interpretation) sends copies of the script for budget estimates to various studio departments, including casting, art, camera, wardrobe, makeup, hairdressing, music, sound and special effects. The script is also broken down to determine location requirements. For example, if scenes in a tavern were required at the beginning and end of the film, both bar scenes would be scheduled together. These budget estimates and the proposed shooting schedule yield the movie's estimated cost.

With an approved budget, the film moves into the **production phase.** The cast begins rehearsals with the director, sets (designed by the art director) are constructed, wardrobes are made and fitted, makeup is created and tested, music and titles are ordered, hairstyles are selected, and special effects work begins. In addition, the Hollywood publicity mill begins to grind.

Photography, which generally runs from early in the morning until late at night five and sometimes six days a week, will take from a few weeks to a few months to complete. For example, "Gone With the Wind," although hardly a typical film, required 21 weeks of principal photography.

Shooting techniques vary with the director, who has responsibility for transforming the script into sight and sound, but the most common

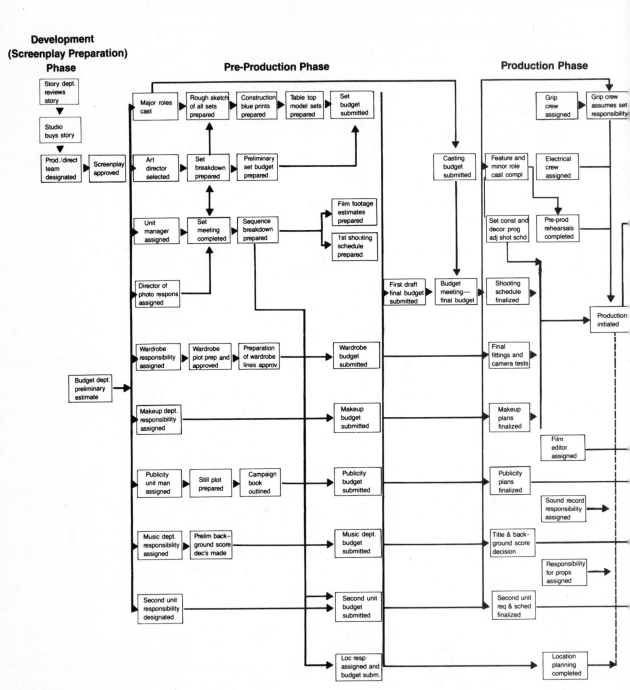

Figure 10.1
Overview of the Motion Picture Production Process
Source: Courtesy of Universal Studios. Reprinted by Permission.

Daily Production Cycle

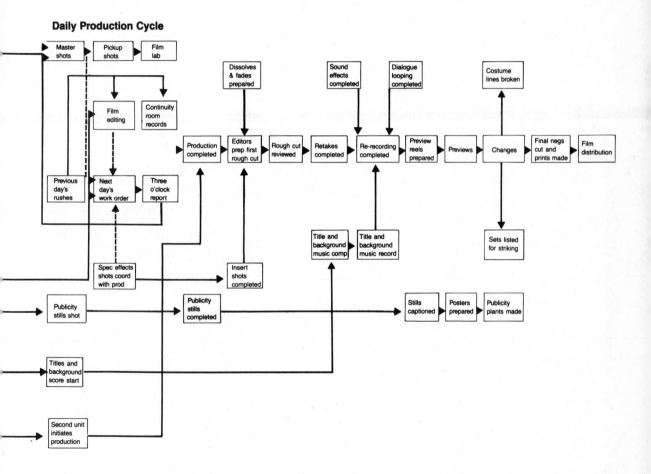

method is to photograph a wide-angle or "master shot" of an entire "scene," followed by medium and close-up versions or "pickup shots." Obviously, this approach requires that the action be repeated numerous times. As work goes on, shots make up scenes, which eventually become part of "sequences."

After each day's work, film is developed and those shots or "takes" the director thinks are best are printed, or transferred from negative to positive film so that they can be viewed. The producer, director, director of photography, editor and others usually view these unedited segments, called "rushes."

The film enters the **postproduction** phase when all principal photography has been completed and editing begins. Editing can take longer than filming—23 weeks in the case of GWTW—and can make or break a movie. The process works like this: A finished version of the film, without titles and music, is prepared. This version, called a "rough cut," allows the production team to see if retakes or rerecording are needed. After retakes and new sound recording are completed, a polished version of the film, with titles, music and effects, is made. The movie is shown or "previewed" to test audiences and changes are made if needed. For example, preview audiences may detest a sad ending and a new, happier one may be

The Voluntary Movie Rating System

American movie producers have avoided federal censorship by exercising self-regulation, first through a group called the Motion Picture Producers and Distributors of America and more recently through the Motion Picture Association of America.

The MPPDA, better known as "The Hays Office" after MPPDA head Will Hays, was formed in 1922 when film themes became unacceptable to many Americans. For example, despite Prohibition, movies featured drinking. Despite narcotics laws, movies showed the use of drugs. And despite conservative moral standards in many communities, movies depicted seduction, sex and divorce. As a result, city and state censorship boards appeared everywhere, and the MPPDA, in an effort to defang them, adopted many of their standards. Members' scripts and films were reviewed and altered where necessary.

By the early 1930s, the Hays Office had lost some of its influence and unpleasantries were starting to creep into movies again. Catholic church leaders, with the help of Protestant denominations, pressured the Hays Office in 1934 to adopt a new production code. The code was stern: If a film didn't get MPPDA approval, it probably wouldn't be released. The production code rules stood until 1968, when the MPAA, supported by member studios and distributors, adopted guidelines to replace them.

As MPAA president Jack Valenti tells it, the current voluntary ratings system, aimed at parents, had its roots in 1966 with the film "Who's Afraid of Virginia Woolf?" In it, for the first time on the screen, the word "screw" and the phrase "hump the hostess" were heard. After discussions, "screw" was deleted, but the other phrase remained.

By late 1968, a formal rating system had been created: "G" for general, "M" for mature audiences, and "R" and "X" for restricted admission. Later, "M" was changed to "PG," and in 1984 "PG-13" was added. In 1990, "NC-17" replaced "X."

After more than two decades, nearly 10,000 pictures have been rated, according to the MPAA and *Variety*.

ordered. After final previews, advertising is prepared, and the film goes into distribution.

By the time the project is finished, sets and properties will have eaten up 35 percent of the budget, with cast and studio overhead each accounting for another 20 percent. The remaining 25 percent of costs will have been spent on acquiring the story and writing the script, filming the movie, and paying taxes.

Motion Picture Dollars and Cents

Making movies is expensive. "The Last Emperor," winner of nine Academy Awards in 1988 including Best Picture, was filmed in the People's Republic of China for authenticity and to help keep costs under control. However, the bills were still big enough to make an accountant weep. For example, while shooting one scene in Beijing involving thousands of extravagantly dressed extras, a film investor told producer Jeremy Thomas how much he liked what he saw. Thomas answered, "You'd better like it; it's costing you $10,000 a second." That's understandable considering "Emperor's" $23.5 million budget.

Other movies have cost more. The Soviet Union's 1967 production of "War and Peace," reportedly the most expensive film ever made, cost $100 million. The most expensive movie in Hollywood history was 1991's "Terminator 2," which cost $94 million, according to *Variety*. Hollywood's four other most expensive movies were "Batman Returns," a 1992 release that cost $80 million; "Who Framed Roger Rabbit," a 1988 production that cost $70 million; "Jurassic Park," which hit theaters in 1993 and cost $60 million; and "Rambo III," a 1988 film that cost $58 million.

Let's follow the money trail of a typical movie from production to exhibition. Before starting, remember two important economic concepts. First, understand that making and marketing a movie costs big money. For example, the average cost of a theatrical film made by a member company of the Motion Picture Association of America in the early 1990s was nearly $40 million—about $29 million to make the movie's master negative and another $11 million for duplicate print and advertising expenses. The second concept is that a film must generate ticket sales worth many, many times its negative cost in order to break even. This ticket sale money is called *gross* revenue.

"Coming to America," a 1988 Paramount comedy starring Eddie Murphy, provides a good example of these concepts at work. Paramount, the movie's producer and distributor, began the process of recouping its investment by licensing "Coming to America" for exhibition at thousands of U.S. theaters. Exhibitors, by the way, make most of their money—80 percent of their profits, in fact—from concession sales, with their share of the ticket sales providing the rest of the profits and all of the theater's operating costs. Thus, contrary to popular belief, the exhibitor gets to keep only a portion of ticket monies—10 to 50 percent, depending on the contract terms, which in turn depend on the potential of the movie. The

	Costs	Revenues
TABLE 10.1 "COMING TO AMERICA"		
Negative cost (including studio overhead):	$48 million	
Interest:	$6 million	
Markets:		
Domestic theatrical	$36 million	$63 million
Foreign theatrical		$43 million
Domestic and foreign home video		$5 million*
Domestic and foreign cable		$13 million*
Soundtrack, book publishing and nontheatrical		$1 million*
Syndication	None as of 1990	
Network TV	None as of 1990	
Subtotal:	$90 million	$125 million
Distribution fee (30 percent of domestic, 35 percent of United Kingdom and 40 percent of foreign theatrical revenues):	$42 million	
Gross participation fees (for star Eddie Murphy and director John Landis):	$11 million	
Total:	$143 million	$125 million
Net profit (or loss):	($18 million loss)	

*Costs have already been deducted from these revenues.
Sources: Paramount Pictures and *Variety*, March 28, 1990, p. 5.

money returned to the distributor—Paramount in this case—is called *rental* revenue. Released in June 1988, "Coming to America" grossed hundreds of millions of dollars worldwide, according to *Variety*. Theatrical rentals amounted to $106 million—$63 million from the United States and Canada and $43 million from elsewhere. "Coming to America" produced other revenue later, of course. After its theatrical release, Paramount released "Coming to America" on videocassette and received an estimated $5 million in worldwide revenue. World cable television produced perhaps $13 million, and soundtrack, book publishing and nontheatrical showings brought in another $1 million.

There were staggering expenses, however. Paramount said the movie cost $48 million, including studio overhead. Interest charges added another $6 million. In addition, Paramount absorbed $78 million in distribution expenses. These expenses included a distribution fee—ranging from 30 to 40 percent of rentals—as well as prints, which cost at least $1,500 each, and advertising costs. Individuals who helped make the movie took another $11 million in fees.

"E. T."—the box office champion of all time–grossed more than $700 million worldwide by the late 1980s.

When a lawsuit forced Paramount to reveal these figures in 1990, "Coming to America" had taken in $125 million against $143 million in costs—thus producing an $18 million loss, Paramount said (see Table 10.1). However, yet to come were network and syndicated television revenues, which would bring in millions of additional dollars during the 1990s. Result: a profitable film, eventually.

"Coming to America," however, will earn just beer money when compared to the all-time box office champ, "E.T., the Extra-Terrestrial." "E,T.," a 1982 Universal film, cost about $11 million. By the 1990s, it had grossed more than $700 million worldwide (excluding revenues from the sale of 15 million videocassettes and television sales figures). Rentals were less, of course, but probably enough to make Universal's stockholders delirious.

An easier and increasingly more popular way to quickly gauge the financial success of a typical feature film is to compare the movie's negative cost against U.S. and Canadian theatrical rentals. If rentals equal the cost of the film, the movie will probably be a financial success, *Variety*'s experts say. This approach omits some costs, such as print, advertising and distribution expenses, but also ignores some revenues. For example, consider Bill Cosby's 1987 movie, "Leonard Part 6." The movie cost $31 million but took in only $2.5 million in U.S. and Canadian rentals. Result: a financial disaster. Of course, Cosby's film eventually made a little more money because after a movie is exhibited in the United States and Canada, it is shown abroad and then goes into U.S. and foreign home video release, where it can earn millions more. Then, as you have read, the typical movie is leased to pay television, such as Home Box Office or The Movie Channel, and later to network television. Toward the end of its economic life, the movie is leased for broadcast to television stations in the United States and elsewhere.

In all, worldwide film rentals usually bring in about 32 percent of the dollars a movie will ever earn (with 60 percent of *that* money supplied by U.S. and Canadian theaters). Videocassette sales provide another 44 percent. Pay and broadcast television provide 24 percent of a movie's overall revenue (HBO, for example, reportedly paid $30 million to air "Ghostbusters"), and various ancillary activities, including licensing of music from the film and merchandising, yield less than 1 percent (see Figure 10.2).

If videocassettes provide 44 percent of a film's revenue, can't cassette sales save a box office disaster? Yes and no. Some low-budget features that don't reap good U.S. rentals can sometimes be salvaged by hundreds of thousands of videocassette sales, but the usual industry thinking is that big box office hits are the biggest videocassette sellers.

**Figure 10.2
Theatrical Films' Revenue Mix, 1980 and 1990**

Most movie revenues came from rentals to theaters in 1980. By 1990, less than half of all movie revenues came from theatrical rentals.

Source: Courtesy Goldman, Sachs & Company. Reprinted by permission.

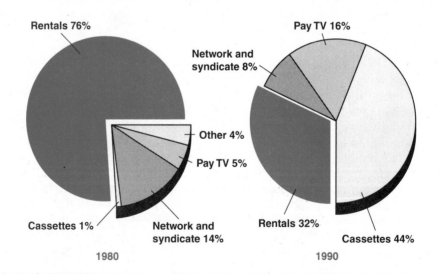

Rentals 76%

Cassettes 1%

Network and syndicate 14%

Other 4%

Pay TV 5%

1980

Pay TV 16%

Network and syndicate 8%

Rentals 32%

Cassettes 44%

1990

More About Money: The Critics and the Oscars

Reviews are also a factor in the motion picture distribution and exhibition business. As you might expect, good movies often get good reviews, which may enhance profits. However, even a very good film with outstanding reviews may not be able to attract an audience. For example, most critics loved "The Bear," but the 1989 movie cost $21 million and made only $13.5 million in U.S. theatrical rentals.

Bad movies often get bad reviews, which can reduce profits. The distributor's traditional solution? A miserable movie is often heavily advertised and then opened simultaneously in perhaps 1,000 theaters across the nation. The procedure, called a "saturation release," is based on the premise that the film might make a profit if it can be marketed before reviewers scare off patrons.

And mediocre movies often get mixed reviews. The most amazing characteristic of the mediocre movie is that it can be a huge hit despite indifferent reviews. For example, "Top Gun," a steamy 1986 naval aviation soap opera, received lukewarm reviews but made nearly $80 million in U.S. rental fees against a $14 million budget.

In short, experts agree that most movies don't live or die by reviews. However, most producers and distributors do what they can to garner good reviews. For that reason, critics such as Pulitzer Prize-winner Roger Ebert of the *Chicago Sun-Times* and Gene Siskel of the *Chicago Tribune* are courted.

Siskel, Ebert and their colleagues are offered special screenings not only because good reviews can't do any harm, but also because good reviews can influence Academy Award nominations. Being nominated for an Oscar— or better yet, winning one—is very, very good for business. An Oscar can double a film's revenue, distributors say, which explains why producers and studios buy millions of dollars worth of $5,000 full-page ads in movie trade publications around Academy Award time. The Academy tells its members to ignore the Oscar campaigns, as it did in 1992 with this warning: "This year, as in the past, you may be importuned by advertisements, promotional gifts, dinner invitations and other lobbying tactics in an attempt to solicit your vote. Excellence in filmmaking is the only factor we consider in casting our Academy Award votes." Alas, Academy members were being asked to ignore hyperbole—"hype" for short—and hype, more than art, is what built Hollywood.

Retrospective

Movies, like most mass-communication media, are international in origin. The first movies, both in Europe and the United States, consisted of motion for motion's sake, but soon filmmakers started telling stories. European nations and the United States intensely competed for movie audiences until World War I, when conflict damaged much of the European film industry and the United States took the economic (and some say artistic) lead in world filmmaking. American producers achieved distinction first in comedy and action movies, and later in other genres.

Sound movies replaced silents in the late 1920s, and 25 years later television and government antitrust action forced additional technological and economic changes such as color, wide-screen, enhanced sound and small, efficient and often automated theaters.

Despite continued American economic dominance, filmmaking today is still international in nature, with movies often financed by multinational concerns and dependent upon international theatrical, video and broadcast markets for profits.

1. What is "persistence of vision?" Why is it important to the development of motion pictures?
2. What was the primary difference between the very first motion pictures and somewhat later films such as "The Great Train Robbery?"
3. If war had not come to Europe twice in the 20th century, do you think Hollywood would have become the center of world filmmaking?
4. Based on what you have read, would you say that movie-making is a relatively risk-free business?
5. What themes do America's biggest money-making films have in common? Do you think the themes of American-made films of the future will have to change in order to retain the international market?
6. What technological changes can you recall occurring in movie theaters in the last few years? Do you think competition from television was responsible? Will television competition be responsible for continuing changes in the movie business? Will the videocassette rental market make movie theaters obsolete?
7. Do you think the federal government should continue to allow movie studios to acquire theater chains?

Suggested Readings

Bohn, Thomas W., and Stromgren, Richard L. *Light & Shadows*. Mountain View, Calif.: Mayfield, 1987.

Jowett, Garth, and Linton, James M. *Movies as Mass Communication*. Newbury Park, Calif.: Sage, 1989.

Kael, Pauline. *The Citizen Kane Book: Raising Kane*. New York: Limelight Editions, 1984.

Kindem, G. A. *The American Movie Industry: The Business of Motion Pictures*. Carbondale, Ill.: Southern Illinois University Press, 1982.

Knight, Arthur. *The Liveliest Art*. New York: The New American Library, 1979.

Mast, Gerald. *A Short History of the Movies*. New York: MacMillan, 1986.

O'Donnell, Pierce, and McDougal, Dennis. *Fatal Subtraction: The Inside Story of Buchwald v. Paramount*. New York: Doubleday, 1992.

Schulberg, Budd. *What Makes Sammy Run?* Cambridge, Mass.: Bentley, 1979.

Advertising

We've all seen the Energizer rabbit—that pink bunny in Ray-Ban sunglasses that marches into the middle of dumb commercials and stops them dead, something we all wish we could do from time to time. You know how it works. A familiar-looking commercial gets underway, touting some mythical antacid or mouthwash, and the rabbit rolls in and rudely interrupts by beating away at a bass drum, while an off-camera voice intones, "Still going. Nothing outlasts the Energizer battery. It keeps going . . . and going . . . and going. . . ."

The Energizer rabbit, a send-up of traditional Madison Avenue commercials, was the brainchild of Chiat/Day/Mojo, a West Coast agency that belongs to a brash school of advertising known as the California Revolution. Chiat/Day/Mojo invented the rude rabbit in response to a series of competing Duracell ads. Duracell, capitalizing on an Ogilvy & Mather campaign that used battery-operated toys to show the staying power of Duracell batteries, had been nibbling away at Eveready's share of the market. Among the Duracell ads was one that showed a batch of toy rabbits banging snare drums. The bigger Energizer bunny, with its more powerful bass drum, was Chiat/Day/Mojo's creative answer to the Duracell bunnies.

The Chiat/Day/Mojo rabbit caught so much attention that other agencies took notice. Coors Brewing Co. did a take-off on the Energizer rabbit in 1991, outfitting movie star Leslie Nielsen ("Airplane" and "Naked Gun") with bunny ears, fluffy tail and bass drum. Nielsen marched onto a rotating platform in front of a giant glass of beer and spun crazily while a voice murmured, "Coors . . . is the fastest growing light beer in America. It keeps growing . . . and growing . . . and growing. . . ." The Energizer people, masters at poking fun at other commercials, didn't think the Coors spot was funny. They took Coors to court and tried to make them stop, but the judge denied their request.

The rabbit even made the 1992 political campaign, in a way. In Ohio, where Senator John Glenn, the former astronaut, was running for reelection, his opponent, Michael DeWine, aired an attack spot titled "Astro," which accused Glenn of owning an expensive home on a golf course, his own private airplane and a spacious 53-foot yacht. DeWine then tried to paint a dark cloud over Glenn's financial judgment by saying that he still owed $3 million from his 1984 presidential campaign. At this point, a tiny astronaut, brazenly modeled on the Energizer bunny, tore through the screen and banged away on a toy drum while an off-screen voice rumbled, "John Glenn. He just keeps owing . . . and owing . . . and owing. . . ."

Glenn responded to the ad with an attack ad of his own, pointing out that it is illegal to repay campaign debts with personal money and suggesting that DeWine was asking Glenn to break the law—"not an unusual request," Glenn's ad went on, "from a former Congressman who saw nothing wrong with bouncing thousands of dollars of bad checks at the House bank."

Glenn was reelected in spite of DeWine's Energizer astronaut, but that isn't the point. The point is that a political campaign used a parody of a commercial that is famous for parodying other commercials, all because the viewing public would instantly recognize the parody and theoretically be amused by it while absorbing the message.

Shrewd commercials, such as those featuring the Energizer bunny, rapidly modified public perceptions about advertising. People started watching and enjoying again. Oh, we might deny it. Most of us enjoy muttering under our breath at the glut of print advertising. We take pleasure in complaining about the irritating commercial messages that interrupt our radio and television programs. We raise a jaundiced eyebrow and scoff at seemingly outrageous advertising claims. But we still go out and buy the products they extol. If we didn't, advertising would be a dead art.

Advertising: What Is It?

And we need advertising. America is an information-oriented society, and advertising pays the bills for most of the information. Because of print and electronic advertising, the American media consumer has access to an enormous amount of information and entertainment at a relatively low cost. Without it, the average newspaper or magazine would be thinner and could cost three times as much. Radio and television stations would probably be on the air only a few hours a day. Even then they would have to seek government subsidies, charge viewing fees or run funding campaigns like public broadcast stations do.

Modern advertising is built on mass production. American manufacturers create a product for which they believe there is a need, design it to be attractive or tasty, test it on small sample of representative consumers, shave costs by producing it on a mass scale, then package and market it by seeking a mega-audience of buyers who will accept it and buy it in mass quantities. Advertising is a fundamental part of the marketing process.

It hasn't always been that way. Advertising was used casually and occasionally in the old days. Someone might pop a small notice in the paper if an indentured servant ran away or a sailing ship arrived from Europe with fresh spices and some new bolts of material for sale. But no one bothered to advertise products that were always available and easy to spot in windows along the main street. If you baked a good loaf of bread and your price was fair, word would get around, and local people would come to buy bread from you. If your town were big enough to attract strangers, you could hang a sign over your door. No point in wasting money on a newspaper notice that told people what they already knew.

What caused the change? Think about your own closet for a moment. How many pairs of shoes do you have? Six or seven? Maybe more, counting your school shoes and your work shoes and your dress shoes and your sandals and your tennis shoes and your jogging Adidas. There was a time when products like shoes were tailor-made. If a man wanted a new pair of shoes, he went to the local cobbler for a fitting and had a pair made. They were expensive, but they were usually pretty good shoes, and the man might wear them for seven or eight years with only an occasional visit back to the cobbler for a new set of soles and heels. Then, when the shoes finally broke down, he went back to the cobbler for a new fitting and a new pair. Most people got along with only one or two pairs of shoes at a time. Cobblers didn't have to advertise. They hung out a shingle, set up their tools and waited for business to come walking in.

Then someone got the bright idea of cranking out shoes by the car lot, all alike and in various sizes. By making them on an assembly line, the shoe manufacturers discovered that the costs went down. The more they made, the cheaper the production costs. They could afford to offer their shoes at a much lower price than the average cobbler and still make a good profit. They knew people would buy them if they knew about them. Everyone likes to save money. So all the manufacturers had to do was make sure masses of people all over the country heard about their mass-produced shoes. Mass advertising was the natural by-product.

Advertising Yesterday: A Brief History

Advertising in one primitive form or another has probably been with us since the invention of trade, but the first advertising professionals were the public criers who circulated through the streets of ancient cities to notify citizens of impending sales of cattle and exotic imports. You can still see a form of this oral advertising in many countries. In Mexico, for example, hawkers still wander the streets of villages announcing the availability of their wares in sing-song fashion. "Pa-le-tas," they call, pushing small ice carts containing what we think of as popsicles. Or they go from street to street chanting that they are available to sharpen scissors. Or to sell strawberries. Or to repair the leather chairs called "equipales."

You can trace the history and progress of almost any country through its advertising. To show you how it works, let's examine some of the links between advertising and the history of our country.

Past Pointer Media Mileposts: And Now a Word from Our Sponsor

1704	First American newspaper advertisements appear in the inaugural issue of *The Boston News-Letter*.	1914	Federal Trade Commission issues guidelines for truthful, ethical advertising.
1812	First advertising agency does business in Great Britain.	1922	First radio commercial (a 15-minute real-estate spot, purchased for $100) is broadcast in New York by WEAF.
1842	Volney B. Palmer opens first American ad agency, acts primarily as space broker for publications.	1938	Federal Trade Commission Act gives added weight to FTC control of advertising.
1869	F. Wayland Ayer founds N. W. Ayer & Son, which soon becomes first ad agency to offer services to advertisers.	1971	Cigarette advertising is banned from radio and television.
1906	Pure Food and Drug Act brings a halt to spurious patent medicine ads.	1978	Supreme Court gives FTC authority to require remedial, or corrective, advertising.

From Slaves to Patent Medicines

Early advertisements in the United States came in the form of handbills and posters. Commercial newspaper notices began to appear in 1704, in the very first issue of John Campbell's original continuing newspaper, *The Boston News-Letter*. These earliest newspaper ads were usually very small, much like our classified advertising today, and they dealt with lost items, the sale and rental of farms, ship arrivals, exotic foodstuffs, and—a sad comment on our Colonial forebears, both North and South—slavery. Here's a 1735 ad that ran in Benjamin Franklin's *Pennsylvania Gazette*:

Just Imported
A Parcel of likely Negro Men, Women, and
Children: As also, choice London double and single refin'd,
clay'd
and Muscovado SUGARS, and GINGER; to be sold by Joseph Marlo
at the Corner of Walnut and Second-Street, Philadelphia.

Franklin was one of the first newspaper publishers to realize that advertising could be a major source of revenue. He also made advertising more attractive through the judicious use of space and changes in typeface. Nor did he mind touting his own products, including the Franklin stove and lightning rods. One of his most popular products was *Poor Richard's Almanack;* in addition to passing on knowledge and sayings, it was designed to predict everything from weather to the exact minute of sunrise and sunset for the American farmer. When the 1741 edition of *Poor Richard's Almanack* was printed in 1735, this is the way Franklin announced it:

Just Published
POOR Richard's ALMANACKS, for the
Year 1741. Also Jerman's Almanacks, and Pocket and Sheet
Almanacks. Printed and Sold by B. Franklin.

As grievances against the Crown mounted and the seeds of revolution were sewn in the young American Colonies, other ads mirrored the temper of the times. For example, American patriots, irritated at a Boston merchant for importing and selling British goods, called for a boycott by printing the following placard and posting it for all to see:

WILLIAM JACKSON
an *IMPORTER;* at the
BRAZEN HEAD,
North Side of the TOWN-HOUSE.
and *Opposite the Town-Pump, in*
Corn-Hill, BOSTON.

Advertisments have been used since the beginning of trade. In this late 18th century woodcut a colonial post rider announces a new route.

NEWS! NEWS!!

AARON OLIVER, *Post-Rider,*
WISHES to inform the Public, that he has extended his Route ; and that he now rides thro' the towns of *Troy, Pitistown, Hoosick, Mapletown,* part of *Bennington* and *Shaftsbury, Petersburgh, Stephentown, Greenbush* and *Schodack.*
All commands in his line will be received with thanks, and executed with punctuality.
He returns his sincere thanks to his former customers ; and intends, by unabated diligence, to merit a continuance of their favours.

O'er ruggid hills, and vallies wide,
He never yet has fail'd to trudge it :
As steady as the flowing tide,
He hands about the NORTHERN BUDGET.
June 18, 1799.

It is desired that the SONS and
DAUGHTERS of *LIBERTY,*
would not buy any one thing of
him, for in so doing they will bring
Disgrace upon *themselves,* and their
Posterity, for *ever* and *ever,* AMEN.

After the War for Independence, the nation began to look westward. New frontiers and fresh prospects were touted by ads for adventurous pioneers, and when people pulled up roots to head west, they usually advertised their homes and bulkier goods for sale. Ads for railroads, homestead sites and barbed wire testify to the taming of the new frontier. And when the nation needed a faster line of communication for its expanding horizons, this ad appeared:

PONY EXPRESS!
10 Days to San Francisco
LETTERS
will be received at the
OFFICE, 84 BROADWAY,
NEW YORK,

Which will be forwarded to connect with the PONY EXPRESS leaving
ST. JOSEPH, Missouri,
Every WEDNESDAY and SATURDAY at 11 P.M.
EXPRESS CHARGES:
LETTERS weighing half ounce or under $1.00
For every additional half ounce or fraction of an ounce 1.00

Along with westward expansion came railroads, population growth and the industrial revolution. America learned to produce goods in abundance for a much larger market, and modern advertising was born. In 1830, there were some 800 newspapers and magazines carrying advertising in the United States; by 1861, that number had swelled to more than 5,000 newspapers and magazines. Improved printing techniques and better transportation allowed magazines to circulate nationally, reaching more and more people with products of a nonlocal nature. By the turn of the century, some magazines were carrying as many as 100 pages of advertising in each issue.

Early Excesses

Of course, placing ads right along with the makers of soaps and watches and baby prams was a band of snake-oil charlatans, selling patent medicines with extravagant unproven claims. Patent medicine ads gave advertising a bad name that lasted for years. Among the hundreds of surefire medicines, you could get *Brown's Iron Bitters* to cure dyspepsia, indigestion, weakness, impure blood, malaria, chills and fevers and neuralgia (it also cured diseases of the kidney and liver, as well as "Diseases peculiar to Women"). *Cuticura Remedies* was said to heal "Disfiguring Humors, Humiliating Eruptions, Itching Tortures, Scrofula, Salt Rheum and Infantile Humors." *Dr. Owen's Body Battery* cured general, nervous and chronic diseases. *Arabian Eye Lotion* cured weak eyes, sore eyes or dim eyes in both young and old. Dr. H. H. Kane promised a quick, painless cure for the opium or morphine habit, and even Thomas Edison got into the act with a product called *Polyform,* which he swore would "cure Rheumatism, Neuralgia, Sciatica and all Nervous Pains."

Some of the patent medicines were patently phony, with no medicinal qualities at all. Others contained "the real thing." In 1886, a pharmacist named John Styth Pemberton brewed up a potent secret formula that included water, corn syrup and other sweeteners, added a dash of coca leaf, including the narcotic cocaine, and called it Coca-Cola. He sold it as "brain tonic and intellectual beverage." It proved to be quite popular. The cocaine was removed from the recipe a few years later, just after the turn of the century, and the drink quietly slipped from the patent medicine list and became a recreational beverage. As Coca-Cola grew and became an international giant over the decades, the recipe of remaining ingredients stayed secret. But after a commercial importer broke silence in 1988, Coca-Cola authorities finally admitted that one of the secret ingredients is still, after almost a hundred years, a nonnarcotic extract of the coca leaf.

We can't really blame all the extravagant advertising excesses on phony patent medicines. In the early days of freewheeling and uncontrolled copy-writing, other products made unsubstantiated claims as well. You could buy *Dr. Scott's Electric Flesh Brush* to produce beautiful, clear skin, as well as new energy and new life. Dr. T. Felix Gouraud's *Oriental Cream, or Magical Beautifier* would remove tan, pimples, freckles, moth patches, rash, skin diseases and every other blemish on beauty. *Arabian Joint Oil* produced a high degree of elasticity to the joints and muscles of gymnasts and acrobats.

Just about every product was the "very best" or "absolutely pure" or "perfect" or "unrivaled." *The Hoffman House Cigar* was "absolutely unequaled." The "only perfect cycle seat" came from the *Automatic Cycle Seat Company* in Grand Rapids, Michigan. *Stearn's Electric Rat and Roach Paste* called itself sure death and swore it killed every kind of vermin—rats, mice, roaches and bugs. *Riker's Compound Sarsaparilla* (that's a kind of root beer) claimed it was the "Best Blood Purifier In The World" and backed the claim by saying, "It is legally guaranteed to do all you expect, or *it don't cost you a cent.*"

You get the idea. Advertisers were making so many wild statements that wary consumers stopped believing them. That made life difficult for the advertisers who had good products to offer and didn't need to resort to exageration and fraudulent claims. By the turn of the century, a series of public moves was underfoot to straighten out the kinks in advertising. Edward Bok, editor of *Ladies' Home Journal,* attacked quack medicines with a series of investigative exposés in the winter of 1904. *Collier's Weekly* did the same thing the next winter. Congress passed the Pure Food and Drug Act in 1906, requiring medicines to meet certain standards and advertisers to withdraw their spurious claims. In 1911, a trade paper for publishers, *Printer's Ink,* began to advocate across-the-board federal legislation against misleading advertising. That same year, the Associated Advertising Clubs of America issued an advertising code and coined the phrase "truth in advertising." By 1914, the Federal Trade Commission, charged with the protection of the marketplace from unfair competitive practices, decided to draw up its first set of guidelines for truthful, ethical advertising.

The Ad Agency Is Born

The first advertising agency, Reynell and Son, was operating in England by 1812, but it was in America that the advertising agency eventually developed to its full potential as a professional marketing arm. It wasn't until 1842 that Volney B. Palmer opened an office in Philadelphia and became America's first advertising agent. Palmer wasn't an ad agent as we know them today, working with clients to plan and implement advertising campaigns. Actually he worked more as an agent of newspaper and magazines than he did for the advertisers. He was, in a way, a space broker.

Publications had a confusing array of page sizes, column widths, measurements and deadlines, and the average advertiser found it difficult to keep them all in mind. Palmer made things easier by buying large quantities of advertising space from various publications (space then, as now, was cheaper in bulk). Then he sold the space to advertisers at a higher rate. He didn't offer advice or ideas, only space.

Palmer's space-buying gimmick (he could sell you space almost anywhere in the country) attracted imitators, and by 1860 there were as many as 30 agencies selling space in just about every publication in the United States. As the market became cluttered, agencies began to look for new ways to expand. A young man named F. Wayland Ayer got into the business in 1869, determined to plan and buy space *for advertisers,* rather than just sell it for publishers. He was afraid his clients wouldn't have much faith in anyone so young (he was only 20 at the time), so he used his father's name for his new agency, N. W. Ayer & Son. By the late 1800s, Ayer and other agency pioneers were offering additional advertising services as well, such as selecting the most effective media, writing the copy, designing the ads and managing the campaigns. From that point on, the advertising industry grew and prospered.

It was in this same general time frame that manufacturers realized that an inexpensive and trustworthy product wasn't always enough. Competition was too fierce. Someone down the line was usually producing a similar product that was just as trustworthy and just as inexpensive. To capture the loyalty of consumers, manufacturers needed quick, memorable product identification. Few people seemed interested in underwear made by a Mr. Bradlee, a Mr. Vorhees and a Mr. Day, so the three men changed the company name to BVD and sales took off. Other product manufacturers

These ads from the early 1900s promote brand names still in use in the 1990s.

also turned to brand names and easily recognizable trademarks. In 1871, there were 121 brand names registered at the U.S. Patent Office. Four years later, there were 1,138. Many are still with us today. The arm and hammer on Arm & Hammer Baking Soda made its public debut in 1867. The smiling old Quaker first decorated a Quaker Oats box in 1877. Those two bearded Smith Brothers (known for years as "Trade" and "Mark" because one head appeared over each word) showed up on glass jars of cough drops in 1886. Aunt Jemima, inspired by a popular vaudeville tune of the time, first graced the pancake mix in 1889. Psyche, the scantily clad goddess on White Rock products, began peering into pools in 1894. And those chubby-cheeked cherubs who appear in Campbell's Soup ads have been doing so since 1904.

Advertising Goes to War

By the time the United States entered World War I, advertising was on its way to sophistication. Products had improved. Ads were bigger and more persuasive. Revenues were up. When the call came, advertising embraced the war effort with recruiting posters, patriotic themes and general boosts to the morale of the country. Uncle Sam posters bearing the stylized artwork of magazine illustrator James Montgomery Flagg told readers "I Want You!" or challenged them to "Buy More Liberty Bonds." Even regular product ads showed patriotic spirit. Doble-Detroit's steam car bragged that it met wartime requirements of economy and fuel conservation by using only kerosene for fuel. Biddle Motor Cars burned regular fuel but claimed it could be found "in the training camps or at the front." Allen's Foot-Ease advised consumers to mail a packet of its antiseptic powder to sweethearts, sons and brothers in Army and Navy training camps. One ad showed a grinning soldier relaxing over his White Owl cigar and saying, "Did I bayonet my 1st Hun? Sure! How did it feel? It doesn't feel! There *he* is. There you are. One of you has got to go. I preferred to stay." Another cigar ad pictured a man saying, "I don't fancy pacifist cigars that weakly proffer peace. Nor do I like barbaric autocrats who war upon my day's efficiency. In Robert Burns, I have found the mildly militant cigar I thought did not exist."

After the war, advertising enjoyed a boom period. American factories were cranked up for full production, and advertising became an essential selling tool. Automobiles and soaps topped the marketing list. Everyone wanted to live the good life. Ad agencies like Lord & Thomas, owned by the brilliant Albert Lasker, became aggressive teams of highly paid specialists. Ad revenues jumped from $1.5 billion at war's end in 1918 to almost $2.5 billion a year later. A new medium, radio, came along in 1920, and two years later station WEAF sold the first commercial air time. By 1927, advertisers were spending $4 million a year on air time. A year later, they were spending $10 million. Advertisers discovered the value of the testimonial—if you could get a movie star to endorse a soap or a cigarette or a soft drink, sales seemed to shoot up. Then came the Depression, and the bottom fell out. Ad revenues, which had reached a peak of $3.5 billion a year in 1929, dropped to just over $1 billion by 1933. Most people blamed the economic system for the Depression. Advertisers caught their share of blame, too. Consumer groups complained that advertising was manipulative. Authors attacked the advertising industry in both fiction and nonfiction. The government tried to ram through a restrictive bill to control industrial quality and advertising (it was defeated in 1934). Advertising managed to weather the terrible 1930s, but the good times seemed to be over.

Another big European war came on the heels of the Depression, and American advertising once again dusted off its wartime uniform. The War Advertising Council, made up of top advertising people, helped recruit troops and sell war bonds. World War II stopped the production of most nonessential durable goods (such as automobiles, refrigerators and radios), but the companies that produced them decided to keep on advertising to maintain goodwill. And again, almost every product, whether production had been frozen or not, looked for some way to tie itself to the war effort. Handsome young men in uniform, American flags, war scenes and patriotic messages appeared in ads for everything from refrigerators to shoe products. A fruit-juice company showed a fighter pilot by his plane, drinking straight from the bottle. The display line read, "Between dogfights he guzzled grapefruit juice—so don't feel too bad about missing your glass this morning!" Borden's Elsie the Cow, informed of a milk shortage, gasped, "Are you trying to say I'm a slacker?" One popular cigarette company, stuck for years with an ugly green-and-red package, seized the opportunity to switch to a handsome white-and-red package and proudly proclaimed, "Lucky Strike Green Has Gone to War!" But cynics noticed that the green, apparently a battle casualty, never came home when the war was over.

But prosperity did. After the war, young men, glad to be alive, came home to make up for lost time. Manufacturers geared up to produce cars and tires and soaps and clothes and oscillating fans and all the comfort products that wartime production had curtailed. There were things to buy and money to be spent. At about this same time, television, held captive in experimental studios for the duration of the war, finally burst free on an eager, anticipating audience. Advertising has never been the same since.

When you divide up the advertising pie to see which media get major shares of the advertising dollar, it all depends on which pie you slice. Magazines and television like to emphasize their success selling the national pie. And why not? *Advertising Age,* reporting on national billings of $34.6 billion by 424 agencies in 1991, showed almost $19 billion going to television (over $10 billion to network television and another $8.7 billion to spot TV). That's almost 55 percent of the national advertising dollar. Magazines drew the next biggest chunk, $4.8 billion (14 percent). Newspapers earned about $3 billion (8.7 percent) in national billings during the same period. Because newspapers are primarily local in nature, they prefer to look at the much

Advertising Today: Structure of the Industry

larger $80 to $90 billion in combined annual billings for both national and local ads. Local newspaper ad revenues usually pile another $20 to $25 billion a year on top of the $3 billion for national ads, giving newspapers the lead on combined ad dollars and leapfrogging them ahead of television's combined total by about $4 billion a year.

Advertising Agencies: What They Do

In the old days, advertising was run largely on intuition. Early experts could look at a proposed ad campaign and determine, often with a fair degree of accuracy, whether it would do the job. But advertising is no longer a seat-of-the-pants operation. Too much is at stake. Costs have spiraled and a slight misjudgment can cost a fortune. Therefore, research has become very important to the industry. Proper market research can, at least theoretically, narrow the chances of failure. Unfortunately, mistakes are still common, and ad campaigns frequently flop. Miffed clients pick up their marbles and switch agencies, leaving a trail of ulcers and broken careers. It's a competi-

GLOBAL GLANCE
Indian Ad Agencies:
Bangalore to New
Delhi

Advertisers in subcontinent India have to struggle with the copywriter's worst nightmare—a country of 750 million people, second in population only to mainland China, with a staggering communication problem. Indians speak a polyglot of 14 major languages (Hindi, Assamese, Bengali, Gujarati, Kannada, Malayalam, Marathi, Oriya, Punjabi, Sanskrit, Tamil, Telugu, Urdu and English) and some 830 local and regional dialects. In many ways, the diversity of languages and culture is invigorating. But it does create problems for the advertiser. Cranking out multilingual ads for such a widespread and disparate population can be enormously expensive. Translators not only have to be fluent in major tongues, they also have to be familiar with local idioms.

The most common language for advertising in India is English. English, a linguistic leftover from the days of British rule, is often used as a communication bridge, one that can transcend geographical and cultural boundaries. Though English is spoken by only 10 percent of the total population, they are an elite and affluent group, including government and opinion leaders. More than 50 percent of total print media advertising revenues ($350 million) goes to English-language publications. Hindi publications, though Hindi is spoken in some form by 50 to 70 percent of the population, have managed to capture only 14 percent of those revenues.

Television presents a more difficult picture. Language problems are partially responsible for slowing the growth of television as a communication medium in India. Networking is difficult. With so many different linguistic audiences scattered about the country, programming has to be created on a regional basis and broadcast in a variety of languages. The same language barriers have obviously affected the growth of electronic advertising. Advertisers are forced to redub commercials in order to air them with regional broadcasts or to do a voice-over with a variety of languages. Some advertisers have found it more effective to reshoot commercials with different actors or multilingual actors, but reshooting can drive production costs up another 50 percent.

tive business, full of stress and tension, but it's also creative, challenging and totally consuming.

Agencies can range in size from small one-person organizations and hot, creative boutiques to something as large as Young & Rubicam, with 10,000 employees and more than 275 offices around the world. The top ten American-based giants, in order, are Young & Rubicam, Saatchi & Saatchi Advertising, McCann-Erickson, Ogilvy & Mather, BBDO, Lintas, J. Walter Thompson, DDB Needham, Backer Spielvogel Bates and Foot, Cone & Belding. Nine of these top ten agencies (many of which combine public relations functions with advertising services) have headquarters in New York. The tenth, Foot, Cone & Belding, is situated in Chicago. Together,

Ads like this are the product of hundreds of hours of work by dozens of different advertising industry workers.

the top ten grossed a worldwide annual income of more than $7.5 billion in 1991.

Except for the very large ad agencies, specialization of media is beginning to affect the agency-client relationship. There was a time when most full-service ad agencies were prepared to manage all of their clients' needs, from creative inception to finished campaign. Now, with vastly fragmented media audiences waiting to be sold, there are too many new problems and different techniques to master. Some ad agencies have been forced to act as contractors, enlisting the aid of smaller, highly competent firms to handle each specialized step in the advertising process.

What kind of valuable expertise is available from the bigger full-service agencies? Just about everything a client would need, including market research, full creative services, account management and media buying. When a potential customer brings a new product to an experienced advertising agency, the following people will deal with it.

Account Management. If you ever read a novel or see a movie about the advertising business, the advertising account executive is probably the job that will get most of the ink or the greatest part of the film. These are the men or women assigned to manage product campaigns from the moment they enter the office until they reach the media. The account executive deals directly with clients and acts as liaison with other agency departments, tending to their needs, answering their questions, keeping them informed and generally babying them through the marketing process. The job requires administrative and organizational abilities, experience, an eye for detail and the tact of a diplomat.

A Young & Rubicam creative team meets to discuss a news idea for a print-oriented advertising campaign.

Creative Services. This is the soul of the agency. It is made up of bright, creative people who will look at the product, get to know it and toss ideas around, discarding some and seizing on others until they brainstorm an effective campaign. They include writers, designers, artists, editors, photographers, talent specialists and music arrangers. They deal with concept, copy, visuals, color, impact, music, humor—in short, they must understand every phase of the creative process and make each work to provide a solid, persuasive message. They will design a print or electronic campaign, draw it up on storyboards, tinker with it, develop it, refine it and present it.

Market Research. The research department may be called in at almost any stage. These are the brains-and-numbers people. They deal with such things as motivation and behavior, message content, product acceptability, demographics and consumers' psychological characteristics. They may be asked to test the product before it goes to the creative process, to test the campaign after it has been conceived, or to test media to see which reach the most productive audiences. Not all research is done in-house, of course. Most resident advertising researchers can crunch numbers as well as anyone else, but some research problems can be so specialized that they may need to be assigned to outside experts—to a sociologist, perhaps, or a psychologist. To get the necessary results, a good agency is willing to pay premium prices to polling organizations, academicians who act as consultants or professional research teams.

Media Buying. Once the campaign is ready to go, ads must be placed in the most effective settings if they are to reach the proper consumers. At this point, market research comes into its own. Media selection is a complex process. You have to know which people are most likely to buy a product and where to find them. You can't just buy the cheapest newspaper space or biggest television audience or most popular radio program or slickest magazine. In these days of fragmented audiences, specialized print publications and specialized broadcast programming, it's too easy to miss the target. You must isolate the media audiences that most closely match the demographic profile of your prospective buyers and go directly to them. We'll talk more about media selection later.

Advertising Strategies

There are several basic theories of advertising, most of which matured over the years as the philosophy of some singularly successful advertising agency before being adopted by others in the industry. These philosophical theories (advertisers prefer to call them *strategies*) weren't developed by academicians in science labs or think tanks. Most of them came directly from the trenches as the result of competitive experimentation. Creative advertising people, seeking a business edge, cast about in search of techniques that would put them ahead of their competitors. When they found a strategy that worked, they used it and rode it to success. Here are some of the more successful techniques and the agencies that made them work.

Unique Selling Proposition. The Ted Bates agency, faced with a glut of competitive *parity products* (mass-produced goods that are all basically the same—bread, soft drinks, toothpaste, cigarettes), developed the **unique selling proposition** (or **USP**) shortly after World War II. Introduced by veteran ad expert Rosser Reeves, chairman of Ted Bates, the USP concept suggests that a product possesses superior qualities. It makes a specific promise to the consumer, offering some unique benefit if the consumer buys the product ("Wonder Bread Helps Build Strong Bodies Twelve Ways" or "Colgate Cleans Your Breath While It Cleans Your Teeth"). The statement is nearly always true, but it may not necessarily be unique. It may be only a *preemptive* statement, claiming a benefit for the product before a competitor can say the same. It's an effective technique. If you're advertising petroleum products, you might use the line "Mobil—the detergent gasoline." The slogan implies that only Mobil gasoline will help clean the impurities from your engine. Actually, there are numerous detergent gasolines. In fact, they may all be detergent gasolines. But if Mobil gets there first with the preemptive claim, competitors must think of a new way to say the same thing without sounding imitative, or they concede the advantage to Mobil.

Brand Image. David Ogilvy (of Ogilvy, Benson and Mather), building on Rosser Reeves' USP concept, came up with the idea of **image** or **status advertising** to lift parity products above the crowd. He decided to give his products a special aura, something that would make them seem just a little bit better, haughtier, even more expensive than competitors. He felt that people would prefer to be seen eating, drinking, wearing or driving first-class products, rather than be caught using what friends and neighbors might consider "cheap" or "inferior" products. So he invented Commander Whitehead, a sophisticated, bearded British naval officer, to create snob appeal for Schweppes Tonic. Whitehead's cultured upper-class British accent wrapped itself for years around the unlikely descriptive term "schweppervescence" and said the bottled tonic was available "for only a few pennies more." A similarly snobbish salesman, ritzy Baron von Wrangel, pushed Hathaway shirts. Ogilvy also coined the classic Rolls-Royce line, "At 60 miles an hour the loudest noise in the new Rolls-Royce comes from the electric clock."

Motivational Research. Norman B. Norman (of Norman, Craig and Kummel) preferred to ignore both USP and image advertising. A social scientist by training, Norman was convinced people bought products for deep Freudian reasons, and he called on Ernest Dichter, president of the Institute for Motivational Research, to help him ferret out some of those reasons. One of the findings was that cosmetics and lingerie were often bought for consciously or unconsciously sexual reasons. A classic example of what Norman called **empathy advertising,** based on Dichter's motivational research, was the Maidenform brassiere campaign, which began in 1949 and continued for 20 years. In print ads, women were shown

The man from Schweppes is here

The man in the Hathaway shirt

The Ogilvy, Benson and Mather advertising agency successfully uses "image" or "status" advertising to promote Schweppes Tonic and Hathaway shirts.

half-dressed, usually in slip and bra, in unusual dream circumstances ("I dreamed I visited the Roman Coliseum in my Maidenform bra"). The implication was that it was acceptable to be sexy and half nude in public if the scene was clothed in pure fantasy. As long as a woman was dreaming, she couldn't be held responsible. The campaign pushed Maidenform to the number two spot in the lingerie industry. Norman also did a highly successful ad campaign for Ronson cigarette lighters after motivational research indicated the flame from the lighter would be viewed as a sexual phallic symbol, and he built an Ajax cleanser campaign around a knight in shining armor who rode through suburban streets zapping dirt by poking his lance in kitchen windows.

Subliminal Advertising. Another startling (and highly controversial) development of the 1950s came as the result of a field experiment by advertising researcher James Vicary. Vicary, wondering what would happen if messages were directed to the **subliminal** awareness of a consumer (subliminal means below the conscious threshold of perception), set up a six-week study in a Fort Lee, N.J., theater. Single frames were inserted in

CHAPTER 11 Advertising

movie film with messages such as "Hungry? Eat popcorn" or "Drink Coca-Cola." Since movies are shown at 24 frames a second, the single frame flashed by too quickly (1/3000 of a second) to be seen by the conscious eye. Vicary, however, was sure the messages would be noted and registered by the subconscious mind, and he wanted to see if consumers would react to them. At the end of the study, he claimed popcorn sales went up 57.5 percent and Coke sales rose by 18.1 percent. The clamor was instantaneous. People resented the idea that they could be brainwashed by sneaky subliminal messages into buying a product, a service, or even a political candidate.

Does subliminal persuasion work? No one seems quite sure, but the evidence is against it. Vicary's research structure was flawed (among other things, it failed to consider weather conditions, change of season, nature of the film being shown, audience characteristics and special snack-bar displays). Most attempts to replicate his findings have failed. Some large department stores are still experimenting with subliminal messages inserted in background music and directed below the normal range of hearing. These messages supposedly say such things as "Don't steal" and "Be honest." But if the antishoplifting messages are found to be effective, they could just as easily say "Buy more" and "Charge it."

Positioning. As advertising moved into the 1960s, a new advertising theory was conceived to take advantage of the growing fractionalization of audiences. Ideally, a product manufacturer would prefer to capture an entire

Marlboro cigarettes, once considered a woman's brand, are "positioned" to appeal to men through the use of macho images like rugged cowboys.

market. A product that sells to absolutely everyone would be hard to beat. But competitive circumstances nearly always rule against such luck. Since capturing the total market is almost impossible, advertisers, led by Al Ries and Jack Trout, decided the next best thing would be to capture a large, dependable share of the market. So they began to **position** their products by looking for segments of the audience that they could rope off and call their own. In the cigarette industry, for example, Virginia Slims went after the lucrative female market with "You've Come a Long Way, Baby," while Marlboro cigarettes (once considered a woman's cigarette) hardened its macho image with rugged cowboys and invited he-men to "Come to Marlboro Country." Positioning is a standard practice now. Soaps may attract hygiene-conscious consumers who worry about body odor ("Aren't you glad you use Dial? Don't you wish everybody did?"), or they may reach for complexion-oriented consumers who want to be beautiful (Dove's beauty bar, with its one-quarter moisturizing cream). Beers may go for swingers ("The night belongs to Michelob"), for hard-working men on their way home from tough jobs ("It's Miller time") or for weight-conscious people who would like to swill without guilt (a whole bevy of "light" beers).

"Advertorials" and "Infomercials." When economic recessions come along, advertising dollars are among the first expenses to be cut by cost-conscious corporations. Newspapers suffer. Magazines hurt. Radio. TV networks and local TV stations. The dollar shortage means editors and broadcasters are forced to compete for a survivable share of the remaining advertising income or risk cutting their editorial products to the bone. At the same time, advertisers, with less to spend, begin looking for new ways to reach potential markets.

When the recession of the 1990s came along, traditional advertising media began to tighten their belts and look for new ways to accommodate advertisers. Two innovations that attracted both advertisers and media were "Special Advertising Sections" and half-hour commercials masquerading as entertainment (called **advertorials** and **infomercials** by critics, though media people and advertisers dislike those terms). These particular advertising vehicles are presented in a way that sometimes makes them hard to distinguish from regular editorial copy or standard programming. The print version, for example, may look like normal paper or magazine editorial presentation, with stories and articles interspersed with ads, though most of these special sections are prepared entirely by the advertiser who writes the copy and designs the ads. The insert usually carries an indication on each page that labels it as advertising, but the labels are often small and subtle, sometimes leading to confusion. The American Society of Magazine Editors, concerned in the early 1990s that the confusion might damage the credibility of member magazines, sent warnings to such stalwart publications as *Newsweek, Business Week, Esquire* and *Harper's Bazaar* pointing out that their special advertising sections looked very much like regular news coverage to the casual reader.

The electronic version of the special advertising section is a full-length

Sex, the Ultimate Sales Pitch

It started like any macho, male-bonding beer commercial. Young men, camping out in the Rocky Mountain wilderness, relaxed around a campfire. One popped an Old Milwaukee and murmured, "Guys, it doesn't get any better than this."

But then it did. One of the campers reached for another cold can, stashed in a rushing creek bed, and discovered gold. From upstream, rounding a bend, came a bevy of bouncing blonds, the Swedish Bikini Team, bobbing on a giant rubber raft. The raft stopped at the campsite and the bikini-clad blonds bounced to shore, flashing teeth and jiggling flesh. A plane flew overhead and dropped a load of fresh Old Milwaukee. Dozens of six-packs floated gently to the ground on tiny parachutes. Cue the lively music. Party time.

Maybe the bikini cuties made things better for the guys, but they brought big problems to Stroh's Brewery in late 1991. Stroh's trotted out the Swedish Bikini Team (actually American actresses wearing blond wigs) for a sexy ad campaign designed to help sell Old Milwaukee beer. Women across the land objected, not only to the "sexual stereotyping" in the Stroh's campaign, but to oversexed beer commercials from other breweries as well. A watchdog group called the Center for Science in the Public Interest announced its yearly awards for 1991's most "unfair, misleading and irresponsible" television commercials and specifically named the Swedish Bikini Team spots for "associating sexual conquest with drinking."

Did the Stroh's ads go too far? A lot of people, both men and women, thought so. The Stroh's Brewery brain trust listened to protesting voices, realized the company was about to reap more embarrassment than sales and eventually phased out the commercials. The Swedish Bikini Team vanished into the oblivion of canceled ad campaigns.

But the Old Milwaukee spots weren't the first to use a wink and a leer to sell a product, nor will they be the last. There's a popular belief on Madison Avenue that "sex sells!" Grabbing the consumer's attention with sexual themes and undraped bodies may be more prevalent today than ever before, but advertisers have relied on sex appeal as a sales device for years. Sex is one of the stronger emotional appeals, right up there with health, motherhood and patriotism.

Perhaps the most famous double-entendre ad of them all featured a blond Swedish bombshell named Gunilla Knutson, who nibbled on a string of pearls in 1965 while watching her man shave with Noxzema medicated cream to stripper music and begged him to "Take it off. Take it all off." The sensuous ad caused a national stir and made both Noxzema and Knutson famous.

Most television commercials are carefully planned. Not so with this one. Noxzema (now the Noxell Corporation) was a small, unknown shaving cream company barely keeping its head above water when ad expert Bill Grathwohl was given the ad account in 1956. Grathwohl spent the next nine years operating on a budget so small that he could advertise in only two cities at a time, but the product seemed to do well in the cities where the ads ran using the line, "The closer you shave, the more you need Noxzema." Finally, in 1965, working with a new advertising agency, William Esty Company, Grathwohl was kicking ideas around with the head copywriter who suggested a new musical background, David Rose's famous old burlesque song, "The Stripper."

The music sounded great, and they decided to do a facial strip tease, with a male model timing his strokes to the strains of the music. The concept went to storyboards and then to production. Everyone at Esty liked the rough cut, but there was something missing. Someone suggested a girl. Gunilla Knutson, Miss Sweden of 1961, who had been trying unsuccessfully to break into modeling, happened to be sitting in the casting reception office. There was no talent search or long list of auditions. The casting director, in a hurry, spotted Knutson and told her to come back the next morning to try the lines and test in front of the camera. Knutson's Swedish-accented whisper, "Take it off. Take it all off," sent Noxzema stock soaring. The rest is history.

half-hour paid program designed to push one specific product—a lipstick, a shampoo, a slicer and dicer or a fitness machine, such as the Thighmaster. Like the print versions, these electronic commercials are designed to look like news or entertainment programs. Famous faces carry on as if they are guests on a talk show. Somber men and women deliver mock news. Chefs burble amusing patter while sharing their cooking secrets. Satisfied customers gush about how their lives have changed. Surprisingly, people watch, and then they spend money on the products. Infomercials generated some $750 billion in sales in 1991 for their sponsors. One of the sponsors, Richard Simmons, grossed $40 million all by himself after showing off his "Deal-a-Meal" diet plan.

Blurring the line between editorial content and television programming on the one hand and advertising on the other no doubt concerns many people. But as long as advertising dollars are short and the advertising pitch works, expect to see more advertorials and infomercials.

Media Selection

No amount of excellent technique will work, however, if the messages fail to reach the proper potential consumers. Some choices are obvious. An ad for Pampers or baby food would be out of place in a man's magazine like *Playboy* or a teen magazine like *Seventeen*. Retirement centers and investment counselors would waste time and breath advertising on MTV or the Saturday morning network cartoon ghetto. Back-to-school clothes would be equally out of place in *Dynamic Years* or *Field and Stream*.

Media selection requires training, sophistication and business acumen. It also calls for an experienced working knowledge of media outlets, since no two media plans are alike. There are nearly 1,700 daily newspapers in the United States alone, not to mention about 8,000 weekly newspapers, 10,000 or so magazines, close to 1,000 commercial television stations and another 7,000 radio stations. A media buyer must determine not only which media units are most likely to reach proposed target audiences, but also how to budget them at the lowest possible cpm (cost per thousand), which represents the cost to the advertiser for every thousand readers, viewers or listeners. A good media planner must keep in mind the following media factors.

Print Media. Words, not images, are still the advertiser's greatest tool. Newspapers and magazines offer the versatility and space to develop a message in depth, and the message doesn't disappear after 30 seconds on the air. Since advertising is used to convey information, print media usually form the backbone of any strong ad campaign.

Daily newspapers are still considered kings in the world of retail advertising. Because they are local in nature, geographical audiences are easier to target. Flexible deadlines allow last-minute changes. Ad copy can be read and reread, at least for the life of the newspaper. Coupons offering special bargains can be inserted in the ads. Newspapers also accept pre-printed tabloid advertising inserts.

Magazines offer greater selectivity in audiences. Since most modern magazines are targeted to a specialized group of readers, it becomes easier for advertisers to pick a precise publication aimed directly at a specific group that matches a consumer profile. Magazines are also more permanent than newspapers, so the ads have a longer life and increased chances of being read. Color is also better in magazines than in newspapers, but magazine deadlines close earlier, ruling out most last-minute changes. In addition, it's hard to isolate a geographical audience unless a magazine offers regional zoning (as do *Time* and *TV Guide*).

Both newspapers and magazines bill according to the amount of space used, based on the circulation of the publication. Newspapers charge by the column inch. Magazines charge by the page or fraction of page. Newspaper and magazine ad rates vary according to size of the ad, frequency, use of color, and position in the publication. Costs can also go up for special effects. If you're willing to pay, you can add odor to the ad, thanks to scratch-and-sniff polymer scents. Magazines can give you die-cut windows opening to following pages or pop-up cutouts that rise above the page. Experiments are now underway to prepare computer-programmed advertising that will print a subscriber's name directly into an ad ("Hello there, Joan Student. Can you see yourself behind the wheel of this Buick Zippo-6?").

Electronic Media. Some campaigns are designed entirely around electronic presentation. But even if a campaign leans heavily on print media, electronic media can be used as excellent supplementary vehicles. Radio and television can give you super music in the background as a selling device, or mini-dramas with dialogue and emotion, or testimonials by celebrities whose voices are instantly recognizable. Television offers such added advantages as huge audiences, sophisticated filming techniques, cartoon and computer animation, color and imagery capable of evoking strong emotion, and actual product demonstration (especially useful with products that show well in motion—cars accelerating from 0 to 60 in a cloud of dust,

A commercial artist prepares an advertisement.

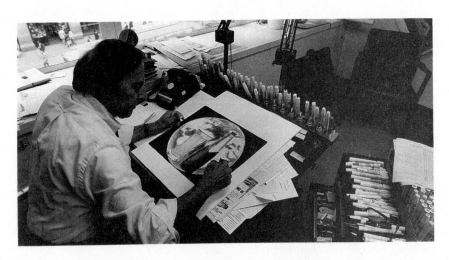

Ad executives look over a storyboard for a television commercial in production.

hand drills and band saws performing household miracles, children's toys crawling over miniature hills and roads, and the latest athletic hero slurping up a bowl of Wheaties). On the disadvantage side, radio and television ads are fleeting. If a viewer or listener leaves the room or shuts off the set, the message is lost. And, since commercials are usually bunched together, there is a "clutter" effect that weakens audience attention. If a commercial isn't carefully constructed to grab the audience member by the ear or the eyeball, the message may be ignored. The viewer may choose to visit the refrigerator or the bathroom or, as you learned in Chapter 9, if the program is recorded on a video machine, the viewer may resort to "zipping" and "zapping."

Radio and television bill on the basis of time units (15 seconds, 30 seconds and 60 seconds) and size of the audience. Network time can be very expensive, depending on the hour and popularity of the broadcast. Prime-time programs, with their big audiences, are the most expensive. The average prime-time 30-second commercial will cost about $120,000. The price is higher for hit programs ("Murphy Brown" has gone as high as $350,000 per 30-second spot) and lower for duds (some are lucky to get $50,000). Daytime soaps and late-night talk shows cost less (the Arsenio Hall show has charged $20,000 per 30-second spot, and NBC's "Tonight Show" has sold spots for $35,000). But if a national audience is guaranteed to be huge, it doesn't matter what time of day the program is aired, the price goes way up. The 1993 Super Bowl, for example, pulled in between $850,000 and $900,000 for each 30-second spot.

Time units can also be purchased on the local level for both radio and television. Not only are local spots cheaper, they are often far more sensible. If you were Goodyear Tire, for example, and you wanted to demonstrate a new snow tire, you would be wasting half of your money on network time since people in Southern states don't buy snow tires. It would be smarter to place your ads in key Northern cities.

Billboards. We've all seen billboards. They stack up in a jumble on busy city streets, hiding trees and buildings. They clutter the countryside like crazy-quilt sails, blocking the view. On long, boring trips, children use them to play travel games such as alphabet, searching for ad messages that use the tougher letters—*j, q,* and *z.* Vandals use them for target practice or as canvases for spray-paint greetings. No one reads them, right? Wrong. Think back to your last long automobile jaunt. Hungry? You looked for burger signs or ice cream stops. Time to spare? Signs may have encouraged you to stop in to see the "whatsit monster" at a roadside zoo, to pull off to check out the ruin of an old fort, or to buy Indian jewelry and souvenirs. And after a long day of driving, when you were tired and ready to stop, you started looking for motel and restaurant signs, didn't you?

Billboards can be highway displays designed to attract the attention of travelers or city signs calculated to take advantage of traffic patterns. If they are placed well and properly lighted, they can offer their messages on a 24-hour basis, in all kinds of weather. Anyone who passes will be exposed to the message, though not everyone will read it. Billboards may not have the informative depth of newspaper or magazine ads, nor the impact of radio and television, but they can be a superior way to reach anyone who drives, and in our modern, far-flung society there are few who don't. Politicians and travel-oriented products find them especially valuable. Charges come in the form of rental. An advertiser pays so much per month, based on location and the number of potential exposures of the billboard.

Direct Mail. Direct mail is a real comer in the advertising business; the very words cause print media executives to cringe. And why not? Direct mail income is growing every year, usually at the expense of a local newspaper. Direct mail pieces are the flyers, coupons and catalogs that come directly to your door, stuffed in your mailbox by your neighborhood mail deliverer. Advertisers get their materials printed by an independent printer and pass them along to a mailing service that attaches labels. They are then put into the mail system as third-class matter and delivered. This form of advertising has one very distinct advantage—total saturation. An advertiser can reach every single household in any given zip code. No other advertising medium can make the same guarantee.

The only problem is that direct-mail advertising can be pretty expensive, depending on how wide a mailing is sent out. Each piece costs a set rate, depending on weight and the escalating costs of postage, so there is no discount break for larger or more frequent mailings, as is usually the case with newspapers and magazines. A new cost-cutting kink is the device known as **marriage mail,** in which a mailing service may combine as many as 20 or 30 unrelated advertising messages and coupons together in one envelope. The coupons are almost mandatory. Most recipients wouldn't bother to shuffle through the messages unless there were some promise of recompense or savings among the clutter.

Specialized magazines have been filtering into the American media system for years. But it wasn't until the collapse of the major general-interest magazines that specialized publications assumed a position of almost total dominance in the magazine field. Why? A big part of the answer is advertising. Since television ad rates are so high, and since specialized magazines automatically target specific audiences, an advertiser with a clearly defined market and a limited budget can make effective use of them.

Let's use an extreme example. Say you're a dog-crate manufacturer who has just come up with a new air-conditioned crate for Doberman Pinschers, perfect for airline use. Where do you advertise? Network television will cost you a bundle, from $100,000 to $150,000 for a 30-second spot. Your audience would be huge, admittedly, and you might even reach a few Doberman owners. But each of them will cost you an arm and a leg. You could try *Time* magazine, but you'll have the same problem—lots of readers, most of whom are not Doberman owners. And a four-color page in *Time* will set you back about $120,000. A black-and-white ad is pretty expensive, too, at $77,000. You could try one of the all-breed dog magazines, like *Dog World* or the *AKC* (American Kennel Club) *Gazette*. Ad rates will be considerably cheaper, and you'll be dealing primarily with dog owners. But for an even better bargain, suppose you go directly to one of the small-circulation magazines designed specifically for Doberman fanciers, like *Doberman Quarterly* or *Doberman World* (yes, both magazines really do exist). *Doberman Quarterly* is a slick, handsome magazine that goes to 3,000 committed Doberman owners, and a four-color page will cost you only $600. A black-and-white page is a steal at only $115. See why advertisers are so fond of the magazine trend toward specialization?

It works across the board. If you're selling a mass product like toothpaste or cigarettes or soft drinks, then television or newspapers or the big circulation magazines may still be best. But if you want to sell special-interest products, such as surfboards, model-train kits or duck decoys, you go where the high-potential audiences are already primed—to magazines like *Surfer* or *Model Railroader* or *Waterfowler's World*. You get the specific readers you want at much lower cost per thousand.

Videotapes. The 1990s brought another new wrinkle in direct-mail advertising—the videotaped pitch. With television commercials reaching the saturation point, ad agencies started looking for new ideas to catch the attention of consumers. Since videocassettes are often cheaper (about $2 each) than expensively printed catalogs, and close to 70 percent of all American homes now have VCRs, the videos made sense. Advertisers of luxury products such as jewelry, clothing and perfumes started putting together taped video sales pitches. Estée Lauder sent out some 250,000 copies of a brief video promoting a new perfume, SpellBound, direct to the consumer's door, in mass mailings to homes in high-income neighborhoods. Car companies sent out another half-million to show off a new van. Still other videos were available to anyone who called or wrote to express an interest.

It sounds like a great way to accumulate free videotapes, but before you start dialing those 800 numbers to request free video commercials, convinced you can record over them with your favorite movie or TV sitcom, be aware that most of these messages are brief, anywhere from 2 minutes to 12 minutes, and the tapes that carry them are short, too. It's cheaper that way.

T-Shirts and Bumper Stickers. One last set of advertising media is worth consideration. These are the *novelty items*—key chains, wallet and wall calendars, appointment books, mugs, books of matches, pencils, ballpoint pens, baseball caps, campaign buttons and any of the hundreds of other giveaway products that sport free advertising. Look at your own pens and pencils. You've probably got a few that make some commercial statement. Or take a look at the T-shirts around you the next time you're in class or in a large crowd. You'll see a dazzling array of commercial and noncommercial messages, including some that probably aren't fit for mixed company.

Keeping the Monster on Leash

Without advertising and the many mass-media vehicles that carry advertising messages, the wheels of the American economic system would grind to a halt. Advertising keeps the economic wheels greased by informing consumers of available goods and demonstrating the advantages of buying those goods. But even symbolic grease can get dirty. Remember, advertising messages can lie or mislead. Consumers, once bitten, may mistrust even honest ads. And that hurts the whole industry. To protect consumers and the reputation and integrity of scrupulous advertisers, a number of controls have been fashioned. Some come from the government. Some have been formulated within the industry. In addition, consumer groups and other outsiders, including the media themselves, are always ready to exert pressure on any advertiser or advertising message that seems to skirt the ethical edge of these controls.

Self-Regulation

There may be a fair share of selfishness in self-regulation. It works two ways. In the first place, most advertising people are serious about cleaning up their own act. Without consumer confidence, advertising won't work. And the best way to improve product credibility is to pressure industry members to avoid deceptive ads and unfair practices. At the same time, advertisers are quick to realize that a moderately successful program of self-regulation means that the government is less likely to step in with tougher restrictions. Anyone who's ever paid taxes knows that government regulations are seldom flexible. It's too easy to end up in court or find oneself scrapping an expensive ad campaign because of some little provision that no one noticed.

At least three industry organizations—the American Association of Advertising Agencies, the Advertising Federation of America and the Association of National Advertisers—have adopted an ethical code of conduct drawn up by the National Better Business Bureau. Called "The Advertising Code of American Business," the code contains four main provisions dealing with truthfulness, accuracy, responsibility and decency. The code's provisions aren't binding on members, the way that government laws and regulations would be, but they are effective. If responsible agencies or independent advertisers stray beyond industry guidelines, peer pressure usually drives them back.

Outside Regulation

Outside controls in the form of group pressure can come from many quarters, including customers, religious organizations, political action groups, and parent/teacher associations. Advertisers are usually sensitive to organized public pressure, especially if it might prove damaging to the company's reputation or, worse yet, profits. Try writing an angry letter to a manufacturer some day. You'll see how quickly you get a response. The response may not satisfy you, but few businesses will ignore you. Multiply that letter by enlisting the aid of like-thinking individuals, and you may get better results. The more people writing, the bigger the impression you'll make. Pressure groups frequently use letter-writing campaigns. They also take their causes to the press in an attempt to sway public opinion. Or maybe they just set up a few picket lines to show their displeasure. But the big gun, the main weapon of pressure groups, is the economic boycott. Nothing can force an advertiser back in line faster than an organized and successful refusal to buy his or her goods and services.

Media can also exert control from outside the industry by refusing to accept dubious and borderline ads. Some print media, concerned about their own reputations, regularly review advertising materials and insist on proof of extravagant claims before they'll run them. Many newspapers and magazines won't accept ads for X-rated movies. Those that do carry them often alter the ads, airbrushing extra clothing onto the illustrations or changing the format to exclude material considered to be in poor taste. The

Future Focus Some Predictions About Advertising

- Audience members will be more sophisticated by the year 2000 and will become increasingly resentful of the heavy-handed, repetitive, intrusive, and disruptive nature of some advertisements.

- People will protest more and even boycott products when advertising insults and defrauds. Advertisers, however, will escalate their own sophistication and lessen the obvious weaknesses of their techniques.

- Government will play a more important role in controlling advertising—especially on television.

- Prospects of TV advertisement improvements are not good, with programming continuing to be largely controlled by and for advertisers and agencies.

- Political advertising, already out of hand, will steadily increase—making media richer and the voting public more exasperated.

- Newspapers will get thicker, padded largely by advertising, and by the end of the 20th century the proportion of advertising in American newspapers will be up to 70 percent of the total space.

- Advertisers will talk more and more about ethics, but as it has been with news people, little will change.

- Advertising, if it does continue to proliferate and dominate the media, will serve as a chief catalyst for increasing intellectual criticism of capitalism.

major television networks are even touchier about taste. They have provided advertisers with detailed lists of items that they won't allow in commercials. You can sell aspirin and cold pills and talk about them, but you can't show people popping pills into their mouths. You can advertise beer and wine, but you had better not show someone actually lifting glass to mouth and drinking. As for hard liquor, forget it. Gin, bourbon and vodka are verboten. So are fortune tellers and astrologists. Toilet paper? Feminine hygiene products? Sure, up to a point. Mr. Whipple can squeeze the life out of a roll of toilet paper and Cathy Rigby can talk all she wants about tampons, but don't show the toilet paper hanging in the bathroom or hold up one of those tampons where the viewer can see it. Neither visual is allowed.

Government Regulation

Why should the government exert any controls at all on advertising? Doesn't the First Amendment guarantee free speech? Yes, but there are limits. It depends on what is being advertised. As recently as 1976, the Supreme Court confirmed a "commercial speech" doctrine, ruling that while *idea* advertising may fall under the protective umbrella of the First Amendment, *product* advertising does not. That means a politician seeking public office may prepare a paid television advertisement full of bald-faced lies and get away with it. Commercial products have to be advertised more carefully.

Government regulation of ads is very complex, mainly because there are so many different agencies that can get into the act. It started with the Federal Trade Commission as an extension of business regulation, a way to combat unfair trade practices (remember the patent medicines?). The FTC used its power to protect consumers as well, regulating consumer product ads for almost 20 years. Then, in 1931, the Supreme Court said the FTC charter didn't include consumers and that the agency couldn't punish a phony fat cure unless it could show that competing dietary products were being hurt. Amendments to the Federal Trade Commission Act of 1938 put the FTC back to work by including consumer protection and allowing the prohibition of unfair and deceptive advertising. The FTC now regularly peruses advertising messages for factual content (advertisers must document their claims), clarity, taste, misleading demonstrations and proper explanation of warranties. And in 1978, the Supreme Court armed the FTC with another weapon, the authority to require expensive remedial advertising to correct false or misleading claims.

The FTC is the major federal guardian against unfair advertising practices, but it isn't the only one. The Federal Communications Commission often exerts direct influence on broadcast advertising. Government control and/or pressure can also come from the Food and Drug Administration, the Post Office, the Patent Office, the Internal Revenue Service, the Public Health Service, and the Securities and Exchange Commission. That's a lot of peeled eyes watching out for the consumer's interests.

Even so, perhaps the best way for the individual consumer to avoid disappointment in a product is to approach advertising warily. Be a smart consumer. If a television commercial or a print advertisement catches your attention with a product that interests you, watch it or read it over carefully. Approach it with suspicion. Check the language for vague, meaningless phrases. Be aware of emotional appeals. Use your knowledge and experience to test each claim. If the ad makes good sense and offers attributes that are useful to you, go ahead and buy the product. If the ad seems flawed in any way, or if the product doesn't really fit your needs, use self-control and consign the ad to the junk heap. Everybody will be happier. The honest advertiser will love you for paying such close attention to all those carefully selected words, particularly if you buy the product, and you'll like yourself for being a smarter consumer.

And you might as well get used to it. Advertising is here to stay. Those commercials keep showing . . . and showing . . . and showing. . . .

Retrospective

Modern advertising is based on mass production and is used as part of the marketing process to create an audience of buyers. An important corollary is that advertising pays for a sizable share of the information made available to an information-hungry society.

Advertising agencies range in size but generally provide clients with *account management, creative services, market research* and *media buying*. Some of the strategies developed over the years by advertising agencies are the *unique selling proposition* (for parity products), *brand image* (image or status advertising), *motivational research* (empathy advertising), *subliminal advertising* (below the conscious threshold of perception), and *positioning* (segmenting the audience).

Media selection is important to advertisers. There are advantages and disadvantages to print and electronic media, as well as to some of the lesser-known advertising vehicles.

Because advertising is so competitive, regulation is often necessary. It comes from advertisers themselves, from media and pressure groups, and from the government.

Questions

1. Why is advertising important to the American economic system? To American mass media? To the consumer?

2. Why did early advertising earn such a shady reputation? How was that reputation corrected? Or do you think it has been?

3. Who benefitted most from the first ad agencies—media, advertisers, or consumers? Why did the focus of those agencies eventually change?

4. What brought about the development of brand names and trademarks? How do you think such devices might eventually affect the quality of products?

5. Name the four most likely services to be found in a modern full-service ad agency. If you had to choose one of the four as the most important, which would it be? Why?

6. A number of advertising strategies were developed in the 1950s and 1960s. Name and describe at least four of them. Which do you think would be the most effective today? Why?

Suggested Readings

Arlen, M. J. *Thirty Seconds*. New York: Farrar, Straus & Giroux, 1980.

Busch, H. T., and Landeck, Terry. *The Making of a Television Commercial*. New York: Macmillan, 1980.

Buxton, Edward. *Promise Them Anything*. New York: Stein and Day, 1972.

Della Femina, Jerry. *From Those Wonderful Folks Who Gave You Pearl Harbor*. New York: Simon & Schuster, 1970.

Gartner, Michael. *Advertising and the First Amendment*. Winchester, Ma.: Priority Press (Unwin Hyman Media Studies), 1988.

Miller, E. G. *The Art of Advertising*. New York: St. Martin's Press, 1980.

Nelson, Roy Paul. *The Design of Advertising*. Dubuque, Iowa: Wm. C. Brown, 1977.

Ogilvy, David. *Confessions of an Advertising Man*. New York: Atheneum, 1963.

Patti, Charles, and Frazer, Charles. *Advertising: A Decision-Making Approach*. Hinsdale, Ill.: The Dryden Press, 1988.

Price, Jonathon. *The Best Thing on TV*. New York: Viking, 1978.

Ries, Al, and Trout, Jack. *Positioning: The Battle for Your Mind*. New York: Warner Books, Inc., 1986.

Rosden, George, and Rosden, Peter. *The Law of Advertising*. New York: Matthew Bender & Co., 1987.

Turnbull, Arthur, and Baird, Russell. *The Graphics of Communication*. New York: Holt, Rinehart and Winston, 1980.

Public Relations

The mountain stillness of Eureka Springs, a little town nestled in northwest Arkansas' Ozark Mountains, was shattered recently with the roar of hundreds of huge Harley-Davidson motorcycles. The thunderous Harleys were in Eureka Springs because their owners— some 500 members of the notorious Hell's Angels motorcycle club—had selected the quaint Victorian village for a week-long national convention.

If the visit to Eureka Springs had been a recipe for a cake, it might have read:

> Take one rural Arkansas town with 1,900 apprehensive citizens and add 500 Hell's Angels. Stir the Hell's Angels and the citizens together well. Add extra measures of steely, heavily armed state police and sheriff's deputies. Mix with nosy reporters from three states. Bake well and wait for the results.

The Angels settled in at a campground five miles west of town. The reporters, who wanted to discover why the Angels had picked the isolated community for a national meeting, gathered at the campground gate to shell them with questions. And that's when the Angels gave incredulous reporters the awful news: "We aren't allowed to talk to you," Angel after Angel said. "You'll need to talk to our *PR* man. He'll be around later in the week. We'll call you."

The garrulous, omnipresent public relations counsel, long a fixture in business, government and entertainment circles, had infiltrated the world of outlaw motorcycle clubs. One appalled newspaper reporter summed it up in a story this way: "Here's another sign of the impending Apocalypse: The Hell's Angels have a PR person."

Public Relations: What Is It?

What could a PR person do for the Hell's Angels? the reporters wondered. And you may ask, what exactly is PR?

Fair questions both. Let's answer the last first. Edward L. Bernays, considered by many to be one of the two founders of PR (the other is Ivy Ledbetter Lee, whom you'll meet a little later), explained PR this way in his 1923 landmark book, *Crystallizing Public Opinion:* Public relations, Bernays wrote, is the "engineering of public consent." Scott Cutlip, one of America's leading PR scholars, defined the field more formally some years later. He wrote, "Public relations is the planned effort to influence public opinion through good character and responsible performance, based upon mutually satisfactory two-way communication." Building on the definitions by Bernays and Cutlip, many practitioners in the 1990s agree that **public relations (PR)** is an umbrella term for a series of complex activities that include the *measurement and evaluation of attitudes* about an individual, product, company, institution or concept, and the *use of various techniques to influence those attitudes*.

Let's explore the definitions offered by Bernays, Cutlip and contemporary practitioners in more detail.

Hell's Angels member, in regalia.

Typically, PR uses a four-step process. The first step is a formal or informal gathering of information, such as a measurement of public opinion. In short, it's listening; it's *research*. Step two is *planning*. The plan may be short- or long-term and may involve modifying the organization as well as influencing public opinion about the organization. The plan itself comes next—call this the *communication* step—and it is here that many familiar PR tools are used, including news or press releases, press kits, publications, videotapes, news conferences, interviews, speeches and special events. *Evaluation* or measurement of results is the final step. The results often lead PR practitioners back to the first step, which means that the process is continual.

Now, let's apply this process to the Hell's Angels and their visit to Eureka Springs. Let's assume that you are the Angels' PR counsel and it's a month before your clients' visit. You don't have to be a rocket scientist to know that your clients suffer from what politicians and pollsters call a "high negative rating." You suspect the reason may be that members of various chapters had been charged with numerous crimes over the years. Too, there's probably an overall image problem, thanks to those 1960s and 1970s biker movies that featured fierce, barrel-chested, bearded motorcyclists who pulled motorists from four-door sedans and beat them senseless for staring without permission.

But if you were the Angels' PR counsel, you still might undertake a public opinion survey to see if specific constituencies or "publics" were neutral or positive in their attitudes and *why* unfriendly publics felt the way they did. The Angels would have six major nonorganization or *external* publics with which to contend: the police, city officials, merchants, tourists, townsfolk and reporters. If you informally surveyed these publics, you might discover that the Angels were feared more than they were disliked and that they were feared because they drove huge, noisy motorcycles, had long hair and beards, and wore motorcycle jackets adorned with flying skulls.

Based on your information, you concoct your plan, which is the second step in the four-step process. Remember that PR is a two-way procedure. The counsel passes on the attitudes of the publics to the organization—in this case, to Angel leaders—and, in turn, provides the publics with the organization's views. At its simplest, you might recommend that the Angels leave the motorcycles at home and dress more conservatively—say, Bermuda shorts and flowered shirts.

Organizations, however, sometimes elect not to change, so you adopt another plan. You will send an advance team to Eureka Springs to meet with police, city officials, merchants and the local media. The advance team will provide these external publics with positive information about club members—for example, that a group of former bomber pilots created the Angels in 1948 and that most members have jobs and families. In addition, the team will tell the publics the Angels will obey the law, stay at an isolated campground and have little contact with tourists or townsfolk. Finally, as a gesture of goodwill, the Angels will make a donation to the city police benevolent fund. Club members, an *internal* public, will also have to be told about the promises made to the external publics. If the Angels approve of your plan, you move to step three and execute it, and then to the final step, evaluation of the results.

Public Relations Yesterday

If public relations at its simplest is presenting yourself or your ideas in the best possible light to neutralize criticism, the field is as old as human communication. Greek poets wrote verses of praise for those who needed it and could afford it; they also publicized the ancient Olympics. Later, Julius Caesar, leading his army in what is now Spain, France and Great Britain, commissioned written "Commentaries" about his military efforts in order to maintain his popularity at home. The first Christians publicized Jesus Christ's work, and later the Catholic Church created an organization called the Sacred Congregation for Propagating the Faith for similar purposes.

A Brief History: From Poetry to P. T. Barnum

As printing became cheaper, pamphlets, books and newspapers—the mass media of their time—were used to promote people and philosophical positions. For example, U.S. revolutionaries such as Sam Adams and Thomas Jefferson used the mass media and reports about events (such as the staged Boston Tea Party and the unstaged Boston Massacre) to whip up sentiment for a break with Great Britain. American presidents used the press to drum up support for the Mexican War and later the Civil War. And then there was Phineas T. Barnum, whose name is synonymous with the circus

1773	The Boston Tea Party, a staged event, is used to whip up sentiment against repressive tax law.	1903	Ivy Ledbetter Lee opens public relations firm, is called in to help John D. Rockefeller after muckraking Standard Oil magazine series.
1842	P. T. Barnum opens his American Museum in New York and instantly becomes famous for his extravagant claims.	1909	American Newspaper Publishers Association warns members about dangers of publicists.
1883	William Frederick Cody is heavily promoted through dime novels, organizes Buffalo Bill's Wild West Show.	1923	Edward Bernays is first to call himself *public relations counsel.*
1896	Posters and publicity move into politics in McKinley/Bryan presidential race.	1948	Public Relations Society of America is formed from earlier organizations.

and with "press agentry," with getting free media coverage even at the expense of the truth. Barnum manipulated the media perhaps more effectively than any other 19th-century American. In doing so, he refined what scholar Daniel J. Boorstin has called the "pseudoevent," an occurrence, such as a circus parade, that is staged *mainly* because it will be reported.

But these exploits are *not* examples of modern public relations. They are parts of the whole, examples of simple persuasion and, later, sophisticated "press agentry" (or what today would be called "publicity"). Today's PR—listening carefully to what is being said and then carefully crafting numerous tools (one of which is publicity or free media coverage) to responsibly modify those attitudes—is really only a century old.

Lee, Bernays and the Modern Era

Public relations has been called an American invention. That is arguable, but no one can deny that it was in an expanding United States, home to huge corporations that exploited the wilderness while building great cities and vast railroad networks, that the first sophisticated practitioners of the art came forward. One such man was Ivy Ledbetter Lee.

Lee, a Princeton University graduate and a former *New York Times* reporter, opened his public relations firm, then called a "publicity bureau," in 1903. The publicity bureau trend perhaps had its beginnings in 1888 when the Mutual Life Insurance Company hired a former newspaper reporter to write news releases. Westinghouse Corporation created a somewhat bigger corporate publicity department in 1889, and by 1900 many large corporations had in-house publicity offices. Some organizations, however, turned to outside businesses to handle publicity chores; in 1900 the first such major, independent firm, the Publicity Bureau, was created in Boston. It was Lee's model. Lee's approach, however, was unusual in that as his counseling practice grew, he became convinced that he needed to meet a client's total PR needs rather than concentrate only on obtaining pos-

Public relations pioneer Ivy Lee.

itive newspaper and magazine coverage, as many of the publicity bureaus did.

Within a few years, Lee had several important clients, including the Pennsylvania Railroad and John D. Rockefeller Jr. Businesses and business-people such as Rockefeller badly needed Lee's services because segments of the public had turned against firms and people who displayed callousness toward employees and consumers. Some of the public's coldness toward business was traceable to successful attacks on corporations by investigative reporters working for muckraking magazines such as *McClure's*. Theodore Roosevelt, who became president in the fall of 1901, was also a factor in the public's skeptical attitude toward business because he favored rigorous antitrust prosecution and legislation to regulate railroad rates and food and drug manufacturing.

Lee told his clients that they would be well served to serve the public well and that they should provide the media with fast and accurate information when newsworthy accidents or incidents occurred. In addition, he insisted that his PR efforts have the support of top management. And he meant what he said. For example, when Lee was retained by the Pennsylvania Railroad after a derailment, he persuaded management to take reporters to the scene and provide full information, an unprecedented concept that eventually gained the railroad better media relations.

Still, like modern public relations representatives, Lee was not without his critics. For example, the American Newspaper Publishers Association in 1909 created a committee to educate its members about the dangers of publicists. Pulitzer Prize-winning poet Carl Sandburg said of Lee regarding his work for Rockefeller during a bloody strike in Colorado: "It was coarse. It was cheap. It was done by the cunning, slimy brain of a cunning, slimy charlatan. . . ."

While Lee and others were refining their art, a first cousin of public relations called *public information* was born as a result of two separate federal government actions. First, Congress passed a law in 1913 that prohibited the government from hiring PR or publicity professionals but permitted agencies to employ public information representatives. The concept was that public information specialists would provide information without persuasion. The second government action spotlighting public information was the creation of a committee headed by a former journalist named George Creel to drum up public support for America's entry into World War I in 1917. It was technically known as the Committee on Public Information but was quickly dubbed the Creel Committee. The creation of this committee somewhat obscured the distinction between public information and what would come to be called PR because the group, despite its official name, eschewed the more narrow concept of public information and successfully urged support of the draft, purchase of war bonds and conservation of commodities in short supply.

Many public relations professionals assisted Creel, among them Edward Bernays who, as you have already read, is considered one of the founders of PR. Bernays, who in 1923 first used the name *public relations counsel,* echoed Lee's concept that the public relations professional must be a part of the management team in order to guarantee full support of all approved policies. He continued to influence his profession with counseling, lecturing, seminars and books even into the 1990s.

The development of public opinion polling techniques in the 1930s,

---

A Critic's Critique

Ben Bagdikian, a U.S. journalism critic, makes these observations about public relations and the news media:

- About 80 percent of a newspaper's news-editorial content originates with the news source itself.
- News organizations consider this situation "harmless and profitable."
- PR people know that the media have limited resources and are glad to get "free" help, and they take advantage of this knowledge.
- PR executives are the real news decision-makers. They know they are more important than newspaper editors.
- PR people are in the business of creating news that puts their clients in a favorable light.
- PR people are like stage managers—turning up their lights when it is to their best interests and dimming them when it serves the purpose not to let the audience see too clearly.
- The truth is this: Public relations people are doing their job when they do PR. Media people often do PR themselves and they are hypocrites.
- News media staffers need to know much more about PR, about its strategies and tactics. The press needs to be more discriminating and ruthless in its selection of PR material.

Source: Ben H. Bagdikian, *The Effete Conspiracy and Other Crimes of the Press* (New York: Harper & Row, 1972).

Tylenol brand pain reliever is removed from store shelves after fatal poisoning incidents in 1982. Johnson & Johnson, which makes Tylenol, gets good treatment from the media because its officials are candid.

1940s and 1950s further aided the field, but make no mistake: Lee, Bernays and other PR pioneers have not legitimized the profession in the eyes of many journalists, even in the 1990s. Many journalists—especially those who see themselves as virginal truth-seekers—consider PR practitioners to be their adversaries. These journalists refer to PR representatives as "flacks" or informational prostitutes (but they usually use a less polite word) who have sold their talents to the highest bidder with little regard for the truth of their information.

On the other hand, many PR practitioners see their role as that of a client's attorney in the court of public opinion. PR professionals say that everyone is presumed to be innocent until proven guilty under the American system of justice and that the PR practitioner is simply a skillful lawyer pleading a client's case before the jury of public opinion. To put it another way, professional PR people help guarantee a story's balance, and a balanced story is good for the media, consumers and the organization, practitioners explain. To support this, practitioners frequently cite Johnson & Johnson's PR approach in 1982 when someone poisoned its popular Tylenol pain reliever with cyanide, killing a number of people and ultimately leading to the withdrawal of 31 million bottles of the product. Johnson & Johnson was candid and open with the media and in return received fair treatment, both PR and media observers agree.

In addition, PR people proudly point to studies that show that perhaps half of the stories in newspapers and a lesser amount on radio and television newscasts are generated by PR sources, which they say means that public relations people perform an important societal role in getting basic information to readers, viewers and listeners.

Because of the controversy over their role and in an effort at self-improvement, American PR practitioners have launched a campaign to polish up their own public image. The campaign is being led largely by the Public Relations Society of America and the International Association of Business Communicators. PRSA and IABC hold numerous seminars and short courses for members and accredit them. Of PRSA's more than 15,000 members, about 4,000 are accredited. Accredited members must have at least five years' experience, pass a grueling written and oral exam (which one Southwestern U.S. member called the ". . . worst experience of my life except for childbirth") and submit to a code of ethics with the possibility of censure by peers. IABC also has more than 12,000 members and a difficult accreditation exam, but few IABC members are thus far accredited because IABC's process is newer.

Structure of the U.S. Public Relations Industry

Bernays has pointed out that PR people use at least 62 different titles. These include director or manager of communication, community affairs, corporate communication, public affairs, public information, public issues and publicity. Because of the variety of titles by which PR practitioners may be known, it's difficult to determine exactly how many PR people are at work in the United States.

Still, U.S. government and industry statistics provide some hints. Be forewarned, however: Statistics about the number of practitioners are misleading because many people call themselves public relations representatives who are, in fact, customer service representatives or even door-to-door salespersons. Still, the industry sources suggest that about 400,000 full-time PR people in the 1990s were employed by U.S. advertising agencies, PR firms, government and military agencies, social service and nonprofit groups, cultural organizations and foundations and businesses. Twenty percent of those PR representatives are in government service—either in civil service or in the military—and are usually labeled *public information* or *public affairs* specialists. The rest of the work force is scattered among PR

Women in Public Relations

Women have been very successful in entering agency and corporate public relations in recent years. As evidence, look no further than the membership rolls of the Public Relations Society of America and the International Association of Business Communicators. More than half of PRSA's members are female (a percentage larger than the percentage of women in the U.S. work force), and more than 6 of 10 IABC members are women.

Even more women will enter PR in the 1990s, if U.S. college and university enrollment patterns are reliable predictors. Public relations is a particularly popular area of study for women in journalism and mass communication programs, and two-thirds of the students in those programs are female.

firms, advertising agencies with PR departments, businesses, associations, not-for-profit organizations, political campaign groups and unions.

Many of these public relations professionals, whether in the public or private sector, try to conduct business using *management by objectives*. MBO, in short, requires that tasks be planned and executed so as to allow results to be specifically measured. For example, if a company's goal is to make 25 percent of the adult population of the city where its plant is located aware of its presence, a PR professional can conduct a public opinion poll before and after a campaign to measure attainment of the objective.

Let's look at the two biggest employers: PR firms (or ad agencies with PR departments) and major corporations.

The Public Relations Agency

There are several thousand public relations firms in the United States. They range in order of fee income in the 1990s, from the top five—Shandwick, Hill and Knowlton, Burson-Marsteller, Ogilvy Public Relations Group and Omnicom PR Network—to hundreds and perhaps thousands of one-person shops. Some firms provide no advertising services but recommend or contract with ad agencies when those services are required. Others are affiliated with or owned by advertising agencies.

Why would a corporation—especially a big firm with a well-developed PR department—hire an outside public relations firm? An independent PR firm might be able to provide a client company with a fresh view of a problem or creative excellence or even special knowledge, such as experience with crisis communications. The outside PR firm also might have the people-power to accomplish a major, tedious task quickly.

The twin King Kongs of American PR firms—Shandwick and Hill and Knowlton—each employ between 1,000 and 2,000 people, including support staff. The next three largest PR firms have several hundred staffers each. The organizational structure of a PR firm will vary with its size, of course. Small firms with few employees often subcontract many services.

GLOBAL GLANCE
Public Relations Around the World

Public relations' horizons are expanding rapidly around the world. Many countries are fascinated by PR and what it can do for their governments and other institutions. The International Public Relations Association (established in the early 1950s) today has more than 1,000 members in about 70 countries. PR is one of the most popular courses in journalism and communications programs in foreign universities.

Some countries, such as Canada, have well-developed public relations activities, rivaling the United States in quality. Although PR is a thriving vocation in Europe, it is generally low-keyed and often hidden in European corporate organizations. British and French public relations activities are increasing at a very fast pace; in Germany, growth is slower due to the prevailing image of PR as gimmicks, show business and stunts.

Japan has the most highly developed PR practice in Asia. However, most Asian countries find PR fascinating, and practitioners are found everywhere—especially in government service. PR is especially prominent in the Philippines, India, Hong Kong and Singapore, and it is even developing in China.

"Relaciones públicas" is a hot field in Latin America where it is closely related to advertising and marketing. Mexico, Chile, Argentina and Brazil probably are the most advanced Latin American countries in the field of PR.

Africa affords another example of the growing interest in PR. In almost every country there is a deep interest in public relations, and courses are proliferating in African colleges and universities. Illiteracy and lack of funds, of course, make the field still rather primitive—as in most Third World areas—but the interest is certainly there for PR development. There are many local associations and institutions concerned with PR, and there is now a pan-African group, The Federation of African Public Relations Associations, with which local associations are invited to affiliate. Cities such as Nairobi, Lagos, Dakar, Abidjan, Accra, Harare, Johannesburg, Cape Town and Durban have the most PR activity.

Public relations firms are found around the world. Here, a practioner in Paris advises a client.

Larger firms, and especially very large firms and those affiliated with full-service advertising agencies, have numerous specialized departments.

A public relations organization of moderate size that is housed within an advertising agency would probably use someone called an account executive to supervise the PR work. The account executive might draw upon a creative services department for writers, artists and production help and upon a research and marketing department for tasks such as public opinion polling and the purchase of media space and time. An accounting department would handle billing. Special tasks, such as sophisticated typesetting, printing, photography and even the assembly of a press kit, could be subcontracted to freelancers or other firms.

If you were a PR account executive at this agency, you or your boss would probably listen at length to a client's concerns, then hook the client with a presentation. After that, you might perform as a counselor on an hourly fee arrangement—for example, x dollars per hour spent on a project such as a new store opening or a publication—or you might agree to a fixed fee for a particular project. The fixed fee might include charges for services such as photography or typesetting, or those charges might be extra. The extra might be for actual expenses or might carry a surcharge for agency overhead.

Your media relations tools might include news releases, feature story suggestions, photographs and perhaps video- and audio-tape segments, press kits, news conferences, interviews, speeches, special events and tours. You might service other external publics—customers, the community and government agencies, for example—with tools that include additional

---

Ten Common
News Release
Mistakes

Most news releases are thrown away when they reach a newsroom. A survey of the complaints of reporters and editors who work for a metropolitan newspaper in a southwestern U.S. city may explain why.

- Releases from the same organization are sent too frequently.
- Releases are delivered too close to deadline, leaving too little time to get them into the newspaper.
- Releases lack news value in general.
- Releases lack *local* news value.
- Releases lack names and telephone numbers of sources to contact for additional information.
- Release leads are "featurized," or too cute.
- Releases are incomplete, lacking times, dates and places and exact positions and titles of key sources.
- Releases do not follow wire service style.
- Releases use too much technical jargon.
- Releases are too long, despite their incompleteness.

Source: "News Release Flaws as Identified by Arkansas Journalists," University of Arkansas at Little Rock, 1993 survey.

special events and tours, exhibits, brochures, nonbroadcast audio-visual productions, broadcast public service announcements and even commercials. You might also deal with internal publics—stockholders, employees and dealers, for example—with tools such as annual reports, employee publications, open houses and parties, sales kits and direct mail pieces.

The list is endless: You do what is required to accomplish the objectives set by you and your client.

The Corporate Public Relations Department

The public relations departments of major American corporations often employ as many people as medium-sized PR firms. Take Phillips Petroleum of Bartlesville, Okla., for example. Phillips—in the 1990s America's 32nd largest business and ninth largest oil company, with over $13 billion in annual sales—has more than 90 employees in its United States, British and Norwegian PR operations. If Phillips' PR organization were an independent public relations firm, it would be in the nation's top 25 in terms of number of employees.

Let's take a look how Phillips' PR organization, which is housed in a division called Corporate Relations and Services, operates (see Figure 12.1). Corporate Relations, which has both public relations and human resources responsibilities, is headed by a vice president who reports directly to Phillips' president. Eleven managers report to the Corporate Relations vice

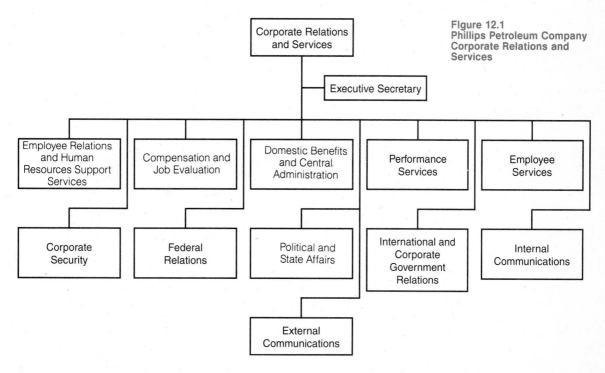

Figure 12.1
Phillips Petroleum Company
Corporate Relations and Services

A Day in the Life
of Jere Smith

Jere Smith is media relations director for Phillips Petroleum Company in Bartlesville, Okla. Although there are no "typical" days in media relations, here's what Smith did on one Thursday in March.

6:30 a.m.   Arrive at office. Make coffee and start through in-box.

7:00 a.m.   Call corporate relations office in London to get names of British journalists coming to international oil industry conference in Houston in May. (We're hosting a dinner for 10 key oil journalists during the conference.)

7:15 a.m.   Call office in Stavanger, Norway. Same reason as above.

7:30 a.m.   Read *The Wall Street Journal,* looking for stories that might be of interest in daily morning staff meeting.

7:40 a.m.   Call company's federal relations office in Washington, D.C., to check on congressional or regulatory action that might be of interest to Phillips.

7:50 a.m.   Call company's investor relations manager in New York to discuss previous day's market activity and implications for company.

8:00 a.m.   Staff meeting. Attended primarily by corporate writers and media relations types. Usually lasts about 10 minutes. We review overnight news items of interest and any intelligence picked up from morning phone calls to London, Stavanger, New York City and Washington. Our video section provides tapes of any overnight network or cable news stories related to oil industry.

8:15 a.m.   Put together a short report for community relations director on a problem our pipeline company is having in Decatur, Ill. Problem started as a media event and is now a little broader in scope.

8:35 a.m.   Visit with a member of my shop about upcoming visit by *Wall Street Journal* reporter. He's coming in before the end of our first quarter, and we discuss the feasibility of using this interview to signal the market that company is going to have a good first quarter. Decide we're going to have to talk with Legal about SEC rules covering "signaling of earnings."

9:00 a.m.   Our section puts out a news release announcing that our coal company subsidiary has just signed a contract to provide fuel for a power company in Louisiana. We've already decided to send the release to Louisiana and Oklahoma

president. Five of those managers deal with public relations matters and six handle human resources tasks. One such PR administrator is the *external communications* manager. This manager coordinates corporate "image" advertising through Phillips' national out-of-house ad agency. And like the other managers, the external communications manager oversees numerous coordinators and directors, including, for example, supervisors who direct the following four units:

- *corporate contributions,* which supervises the Phillips Petroleum Foundation, the unit responsible for making all nonpolitical contributions;

- *media relations,* which maintains contacts with the news media, arranges interviews with company personnel, provides media spokespersons,

media as well as to financial publications. This is a small contract but it's good news because we haven't had much luck selling our coal reserves since the price of oil dropped so low.

9:15 a.m.   Start preparing for a meeting later this afternoon with the vice president for corporate relations. Since we've just merged corporate affairs with human resources to form "corporate relations and services," we're all trying to get a feel for who does what. (Naturally, we're all trying to protect our turf.)

10:25 a.m.   Handled phone inquiry from reporter in Amarillo asking about our long-term debt load in early 1985. (Can't imagine what kind of story he's working on requiring that information.)

10:30 a.m.   Went back to in-basket.

10:50 a.m.   Informal meeting with community relations director and member of PR shop regarding a zoning problem near one of our refineries along the Texas Gulf Coast. Legal told us this morning that they got scorched in a public meeting last night and would now like to have guidance from corporate relations. (Better late than never.)

12:00   Short lunch break.

12:40 p.m.   Informal meeting with video communications supervisor regarding taping of company activities at big Houston oil industry show in May.

1:00 p.m.   Play around with word processor.

1:30 p.m.   Meeting with V.P. We're still trying to lay out responsibilities for staff members.

2:30 p.m.   Return miscellaneous phone calls.

3:15 p.m.   Call my counterparts at some other oil companies to see what's going on in the industry. Not much, it turns out.

4:00 p.m.   Draft monthly media highlight report for Board of Directors' Public Policy Committee.

5:05 p.m.   Leave for the day.

Source: Jere Smith, media relations director, Phillips Petroleum Company, 1992.

prepares news releases and handles emergency or crisis public relations at field locations;

- *community relations,* which has two tasks: coordinating community efforts where many Phillips employees are located and distributing educational films produced by an outside production company for Phillips; and

- *issues management,* which tracks environmental issues and recommends appropriate policy and educational programs.

Before looking at the other four public relations managers and their tasks, let's take an in-depth look at just one responsibility of the media relations section: issuing news releases.

The procedure for distributing news releases, although just one function of Phillips' media relations unit and its public information subdivision, reflects the complexity of the corporation's media relations efforts. News releases fall into four categories: disclosure, personnel, general information and feature, and outside releases.

- *Disclosure* releases contain information that the federal Securities and Exchange Commission would consider significant because an investor might buy or sell shares of Phillips based on that information. Examples include news about major oil or gas discoveries, plant openings or closings and quarterly or year-end earnings. Strict SEC rules govern the release of this kind of information.
- *Personnel* releases announce the promotion or hiring of middle- or upper-level management.
- *General information and feature* releases cover everything else of news or feature value, except for information about business ventures with Phillips' partner companies.
- *Outside* releases involve information written by Phillips about the company's partners or by those partners about Phillips. For example, Phillips operates a major oil and gas production facility in the middle of the North Sea. Seven partners have varying amounts of financial interest in the project, along with approval rights of releases dealing with the project. Their corporate headquarters are in Norway, Belgium, France and Italy, and Phillips must get approval from each company before a release is issued.

Requests for news releases generally come from a Phillips' operating division, such as the Petroleum Products Group, which makes gasoline, among other items. After a request is made, a writer is assigned. The writer gathers information by phone or in person and produces a draft of the release, which must be approved by the person requesting it. If the release is acceptable, it enters a formal approval system, beginning with the operating group head, moving to Phillips' legal department, then to the vice president for corporate relations and finally to the company president. The approval process may take from a few hours to a few days, depending on the nature of the release. Outside releases may take longer.

Distribution of releases varies, depending upon subject matter and potential interest. Some releases go to only one city, others go to specific lists of editors such as newspaper and magazine energy editors, and other releases are distributed worldwide. Phillips' media relations and public information employees analyze the use of the releases through the kind of follow-up questions asked by reporters receiving the releases and also through clipping services that search for stories about Phillips.

Complicated? Yes. Now let's look at those other four managers, who also have complex duties.

Under the *internal communications* manager are directors and supervisors who oversee the following units:

- *corporate communications,* which provides executive speeches, produces annual and quarterly financial reports, arranges for employee meetings and publishes company bulletins, field office newsletters, company benefits communications, a monthly company newspaper and a quarterly company magazine;

- *creative design,* which provides corporate artists who create new product packaging, layout experts who design all publications and photographers who take pictures worldwide for the company;

- *graphic production,* which provides typesetting;

- an *exhibit center,* which designs and fabricates exhibits used in trade shows; and

- *video services,* which produces a monthly news program for companywide distribution as well as videotapes for training purposes.

Three executives oversee international, national and state legislative activities, which are PR-related responsibilities. The *federal relations* manager, based in Washington, D.C., handles federal lobbying, maintains contact with federal agencies, embassies and legations of countries affecting Phillips' business and is a liaison with national trade organizations. The *political and state affairs* manager maintains memberships in various oil-related associations and supervises legislative offices in Oklahoma City (for legislatures in Oklahoma and New Mexico), Austin (for Texas and Louisiana) and Denver

---

The Electronic News Release: Dawn of a New Day?

News releases are traditionally mailed, faxed or hand-delivered to news organizations. However, paperless or electronic delivery of releases, started on a limited basis by PR Newswire in 1954 in Chicago, is becoming more common and offers some advantages for both news organizations—newspapers in particular—and public relations counselors.

The advantage for the newspaper is that the release is electronically delivered to the paper's computer system, making editing easy and eliminating the need for typesetting.

PR advocates of electronic distribution of news releases argue that reducing releases to bits and bytes is an efficient way to meet Securities and Exchange Commission requirements for quickly and broadly distributing financial information.

However, the key advantage for the PR person is that at least one study shows that the electronic news release is edited differently from its paper counterpart. The study, by four University of Wisconsin at Madison researchers in the mid-1980s, measured the amount of editing done to University of Wisconsin News Service releases by reporters and editors at the two Madison daily papers. The researchers found that electronically delivered releases were less heavily edited than stories delivered to the papers in the traditional way.

Although the publication of virtually unedited news releases may be a journalistic nightmare, it's a dream come true for most PR counselors.

Source: "The Effect of 'Electronic' News Sources on News Production," a study by Kurt Neuwirth, Carol M. Liebler, Sharon Dunwoody and Jennifer Riddle, School of Journalism and Mass Communication, University of Wisconsin-Madison, 1986.

Future Focus Public Relations Tomorrow

Public relations in the late 1990s and beyond will be far more complex than it is today. Changing organizational and social trends are requiring that the scope of public relations practice be redefined.

To be specific, those who employ practitioners require that PR programs produce measurable beneficial results, and those results must be obtained in a society in which mediated communication has become progressively more difficult.

Mediated communication—transfer of information through messages transmitted by mass media—long has been the primary function of public relations. Practitioners' efforts traditionally have been focused on message design, media selection and—in more recent years—measurement of results.

The efficiency of mediated communication has been deteriorating, however, in almost direct proportion to mounting demands for measurable results. Several factors are involved. They include social demassification, as first defined by futurist Alvin Toffler, fragmentation of media audiences and mounting public skepticism and distrust of organizations.

Demassification, as Toffler uses the term, refers to the progressive process of fragmentation that has recast a once largely homogeneous U.S. society into a host of special-interest groups. Demassification has created conditions in which no communicator can deal successfully with a "general" public. Instead subgroups must be addressed in terms of their demographic and psychographic characteristics.

Demassification has been accomplished by progressive *fragmentation* of media audiences. Publishers and broadcasters motivated by profit and intent on their own survival have launched hundreds of special-interest media. They include nationally circulated newspapers that compete with once-dominant local publications, a host of specialized magazines that largely have supplanted their mass-circulation predecessors, independent television stations and cable systems competing with earlier-established network outlets and growing numbers of new media spawned by computer and satellite technology.

Each new medium must capture an audience of sufficient size to engender the advertiser support necessary to survive. More than survival is involved, however, from the perspective of public relations practitioners. In capturing audience, each new medium absorbs part of the limited amount of time that media users devote to information gathering. Successful new media, in other words, survive at the collective expense of their predecessors. In the process, they render all media individually less effective from the standpoints of those who seek to reach large audiences. Progressive audience fragmentation thus is making the term "mass media" increasingly contradictory.

Increasing *skepticism* on the part of message recipients further erodes the efficiency of mediated communication. Public confidence in government, in business and even in the media has deteriorated steadily for more than two decades. The Vietnam War, Watergate and economic problems that followed destroyed public trust in institutions and organizations. Politicians, corporate executives and others in responsible positions now are viewed with little more credibility than once was granted to used-car salesmen. Individuals more and more base decisions on experience and observation rather than on messages.

These circumstances are the primary drivers of change in public relations practice. They are forcing practitioners to broaden the scope of their activities—to redefine "public relations" to encompass interpersonal, behavioral and environmental as well as mediated communication. Success in public relations practice now depends on the ability of practitioners to ensure that all message sources are functioning harmoniously at all times. Any hint of disharmony can be fatal.

Mediated messages are necessary but don't guarantee success. Messages convey information. Success requires that message content be accepted, assimilated and acted upon, responses that can be logically expected only when message content is supported by reality. Organizations' professed commitments to service are too readily defeated by inept personnel. Product advertising claims are as easily contradicted by poor quality. Discourtesies on the part of personnel and crowded or unclean business premises are damning for any organization. Success or failure, in other words, ultimately is produced by the environments and behaviors that shape the experiences of those who respond to practitioner messages.

Under increasing pressure to produce measurable results, public relations practitioners are responding to the diminishing role of mediated communication and the increasing relative importance of interpersonal, behavioral and environmental communication. They seek consistency in message content that can be accomplished only when all messages transmitted are accurate reflections of reality. If organizational realities are inadequate to support proposed message content, only two options exist: either realities or messages must be changed.

Public relations programs, as a result, increasingly extend beyond communication. Personnel training and incentive components may be necessary to induce appropriate interpersonal and behavioral communication on the part of organizational personnel. Redesign and refurnishing of organizational premises may be required to produce "user friendly" environments.

Public relations professionals may or may not become personally involved in interpersonal, behavioral or environmental communication. Their roles are usually limited to program design and development. Professionals in training, decorating and other disciplines are then called upon as necessary (much as PR practitioners traditionally have obtained the services of graphic designers and printers). The ultimate results are usually highly satisfactory. Mediated messages are incapable of overcoming practical realities, and public relations of tomorrow demands that practical realities be changed and improved.

Source: Prepared for this textbook by E. W. Brody, University of Memphis.

(for the western United States and Alaska). Those offices are maintained all year but provide extensive lobbying support when the state legislatures consider legislation affecting Phillips. An *international and corporate government relations* manager tracks international legislative and regulatory matters affecting Phillips' *upstream* and *downstream* operations. *Upstream* operations refers to oil and gas exploration and production activities; *downstream* operations are transportation and supply and sale of petroleum products and chemicals.

In all, some 80 people with a variety of skills work in the public relations units of Phillips' Corporate Relations division in the United States—mainly in Oklahoma—and another 15 work in Great Britain and Norway for related companies.

Retrospective

Public relations is a relatively recent and some say distinctly American adjunct of mass communication. Some of its techniques are ancient, but its modern form is traceable to 20th-century practices and attitudes refined by people such as Ivy Lee and Edward Bernays. Both Lee and Bernays believed that PR was a management function requiring cooperation of a company's senior officials, ideally within an atmosphere of public service. They also both believed in being cooperative and candid with the news media, unusual notions at the time.

Contemporary public relations—two-way communication in which the PR person is a conduit for information from various external and internal publics to management and from management to those publics—exists in both agency and nonagency settings.

Despite the free flow of information suggested by the two-way model, PR still has more than its share of media critics. The critics charge public relations practitioners with many moral crimes, but the critics' most common complaint is that some PR representatives shade the truth and even lie when they realize media coverage will not be positive. PR practitioners counter that organizations have a right to tell their side of the story and that they are simply lawyers representing their clients in the court of public opinion.

Questions

1. What do PR practitioners mean when they talk about two-way communication? Can you think of a circumstance in which one-way communication might be appropriate?

2. What are the four steps used by many PR practitioners?

3. What was Ivy Lee's primary contribution to PR? What was Edward Bernays?

4. If you were a PR representative answering questions posed by a news organization, would you tell the truth at any cost? Would it be appropriate to withhold information or even lie in the face of a disclosure that would seriously damage your employer of your client?

5. Given the entire spectrum of PR—government, military, corporate, association, not-for-profit, political and union—do you think public relations is basically helpful or harmful to society?

6. Why would a corporation with a good company PR department hire a public relations agency?

7. Name some publics you would have to deal with if you were the corporate relations vice president for Phillips Petroleum.

Suggested Readings

Baskin, Otis W., and Aronof, Craig E. *Public Relations: The Profession and the Practice.* Dubuque, Iowa: Wm. C. Brown, 1992.

Brody, E. W. *Public Relations Programming and Production.* New York: Praeger, 1988.

Cutlip, Scott M., Center, Allen H., and Broom, Glen M. *Effective Public Relations.* Englewood Cliffs, N.J.: Prentice-Hall, 1993.

Fink, Conrad C. *Media Ethics.* New York: McGraw-Hill, 1988.

Hendrix, Jerry A. *Public Relations Cases.* Belmont, Calif.: Wadsworth, 1992.

Hiebert, Ray E. *Courtier to the Crowd: The Life Story of Ivy Lee.* Ames: Iowa State University Press, 1966.

Nager, Norman R, and Allen, T. Harrell. *Public Relations Management by Objectives.* Lanham, Md.: University Press of America, 1991.

Newsom, Doug, and Carrell, Bob. *Public Relations Writing.* Belmont, Calif.: Wadsworth, 1991.

Newsom, Doug, Scott, Alan, and Turk, Judy Van Slyke. *This is PR: The Realities of Public Relations.* Belmont, Calif.: Wadsworth, 1993.

Olasky, Marvin. *Corporate Public Relations and American Private Enterprise.* Hillsdale, N.J.: Lawrence Erlbaum Associates, 1987.

Issues & Concepts

It isn't enough to understand media and their functions. In this rapidly evolving world of ours, there are incandescent issues and complex concepts that relate directly to mass media and the way they operate—the tenuous relationships of press and government, controversial issues of media freedom, developing concepts of media ethics and the broadening importance of international communication. We would be remiss not to examine them all.

Governments and media must coexist, sometimes in partnership, sometimes in apparent opposition. The form of government in a given situation usually determines the purpose and makeup of the media. Closed, totalitarian governments frequently use media as support systems. Open, democratic governments often depend on media to keep the governmental process honest. Whatever the relationships between government and media, there is usually a correlation to the amount of media freedom that may be practiced. Controls exist in all media situations, though some media controls are more severe than others.

Also of growing concern in recent years is the seeming decay of ethics on all fronts, media included. If we are to protect ourselves from an inevitable erosion of ethical sensitivities in media, we must—as media consumers and media practitioners—examine the importance of ethical media decisions. It isn't easy. Ethical choices, unlike government statutes and regulations, are seldom carefully delineated, and proper ethical conduct can't easily be forced. Ethical decisions must spring from the individual. But we can at least insist that an understanding of ethics be stressed in the training and education of our future media personnel. Only then will they be prepared to make the proper decisions.

And finally, in this shrinking world, it's time to break away from provincial attitudes and become more thoroughly versed in issues of global communication. The American media system is very special, but it has its problems. We can recognize our strengths and our weaknesses and more easily put our own media into perspective by studying the problems and solutions of other countries.

The media's infatuation WITH THE NEW ADMINISTRATION IS already fading and soon the honeymoon will be over. But This past week Americans from all over the country came to the nation's capitol to celebrate America's reunion on the mall. STAY WITH US!

Press and Government

Toward the end of 1992 presidential campaign, George Bush found himself running behind Bill Clinton in the polls. Modern polls, if properly administered, are notoriously accurate. That left President Bush little latitude. To keep his supporters charged up, he had to denigrate the polls and take on another opponent—the press. Bush began to carry a red bumper sticker around. He flashed it at every campaign stop, holding it up to show to the partisan crowds who turned out to hear him. They loved it. The sticker said, "Annoy the Media. Re-elect Bush."

Press-bashing is a favorite ploy of politicians who drop behind in the numbers. It gives them a way to try to explain their low position in the polls. However, contemporary political candidates are not the originators of the sport. Former President Dwight Eisenhower ridiculed "sensation-seeking columnists and commentators" on the floor of the 1964 Republican convention, provoking massed delegates to a chorus of boos and hisses at press people covering the proceedings. In 1969, Richard Nixon's vice president, Spiro Agnew, began taking swipes at the press in public speeches, referring to them as "nattering nabobs of negativity" and an "effete corps of impudent snobs."

But attacks belittling the integrity of the press were particularly strident in the 1992 campaign. From both sides. Or rather all three sides. Clinton, dogged during his primary race by continuous charges of womanizing, called the rumors "trash" and lashed out at reporters. Dan Quayle started it for the Republicans by labeling news media part of the "cultural elite" determined to undermine the American family. Ross Perot, after receiving what he considered rough treatment from the media on his accusations of Republican dirty tricks toward the end of the campaign, held a hostile press conference in which he told reporters that the subject was none of their business.

But the Republicans were the angriest. The most popular T-shirt on sale at the 1992 Republican convention was one bearing the message, "Blame it on the Media." President Bush's son, George, went on CBS's "This Morning" and CNN's "Larry King Live" to accuse the press of "hammering" his dad with "unbelievable allegations." And things got so bad when Bush started showing off his red bumper sticker that crowds started spitting on press photographers and poking reporters with American flags. After one reporter was hit in the back with a thrown bottle, members of the Bush press delegation finally petitioned the president's press secretary, Marlin Fitzwater, to ask his boss to tone the attacks down. Bush, not wanting to see anyone hurt, told his next assembled crowd, "Don't take it out on these guys with the cameras and the boom mikes. They're all good folks. Take it out on those talking heads in the national press that come on and tell us everything that's bad about America."

At the end, after losing to Clinton, Bush had one bitter parting shot for the press. He called the 1992 campaign "the most biased year in the history of presidential politics."

Was it? That's probably an unanswerable question, but several organizations took a shot at answering it shortly after the election. The methodologies and political leanings of the groups varied, so the results were mixed. At least two of the groups, Accuracy in Media (which leans to the right) and Fairness and Accuracy in Reporting (which leans to the left), came up with opposite conclusions. AIM claimed that reporters ignored stories damaging to Clinton, while FAIR insisted that media spent more time on Clinton's draft record than on Bush's involvement in Irangate. Two largely nonpartisan organizations, the Center for Media and Public Affairs and the Joan Shorenstein Barone Center on the Press, decided that both Bush and Clinton received mostly negative coverage. A fifth group, the Freedom Forum, tackled the issue in yet another way and tried to identify the political affiliations of the working journalists themselves (the results labeled 44 percent as Democrat and 16 percent as Republican).

Media people denied all charges of favoritism. Tom Brokaw, NBC news anchor, defended the press's role in the election by saying, "We're not in the business of being biased. I think most bias exists in the eye of the beholder." That isn't to say there wasn't negative coverage. The various studies seemed to verify it. But most journalists argued that Bush obtained his negative coverage the old-fashioned way—he earned it.

Four Theories of the Press

The disputes between presidential candidates and the press couldn't have happened in many countries. Only a nation with a robust press/government environment could provide the climate for such a campaign collision. When Bush and Clinton (and Perot) stood behind a podium and faced massed reporters, they were playing roles in a time-tested, 200-year-old script, and the stage from which they spoke was as American as apple pie.

And in spite of the complaints, most Americans wouldn't have it any other way. A democratic society calls for the rule of the people. Citizens make important majority decisions, debate public issues, correct social ills and elect their leaders by democratic ballot. Only if citizens are kept informed can they fulfill their potential. That's where media come in. The crucial mission of mass media in an openly democratic society is to provide a meeting ground for an exchange of ideas. Without a free and pluralistic media system to feed ideas and information to all elements in society, democracy would shrivel and die.

But media systems have not always been used as open information links between people and their governments. Indeed, some are still not used that way today. Media systems are closely related to the political systems under which they operate. They must be tolerated by the government in power. As a consequence, they are usually supportive of that government and reflect the political philosophy of government. Perhaps the best known typology of press and media systems is the "four theories" concept. Three noted communication scholars, Fred Siebert, Theodore Peterson and Wilbur Schramm, wrote a series of essays in 1956 examining the social and political structures under which various world media historically have functioned. The rush of history has overtaken some of the theories, but they are still considered important for journalists and communication

Then-Presidential candidate George Bush complains about media bias in the 1992 election, as he did during the 1988 election. Later, his successor, Bill Clinton, also complains about the media's lack of fairness.

students because they help explain how we got to where we are. Let's take a look at these four original government types and their concomitant press theories.

Authoritarian Press Theory

Closed totalitarian societies have existed since the beginning of governments. They are often elitist, authoritarian regimes with a single strong leader—usually a king, queen, czar or dictator. Under an authoritarian orientation, the people are not considered intellectually capable of making decisions for themselves. From the moment Gutenberg cranked out his first printed tome, early authoritarian kings (and queens) quickly recognized the danger of the printing press. It was one thing to have a few petty dissidents speak out against the status quo; all governments and monarchs have had to face dissatisfied elements among their subjects, no matter how benign their rule. As long as these insignificant elements spoke only to one another and passed potentially dangerous ideas along to others by word of mouth, they could be controlled. But the printing press made possible the mass production of hazardous thought. What's more, the thought was offered in more or less permanent form. Dissidents could be exiled. Rebels could be pilloried or drawn and quartered. Printed ideas, available to the masses, wouldn't be so easy to manage.

Such a threat could not be ignored. Nor was it. The printing press reached England in 1476 during the reign of Edward IV, when William Caxton opened his print shop. Henry VIII, known for his interest in multiple wives and the chopping block, came to the throne in 1509 and saw nothing but peril in the new print medium. By 1530, he had banned the publication of certain books and established a requirement that all English printers obtain a royal license before they practice their trade. Since printers couldn't publish without a license, and the license could be lifted if they printed anything unacceptable, the new print medium was effectively muzzled. Succeeding monarchs maintained the licensing provision and added a few new twists. Queen Elizabeth I introduced the Star Chamber, an organization that punished all printers foolish enough to offend the Crown. Other rulers used selective taxation to drive printers out of business or enacted heavy-handed sedition laws that frightened printers into silence.

Media have grown up, of course, but under present-day authoritarian rule, nothing much has changed. Muzzling the press is still a vital step in the creation of a totalitarian state. Media, generally privately owned, are allowed to operate as a special privilege granted by the national leadership. The media, therefore, owe their existence and their allegiance to the leader. If there is an item of importance that the national leader feels the people should be told, the media must make these things public. If, by contrast, the leader wishes to deny other information to the public at large, the media must keep the information secret. Media will have only as much freedom as the national leadership will permit them to have.

Libertarian Press Theory

A new philosophical stance, one that despised secrecy, began to develop under England's early authoritarian yoke. Though press licensing and various forms of censorship remained in place for almost 200 years, new ideas struggled to the surface. A few isolated 17th-century thinkers believed free criticism was essential to happiness and growth, and they wanted an end to prior censorship. During a brief relaxation of press control in the

---

Past Pointer: Hutchins Commission: Why Press Freedom Is Threatened

The Commission on Freedom of the Press (Hutchins Commission), reporting in 1947 after several years of studying the American press, concluded that press freedom was threatened mainly for three reasons:

1. Access to the press by citizens had become more restricted, although the importance of the press to society had grown tremendously;

2. Those limited persons who did have access to the press had not done what they should to provide societal needs;

3. Press management often engaged in activities respecting their media that were generally disapproved of by society.

The Hutchins Commission concluded that if such press practices were to continue, press freedom could be lost or lessened in the country through increased regulation or control of the press. Many media critics, following the Gulf War of 1991 and the American presidential campaign of 1992, have reiterated the criticisms of the Hutchins Commission.

mid-1640s, English poet John Milton published *Areopagitica*, an impassioned plea for an end to press licensing and the establishment of a free marketplace of ideas. Milton's pioneering thought, coupled with the writings of John Locke some 50 years later, suggested that common people could be trusted to make the right decisions, but only if all kinds of information and ideas were made public to assist them. The writings of Milton may have aided the eventual rise of libertarianism, but not at that moment. Authoritarian rulers weren't ready to relax their control. English printing presses continued to be licensed, and their products were subjected to varying degrees of censorship for another 50 years.

But the concept of press libertarianism continued to grow. It was fundamentally a democratic stance, one in which the leadership relates closely with the followers. Under a libertarian orientation, there is a trust of the masses, a belief that the majority, through free expression, will come closest to the truth and make rational decisions. The media of a libertarian society must, therefore, be free to seek and present the truth so that the people will be informed and can act intelligently to elect their representatives, direct them in their duties, and, if necessary, change them when they do not function properly. Without a free and unmuzzled press to act as a link between the people and the government, the libertarian concept is largely invalidated.

Providing a meeting ground for an exchange of ideas is a crucial mission of the mass media in a democratic society.

Soviet Press Theory

A new press theory appeared in the early part of this century with the success of the Marxist revolution. As Communists came to power in Russia, they proclaimed a new role for mass media: Basically, the function of mass media in Soviet society was to be the same as the ruling apparatus—to ensure the perpetuation and expansion of socialist ideals. No longer were the media to aid in a search for truth. Soviets said the truth—as expounded by Karl Marx, the original philosopher of world communism—was already known. Therefore, media should exist to transmit social policy and spread that truth.

You may see similarities between the old authoritarian and the newer Soviet press theories. They surely existed. Some scholars preferred to lump the two together for discussion under the single heading of *totalitarian press theory*. And it made a kind of sense. Both authoritarian and Soviet governmental systems fell under a form of elite leadership. And both held that the masses were generally too ignorant, too uninterested in the workings of government to be told much about it. But there were differences. The media under authoritarian rule are usually owned by private individuals who follow authoritarian dictates as a matter of survival. Media under the Soviet system were instruments of the state. They were owned and operated by the government and undertook their functions under the direct control of the Communist Party or its agencies.

Just as controlled freedoms may vary under different authoritarian leaders, the extent of control varied in the Soviet system, as well. The introduction of *glasnost* (former Soviet leader Mikhail Gorbachev's favorite catchword for greater official tolerance of public expression) in the late 1980s led to a loosening of the Party grip in the Soviet Union, as evidenced by a somewhat improved image of America in the Soviet press and on Soviet television. Officials lifted restrictions on the sale of American and West European newspapers and magazines. In 1988, Soviets were even exposed to American-produced television commercials for Pepsi and Visa credit cards. But the role of the Soviet press was essentially the same, and news for public consumption was still strongly colored by doctrinaire Marxist ideology.

Communist press systems still exist in countries like Cuba and China and other regional pockets of the world, but Soviet press theory lost most of its bite when the Soviet Union collapsed in 1991 to be replaced by the Coalition of Independent States. Under the new independent regimes, democratic ideals are more appealing to the masses, and the splintering press systems are beginning to reflect it.

Theory of Social Responsibility

When libertarian press theory began, it was still possible for the average individual to air personal views by publishing a pamphlet or starting up a newspaper. The whole point of libertarianism was to guarantee the free exchange of ideas and to give every citizen a voice. But times have changed. In these days of mass communication, it costs a bundle to start a newspaper or launch a broadcast station, and relatively few people have the economic means to do it. Even existing newspapers and broadcast stations are often too expensive for independent owners to maintain. More and more of them are being absorbed by larger media chains. As the number of independent media shrinks, so does the necessary pluralism of voices required to air the wide variety of social and political thought.

In the middle of this century, an assortment of educators, lawyers and businesspeople expressed concern over this concentration of media outlets in fewer and fewer hands. They formed a group called the Commission on Freedom of the Press, later known as the Hutchins Commission, and suggested that the economic interests of modern media often interfere with original libertarian ideals. Modern society, they said, makes it mandatory that an obligation of social responsibility be imposed on media. Only if media are required to report events accurately and fully in a meaningful context, with all viewpoints made public rather than just those of the media owners, could the concept behind libertarianism be revived.

This theory, then, has its roots in libertarian theory, but goes beyond it. It places moral and ethical restrictions on the press. The emphasis shifts from press freedom to press responsibility. Indeed, to make certain the media live up to their new responsibilities, the Hutchins Commission suggested that government might have to step in. The proposal of government enforcement was instantly controversial. Supporters of the social responsibility theory held that improvements in the press would outweigh any slight erosion of press freedoms. Critics were convinced that social responsibility could not be required; they contended that a government hand at the press throttle would do far more damage to the original concept of libertarianism than would the so-called weaknesses it was designed to correct. The Hutchins Commission was alternately dubbed "Hutchins and his Twelve Apostles" by supporters of the social responsibility concept and "Hutchins and the Twelve Dwarves" by opponents.

In the decades that followed Hutchins Commission criticism, American journalists worked quietly to clean up their own house. Social trends have become more important to media reporters. Such issues as health, environment, economics, energy, education, race, poverty, the aged and science are now regularly and insightfully examined by both print and broadcast media. Background and interpretive articles have increased sharply in number. Newspapers have established "op-ed" (opinion-editorial) pages to increase the range of opinion. Modern editors and reporters are far more willing to investigate complex stories and institutions rather than merely reporting simple one-note events. Compared to the ideological press systems that permeate the rest of the world, modern American journalism is demonstrably fair and balanced.

Yet, in spite of better coverage and improved balance, more and more Americans have grown suspicious of the press. Too hostile, they say. Too powerful. Too biased. Government officials and political campaigners have learned that taking swipes at the press in speeches almost inevitably produces applause. Media-bashing has become a popular sport.

Why? If the American press system is among the best in the world, why do critics assail it so? We'll examine some of the charges in the course of this chapter and attempt to analyze them. But we saw part of the answer in our opening situation—the 1992 presidential campaign and the spirited confrontations between wary presidential candidates and the relentless reporters who followed them on the campaign trail, classic examples of the traditional adversarial relationship between government and the press.

The press and the government have always appeared to be adversaries. Every government official, from the president to the lowest filing clerk in some small bureaucratic backwater, has a job to do—running the massive machinery of government. Reporters, especially those who make up the Washington press corps, also have a job to do. They scrutinize the operation of government and keep the public informed on the successes and failures of various policies. If government business is conducted properly, the public hears of it and often reflects its satisfaction at the ballot box. If the press passes word of embarrassing government improperties to the public, that too may be reflected at the ballot box. That's the basis of the American democratic system. As long as things go well, government and press coexist. If something goes wrong—money is misspent, power is abused, laws are ignored or misused or any of the myriad mistakes that can affect the public welfare—it's the job of the press to uncover the facts and make them public.

Unfortunately, such information does not come easily. Government today, particularly the national government, has a wide-ranging ability to manage the news and mislead the public. Government officials can often conceal improperties, walling them off from the press and public until their discovery is no longer damaging. Aware of this human tendency to hide mistakes, reporters often view their official beats with a jaundiced eye. They step back from their subjects and try to maintain a detached attitude. They know that damaging information, if it exists, can be unearthed only through perseverance and constant digging. This is one way in which the adversarial relationship can begin.

Is this seemingly antagonistic approach also one of the reasons the American public is so critical of modern American journalism? Let's look more closely at the workings of press and government—starting at the top level.

Many readers and viewers question the manner and attitude of the Washington press corps. They see reporters as not only detached but actually hostile to the government whose doings they report. Those assigned to cover the White House seem especially hostile. The average viewer doesn't see the democratic process at work when reporters shout sharp questions during a televised presidential news conference. What the viewer sees is the president at bay, assailed from all sides by rude, chaotic journalists—the highest official in the land forced to field prosecutorial questions like a prisoner in the docket.

The press and government have long been adversaries in the United States and in many other countries.

But this question-and-answer session is not as chaotic nor as accusatory as it may seem. Only the president can call a press conference, and he can hold them as often or as seldom as he likes. When he does, it is usually because he has something he wants to say or something about which he is willing to be questioned. Certain traditions are maintained. The most senior correspondent always asks the first question, but from that point on the president selects his inquisitors. He usually knows the White House press corps well enough to know who will ask the hard questions and who will ask the soft questions and can pick accordingly. Yes, there's a lot of shouting and vying for the president's attention, sometimes because reporters have newsworthy questions they are eager to have answered, sometimes (sad to say) because reporters want to be seen on live camera back home, to prove to their editors or client newspapers that they are hard at work. But the president sets the pace, selects the questioners and controls the answers. And though most modern televised press conferences last just long enough to fill thirty minutes of airtime, the president can end it when he wishes.

The president can control news in a number of other ways. He can arrange private discussions with tame or favored reporters. He can schedule speeches before sympathetic audiences. He can restrict himself to photo opportunities at which no questions are allowed. He can arrange high-profile foreign trips that will guarantee upbeat press coverage. He can pass the "bad news" buck to his press secretary, who holds regular press backgrounding sessions, a method that shields the president from questions. He can bypass reporters and command network television time, going directly to the people. He can issue executive orders limiting contact between his administration officials and reporters. He can even affect the scope of the Freedom of Information Act to make information more difficult to obtain. In all, the president has extraordinary powers of communication and numerous methods available for news management. Even so, most reporters and editors consider the White House beat one of the most productive assignments in Washington.

Press Conferences

Press conferences are relatively new. Early presidents, from George Washington on, summoned writers from one or more of the chronicles when they had something to say and avoided them the rest of the time. Not that early reporters were that easy to avoid. If a writer was determined to confront the president on some issue of public importance, he could usually walk into the White House without appointment and corner the president in his office. Or he could wait outside the White House and catch the president taking his family for a leisurely carriage ride in the afternoon sunlight. Bodyguards and Secret Service protection were a long way in the future.

Not that some of the earlier presidents might not have wished for a bit of protection from the press. In the early days of the Republic, most of our newspapers were strident, scandalous partisan rags, far less reliable than some of the flashy gossip sheets you can buy at today's supermarkets. Presidents were scurrilously attacked in print. Even George Washington took body blows from the press. John Adams was so irritated by journalistic excesses that he encouraged the passage of the restrictive Alien and Sedition Acts (more about this in the next chapter). Thomas Jefferson, a devout supporter of press freedom, wrote to a friend, "They [editors] fill their newspapers with falsehoods, calumnies, and audacities." But for every raucous enemy newspaper, a president could rely on a feisty newspaper ally to do battle in his favor. When Andrew Jackson became the seventh president of the United States, he even brought several newspaper cronies with him as advisers (known as the "kitchen cabinet").

As government grew more complex over the years, more and more reporters were sent to Washington to report on government activities. Coverage of the president increased in importance. Simultaneously, personal access to the president became more difficult. The job was too demanding. A president couldn't give private audiences to all the reporters who wanted to see him and still have time to run the government. He could make himself available to only a favored few. By the time Woodrow Wilson came to office in 1913, the situation had become almost intolerable. In an effort to be fair and to give every reporter a chance, Wilson devised the concept of the press conference. All accredited reporters were invited to attend these twice-a-week briefing sessions. They had to submit written questions in advance, giving Wilson plenty of time to prepare his answers.

And so the presidential press conference was born. It's been with us ever since, though the style and substance have changed. Franklin Roosevelt, unlike Wilson, permitted direct questions and answered them on the spot. Roosevelt was a master of the press conference and held almost 70 a year, usually summoning members of the press corps to the Oval Office where they crowded around his desk and traded repartee. By the time Harry Truman succeeded Roosevelt, the White House press corps had grown too large for informal office sessions. Truman made the press sessions more formal. Instead of casual give-and-take, reporters rose to ask their questions, then sat quietly through the answers. Dwight Eisenhower was the first to lead off each press conference with a prepared statement. Jack Kennedy set another precedent by allowing live television coverage. Television has been a major participant ever since.

Like style and substance, the frequency of press conferences has also varied from president to president. Wilson and Roosevelt set very high early standards, meeting with the press at least weekly, often twice a week. Truman dropped off a bit, managing no more than 40 meetings a year. The next three presidents also scaled back. Eisenhower, Kennedy and Lyndon Johnson each averaged roughly 20 to 25 sessions a year. Then the numbers took a plunge, Richard Nixon, never fond of the press, averaged only eight press conferences a year before Watergate. After Watergate, he gave them up almost entirely. Gerald Ford and Jimmy Carter tried to breathe new life into the news conference, meeting with the press every two weeks or so, about the same pace as that of Eisenhower, Kennedy and Johnson. Ronald Reagan, though widely hailed as "the great communicator," returned to the low Nixon numbers, holding an average of only seven press conferences a year during his first four-year term. His second-term average was even lower. At one point in 1986–1987, he went a full five months without a televised news conference. Reagan preferred to make weekly radio broadcasts, knowing they would be quoted and reported in the press. Frequency improved with George Bush, but lasted only the one term. President Clinton's aides announced soon after his inauguration that the new president would hold fewer full-fledged press conferences than President Bush. Instead, they said, Clinton would continue a technique developed during the campaign and deal more directly with ordinary voters through the use of televised town meetings, radio addresses and appearances on call-in shows.

Press Secretary

The president's press secretary, like any public information officer in Washington, is basically a public relations expert. The expanded scope of the modern executive branch and the huge numbers of reporters assigned to cover it mean that most reporters can spend weeks at a time without actually seeing the president. The press secretary's job becomes especially important. He is the White House liaison, acting as a buffer between the president and the press. It is the press secretary who briefs the White House press corps at regular intervals, answers questions, arranges photo sessions, announces presidential decisions and in general keeps the president on television screens and the front pages of American newspapers, preferably in a positive light.

There have been a number of effective press secretaries in recent decades, but the job isn't easy. A good presidential press secretary must walk a delicate line. He owes loyalty to his boss, the president, but he must also maintain his own reputation for integrity. If a press secretary lies or tries to cover up for the president through obfuscation, and the press learns of it, his usefulness is frequently at an end. Ron Ziegler, Richard Nixon's press secretary, learned this lesson the hard way during the Watergate era when he treated the press corps to a consistent pattern of angry denials, falsehoods and sweeping cover-up statements, and then, as Watergate revelations continued to unfold, was forced to backpedal furiously. Larry Speakes, who became Ronald Reagan's spokesperson after press secretary James Brady was seriously wounded in a 1981 assassination attempt against the president, erred in the opposite direction, showing a basic lack of loyalty when he wrote an embarrassing "kiss-and-tell" book after leaving the administration.

Presidential Addresses

Presidential speeches are always worth covering. And presidents, knowing a public address is often the best way to make a point for public consumption, often schedule such speeches before predictably sympathetic organizations. The president advances to a speaker's lectern, makes his views known, usually to stirring applause, then retires without having to entertain questions. It may be an address before Congress, a speech at a university or a rousing talk before some veteran's group. The press will be there, and the speech will be duly reported by print and broadcast media. The president also knows he can circumvent the press entirely by asking for network time to present a message directly to the public. The three networks are generally generous with their airtime, though they have been known to reject such requests.

Covering the Government: National, State and Local

The president frequently dominates the news from Washington, but there is much more to covering the government than just zeroing in on the White House. In fact, government is so huge, stretching from Congress and the judicial system down through a bewildering maze of government agencies and bureaucratic offshoots, that it may seem at times simply too awesome in size and complexity for mortal journalists to understand, much less report in a meaningful way to the public. Indeed, government size and complexity have proved so daunting to some members of the Washington press corps that they have taken the easy way out, focusing on politics and the president because they are simpler to comprehend and flashier to report. But many reporters, including some of the best in Washington, are always ready to probe the probity and performance of Washington's tangled departmental bureaucracy. It is these masses of government agencies and departments, after all, that swallow the bulk of this country's massive budget.

Nor does government coverage stop at the national level. There are state governments to consider, with governors, legislatures and their own smaller webs of bureaucracy. There are county governments as well as city township governments with mayors and commissioners and city managers. There are sheriff's departments, police departments, city councils and boards of education. We are a nation of local and regional governments, and all must be reported if the electorate is to make rational decisions when it is time to select new leaders.

How do the media cut through this Gordian knot of governmental intricacies and make sense of it to their audiences? Through perseverance, primarily. Familiarity helps. By getting to know government and its inner workings, reporters learn to recognize important stories. Some are easier than others. There are public information officers and governmental devices to smooth the way to positive stories, news that makes the government look good. For less flattering stories, the reporter must often resort to curiosity, shoe leather and old-fashioned digging.

Public Information Officers

Practically every governmental agency and department in the country, from the biggest bureau in Washington to the smallest state investigatory task force, has its own public information officer. (Even the secretive Central Intelligence Agency has a public information office, though the traditional response to all queries is a standard "no comment.") Since government agencies exist on public funds and are always eager for public notice and approval, most information officers are quick to help journalists, particularly if the information sought is favorable to the agency in question. They not only stand ready to answer queries but also frequently seek attention through departmental press conferences, carefully prearranged interviews and news tips. But they have also been known to do just the opposite—keep information under wraps.

Government Handouts

The mainstay of the public information officer, like any public relations practitioner, is the press release. Governmental press releases are cranked out at a dizzying pace and provide the basis for most of the news we get on the daily process of governance. Since reporters seldom have time to verify the flood of press releases, the situation is ripe for news management. Veteran reporters try to double-check the more important government-source facts before passing them along to readers or viewers, but not all reporters are so conscientious. For a good many years there was a special rack on the 13th floor of Washington's National Press Building that was used solely for the accumulation of daily government handouts. The bustling bar of the National Press Club was only a few feet away. At least one reporter (representing a Western newspaper) unabashedly conducted his entire day's business from the bar, breaking away only long enough to gather handouts and call in his stories. He didn't last long.

News Sources

To go beyond press briefings and government handouts, the successful reporter will also fashion a network of regular news sources. The most difficult task for any newly assigned reporter on the federal or state government level is to find and cultivate these sources. It's easier, of course, for reporters representing highly visible news organizations—a television network or a newspaper such as *The New York Times* or one of the news magazines, for example. With some mild socializing, they often get cabinet officers, committee chairs and high-level officials to become their sources. Journalists from lesser-known publications and local TV outlets usually have to settle for lower-level sources.

How do reporters dig up reliable news sources? Time is often the key. Do your job well, and they'll come to you. Good sources gravitate to journalists with a reputation for fairness and accuracy. But a reporter can't always wait. The job begins the first day you arrive in Washington or some state capital. You need information immediately. Many reporters make contacts at the endless briefings and breakfasts and luncheons where key government officials gather to meet with reporters and each other. In Washington, there is an added advantage, the continuous swirl of cocktail meetings and diplomatic parties. Not only can one make important contacts, but a great

Leaks Can Be
Official

Of particular difficulty for most ordinary citizens to understand is the obvious tendency of government reporters to rely on leaks from government sources. Stories resulting from leaks are usually anonymous, either unattributed or credited to hazy, unknown voices such as "a reliable source in the State Department," "a White House official" or "a highly placed Congressional spokesman." Such vague attributions bring to mind shadowy images of disloyal government employees, out to discredit a hard-working president, cabinet minister or senate committee. Some leaks are manipulative, it's true. And many come from disgruntled people, striking back at imagined wrongs (and some *not* imagined). But more often than not, the leaker being quoted is the president's own press secretary, the Secretary of State or some senator who wants to get word back to his or her constituency.

The leak has become an acceptable mechanism in the machinery of government/press operations. Top-ranking officials use them all the time to test public reaction to ideas and policy proposals, to send messages to other branches of government or to gain the initiative over political colleagues in some ongoing governmental debate. The leaked story, then, is often just another channel used by government officials to communicate information for which they are not yet ready to accept responsibility. When reporters use leaked stories, they often play a part in the governmental information chain. By doing so, they become a part of the governmental process that they are supposed to be watching.

Part of the problem lies in an aging set of ground rules still used for most official government briefings. When a government source calls a briefing or press session, the source sets the conditions. Once a reporter accepts the conditions, he or she is obligated to respect them. And that can lead to trouble.

What are the traditional conditions?

On the Record. Fortunately, the most common condition for interviews, press briefings and news conferences is to go *on the record*. That condition indicates a wide-open reporting status, with no restrictions. The source can be quoted directly and named. The reporter is on solid ground.

Not for Attribution. All too common, however, is the half step away from full disclosure. *Not for attribution* means that the writer can use all the material provided, even full, direct quotes, but without naming the source. If the president's press secretary declares a session not for attribution, you can use his or her exact words and report everything he or she said, but you'll have to credit your story to some

deal of government business is conducted over the rim of a glass at these parties, and an alert reporter can pick up story tips.

Socializing with sources presents its own dangers. Friendships can affect objectivity. Government officials aren't dummies. They know how useful it can be to have a friendly journalist in the pocket. It's called *cronyism*. If a cabinet official becomes your friend, gives you silk pajamas for your birthday and always asks about your family, you may someday find yourself protecting him or her from damaging news. And that can turn you into a very poor reporter. Some news organizations occasionally shuffle their reporters from beat to beat, just to guard against such temptations.

unseen official, like "a source close to the president" or "a White House insider." You've now left solid ground and are walking through sand.

Background. The next step away from reality is the *background* session. Not only can you not use the name of the source, but you also are no longer allowed to use his or her exact words. You can describe what was said, but only in your own words. Your story becomes a series of paraphrases, credited to an unnamed source. At this point, the dangers for the reporter begin to multiply. Readers or viewers may decide the story is suspect and accuse the reporter of fabricating it. If the story is accepted, but public reaction is unfavorable, the reporter is still on the hook. The source can always claim that he or she was misunderstood or that someone else entirely must have made the statement.

Deep Background. When a news source goes into *deep background,* the reporter takes a final step and finds nothing but empty air. This convention requires you to write as if there is no source at all. You can still use the information, but it must read as if you pulled it all together for yourself. Deep background conditions often give stories a suspect aura. Without documentation or a credited authority, stories may sound entirely too speculative. Your credibility can suffer.

Off the Record. There is one final condition, but most reporters prefer to avoid it. *Off the record* is a condition of complete secrecy. If you agree to listen to off-the-record comments, that means you can't use them (not even anonymously). Veteran reporters have learned to interrupt immediately when someone says "This is off the record." If you refuse to accept off-the-record material, the source can either change his or her mind and put it on the record or move on to another subject entirely. But once you allow the off-the-record condition to stand, the information is lost, unless you can find another source who says the same thing *on* the record. Even then you must return to your first source and explain.

Most reporters would rather not use unattributed quotes, just as TV reporters would prefer not to use diffusion screens and voice modulators to hide the identity of sources. So why do reporters allow themselves to be handcuffed in such a way? Actually, reporters can refuse in advance to abide by any condition they find unacceptable. Some do. But it usually means getting up and leaving the room while competitors stay to make notes. And that may mean getting beat on a story. Most reporters would rather not be put in that position.

Access to Information

For reporters who believe in digging up their own information, a government beat can be extremely frustrating. A truism about most bureaucracies is that they seem to grow in a befuddling manner, no matter how carefully organizational charts are tended. In the larger bureaucratic organizations, with their intricate chains of command and diversified duties, it is not unusual to find busy government workers who have no idea what's happening across the hall or two doors down. If a bureau or department chief wants to keep something out of the public eye, it is relatively easy to do so. Public trust scandals and bone-headed decisions are all too often hidden away forever.

Fortunately, federal and state governments have recognized the dangers of obsessive secrecy and have enacted various types of legislation to thwart it. Some are more useful than others.

Freedom of Information Act. Congress, troubled by growing secrecy after the end of World War II and convinced that people had a right to follow and understand the workings of government, passed the Freedom of Information Act in 1966. The FOI Act makes it possible for any citizen to challenge classified public records. The government must then prove that secrecy is necessary or release the information to the public. FOI Act guidelines provide a number of automatic exemptions, including legitimate intelligence and military secrets, trade and commerce secrets, personal medical records and law-enforcement investigatory files. The system has worked better under some administrations than others. Journalists use it occasionally, but often complain about its cost (the petitioner for information is required to pay for all information searches, and the costs can mount quickly) and its ponderously slow pace (it can take weeks, even months, to shake information loose, by which time it may no longer be relevant to a developing story).

Open Records Laws. Legislation also exists on both federal and state levels to force government bodies to conduct their business openly. Congress passed a federal "Government in the Sunshine" law in 1976, requiring more than 50 government boards and agencies to open their meetings and records to the public. There are exceptions to this law, too. Meetings can be closed for specified reasons, and records can be withheld when they pertain to national security matters, trade secrets and the hiring and firing practices of the agency involved.

Individual state governments began passing open meetings and records laws during the 1950s, providing easier public access to meetings, documents and investigatory files. By now, every state in the union, as well as the District of Columbia, has such a law. The impact of each law, however, varies from state to state. Key exemptions fluctuate from mental health proceedings to labor negotiations, and loopholes abound. But the existence of the laws is an encouraging step forward.

Investigative Reporting

When reporters move beyond public information officers, government handouts, public meetings and the other forms of information-gathering that are often too easily controlled at the source, they may be moving into a realm of hard-nosed digging known as *investigative journalism*. Striking off on one's own to track down a story lead requires patience, energy, a well-developed news sense and the deductive powers of a trained private eye. It can also require patience on the part of the reporter's parent medium, because some stories take a long time to put together. Every lead has to be analyzed, double-checked and followed up. Dead ends and unverified facts can bring any story to a halt. Some never fall in place.

But investigative reporting is a time-honored tool of good journalism, and the more prestigious news organizations are always ready to free a reporter or a team of reporters if they sniff a valuable story in the making. Check the yearly list of Pulitzer Prize award winners and you'll usually find one or more excellent examples of the investigative process. The practice isn't new. Trailblazing reporters like Ida Tarbell, Lincoln Steffens and Jacob Riis used investigative techniques in the early part of this century to track down and expose government corruption, social injustice and criminal business practices. They did their jobs so well that they were called muckrakers, a pejorative tag which they, and others after them, have worn with pride.

The best-known example of successful investigative reporting in modern journalism took place when two young journalists from *The Washington Post* took on a minor burglary story in June 1972 and turned it into America's most shocking political scandal. The reporters were Bob Woodward and Carl Bernstein. The burglary was a late-night raid on the campaign offices of the Democratic National Committee, housed at that time in a Washington

Richard Nixon leaves the presidency in 1974, as a result of press coverage and subsequent investigations surrounding the Watergate burglary.

Washington Post reporters Carl Bernstein and Bob Woodward, who broke the Watergate stories, stand in front of the symbol of the presidency.

apartment complex known as Watergate. The break-in was bungled, and the burglars were caught. Most early stories tossed off the incident in a few paragraphs. By the time the Watergate saga had run its course two years later, a total of 18 men, many of them important government officials, were in jail, and a president had been forced to resign.

In the beginning, most editors and reporters missed the significance of the Watergate break-in. A presidential campaign was in full swing at the time, and top political reporters were too busy covering the speeches and electioneering trips of the two candidates, incumbent Richard Nixon and challenger George McGovern. Nixon's press secretary, Ron Ziegler, dismissed the Watergate story as a "third-rate burglary attempt" and refused to comment on it. But Woodward and Bernstein, the two *Post* reporters, were convinced the story was important and kept digging.

Other news organizations drifted slowly to the Watergate story as the winter wore on, but it wasn't until nine months after the burglary that the rest of the Washington press corps piled onto the Watergate bandwagon. That's when one of the burglars, James McCord, wrote a letter to Judge John Sirica saying he was only an agent of higher authority and that pressure had been applied to keep him silent. Sirica made the letter public, and the Watergate story exploded.

The competitive nature of American journalism provided break after break in the longest-running political story this country has ever known. Political tricks, laundered funds, obstruction of justice, payments of hush money, abuses of power—the stories tumbled across the consciousness of a stunned American public. The Nixon administration hunkered down in the White House and tried to weather the storm, but too much had happened. The Senate Watergate Committee discovered the existence of a taping system in the White House. Judge Sirica demanded the tapes. Nixon proposed submission of transcripts only. Special Prosecuter Archibald Cox objected and Nixon fired him, leading to wholesale resignations in the Justice Department, the famous "Saturday Night Massacre." Then, as the House Judiciary Committee began an impeachment debate, a so-called "smoking gun" tape surfaced, providing proof of the president's role in a Watergate conspiracy of silence. The tape, recorded only six days after the initial break-in, exposed a presidential conversation in which Nixon and his chief of staff, H. R. Haldeman, discussed a plan to use the CIA in an attempt to subvert the course of the official investigation. Before the House could start impeachment proceedings, Nixon resigned the presidency.

The press did an extraordinary job of bringing the Watergate story to the public. Though administration officials cried foul, issued denials and accused the press of frequent inaccuracies during the course of the investigation, remarkably few errors made their way into print or onto the airwaves. A few did, of course. And Nixon officials made the most of them. But the bulk of the stories denied by Nixon spokespeople were eventually proven to be factual.

How did the Watergate outcome affect the reputation of the press? Oddly enough, the result came in two forms. The short-term result was a peculiar period of admiration. Woodward and Bernstein wrote a book about their Watergate experiences, entitled *All the President's Men.* It became a best-seller. Robert Redford bought the movie rights to the book and played the role of Bob Woodward; Dustin Hoffman portrayed Carl Bernstein. But Watergate also exposed a number of press weaknesses, and the long-range backlash effects of Watergate, still being felt, have led to an almost paranoid suspicion on the part of many readers and viewers.

Problems for the Reporter

Tune in on some popular television programs and you'll see Angela Lansbury ("Murder, She Wrote") lecturing a pushy newspaper reporter for being more interested in selling newspapers than in telling the truth or Andy Griffith ("Matlock") trying to hustle a client past a swirling mob of rude, jostling men and women with TV minicams, microphones and notepads. Why are reporters so frequently portrayed as semivillains cluttering up the television background? Why is one medium so willing to savage itself and other media in its entertainment programs? Perhaps because TV script writers, squeezed by the time constrictions of the 60-minute TV program, have to resort to stereotypes in order to ensure the credibility of their plots. They need instant villains who viewers are ready and willing to believe: politicians, venal businesspeople, crooked cops, alcoholic doctors —and insensitive journalists.

Attacks on the integrity of the press are as common as breakfast cereal, baseball and backyard barbecues—all distinctly American traditions. Why?

A hard question to answer. Buzz-words and charges abound. You hear them all the time. The press is too negative, arrogant, hostile, biased. Media have grown too large, too powerful. And on and on. Some of the criticism is probably deserved. Much is not. Reporters certainly leave themselves open to criticism when they use information-gathering practices that casual public observers either don't understand or are unwilling to tolerate (such as leaks from anonymous sources, for example). But many of the complaints are based on myth and misunderstanding.

Perhaps it will help if we investigate some of these public perceptions about the press.

Bigness

Size is a problem. Americans seem to resent anything that grows too big: the telephone industry, bureaucracy, the national budget. People used to get most of their news from the local newspaper. These days, more and more people turn to the three national television networks for the bulk of their news. Community newspapers and local TV stations certainly get their share of public shellacking, but the heavy guns of criticism and complaint are most often trained on the remote giants of the news industry—the three major networks, the wire services, the big eastern newspapers in New York and Washington. There's a misguided public tendency to lump together all national media into a sort of great amorphous, monolithic lump. Part of the problem is that far too many people mistakenly use the word *media* in the singular. "The media is unfair." *Media* as a singular noun is not only atrocious English, it's misleading. It gives the impression that the fractious, fragmented media are one solitary, single-minded giant, working to control the flow of ideas and information. The proper singular usage is *medium*. Radio is a broadcast *medium*. Television is a visual *medium*. Books comprise yet another *medium*. Put them all together, and you have a vastly diverse, wildly competitive, often contradictory set of *media*.

Negativism

A frequent complaint is that news media concentrate on bad news: Death, injury, crime, accidents and natural disasters crowd the airwaves and front pages, shrinking the "good news," if there is any, to relatively small items in the back of the newspaper or the tail end of the telecast. Is this true? In some ways, yes. Actually, there's more good news in your newspaper and daily broadcast report than you might realize. Try it some time. Spread a newspaper out on the kitchen counter and count the positive stories and negative stories. You might be surprised. Most of us remember the negative stories because they catch our attention. Conflict and catastrophe fascinate us. The pleasant "happy" items about new hospital wings and fundraising events and charity contributions are often too boring to stick in our memories.

And still, the negatives often outweigh the positives. So is this criticism a valid one? News people bridle when they hear it. A stock answer (perhaps oversimplified) is to remind critics that there is but one modern press-theory system in the world in which news media offer only good news about their countries. And that press system, though changing, is found only in surviving Communist countries.

Inaccuracy

Are media news reports inaccurate? Some, probably. Mistakes are inevitable, considering the human complexities of the news-gathering process and the constrictions of time. Think back to Chapter 1 and the discussion of message entropy. An event occurs and a report of that event has to filter through many layers in the information chain—from participants and witnesses to reporter, from reporter to editor, from editor to copy desk, from copy desk to printer, from printer to page—all under the pressure of imminent deadline and all subject to the many psychological, mechanical and semantic barriers that confound accurate communication. Mistakes are bound to occur. The really remarkable thing is that more inaccuracies don't creep into the news.

But every single inaccuracy, projected on a mass screen for all to see, helps to erode public confidence. In a 1974 Gallup survey following Watergate, a representative sample of Americans were asked to respond to the statement "Newspapers are not careful about getting their facts straight." A staggering 67 percent said they either definitely agreed or partly agreed with that assessment.

A 1984 *Newsweek* poll asked a similar question, "How much of what you read or hear in the news media as a whole can you believe?" Only 39 percent answered "almost all" or "most." The remainder, 61 percent, responded "only some" or "very little." And yet when the same *Newsweek* poll asked respondents whether in their own experience—events they had been involved with or knew about personally—the media had reported facts correctly or inaccurately, 46 percent said media had their facts straight. Only 37 percent (still a pretty sizeable chunk of the audience) claimed to have personal knowledge of inaccurate stories.

Unfairness

The "objective" system of reporting is an American invention, dating from the early days of the embryonic Associated Press. Since a number of newspapers, often with widely varied political affiliations, were expected to use stories produced by a cooperative pool of reporters, it became necessary to write those stories with an even-handed, fair appraisal of events, acceptable to all quarters. So-called "objective reporting" was the result. We know, of course, that complete objectivity is a myth. The best one can do is to try to be objective. The consistent pursuit of objectivity is a basic tenet in all American news coverage. Most reporters follow the principle that a conscious attempt to be fair will, in effect, tilt the scales toward fairness.

But the reading and viewing public doesn't always agree, particularly when it comes to political coverage. A peculiarity of our democratic system is that long, involved process that comes around once every four years, the parade of candidates for their party's presidential nomination. In theory, it's a time for testing. Political reporters follow the candidates around the country and report their ideas, their stands on issues and their policies. But for many disgruntled readers and viewers, the modern campaign process seems primarily to provoke a feeding frenzy of journalistic sharks. We all have our political favorites and basic political beliefs, and we don't like anyone taking potshots at them, not even "objective" potshots. Case in point: the fall of Gary Hart from presidential primary grace when he was caught by a *Miami Herald* reporter in the company of a young woman who was not his wife. The story stirred public outrage, and not all of it was directed at Hart. Critics assailed reporters for bedroom snooping. Poll after poll showed that the majority of readers and viewers considered press coverage of Hart's personal life to be excessive and unfair. A *Time* magazine poll asked "Do you think it is right or wrong for the press to write stories about the sex life of presidential candidates?" A resounding 67 percent of the polled respondents denounced the practice. Only 27 percent considered it permissible. A poll by *Newsweek* magazine verified the findings. Asked "Do you think the media have been fair or unfair in their treatment of marital-infidelity charges against Gary Hart?" 64 percent declared media unfair, and only 22 percent considered the treatment fair. *The Miami Herald* conducted its own survey and found that local figures matched national figures. A hefty 63 percent of its readers challenged the Hart coverage as excessive.

And yet, when Gary Hart, perhaps encouraged by the sympathetic tenor of these poll results, decided later to reinsert himself into the race, vowing

During his 1992 campaign for President, Bill Clinton is accused of marital infidelity by Gennifer Flowers. Here, at a news conference arranged by the tabloid with exclusive rights to her story, Flowers talks about her alleged affair with Clinton.

Dedication To Language

I dedicate myself to words—
    words that spill like flimsy fish
    through the nets of understanding;
    I would become a net-repairer,
    or build new nets of tougher fiber;
    I would constrain the elusive words
    that flash shimmering before the eyes
    and flirt with the mind.
I turn away from weak, wet words
    that wash away at the edges,
    and flop their frigid forms in sad gesture.
    I seek the precise words, the firm words,
    words that pierce to the inner core
    of consciousness with meaning and knowledge.
    I relish those words that alternately growl and purr
    as they rush to do my bidding.
I dedicate myself to language—
    to language that fits the occasion,
    to words that roll to the cadence of the message
    and spark the flames of excitement.
I dedicate myself to verbal precision
    that cuts cleanly through the thickened thought
    and seeks the crystal core of credibility.
I eschew the charred word,
    the undernourished and overused word,
    the weary word
    that flays away at thoughtless minds
    and drones drearily in dark redundance.
I seek words that grab the truth
    and cast it courageously before the crowd,
    intent always on directness and light,
    avoiding the dank darkness of delusion.
In sum, I dedicate myself
    to harness and use that ponderous pounding
    of language that restlessly rolls across
    the barrier reefs of perception
    and persistently probes
    the shifting beaches of humanity.

John Merrill
1971

to ignore the press and take his case directly to the people, he quickly bombed. American media audiences may decry the methods and interests of the press. But they apparently listen.

Bias

Critics also frequently charge the press with bias. Reporters are too liberal, they say. Or too conservative. Or too establishment-oriented. Though a majority of media outlets are owned by Republicans, conservative critics point to an apparent preponderance of Democratic reporters and editors at the working level and profess to see a consistent liberal bias in the choice and handling of news stories. One conservative coalition, headed by Senator Jesse Helms, even made noises about buying the CBS television network, so they could "be Dan Rather's boss" and guarantee fairer coverage of conservative issues.

But accusations of bias can come from all quarters—from liberals, from moderates, from conservatives. It all depends on whose ox is being gored.

Arrogance

Reporters and editors seldom win popularity contests. Nor should they try to. They are in the business of gathering news and presenting it to their readers and viewers. Most of them take that role very seriously. And it is an impressive calling. They spend their waking hours holding a mirror to history (though mirrors never edit), preparing a public record of the grand, great, mean, petty or otherwise important events of the day. They inform, entertain and persuade. They stir the economy and keep the wheels of commerce turning. They function to reflect what is good or evil in society and, consciously or unconsciously, they occasionally shape society's future.

A lofty job description, to say the least. For the journalist who covers government, add the basic concept of the libertarian press system, alerting the public to governmental processes and excesses so that future electoral decisions can be made with the fullest possible knowledge and understanding. With such an idealistic backdrop to motivate them, perhaps we can understand why journalists on the government beat often seem to be prideful, self-righteous, even arrogant. Still, less arrogance would undoubtedly help their image.

Modern American journalism certainly has its weaknesses. It has also made remarkable strides in recent years. Today's newspapers and magazines are immeasurably superior to the brawling, fractious partisan publications that time left scattered across the historical landscape of early American journalism. The two media newcomers, radio and television, have grown from infancy to adulthood, blazing their own trails through a thicket of reportorial brambles. There will always be room for improvement. There will always be room for innovation. But it's still the best press system in the world. And for that we can thank the First Amendment to the Constitution of the United States.

First Amendment freedoms, as we shall see in the next chapter, are not designed for the exclusive use of the journalist but for the good of the country as a whole. A free press functions to preserve our democratic system of government. To keep anyone from tampering with those freedoms, journalists must continue to examine the various valid criticisms and charges that are hurled at them. Only by analyzing and responding to criticism can the press guarantee its ongoing function in the constitutional process.

The term "journalism" doesn't seem to have a clear-cut meaning in any language. And yet "journalism" and such companion words as "journalist" and "news" are used in virtually every country to mean roughly the same thing, but with shades of difference. Let's take a quick look at the three words as they exist in seven of the world's major languages, without attempting to specify the meaning in any of them.

	journalism	journalist	news
English	**journalism**	**journalist**	**news**
French	journalisme	journaliste	nouvelle
German	Journalismus or Zeitungswesen	Journalist or Zeitungsschreiber	Nachrichten
Italian	giornalismo	giornalista	notizia
Spanish	periodismo	periodista	noticias
Russian	Professia Jurnalista	Jurnalist	Novosti or Izvestia
Chinese	hsin wen hsüeh	hsin wen chi che	hsin wen

Retrospective

The relationships between press and government vary according to the governmental press system under which the press operates. Closed *authoritarian* systems usually regulate press units tightly. *Libertarian* systems generally favor an open market of information and ideas. *Soviet systems* used the press as an arm of government. There are critics under all forms of government who favor concepts of *social responsibility* for the press, but these concepts will vary from system to system.

The American system often leads to an adversarial relationship between press and government, in which government officials attempt to conceal some aspects of information and press representatives work just as hard to uncover the information. This shadow-boxing relationship can exist from top to bottom in government—from the hallowed halls of Washington, D.C., to musty offices in small towns.

Adversarial reporting has also led to public criticism of the press. Critics charge press media with being too big, too negative, inaccurate, unfair, biased and arrogant. Some of these negative perceptions are perhaps deserved, but some are based on myth and misconception.

Questions

1. Name the four theories of the press. Which is considered a "democratic" stance? Imagine the press of the United States under any of the three remaining theories. How would it (or could it?) affect the American system of government?

2. What do we mean by "the adversarial relationship"? Do you consider such a relationship to be good or bad? Why?

3. Name some of the ways in which a president can control news. Can you give specific examples in which you have seen the results of any of these presidential controls?

4. In what ways does the president's press secretary differ from a general public relations practitioner?

5. Do you consider the publication of "kiss-and-tell" books to be ethical or unethical? Why?

6. How does coverage of the president differ from coverage of departments and bureaus? Which do you think is more difficult? Why?

Suggested Readings

Abel, Elie. *Leaking: Who Does It? Who Benefits? At What Cost?* Unwin Hyman Media Studies. Winchester, Ma.: Priority Press, 1987.

Bernstein, Carl, and Woodward, Bob. *All the President's Men.* New York: Simon & Schuster, 1974.

Cater, Douglass. *The Fourth Branch of Government.* New York: Vintage Books, 1959.

Crouse, Timothy. *The Boys on the Bus.* New York: Random House, 1973.

Donaldson, Sam. *Hold On, Mr. President!* New York: Random House, 1987.

Hess, Stephen. *The Washington Reporters.* Washington, D.C.: Brookings Institute, 1981.

Hiebert, Ray Eldon, ed. *The Press in Washington.* New York: Dodd, Mead & Company, 1966.

Lee, John, ed. *The Diplomatic Persuaders.* New York: John Wiley & Sons, 1968.

McGinniss, Joe. *The Selling of the President 1968.* New York: Trident Press, 1969.

Merrill, John C. *The Dialectic in Journalism: Toward a Responsible Use of Freedom.* Baton Rouge: Louisiana State University Press, 1989.

Powell, Jody. *The Other Side of the Story.* New York: William Morrow & Company, 1984.

Rivers, William L. *The Adversaries—Politics and the Press.* Boston: Beacon Press, 1970.

Siebert, Fred S., Peterson, Theodore, and Schramm, Wilbur. *Four Theories of the Press.* Urbana: University of Illinois Press, 1956.

Speakes, Larry. *Speaking Out.* New York: Charles Scribner's Sons, 1988.

Thompson, Hunter S. *Fear and Loathing: On the Campaign Trail.* New York: Popular Library, 1973.

Freedom and Controls

As coalition troops headed toward Saudi Arabia in August 1990 to prepare for the Persian Gulf War, American military planners worked feverishly to concoct a plan of battle. Saddam Hussein had a huge army. To confront him properly, air, sea and naval units had to be coordinated, supplies transported, weapons stockpiled, timing approved, attack routes devised. And one other priority item had to be considered: how to handle the 1,500 members of the world press who would shortly arrive on the scene to cover the war.

The military establishment had learned its lesson in Vietnam. Pentagon planners, with the backing of the Bush administration, made a conscious decision to control news in the Persian Gulf conflict and make sure that any information released to the media supported the political goals of the operation. A classified memo detailing the strict news policy went out on military computers. Among other things, the memo told field combat officers, "News media representatives will be escorted at all times. Repeat, at all times." By the time the air war began in January, a pool system had been put into effect. Only a restricted number of reporters and photographers could talk to the pilots or visit troops in the field, and only when accompanied by hand-picked military briefers.

When the ground war began in earnest some five weeks later, massed coalition troops (including Americans, British, Saudis, Egyptians, French and others) swarmed into the sandy wastes of Kuwait and Iraq to encircle and finish off the remnants of Saddam Hussein's beleaguered forces. Only a handful of American news reporters (159) were allowed to accompany the troops, all in controlled military press pools. Every word written by the pool reporters had to be cleared by military censors, causing long delays. The ground war lasted only 110 hours. Some of the copy written by pool journalists didn't reach home until a week after the fighting ended.

Those American reporters who were unable to obtain pool assignments (more than a thousand were left behind) had to rely on sanitized government briefing sessions, accepting filtered information at face value. Complaints from the press establishment were heated and numerous. And all but ignored. As the ground war swept to a quick and bloody conclusion, very little news reached home. Nor did Americans appear to mind. People at home, deprived of independent news accounts, turned on their TVs to hear a succession of generals giving them spoon-fed information at carefully orchestrated press conferences, watched smart bombs perform with perfection like hideous video games and learned only what the military censors wanted them to know.

Did this blatant censorship bother the American public? Apparently not. A poll conducted at the beginning of the air war by the Times Mirror Center for the People and the Press asked whether the military should exert even more control over the press. A surprising 57 percent of those Americans polled said yes. Only 34 percent said decisions should be left to the media. A *Newsweek* poll conducted at about the same time found that 64 percent thought news media made it harder for U.S. officials to conduct the war, while only 32 percent considered Pentagon controls too strict.

Censorship? In a country known for its free press? Yes, it happens. True, the American press system is among the freest in the world. But nothing can be taken for granted. And freedom has never been absolute. In many cases, a free-press guarantee lasts only as long as a government is willing to stand behind it. Events occur. Public perceptions change. A government feels endangered. Press rights are suspended. Sometimes the repression is temporary. Too often it becomes a permanent condition. And freedoms erode.

The basic foundation for our press freedom can be found in the wording of the First Amendment to the Constitution of the United States. It says:

> Congress shall make no law respecting an establishment of religion, or prohibiting the free exercise thereof; or abridging the freedom of speech, or of the press, or the right of the people peaceably to assemble, and to petition the Government for a redress of grievances.

Handsome words. But a finely crafted governmental pledge doesn't automatically guarantee press freedom. Every government on earth offers some form of press guarantee. Even the Constitution of the former Union of Soviet Socialist Republics, for example, once stated in its Article 50, "In accordance with the interests of the people and in order to strengthen and develop the socialist system, citizens of the USSR are guaranteed freedom of speech, of the press, and of assembly, meetings, street processions and demonstrations." Equally handsome words. But they were hardly effective in actual practice.

Pledges of press freedom have failed in so many countries. But not in America. In spite of the occasional slippage, our First Amendment press guarantee has continued to work for two hundred years. Why? The brilliance of 18th-century American Constitutional framers was in linking press freedom with the other guaranteed freedoms—religion, right of assembly and speech and redress of grievances. Americans feel strongly about their individual freedoms and bridle when someone talks of curtailing them. By linking press freedom closely to the other freedoms, our forebears made it doubly difficult for anyone to tinker with the status of the press without infringing on the rights of the individual.

But it hasn't always been easy to maintain our First Amendment freedoms. Public opinion waxes and wanes with the temper of the times, and there have been moments in our history when "public spirited" individuals, perhaps even a majority of America's citizenry, have roused themselves to speak against one or another of the First Amendment freedoms. Occasional attempts have been made to change them. Potentially restrictive laws have issued from Congress. Peaceful assemblies have been outlawed. Censorship tools have surfaced. Whole segments of society have been uprooted during wartime and placed in detention camps. None of these repressive activities have lasted for long. Thanks to the carefully interwoven language of the early framers and our unintimidated judiciary, no individual or group has found it possible to remove permanently one freedom from the others without unraveling the whole fabric.

John Stuart Mill, the English philosopher, writing 80-some years after the U.S. Constitution was written, argued strongly for free expression, thus:

If all mankind minus one were of one opinion, and only one person were of the contrary opinion, mankind would be no more justified in silencing that one person, than he, if he had the power, would be justified in silencing mankind. . . . But the peculiar evil of silencing the expression of an opinion is, that it is robbing the human race; posterity as well as the existing generation; those who dissent from the opinion, still more than those who hold it. If the opinion is right, they are deprived of the opportunity of exchanging error for truth; if wrong, they lose, what is almost as great a benefit, the clearer perception and livelier impression of truth, produced by its collision with error.

Source: John Stuart Mill, *On Liberty* (1859).

A Brief History

Press freedoms came to us slowly and painfully. When the printing press migrated to America, authoritarian control followed right behind. As we have already learned, the first newspaper in the Colonies, Benjamin Harris's *Publick Occurences,* was suppressed by Boston authorities in 1690 after one issue. Later attempts at newspaper publishing also faced careful government scrutiny. John Campbell's *Boston News-Letter* was precensored by the Royal Governor. James Franklin's *New England Courant* was ordered to submit materials for precensorship, and Franklin was twice arrested. And then came John Peter Zenger.

You've already read about the John Peter Zenger trial (in Chapter 5), and you know that it didn't really establish a new legal principle. But it did establish the fact that many American colonists were firmly opposed to a continuation of authoritarian press control. That opposition was to grow over the next 50 years and bear fruit during the American Revolution and, following the American victory, the Constitutional Convention of 1787.

There is a popular conception that our constitutional press guarantee was a direct result of antiauthoritarian sympathies still smoldering after years of oppressive English rule and was intended as a blanket freedom. Was that really the way it happened? Or was the commitment to a free press just a lucky accident? Evidence points both ways. The original draft of the Constitution didn't even mention press freedom. Nine of the 13 new states had already made provision for press freedom in their state constitutions, and some of the men at the Constitutional Convention felt that was enough.

Perhaps the issue of press freedom boiled down to one of the first schisms in the newborn republic. Most new Americans were either Federalists, in favor of a strong central government, or Anti-Federalists, favoring a shadow government that would act as glue for a string of strong state governments. Some historians suggest that the Bill of Rights, which contained a series of amendments including the First Amendment press guarantee, was written

Numb. 1.

PUBLICK
OCCURRENCES

Both *FORREIGN* and *DOMESTICK*.

Boston, Thursday Sept. 25th. 1690.

IT is designed, that the Country shall be furnished once a moneth (or if any Glut of Occurrences happen, oftener,) with an Account of such considerable things as have arrived unto our Notice.

In order hereunto, the Publisher will take what pains he can to obtain a Faithful Relation of all such things; and will particularly make himself beholden to such Persons in Boston whom he knows to have been for their own use the diligent Observers of such matters.

That which is herein proposed, is, First, That Memorable Occurrents of Divine Providence may not be neglected or forgotten, as they too often are. Secondly, That people every where may better understand the Circumstances of Publique Affairs, both abroad and at home; which may not only direct their Thoughts at all times, but at some times also to assist their Businesses and Negotiations.

Thirdly, That some thing may be done towards the Curing, or at least the Charming of that Spirit of Lying, which prevails amongst us, wherefore nothing shall be entered, but what we have reason to believe is true, repairing to the best fountains for our Information. And when there appears any material mistake in any thing that is collected, it shall be corrected in the next.

Moreover, the Publisher of these Occurrences is willing to engage, that whereas, there are many False Reports, maliciously made, and spread among us, if any well-minded person will be at the pains to trace any such false Report so far as to find out and Convict the First Raiser of it, he will in this Paper (unless just Advice be given to the contrary) expose the Name of such person, as A malicious Raiser of a false Report. It is supposed that none will dislike this Proposal, but such as intend to be guilty of so villanous a Crime.

THE Christianized *Indians* in some parts of *Plimouth*, have newly appointed a day of Thanksgiving to God for his Mercy in supplying their extream and pinching Necessities under their late want of Corn, & for His giving them now a prospect of a very Comfortable Harvest. Their Example may be worth Mentioning.

'Tis observed by the Husbandmen, that altho' the With-draw of so great a strength from them, as what is in the Forces lately gone for *Canada*, made them think it almost impossible for them to get well through the Affairs of their Husbandry at this time of the year, yet the Season has been so unusually favourable that they scarce find any want of the many hundreds of hands, that are gone from them; which is looked upon as a Merciful Providence.

While the barbarous *Indians* were lurking about *Chelmsford*, there were about the beginning of this month a couple of Children belonging to a man of that Town, one of them aged about eleven the other aged about nine years, both of them supposed to be fallen into the hands of the *Indians*.

A very Tragical Accident happened at *Water-Town*, the beginning of this Month, an Old man, that was of somewhat a Silent and Morose Temper, but one that had long Enjoyed the reputation of a Sober and a Pious Man, having newly buried his Wife, The Devil took advantage of the Melancholly which he thereupon fell into, his Wives discretion and industry had long been the support of his Family, and he seemed hurried with an impertinent fear that he should now come to want before he dyed, though he had very careful friends to look after him who kept a strict eye upon him, least he should do himself any harm. But one evening escaping from them into the Cow-house, they there quickly followed him, found him changing by a Rope, which they had used to tye their Calves withal, he was dead with his feet near touching the Ground.

Epidemical *Fevers* and *Agues* grow very common, in some parts of the Country, whereof, tho' many dye not, yet they are sorely unfitted for their imployments; but in some parts a more malignant Fever seems to prevail in such sort that it usually goes thro' a Family where it comes, and proves Mortal unto many.

The *Small-pox* which has been raging in *Boston*, after a manner very Extraordinary is now very much abated. It is thought that far more have been sick of it then were visited with it, when it raged so much twelve years ago, nevertheless it has not been so Mortal. The number of them that have

EXAMPLE 401
The first and only number of America's first newspaper

Publick Occurences,
America's first newspaper,
is immediately censored.

CHAPTER 14 Freedom and
Controls

primarily as a sop to the Anti-Federalists, to get them to accept the Constitution more readily. These historians tell us we should read the pertinent portion of the amendment with stress on the word *Congress*. "*Congress* shall make no law . . . abridging the freedom of speech or of the press." In other words, the Federalists were giving up the central government's right to control the press and leaving it to the Anti-Federalists and the various state governments to pass whatever restrictive laws they might wish.

Whatever the intent, the First Amendment to the Constitution of the United States is a powerful statement that has stood the test of time. Without a free press, America would not be the country it is today.

Censorship—An Ugly Word

Even so, it isn't possible for any government to give complete freedom to its press system. Even the most libertarian democracy will recognize the absolute necessity for certain press limitations. Individual property rights must be considered. Reputations must be safeguarded. The populace must be protected from advertising fraud. Guarantees of personal privacy must be observed. The right to a fair and impartial jury trial must be maintained. Laws must be designed to protect and maintain community standards of decency. Without such protections, a free press would be meaningless.

Nevertheless, in a true democracy, such press restrictions are usually kept to a minimum. In cases where press freedom and individual rights collide, America has a better-than-average record of thoughtful courtroom decisions. Only when the government sees itself in danger do press restrictions sometimes get out of hand. If war breaks out, the prudent government will galvanize its forces and lower its risks. The first victim is often the press.

The Press at War, from 1861 to Desert Storm

Censorship is often the first weapon in a wartime arsenal (and truth the first casualty). In some of our American wars, censorship has been wielded like an ax, chopping raggedly and indiscriminately at any target that catches the censor's fancy. In other wars, the thrusts have been more deft, a surgical incision here or there. Now, with the unremitting eye of the television camera focused on the business of war, military leaders seem to have developed a new aversion to media coverage. So much so that when Desert Storm troops swept into Iraq, the American government declared a complete news blackout, allowing nothing to be reported from the field until the order was rescinded a couple of days later. Even then, copy had to be reviewed. Military censors said the review was needed to protect the troops and maintain operational security. And yet protection of the troops and operational plans didn't appear to be the only matters that concerned censors. Journalists complained that peculiar alterations occurred in their copy that had nothing to do with security. For example, one military censor changed the word "giddy" to "proud" in a story about pilots returning from a bombing mission. Another censor substituted "rescued" for the word "captured" in another story about Iraqis taken prisoner.

Early Wars. Wartime censorship was dormant in America's first wars. This is not to say our early journals got off lightly. Although the newly formed rebel government made no attempt during the American Revolution to censor the writings of its citizenry, hot-blooded patriots felt no such compunction. Loyalist newspapers, faithful to the Crown, were badly treated throughout the war, and many were forced out of business. Later wars were treated just as casually by government officials. Coverage of the War of 1812 was spotty at best and largely written from official reports, so the government kept its hands off. The Mexican-American War, the first to be covered by American correspondents in the field, was too far away to pose a threat to governmental security. News stories often took weeks to reach the pages of American newspapers, and when they did, they were strongly supportive of the American position. Censorship wasn't needed.

The Civil War. The situation changed when Confederate forces fired their first shots at Fort Sumter. For one thing, the war was in America's front yard. The telegraph, invented in 1844, had come into its own and provided a speedy way to bring the news to a nation's front pages. Having learned the value of front-line coverage in the Mexican-American War, newspaper editors flooded the battlefields with correspondents. Less than three months after the shelling of Fort Sumter, the Union Army issued an order forbidding the use of the telegraph to send any information of military value (and apparently with reason: some Southern generals devised their strategy based on Northern newspaper accounts of Union battle plans). Northern reporters, who relied on the telegraph, were forced to submit their articles to military censorship. Many field commanders used the new censorship authority not only to strike mentions of troop strengths and deployments but also to excise anything that might otherwise prove embarrassing to them personally.

Reporters quickly learned how far they could go to get through the censorship barrier. Those who wrote favorably about commanders in the field often sent copy through without problems. Those who continued to criticize military tactics and command-level weaknesses often found themselves cut off and speechless. In General William T. Sherman's camp, one reporter went too far and so angered the general that he found himself under arrest as a Southern spy. Sherman wanted to shoot the man, but the president intervened.

Spanish-American War. The next war was so quick and so successful that censorship was never an issue. But if ever wartime censorship was needed, this was the time. For one thing, the war might never have happened if the American press had been muzzled. These were the days of sensationalism,

Any government will try to protect itself from enemies, including those within its own population. That's why nations devise sedition laws—it's a simple matter of self-defense. Sedition can be as simple as criticism of the state or as extreme as a willful determination to overthrow the state. And in order for a citizen to criticize a government or advocate its violent overthrow, something must be said aloud or written. Hence, sedition laws in the United States will automatically touch on our First Amendment freedoms.

Sedition laws, although used effectively in Great Britain for centuries to stifle criticism of the government, have never been a particularly useful weapon in America. The *Sedition Act of 1798,* for example, made it unlawful to publish anything "false, scandalous and malicious" against the government of the United States, its officials or its legislation. It was passed at a time when the American press was actively partisan and was used by Federalists in power to punish the criticism of Anti-Federalist editors and writers. But the act was unpopular and was allowed to lapse three years later when Thomas Jefferson took office.

Over a hundred years later, the *Sedition Act of 1918* made it a crime to use "disloyal, profane, scurrilous or abusive language" about the government, the armed forces, military uniforms and even the flag. It was used primarily to deal with German-language newspapers during World War I and was allowed to expire in 1920.

A third sedition law, the *Smith Act of 1940,* is still on the books. The Smith Act made it a crime to advocate the violent overthrow of the government, but the Supreme Court defanged the law in 1957 when it ruled that the government must prove an active intent, rather than just an abstract doctrine.

What does *active intent/abstract doctrine* mean? If your professor tells you in class that your university is in a terrible state and should be burned to the ground so the educational process can be constructed anew, that would be an abstract doctrine of change. But if the professor goes further, rallies you together and says, "Let's march out right now and corner the Board of Regents and tar and feather them," that may be evidence of active intent. The Smith Act has seldom been used since the 1957 decision. The most recent attempt was a case involving a group of neo-Nazis in Arkansas. They were found innocent in 1988.

with William Randolph Hearst's *New York Journal* and Joseph Pulitzer's *New York World* fighting aggressively for circulation. Critics of the era claim that the Spanish-American War was an inevitable byproduct of that circulation battle. Frederick Remington, a popular artist of the time, was sent to Cuba by Hearst to make sketches of a reported rebellion against the Spaniards. Remington supposedly found no traces of the rebellion and asked permission to come home. Hearst's famous reply, perhaps apocryphal, was "Please stay. You supply the pictures. I'll supply the war." Once hostilities began, newspapers sent some 500 correspondents into the fray and cheerfully printed anything they could get their hands on, including troop movements, battle strategies and naval deployments. Hearst, who proudly called it "the *Journal*'s war," sailed his private yacht to Cuba with a reporting staff of 20 aboard. Journalists even entered the fighting. Reporters led at least two charges against Spanish troops.

World War I. Censors had time to prepare for the European War of 1914. By the time America got into it in 1917, it had become a world war, and national sentiments ran high. Within a week of America's entry, President

Woodrow Wilson had appointed George Creel to head the newly formed Committee on Public Information. The Creel Committee called for voluntary censorship on the part of newspapers and cranked out masses of wartime propaganda in the form of news releases. Most newspaper editors, eager to aid the war effort, censored themselves well beyond Creel's suggested guidelines and cheerfully ran most of the committee's propaganda releases.

In addition to self-censorship at home, war correspondents in Europe had to submit their communiqués to censorship by the press section of the U.S. Military Intelligence Service in France. News of battles, casualties and troop identifications were allowed only if they had already appeared in official releases. All in all, it was a tightly run war.

World War II. Voluntary censorship was again invoked after the Japanese attack on Pearl Harbor. Radio newscaster Elmer Davis was named to head the Office of War Information, modeled after the Creel Committee. And a government censorship office, headed by newsman Byron Price, directed mandatory censorship of all overseas mail and cable and radio communications; newspapers, magazines and books were issued guidelines only as to what they should or should not publish. The voluntary domestic system worked quite well.

Military censorship, on the other hand, went back to its World War I moorings, with the added problem of controlling shortwave radio transmissions. Some military censors were more active at news suppression than others. Navy censors, for example, horrified by the calamitous damage done by the Japanese at Pearl Harbor, withheld details of the disaster for almost a year. General Douglas MacArthur also came under fire for his censorship in the Pacific. Many editors and reporters claimed MacArthur's press officers were more interested in glamorizing their commander than in protecting military secrets.

Later Wars. Until the Korean conflict, wars had generally been patriotic ventures, with a country fully mobilized behind the war effort. But hostilities in Korea came soon after World War II, and a war-weary nation just couldn't gear up its enthusiasm. The fighting in Korea, like Vietnam after it, was unpopular in many quarters. Military censors, sensitive to the lack of popular support on the home front, turned their attention more to maintaining troop morale than to actual suppression of military secrets. Correspondents accused censors of using psychological censorship as well as military censorship. For example, the word *retreat* (a word that occurred too often in the early days of the war) was considered embarrassing by the censors and was disallowed. When General MacArthur was subsequently fired by President Truman, censorship eased. But military censors still complained over what they called inaccurate and biased reporting.

Vietnam was played out interminably before television cameras. It thus became perhaps the most thoroughly reported war in the history of civilization. For the first time, Americans could sit in their homes and watch young men die and kill and weep and grow old before their time. Scarcely a soul was left unmoved. Censorship played a minor role. Government and military leaders turned to a different method of controlling news: They lied. To protect U.S. policies in Southeast Asia, military and government spokespeople deliberately falsified information, ran up dubious daily "body counts" and often simply buried information that they considered damaging. They were caught lying so often by alert correspondents that government credibility suffered gravely. Because the Vietnam War had such a polarizing effect, many Americans were outraged that the press would reveal government shortcomings, and press credibility suffered as well.

The antagonism between the media and the military grew so intense during the Vietnam War that it has never really gone away. By the time the Reagan administration decided to send troops to invade the small Caribbean island of Grenada, an entirely new approach had been devised to control the press. For the first time ever, press representatives were simply left behind. Not until the third day, when things were relatively quiet, were reporters allowed to set foot on the island. Government spokespeople defended the ban, citing as sufficient reasons the possibility of leaks, the safety of journalists and danger to troops required to protect journalists. Journalists responded that they could keep secrets when necessary, that danger was part of their job, indeed that journalists had died in every war and accepted the possibility of death as quickly as soldiers in the field, and that they needed no special entourage of troops to protect them while present in the war zone. When tempers settled, the issue led to a Pentagon study and an eventual (though carefully qualified) agreement on the part of the administration to allow a press pool arrangement for future combat

War correspondents are initially left behind in the 1983 U.S. invasion of Grenada. Here, reporters Morris Thompson *(left)* and Bernard Diederich monitor developments from offshore.

situations. A small number of reporters—six or 10 or 12—would be allowed to accompany military groups. The pool would then make stories and videos available to all media.

This was the pool system that would so antagonize reporters during Desert Storm.

The Gulf War. The new pool system was tested in 1985 when the Defense Department called in 10 pool members and launched a surprise mock attack on a Central American country. The exercise was a mixture of success and failure, but the pool appeared to work. Then in 1987, when the Reagan administration decided to escort reflagged Kuwaiti oil tankers in the Persian Gulf, the pool system got its first actual test. A pool of 10 reporters, photographers and television personnel traveled with the Navy for five days. According to the newspeople who accompanied the escort convoys, the pool system worked well enough, though they noted an absence of women journalists and complained that some of their stories were frequently delayed unnecessarily.

When Saddam Hussein invaded Kuwait, the stage was set. The military, after the embarrassments of Vietnam and the successes of Grenada, began to see a correlation between victory and censorship. This mindset led to the early policy decision to control news from the Gulf. The Gulf War was the first major conflict in this century in which American reporters were restricted to carefully guarded pools that dictated when and how they could talk to troops in the field.

Information was also controlled by the Iraqis, as evidenced by the controversial presence of CNN reporter Peter Arnett in Baghdad. Arnett, who stayed behind when other American reporters were forced out of Iraq by Saddam Hussein, spoke almost nightly from Baghdad, transmitting reports that were monitored on the spot by an Iraqi censor. Some Americans were outraged, accusing Arnett and CNN of acting as conduits for Iraqi propaganda. But the majority of Americans (69 percent, according to one poll) thought his broadcasts were useful, and several members of military intelligence were among his viewers, sifting for useful tidbits of information that might have eluded the Iraqi censor.

The Gulf War was the first major recent confrontation in which American reporters were restricted to pools that limited contact with battlefield troops. Here, a reporter wears a gas mask during an Iraqi attack.

Prior Restraint and National Security

Censorship in time of war makes a grim kind of sense. A country involved in a struggle for survival certainly would not want to provide the enemy with information that could be used against it. But not all censorship occurs in wartime. Under normal peacetime circumstances, the government of the United States, cognizant of First Amendment freedoms, does not censor the press. If someone writes or broadcasts a harmful story, various laws provide for punishment. That punishment, in the form of fines or imprisonment, might be considered a kind of postpublication censorship, but at least the story is allowed to appear. But prior restraint—which means that the government steps in and blocks the publication or broadcast of a story,

GLOBAL GLANCE
Press Suppression
Rampant
Throughout the
World

Frances D'Souza, director of Article 19, a London group that fights censorship, in 1992 provided examples of places where suppression of information was rampant. Top offenders: Islamic countries where fundamentalists regularly ban books and the press is state-controlled; Latin American countries where various kinds of information (e.g., family planning) is prohibited; African countries where journalistic loyalty to the ruling dictatorship is demanded; and China where a free media system is still unknown. She could have also mentioned Cuba and North Korea, two of the world's monolithic and highly controlled media systems.

According to D'Souza, who has headed the organization since 1989, the basic step in establishing a democratic process in any nation is creating a free press. "There is no substitute for the uncensored truth," she believes. Article 19 has been collecting and analyzing press laws from around the world and is also setting up a procedure for bringing suppression of free expression cases to global forums such as the World Court.

Source: "Conversations/Frances D'Souza," *The New York Times,* Aug. 16, 1992.

---

thus preventing it from ever being read or seen—smacks of the old authoritarian regimes and comes dangerously close to thumbing one's nose at the Constitution. Nevertheless, there are times when the security and survival of the nation are at stake, even in peacetime, and when government officials will feel it necessary to take the ultimate step.

The Pentagon Papers. One such case arose in 1971 when *The New York Times* and *The Washington Post* began to print selections from a body of classified materials that came to be known as the *Pentagon Papers.* Although it's true that the Vietnam conflict was raging at the time, the war was undeclared and the papers had nothing to do with military secrets from the war zone. The papers were, rather, part of a 47-volume history of early American involvement in Vietnam, assembled by the Pentagon during the Johnson administration; they detailed the political and diplomatic decisions from 1945 to 1967 that led to America's military involvement. As the fighting in Vietnam became more unpopular on the home front, Daniel Ellsberg, an opponent of the war, leaked the classified documents to *The New York Times.* Even though the documents were illegally removed from government files and covered by a government secrecy classification, the *Times* determined that it was an important story and began to publish portions of the reports.

The Nixon administration rushed to court to stop publication of the papers. It was the first time in American history that a president had ever resorted to the theory of prior restraint. A temporary restraining order was issued, forcing the *Times* to break off publication after the third installment. *The Washington Post* stepped in and began its own publication from the documents, and another restraining order was sought. This attempt failed when a second judge ruled that government could not use prior restraint on "essentially historical data." Within 12 days and after appeals, both cases were hurried to the U.S. Supreme Court. The court found, in a 6–3 ruling, that the evidence supporting national defense needs was not strong enough to override the principle of freedom of the press. *The New York Times* and *The Washington Post* were allowed to continue publication of the papers, and a number of other media also gave the papers wide distribution. Even the U.S. Government Printing Office eventually released a voluminous and almost complete version.

The Progressive **Magazine.** Eight years later, in 1979, government officials tried once again to exercise prior restraint. *The Progressive* was on the verge of printing the Howard Morland article (described in Chapter 7) explaining the manufacture of hydrogen bombs. Justice Department officials, claiming the article contained highly classified materials that would do irreparable damage to national security, obtained a preliminary injunction from a U.S. district court. The case never reached an appeals court nor the Supreme Court, however. Documents containing the so-called "secret data" in the *Progressive* article were found on open library shelves in Los Alamos, home of the hydrogen bomb, and a computer programmer all but duplicated the *Progressive* H-bomb story by stringing together materials available on library shelves. After six months, the government dropped the case.

The CIA and the Book Industry. The Central Intelligence Agency has been more successful in the use of prepublication censorship, forcing the deletion of passages from at least one book and severely punishing the author's pocketbook after another was published. The CIA has a standard contract that all CIA employees must sign, stating that anything written by the employee must be submitted to CIA review and censorship before publication. The first former CIA agent to run afoul of this contract provision was Victor Marchetti. Writing with John D. Marks, he prepared a manuscript in 1974 for the Knopf publishing house. Called *The CIA and the Cult of Intelligence,* the book was duly submitted to the CIA for review and returned with 339 gaping holes where passages had been excised with scissors. The agency later reinstated 171 passages but refused to relent on the remaining 168. The book went to press with gaps of white space representing the deleted passages and boldface type indicating the passages that were returned to the manuscript.

Another former agent, Frank Snepp, in 1980 wrote a book called *Decent Interval,* detailing events leading to the fall of Saigon. In spite of his contractual obligations, he did not submit the book to the CIA for review. The book contained no classified information, but a judge responded to CIA legal complaints by ordering Snepp to forfeit his entire royalty earnings, which eventually amounted to some $200,000.

Censorship from Other Quarters

Not all censorship comes from the government. Various forms of content control can spring from news sources, advertisers, consumers, pressure groups in society and independent media organizations, as well as within the editorial process itself. Let's look at some of the problems faced by individual media.

Books. The CIA isn't the only organization that attempts censorship of books. Parental and religious groups have increasingly challenged public libraries and school systems to force the removal of specific books from the shelves. When a committee of parents met with library officials in Green Cove Springs, Florida, in 1990 and demanded that the children's classic *My Friend Flicka* be pulled because it used the word "bitch" in reference to a female dog and also contained the word "damn," First Amendment freedoms may have been violated, but the action was local in nature and didn't necessarily affect the continued publication of the book. But attempts to censor textbook offerings can directly affect the book industry. Almost half of the states in this country have statewide adoption and approval practices. If a pressure group finds fault with a book and succeeds in convincing a state adoption agency that the book is unworthy, it can no longer be considered by the various school districts in the state. Such decisions create enormous economic pressure. A large state like Texas, with a textbook budget running $60 or $70 million a year, can say, "We don't like your book the way it is. Change it or forget it." Many textbook publishers, rather than lose an economically important share of the market, will buckle under.

Film. The movie industry learned early that it was apparently not covered by the First Amendment. A 1915 Supreme Court ruling upheld the rights of individual states to censor films on the grounds that movies were only show business and not vehicles of thought and therefore didn't deserve the same protection as other media that have come to be known under the general title "the press." Hollywood industry leaders, forewarned by the court decision and alarmed by the high-living lifestyles of some film stars, turned to self-censorship in an attempt to clean up their own act before the government stepped in to do it. The Hays Office, moviedom's famous self-policing agency, was organized in 1930 and continued to censor films until 1968. A list of taboo items quickly appeared. The inside of the thigh was not to be shown. Married couples were not to be filmed in the same bed unless at least one had a foot on the floor. Homosexuality and prostitution were not to be mentioned. Long kisses, adultery and naked babies were out. Tarzan and Jane would have to wear bigger loincloths. And on and on.

In 1952, the Supreme Court changed its mind and placed movies under the umbrella of the First Amendment. An Italian film, *The Miracle,* had been banned by a state board in New York on grounds that it was sacrilegious. The court said sacrilege was not sufficient reason to censor the film and declared the language of the 1915 decision "out of harmony with the views here set forth."

The 1952 court decision set the stage for a new era in film. Hollywood, still cautious however, was slow to respond. Films got a little racier, and language a little tougher, and some of the old Hays Office restrictions began to slip away. There was even the occasional flash of nudity. Nevertheless, the

Hays Office continued to operate until it was replaced in 1968 by another form of self-censorship, the industry-imposed rating system. Movies today are enormously freer in their use of language, themes, bare skin and violence than they ever were under the old Hays Office dictates, but there was still economic pressure to censor. If a film received an X rating, it invited community protest and was likely to suffer at the box office. Most filmmakers were willing to cut scenes and leave them on the floor rather than settle for the X-rated onus. In addition, makers of porn films and hard-core skin flicks appropriated the X rating for themselves as a kind of brag and began to rate their own films "triple X." In 1990, after considerable lobbying from the makers of legitimate adult films, the old X rating was changed to NC-17 to help differentiate mainstream adult films from the sleazier "triple X" skin flicks.

Magazines. In 1988, a Texas jury returned a $9.4 million verdict against *Soldier of Fortune* magazine for carrying a classified ad that led to a 1985 hit-man contract killing. The ad said:

> EX-MARINES—67–69 'Nam vets—Ex-DI, weapons specialist— jungle warfare, pilot, M.E., high-risk assignments, U.S. or overseas.

It sounded innocent enough, but a reader answered the ad and hired the man behind it, John Wayne Hearn, to kill his wife. Hearn was later caught and sent to prison. The woman's family charged that the magazine was negligent in not investigating the nature of the ad and asked for $22 million in damages. Lawyers for *Soldier of Fortune* argued that the First Amendment protected the magazine from responsibility, but a federal judge rejected the magazine's argument and sent the case to the jury. The family won, but a federal appeals court overturned the judgment in 1989 and the appeals court decision was upheld by the U.S. Supreme Court in 1990.

Soldier of Fortune was in trouble again in that same year, when a Georgia family sued in 1990 for another ad that they claimed led to the death of their father. An Alabama jury awarded the family a sizable money settlement and the case once again headed for the appeals court. The new offending ad, placed by a man named Richard Savage, said:

> GUN FOR HIRE: 37-year-old professional mercenary desires jobs. Vietnam veteran. Bodyguard, courier and other special skills. All jobs considered.

The magazine didn't fare so well in the appeals process for the second case. The U.S. Supreme Court, ruling in 1993, rejected the magazine's free-press arguments and allowed a $4.3 million judgment to stand. Not only did the judgment threaten the continued existence of *Soldier of Fortune* magazine, it opened a whole new Pandora's box of possible future problems for magazines of all kinds. If magazines can be held accountable for the actions of readers based on the materials they carry in their pages, editors and publishers may become much pickier about what they will accept as

In a surprising article in China's *People's Daily,* the official Communist Party mouthpiece, readers were told that official secrecy was not good, that it was harming the Government's reforms and keeping the people in the dark about the true situation in the country.

The article went on to encourage criticism and to report on an important conference recently held to discuss such matters. The conferees concluded that Chinese media should be given complete freedom to tell the truth about the society without fear of retaliation.

Although reality and rhetoric are often far apart, this was an unusual and encouraging development for Chinese journalists wanting more freedom of expression. And it was one sign that the Chinese government's drive for faster economic reform may be spilling over into media activities.

advertising. Carried to its extremes, magazines might even find themselves backing away from controversial articles, for fear they might provoke abnormal reactions on the part of readers that could prove injurious to third parties.

Photographs. Photographs are seldom singled out as targets for court cases dealing with pornography. They have been considered as evidence in cases against magazines or books that published them, but the entire content of the publication—copy, drawings, leering advertising—was usually considered equally as important. Until 1990. That's when an art museum, the Contemporary Arts Center of Cincinnati, and its director, Dennis Barrie, were hauled into court on charges of pandering obscenity. At the heart of the case were seven explicit pictures of men in purported sadomasochistic poses and children with genitalia exposed. Robert Mapplethorpe was the homoerotic photographer, a gay artist of some note who died of AIDS in 1989. It was the first time a museum had ever been taken to court on obscenity charges, and the trial stayed in the headlines. A guilty verdict might have presaged more censorship in the art world, including the removal of some classic, but explicit nude paintings. The judge in the case, David Albanese of Hamilton County Municipal Court, ruled that the offending pictures, only a portion of a posthumous photographic retrospective featuring 175 of Mapplethorpe's creations, could be tried separately and not as parts of the whole (theoretically easing the case for prosecutors). But in the end, a jury cleared both museum and director and returned a verdict of acquittal.

Rock Records. Rock music lyrics have also come under heavy fire in the last decade. The battle heated up when a group of concerned people organized the Parents Music Resource Center to deal with what members called "the growing trend in music toward lyrics that are sexually explicit, excessively violent or glorify the use of drugs and alcohol." Two of the group's spokespersons (Tipper Gore, wife of Vice President Albert Gore, and Susan Baker, wife of former Secretary of State James Baker) appeared before the Senate Commerce Committee in 1985 to suggest a voluntary labeling system by which the record industry would attach generic warnings to records containing explicit lyrics that might be considered inappropriate for young children.

If anything, the war against rock, rap and pop records has become more intense. In 1990, the rock band Judas Priest was sued by the families of two young men who committed suicide supposedly after hearing subliminal messages implanted in several Judas Priest recordings, including the album "Stained Glass." A judge later ruled in favor of the band, saying the family failed to prove the presence of the subliminal messages. That same year, a record store owner in Florida was charged with violating anti-obscenity laws by selling 2 Live Crew's sexually explicit record album, "As Nasty As They Wanna Be." The record store owner was found guilty, but in an odd twist, the group 2 Live Crew was acquitted on obscenity charges by a different Florida jury in another trial a month later. Another rapper, Ice-T, came under attack in 1992 for harsh anticop lyrics on his "Cop Killer" album, eventually forcing his parent company, the giant communication conglomerate Time Warner, to withdraw the album. Keep your CDs warmed up. This war is far from over.

The Editorial Process and Self-Censorship. All news must flow through the editorial process before it reaches the pages of your newspaper or magazine or is broadcast on your radio or your television screen. The process is complex, and some messages may be reviewed by a dizzying number of editors, advisers and lawyers. But all media messages, except live interviews on radio or television, usually pass through the hands of at least two people, the writer and at least one editor, both of whom screen facts before selecting what may or may not reach the public eye or ear. These choices are part of a natural editing rhythm, and no news medium could exist without them. Information must be telescoped, quotes deployed, copy made readable. Still, when choices are made, the choosers—known as *gatekeepers*—are practicing a form of self-censorship. The reasons for choices made within the system are usually (but not always) quite different from reasons found outside the system. Writers and editors lean heavily on news judgment, on space or time limitations and on their own knowledge of what may be verified as true or accurate. Some editors may also make biased decisions based on political background, moral or religious upbringing or—more pragmatically—they may choose what they think is least likely to offend their audience, their advertisers or even their employers. In an ideal world, such unprofessional motives would be kept to a minimum. But editors and writers are human, too. That's why circulations and broadcast ratings go up and down. A gatekeeper who consistently uses the wrong criteria for self-regulation will invariably drive portions of his or her audience away.

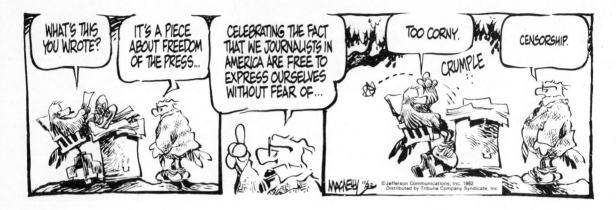

CELEBRATING THE FACT THAT WE JOURNALISTS IN AMERICA ARE FREE TO EXPRESS OURSELVES WITHOUT FEAR OF...

WHAT'S THIS YOU WROTE?

IT'S A PIECE ABOUT FREEDOM OF THE PRESS...

TOO CORNY.

CRUMPLE

CENSORSHIP.

©Jefferson Communications, Inc. 1982
Distributed by Tribune Company Syndicate, Inc.

Some Necessary Limits— Protecting Freedom

Even with a background of censorship and special-circumstance limitations such as those already mentioned, the press of the United States celebrates extraordinary freedom. Nevertheless, too much press freedom, like many other freedoms, can be dangerous. There are still more press restrictions that bear careful scrutiny by the media student. For example, how secure would you feel if there were no libel laws—if any newspaper reporter or TV commentator were free to say anything at all about you, no matter how scandalous or false or how damaging it might be to your personal reputation or your ability to earn a living? How eager would you be to write your own book or record your own music if there were no copyright laws to protect your investment of time and energy—if any publisher could pirate your manuscript or tape your songs and reproduce them at will without any payment whatever for your time and skill? Life could get very complicated.

Let's take a closer look at some of these fundamental restrictions, including libel laws, rights of privacy, copyright, obscenity, antitrust and truth in advertising.

Libel

Libel is a false statement about a living person that does damage to that person's reputation in the community in which he or she lives. It may also cause embarrassment or humiliation or affect a person's ability to make a living. The four most commonly cited classic examples of libel, called *libel per se,* would be to charge someone falsely with the commission of a crime, to charge that someone has or has had a loathsome or contagious disease, to bring discredit on someone in his or her profession or (though this one sounds antiquated) to suggest that a woman is unchaste.

Once a libel case is filed, there are three kinds of damages that a libel claimant can ask a court to award. The first is *general damages,* granted for injury to reputation. The second is *special damages* for specific monetary loss, such as injury to one's business or loss of one's job as a result of the libel. The final form of damages is *punitive;* it is usually sought by the claimant as a punishment against the writer, publisher or broadcast station for making the mistake. Punitive damages are awarded only if the parties responsible for the libel have shown reckless disregard or malicious intent to harm, meaning that someone in the editorial process knew or had reason to suspect that the statement was false.

Let's say you've been hauled into court and charged with libel for something you have written. How do you defend yourself? For years, the most frequently used defenses were the common law defenses: truth, fair comment, and fair report of a judicial or official proceeding. Truth was considered an absolute defense. If you could prove your statements were true, then the plaintiff had no case. By the same token, fair comment refers to legitimate opinions expressed about anything that is offered to the public for its consideration. If you pan a book, savage a play, say terrible things about a movie or even offer criticism of someone's political record, you are within your rights. The writer, entertainer or politician may never speak to you again, but you're off the libel hook. The third common law defense—fair report of a judicial or official proceeding—deals with privileged communication. If a senator says something outrageous on the floor of the Senate or a witness testifies falsely in a courtroom, you can report what was said even if it's obviously libelous, so long as your report is fair and accurate.

Then, in 1964, the U.S. Supreme Court opened a new door to libel defense in the landmark *The New York Times v. Sullivan* ruling. The plaintiff, Sullivan, was a public official, a police commissioner who charged that he had been libeled in a civil rights advertisement that ran in *The New York Times*. The Supreme Court, overturning an Alabama court decision that found in favor of Sullivan, said that a public official could not maintain a suit for damage to reputation unless the official could prove that the libelous statement was published with actual malice. In this case, the term *malice* has nothing to do with the dictionary definition. Actual malice, as defined by the court, means that the writer or publisher either knew the statement was false or went ahead and published it with a reckless disregard for whether or not it was false. This decision has since expanded beyond public officials to include public figures—people who are consistently in the public eye, such as athletes and entertainers.

The decision in *The New York Times v. Sullivan* doesn't mean that courts have declared open season on public officials and public figures. There are nuances, and later decisions have seen that particular defensive door swing wider at times and narrower at other times, depending on the case, the climate and the individual judge. In particular, First Amendment adherents have offered two specific complaints about the way the *Sullivan* case has worked out. First, jurors in libel cases are often confused by the label "actual malice" and continue to think of it as a term denoting hostility or ill will on the part of the publisher or broadcaster. Second, the *Sullivan* decision has become an open invitation for furious plaintiffs to go on fishing expeditions through the editorial process. After all, if the public official has to prove reckless disregard for the truth, he or she should be allowed to explore the editorial state of mind. The Supreme Court, in its 1979 *Herbert v. Lando* decision, endorsed this opinion.

Still, *Sullivan* continues to show its strength. At least two highly visible cases have tested the actual malice provision in recent years. In 1983, General William Westmoreland took CBS to court for airing a Vietnam War documentary that appeared to accuse him of being one of the figures behind a "conspiracy at the highest levels of American military intelligence"; former Israeli Defense Minister Ariel Sharon sued *Time* magazine for a story that suggested he had a hand in the 1982 Beirut massacre of Palestinian refugees. Westmoreland sought $120 million in damages; Sharon sued for $50 million. Both cases ended in 1985. Westmoreland, convinced he no longer had a chance to win, dropped his suit before it went to the jury. Sharon kept to his guns and claimed a moral victory when a jury ruled that *Time* had indeed defamed him but that the magazine was innocent of actual malice and therefore could not be found guilty of libel.

Invasion of Privacy

If you think libel laws are complex, wait until you sample the roiled waters of privacy. Traditionally, a person has a right to be left alone. That means we all deserve protection from unwarranted publicity. But what is unwarranted publicity? According to the courts, there are four different ways in which you can violate someone's right to privacy. The four forms of **invasion of privacy** are:

Casting Someone in a False Light. This one is vaguely similar to libel. You can cast someone in a false light in one of three ways. You can take a factual situation and embellish it (by adding dialogue or thought patterns, for example). You can take a factual situation and fictionalize it (the kind of thing we see in television docudramas, complete with actions and emotions that may not have taken place). Or you can take a factual situation and distort it (by omitting things or changing the meaning). Any of these situations can lead to a "false light" invasion-of-privacy suit. But a key difference between libel and false-light invasion of privacy is that the plaintiff doesn't have to prove the statement is defamatory.

Revealing Intimate Details of Someone's Life. The second tort of privacy touches on the broadcast or publication of intimate and embarrassing personal details of someone's life. It might be as simple as reporting that an athlete bites the heads off goldfish or it might be a shocking revelation of the bizarre sexual preferences of a movie star. The problem here is that even if you are telling the absolute truth and have photographs and signed affidavits to prove it, making public hitherto unknown personal habits may get you in trouble.

Misappropriating Someone's Name or Likeness. This one is a bit easier to understand. It deals with using someone's name or likeness for commercial purposes without first seeking permission. Advertisers can't run a picture of a famous person eating corn flakes, for example, unless that person has agreed (probably for hefty recompense) to endorse the product. Celebrity endorsements are big business. The rules governing endorsements are firmly drawn in mainstream advertising, but news media fall in a different category. Photos and stories about celebrities may be run without permission in newspapers and magazines, even if a cover photo helps sell the product. Usually, those same covers or newspapers can be duplicated in advertising for the news medium. But that may be changing. Isabelle Adjani, a French actress who starred in an expensive Hollywood turkey called "Ishtar," sued *Time* magazine in 1988 for using her picture in a magazine ad campaign. She won a judgment of $300,000.

Intruding Physically into Someone's Private Life. The final area of invasion of privacy usually deals with the way information is gathered, not with the material that is published. It involves wiretaps, trespassing on private property to gather information, seeking interviews under false pretenses, stealing photographs and other unreasonable intrusions in a person's private life.

Copyright and Plagiarism

Copyright law is designed to protect the work of the writer, photographer or artist, yet few writers seem to understand how it works and what it actually protects. For one thing, if you are the author of a copyrighted newspaper story, magazine article or book, you don't own the facts contained in that story; you own the words you used to describe those facts. Facts and ideas can't be copyrighted. The 1976 Copyright Law, which went into effect in 1978, differs from the old copyright law in that a writer no longer has to register material with the U.S. Copyright Office in order to place it under protection. The new law grants an automatic copyright protection to the work at the moment it is created. The automatic copyright continues until publication, and then a copyright notice must appear.

The new copyright act also tells us that anyone who violates the exclusive rights of the copyright owner has infringed on that copyright. Basically, this means you can't pick up someone else's material and pass it off as your own. But there's a fine line here. Plagiarism refers to the use of another writer's words without giving credit. If you're writing a term paper, and you copy a few passages from a book or an article and use them as your own without footnoting them, you may be guilty of plagiarism without actually infringing on anyone's copyright. On the other hand, if you make copies of the entire book or article and hand them out to your friends with thorough credit to the original author, no one can accuse you of plagiarism, but you may be guilty of copyright infringement. It comes down to a ticklish question. How much can you copy or excerpt from another writer's work without stepping across the infringement boundary? There is a hazy doctrine called "fair use." Even without the author's permission, copyright law allows you to copy a portion of another writer's words, so long as you do so within reason. The problem is to determine how much is within reason. Most publishers have fair use guidelines that they use to decide whether permission is required for use of a portion of someone else's work. Typically, guidelines are tied to length and source of material.

Obscenity and Pornography

As everyone knows, pornography is . . . er, come to think of it, just what is pornography? Supreme Court Justice Potter Stewart once admitted that he could not define pornography, but said "I know it when I see it." And therein lies the problem. There is general agreement that pornography and obscenity do not fall under First Amendment protection and can, therefore, be legally punished. But where does one draw the line? Which published materials fall under the free press guarantee, and which are to be declared pornographic?

Current laws against pornography are uncertain and full of loopholes. The U.S. Supreme Court tried to issue a guideline in the landmark *Roth* decision of 1957 when it drew a distinction between sexual and obscene material. What was sexual was not necessarily obscene, the court said. To help us differentiate between the two, it laid down the following standard: "whether to the average person, applying contemporary community standards, the dominant theme of the material taken as a whole appeals to the prurient interest." The court went further in 1966, narrowing the definition to material that was "utterly without redeeming social value." First Amendment libertarians promptly testified that they could find traces of social value in almost any so-called obscenity. Cases kept passing up to the Supreme Court for review. In 1973, the court turned more conservative. It ruled that local juries would have to decide whether standards of taste had been offended. The juries were instructed to convict if they decided a work "taken as a whole, lacks serious literary, artistic, political or scientific value." This standard was much easier for prosecutors to prove, but it didn't help for long. A general relaxation in sexual attitudes began to erode traditional American attitudes. "Contemporary community standards" were changing. Pornography prosecutions were time-consuming, expensive and too often unproductive. Cases began to clutter court dockets, making it difficult to prosecute more important cases. So there has been a general decline in pornography cases over the past decade. In the entire fiscal year of 1986, for example, only 10 people were indicted on obscenity charges by the Justice Department. The battle continues, of course. The U.S. Attorney General's Commission on Pornography released a report in 1985 that concluded that there is a link between some sexually explicit material and violence. (This conclusion has been much debated.) Police still raid porn shops and confiscate books, magazines and films. But most of the government's current court cases are directed toward sleazy and abnormal materials, like "kiddie porn." And in 1988, the U.S. Justice Department promised a series of racketeering indictments against the distributors of sexually explicit material.

Antitrust

In existence for a hundred years, **antitrust laws** are used to control economic concentration—to keep any business, including a media organization, from monopolizing the marketplace. The purpose is to keep one company from dominating others unfairly.

Antitrust statutes have been used against media on several occasions, including an action against the Associated Press in 1945 that reshaped the wire service's exclusivity rules, allowing both newspapers and radio stations in the same community to subscribe to the service. An action in 1955 kept the Kansas City Star Company from requiring advertisers to buy space in all three of its newspapers, the *Star,* the *Sunday Star* and the *Times,* in order to advertise in any single paper. Such cases are typical. And yet antitrust laws have proved all but ineffective when it comes to control of large and burgeoning media chains.

The growth and popularity of television introduced a new monopoly danger. Media critics feared that publishers and owners would gobble up newspapers and TV stations in the same locality, bringing advertising outlets under one roof and shrinking the arena for a robust exchange of public thought. A ban on media cross-ownership was promulgated by the Federal Communications Commission in 1975 to curb such trends. Existing newspaper/television combinations were allowed to continue under a "grandfather" clause; communication companies could still buy several newspapers and even a few television stations, but not in the same market areas.

Broadcast Restrictions—A Changing Scene

Radio and television have always been under a more stringent control than any of the other media units. Very early in the life of the broadcast industry, the Radio Act of 1927 stated that since radio waves belong to the public, any broadcaster using the public air waves would have to be licensed. The act also set up an organization called the Federal Radio Commission to oversee the licensing system. First Amendment freedoms were to apply to broadcast media, but not as absolutely as they applied to print media.

FCC

In 1934, the Federal Communications Commission took over from the FRC and was given expanded powers. The FCC was to act as a regulatory agency not only over the growing radio business but also over telephone and telegraph systems and television, which at that time was an experimental infant in the laboratory. As broadcast media have grown and developed, so has the FCC.

Licensing. The FCC licensing system is simple. All broadcast stations are licensed. An applicant for license must fit an FCC profile that calls for U.S. citizenship, demonstration of technical competence, economic resources, good character and a variety of other criteria. Once the license is granted, a station can begin to broadcast, but the licensing process isn't over. Every license is temporary and must be reviewed periodically before renewal. At the beginning, radio and television licenses came up for review every three years. In 1981, Congress extended the terms of broadcast licenses to seven years for radio stations and five years for television stations.

The Trend Toward Deregulation

In the 1980s, government deregulation of businesses became a watchword. Spearheading the early deregulation movement in broadcast was Reagan-appointee FCC chairman Mark Fowler. Under Fowler's prodding, a number of key regulations were either abandoned or modified. Local broadcasts no longer have to deal with structured assessments of community problems. Restrictions on children's programming were loosened. Strict limits on advertising were waived. Programming guidelines on public affairs were dropped. Program logs no longer have to be kept open to the public. The FCC also increased the number of radio and television stations that can be owned by a single company or individual. The radio limit, once seven AM and seven FM stations, was enlarged to 12 AM and 12 FM in 1984. The television limit was extended from seven to 12 in 1985 (though the 12 TV stations must be in markets reaching no more than 25 percent of all American households).

Cable Control

Cable franchises are usually awarded by local governments, most often as a result of competitive bidding. Some cable systems serve their markets with as few as 12 stations, whereas others may offer as many as a hundred choices. The FCC moved in on cable television in 1960 and over a period of years assembled a 500-page book of regulations. However many of the early restrictions have either been watered down by court decisions or modified as a result of the FCC's recent trend toward general deregulation. In the meantime, cable continues to grow. In 1970, cable enjoyed a 7.5 share of households (some 4.5 million subscribers). By 1987, cable was reaching a 50.5 share of households (almost 45 million subscribers). It's conceivable that such phenomenal growth may eventually provoke a closer look from federal agencies, but not unless the current mood toward deregulation falters.

Unsettled Issues—When Rights Collide

The First Amendment seems precise enough, but we've already seen how truly complex the issue of press freedom can be. Consider, then, how the complexities deepen when the First Amendment crashes headlong into guarantees provided by other constitutional amendments.

Free Press Versus Fair Trial

A problem that has been with us since the Constitution and the Bill of Rights were ratified is the occasional direct confrontation between the First

Amendment guarantee of a free press and the Sixth Amendment guarantee of a fair and impartial jury trial for every defendant. Supreme Court Justice Hugo Black once wrote that "free press and fair trial are two of the most cherished policies in our civilization, and it would be a trying task to choose between them." And yet the choice must occasionally be made. Pretrial publicity and courtroom coverage can sometimes endanger justice. Modern examples include the 1932 Lindbergh kidnapping case, which led to the trial of accused kidnapper Bruno Hauptmann and turned the courtroom into a noisy, raucous circus, packed with 150 reporters and photographers. In 1954, an osteopathic doctor named Sam Sheppard was accused of brutally murdering his wife, and Cleveland newspapers all but convicted him prior to the trial, by publishing editorials demanding his arrest. The newspapers continued their crusade against him during the trial, which was also covered by waves of national reporters and columnists. Remarkably, the jurors were at first allowed to go home every night, exposing them to the news accounts and broadcast coverage. The Supreme Court, citing the prejudicial publicity, reversed Sheppard's conviction 12 years later.

Gag Rules

Because of the First Amendment versus Sixth Amendment collisions, some judges have gone so far as to place restrictive **gag rules** on participants in a trial, barring anyone connected with the case—attorneys, witnesses, police officials—from talking to reporters. If a trial participant ignores the order, he or she runs the risk of a contempt citation and a jail sentence. A Nebraska case went to the U.S. Supreme Court in 1976 after a judge ordered media not to report facts in a murder case that he thought would prejudice the defendant's right to a fair trial. The court found in favor of the media organizations, but the decision dealt with the use of prior restraint, not directly with the issue of gag rules. Judges have since resorted to other strategies, and gag rules are still with us in various forms, including the closure of pretrial proceedings if circumstances warrant.

Shield Laws

Journalists sometimes rely on sources who insist on remaining anonymous. Often it's the only way to get information on government or business improprieties. But if a report leads to legal proceedings, the court will sometimes direct the reporter to name the source. At this point, a dilemma arises. If a reporter refuses to reveal the name of the source, that reporter can be jailed until he or she is ready to relent. On the other hand, if a reporter has promised not to reveal a source's name, that promise must be kept. If reporters made a practice of revealing the names of confidential informants, many valuable news sources would dry up. Important stories, of provable value to the public, would go unreported.

For a number of years reporters responded to such court orders by citing the First Amendment and the indirect effect the orders would have on their right to report freely. The Supreme Court weakened that position drastically in 1972 when it ruled in the *Branzburg v. Hayes* decision that a journalist, just like any other citizen, was required to give testimony when so ordered by the judge. But the ruling was badly split and contained apparent contradictions regarding the conflicting rights of a judge to compel testimony and the rights of a reporter to gather information without interference. Lower courts have been forced to continue on a case-by-case basis to deal with the two competing rights. Further complicating the issue, a number of states passed legislation to help protect journalists from having to reveal news sources. These state statutes, called **shield laws,** have in some cases reduced the legal threat to journalists, but they are no panacea. Journalists are still regularly subpoenaed to testify about stories they have written. Many media organizations now tell their reporters to use the promise of anonymity only as a last resort.

As you can see, there are more restraints and controls on the media than are immediately apparent to the eye. Are they all necessary? You can argue the question from both sides. And you can be right from both sides. But keep your eyes on the main point of this chapter. Freedom of the press is a cherished hallmark of our constitutional heritage. Some controls are surely necessary to maintain stability, but in a democratic society those controls and restrictions will remain minimal. Every new step toward broadening press constraints contributes, like a steady drip of water on stone, to an erosion of the original freedoms. And that could change the fabric of our government.

Retrospective

The American press system is among the freest in the world, thanks to the First Amendment provisions to the Constitution of the United States. But even when press restrictions are kept to a minimum, freedom has its limitations.

Wars provide special situations in which some government censorship is often thought to be necessary, but pressure and censorship can come from other quarters, as well—from parental groups, consumer organizations, courts and the media themselves.

We must also consider the rights of individuals, property rights and questions of taste. Regulations dealing with these rights include libel laws, invasion of privacy statutes, copyright provisions, court rulings covering obscenity and antitrust regulations.

Broadcast media face their own special considerations, thanks to the licensing process of the Federal Communications Commission. Though there appears to be a trend toward deregulation, the FCC still exerts control over radio and television stations and cable systems.

At times, First Amendment rights seem to conflict with other rights guaranteed by the Constitution. Then, usually, the judiciary is called upon to decide the issues in conflict, such matters as free press versus fair trial and the use of gag rules and shield laws.

1. What makes the First Amendment to the U.S. Constitution different from other national pledges of press freedom? Does it work better? Why?

2. Who besides government can exercise control over the publication of books? Movies? Rock records?

3. What are the three common law defenses against libel? How has *The New York Times v. Sullivan* affected libel cases? What do we mean when we refer to someone as a "public figure"?

4. Who decides whether something is pornographic? How are such decisions made? Can you think of better guidelines? Would a majority of people agree with your guidelines?

5. Why does the FCC license broadcast media? Do you think broadcasters should be given more freedom? Less freedom? Why?

6. When two constitutional amendments collide (as the First and Sixth often do), who decides which should be given precedence? Can such problems be solved fairly?

Suggested Readings

Bittner, John. *Broadcast Law and Regulation.* Englewood Cliffs, N.J.: Prentice-Hall, 1982.

Bosmajian, H. A. *Obscenity and Freedom of Expression.* New York: Burt Franklin & Co., 1976.

Chafee, Zechariah. *Free Speech in the United States.* Cambridge, Mass.: Harvard Press, 1967.

Emerson, Thomas. *The System of Freedom of Expression.* New York: Vintage Books, 1970.

Franklin, Marc. *The First Amendment and the Fourth Estate.* Mineola, N.Y.: The Foundation Press, 1977.

Gillmor, Donald, and Barron, Jerome. *Mass Communication Law.* St. Paul, Minn.: West Publishing Company, 1984.

Krasnow, E. G., and Longley, L. D. *The Politics of Broadcast Regulation.* New York: St. Martin's Press, 1978.

Merrill, John C. *The Imperative of Freedom.* New York: Hastings House, 1974.

Nelson, Harold, and Teeter, Dwight. *Law of Mass Communications.* Mineola, N.Y.: Foundation Press, 1986.

Pember, Don. *Mass Media Law.* Dubuque, Iowa: Wm. C. Brown Publishers, 1981.

Zuckman, Harvey, and Gaynes, Martin. *Mass Communication Law in a Nutshell,* 2d ed. St. Paul, Minn.: West Publishing Co., 1983.

Media Ethics

- A disc jockey takes under-the-table money from record companies for playing their records.
- A newspaper reporter intentionally withholds pertinent information from a story in order to protect a friend or to keep a source from "drying up."
- A freelance magazine writer makes up facts to buttress a point.
- A TV interviewer with an obvious bias confronts an interviewee and argues with her positions.
- A photojournalist stands aloof and takes pictures while a man, brandishing a knife, pursues a young woman down a city street.
- A magazine editor accepts a government-paid trip to Central America to see U.S. military and support forces stationed there.
- A book-review editor accepts free books from a publisher wishing to have the books reviewed.

These are just some of the many kinds of situations faced by media personnel every day. Such situations get us directly into the area of media ethics, a field of great complexity and controversy that is growing in importance every year. A consideration of ethics forces the mass communicator to look carefully at basic principles, values and obligations to self and others.

Ethics relates to *self-imposed* duty; it is a field of moral concern that is primarily individual or personal even when it relates to obligations and duties to others. The quality of our work as communicators has to do with both solitude and sociability, thereby making behavior known as "individual ethics" *and* "social ethics" very important. We do right and wrong in that part of our lives lived inwardly and also in that part of our lives in which we respond to other people. Ethics, then, is an area in which each individual makes decisions about both private and public matters.

Ethics: An Introduction

Media ethics has to do with standards and practices of the media, but we must remember that media are made up of *individuals*. Therefore, the ethical practices of a mass medium depend on the ethical practices of its staff members. So when we speak of *media ethics* we are, by definition, talking about the ethics of individuals.

Ethics is that branch of philosophy that deals with what *ought* to be done, with what kinds of actions are *good* (or at least *better*) and with personal values and individual character. Journalism ethics is very much a normative field—helping journalists develop principles and maxims to follow in pursuit of ethical practice. Journalistic conduct, from an ethical perspective, should be self-determined by each journalist, although there is no reason a person's colleagues or family or society's expectations cannot impinge on this ethical self-determination.

The terms *ethical* and *moral* can usually be used interchangeably. Actually they are synonymous etymologically: *ethics* coming from the Greek *"ethos"* and *morality* from the Latin *"mores."* Both terms refer to conventional or customary behavior. Usually, the opposite of *moral* is *immoral.* A moral person is one who acts in a right way, and an immoral person is one who acts wrongly.

We can talk also about a person being *amoral* (but there is no word *"a-ethical"*), meaning that morality or ethics doesn't enter into the situation. If a newscaster mispronounces a word, for example, or unintentionally omits a name, these actions would be *amoral.* If newscasters distort their stories by manipulating facts, they may be called *immoral* in their practices —although in such a case they would usually be called *unethical.*

A Concern for Being Ethical

We may disagree about proper ethical practice while being concerned about ethics. What is important is *ethical concern.* A TV anchorperson who has this concern obviously cares about good or right actions. And such a concern shows itself in a respect for personal responsibility and the public welfare. It also demonstrates that the anchorperson wants to discover norms to be used as guiding principles for the kind of life that he or she considers meaningful and satisfying. Such a concern leads the anchorperson, or any mass communicator, to some kind of commitment, to reasoned decisions among alternatives and to a search for the "summum bonum" or highest good in the field of communication.

Many critics of journalism today (and even more critics of mass communication generally) insist that most practitioners do not have an ethical concern. Journalists are seen largely as lacking moral commitment and a consistent and predictable ethical practice. Too often journalists are seen as *antinomians* (having no principles and simply playing things "by ear") or as arrogant and power-hungry *Machiavellians* (seeking their own success and believing that ends justify any means).

Law is not ethics. They may be first cousins, but they are not the same. We can follow the law and be unethical. And we can break the law and be ethical. Law has to do with outside or external imposition of rules of conduct, which are socially (legislatively) imposed and externally enforced (by police and courts). On the other hand, ethical conduct is personally determined and enforced. If we are unethical, we consider ourselves unethical or are so considered by others, and we go on about our business. If we break the law, we are punished (or may be) by an external force and may lose our freedom.

One basic assumption of ethical behavior is that a person has considerable *freedom.* Another assumption is that a person is *sane.* A person who is enslaved (whose free will is taken away) or insane (whose self-will is absent) is, in a very real sense, *beyond* ethics or amoral. Such a person may do something that is wrong, bad or injurious to society—but such a person cannot accurately be considered unethical.

Philosophers through the ages have suggested many ethical pathways to right actions and a good life. As is clear from the list below, philosophers and ethical leaders disagree about what constitutes the greatest good.

Confucius (551?–479? B.C.): self-sacrifice; love for others

Lao-Tse (604? B.C.–?): seeking the Way; spiritual absorption of personal desires

Moses (1300? B.C.): following the laws of God, especially as set forth in the Ten Commandments

Gautama Buddha (563?–483? B.C.): Self-transcendence; perfect wisdom through meditation

Socrates (470?–399 B.C.): following one's personal *daemon* (guiding spirit); self-discipline

Plato (427?–347? B.C.): seeking knowledge and virtue

Aristotle (384–322 B.C.): moral character; good habits; reason; nothing in excess; having good motives

Epicurus (341?–270 B.C.): attaining the pleasant life

Epictetus (50?–135? A.D.): self-discipline

Jesus Christ (8–4 B.C.–29 A.D.): self-sacrifice; love for others and for God

Mohammed (570?–632 A.D.): faith; chastity; ascetic attitude

St. Augustine (354–430 A.D.): the love of God

Thomas Aquinas (1225?–1274): morality; character; natural law

Thomas Hobbes (1588–1679): self-interest

Jean Jacques Rousseau (1712–1778): society above self

Machiavelli (1469–1527): self-interest and pragmatism

Benedict de Spinoza (1632–1677): reason

John Stuart Mill (1806–1873): bringing the greatest happiness to the most people

Immanuel Kant (1724–1804): duty to principle, reason

Karl Marx (1818–1883): society above self

Friedrich Nietzsche (1844–1900): self-enhancement; will to transcendence

John Dewey (1859–1952): making the effort; forward movement; self-improvement

G. E. Moore (1873–1958): intuitive knowledge; indefinability of the good

A. J. Ayer (1910–1989): ethics as emotive expression

Jean-Paul Sartre (1905–1980): commitment; integrity; use of freedom

Ayn Rand (1905–1982): rational self-interest

John Rawls (1921–): egalitarianism; social justice

Robert Nozick (1938–): self-enhancement; striving for merit

The potential for voluntary actions is important to a person considering ethics. What are voluntary actions? They are those that could have been done differently had the person wanted to. Often journalists excuse their actions by saying that they were not a matter of choice; rather they were *assigned* a certain story or *told* to write it in a certain way by an editor or someone in authority. This is a cop out, for the journalist always has the choice of not doing something. Undoubtedly, a decision *not to do what one is told by an editor can have serious consequences for one's employment;* but the journalist has the choice and may find that a job at another newspaper or magazine is a good thing. Most often, however, it will not come to this. Few editors would force a reporter to write a certain story (or write one in a certain way) if the reporter had *ethical* reasons for his or her reluctance.

Journalism's "Super-Concepts"

Without getting into specific cases at this point, we should note that journalists do seem to recognize a few general or "super" ethical concepts. These are present in almost every code of media ethics, whether broadcasting or the print media.

First, there is the sacred concept of *truth*. Everyone seems in favor of truth; it is the primary watchword of journalism and related communication activities. The American Society of Newspaper Editors (ASNE), in its 1923 "Canons of Journalism," enthrones truth and speaks of "truthfulness," "accuracy" and a "clear distinction between news reports and expressions of opinion." The Society of Professional Journalists (SPJ), in its ethical code, pays the same homage to truth, saying that "truth is our ultimate goal." Codes of various other media groups exhort their members to be accurate and objective. In a sense such admonitions for accuracy and objectivity simply reinforce the standard of truth. If the codes stopped there, things would be pretty clear, but they don't. They proceed on to the second big ethical concept of the news media: *fairness*.

One way we might look at the mainstream of journalistic ethics (and at these two super-concepts) is to use a basic formula that includes both truth and fairness, what the authors have dubbed the *"TUFF" ethical principle* (see Figure 15.1). Basically it summarizes the difficult, basic ethical tenets that say that a journalist must be *truthful, unbiased, full and fair*. The first three concepts focus on the main principle, seemingly common to all journalists: being truthful, accurate, thorough—in a word, *objective*.

But the problem comes with the final or fourth concept in the formulation—the idea of fairness. It is entirely possible that a journalist will *not be fair* if he or she is truthful, unbiased and thorough. So the formula may be

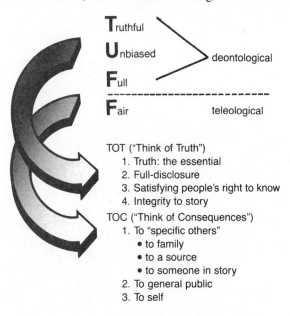

Figure 15.1
The "TUFF" Ethical Formula

Truthful

Unbiased ⟩ deontological

Full

- -

Fair   teleological

TOT ("Think of Truth")
    1. Truth: the essential
    2. Full-disclosure
    3. Satisfying people's right to know
    4. Integrity to story

TOC ("Think of Consequences")
    1. To "specific others"
      • to family
      • to a source
      • to someone in story
    2. To general public
    3. To self

helpful as a kind of ideal ethical objective, but we should remember that it may lead into a quandary where dangerous dragons of contradiction lurk.

For example, if the journalist's main goal is *truth,* as most codes tell us is the case, what does the reporter do when he or she feels the presentation of the truth may not be the ethical thing to do? If the truth implies full-disclosure reporting of verified facts, what about the journalist who shields the source, who decides not to print the name of the rape victim or who (for whatever reason) withholds from the public some information that has been gathered and verified? Certainly the reporter is not being a truthful reporter, but he or she may well be a fair reporter.

It is quite common for *ethical concerns* to take precedence over the basic practical tenets of *reporting.* So, we can see that a respect for truth is important in journalism and is usually looked on as a sacred standard—*that is, until the reporter begins thinking seriously about consequences.* Then a kind of moral rationalization begins whereby certain practices may be condoned because they are felt to result in a higher ethical practice than simply telling the truth.

Two Main Ethical Views

The quandary in which the journalist is pulled between a dedication to truth, on one hand, and a desire to deviate from truth upon a consideration of consequences, on the other, leads us into a brief discussion of the two main ethical viewpoints that have dominated the history of ethics.

Figure 15.2
Two Main Ethical Stances

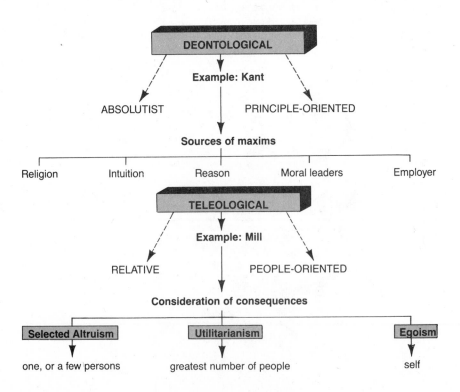

As a kind of super-maxim against which to test all ethical principles, the German philosopher Immanuel Kant (1724–1804) suggested what he called the "categorical imperative." It was based on the rational consideration of the ethical question facing a person. For example, is it ethical for a journalist to lie or distort a story? Using the categorical imperative, the answer would be yes *if the journalist making the decision would be willing to have all journalists lie or distort.*

Thus, the main formulation of the categorical imperative was presented by Kant in these words: "Act only on that maxim whereby thou canst at the same time will that it should become a universal law." A second and equally important form of the categorical imperative, indicating a major thrust in Kant's ethics is this: "So act as to treat humanity, whether in thine own person or in that of any other, in every case as an end withal, never as a means only."

So here are Kant's two main versions of the categorical imperative: (1) Do only what you would want universalized, and (2) never treat others as means to an end, only as an end in themselves.

First, there is the formalistic, absolute, legalistic, duty-bound ethical position known as **deontological ethics.** Second, there is the more flexible, consequence-oriented position called **teleological ethics** (see Figure 15.2).

Deontological ethics is often called *duty ethics,* whereas teleological ethics is commonly referred to as *consequence ethics. Deon* is a Greek word for "duty," and *teleos* is the Greek word for "end" or "result"—hence we have the words *deontology* and *teleology.*

Most communicators are inclined largely toward one or the other of these ethical viewpoints. In fact, the whole history of ethics has found people falling basically into one of these camps. The reporter who accepts as a maxim "to tell the truth or to indulge in full-disclosure reporting" (and who feels an ethical duty to perform in this way) can be termed a *deontologist.* The other reporter, instead of looking on the formal-istic practice of truth-telling as ethical, constructs the story so as to bring about the best consequences; this reporter is the *teleologist.* (Of course, there are those who might consider truth-telling as bringing about the best possible consequences and not as an absolute maxim, but this is the exception.)

I. Kant and J. S. Mill

Immanuel Kant (1724–1804) is philosophy's best example of a strict deontologist. This famed German philosopher would have wiped conse-quences out of ethical consideration. He believed that *only* an action taken out of self-imposed duty could be ethical. Kant formulated what he called the "categorical imperative," which said essentially that what was ethical for a person to do was what the person would want to see everybody do. Another version of the famous imperative (a kind of super-maxim for general guidance) was that no person should ever be treated as "a means to an end," but only as an "end." Together, these formulations capsulize Kant's formalistic *ethics of duty.*

John Stuart Mill (1806–1873), a British philosopher, is usually given as the best example of a teleologist. Mill's variety of teleology was *utilitarianism,* the goal being the greatest happiness—or good—to the greatest number. For Mill, consequences were essential, and a person who failed to consider them could not claim to be ethical.

Although Kant's concept has profoundly influenced Western thought, it is obvious that among modern intellectuals his strict and absolutist "duty ethics" has lost much of its appeal, whereas teleological ethics is in its ascendency. In spite of the fact that many communicators pay lip service to some principles or maxims of the Kantian kind, it is very often seen that they find no difficulty in departing from them. Most communicators, instead, do consider consequences and make decisions based on how the consequences will likely affect others or themselves.

As journalists begin talking about the context or the specific situation determining what they will do, they are straying farther and farther away from Immanuel Kant. If Kant were editor of the *Forlorn Gazette* he would expect all rational staffers to follow journalistic principles *in every journalistic situation,* not just where they suited them. If, for example, a fundamental maxim of a reporter on the *Gazette* were to engage in full-disclosure (truthful) reporting, the reporter would be duty-bound to conduct such reporting in *every case,* not in just some.

In other words, Kant would say: "Take the principle that you have tested against the categorical imperative (would you want it universalized?) and stick to it come 'hell or high water.'" On the other hand, John Stuart Mill (and all the teleologists among us) would say: "Forget hard-and-fast principles or guidelines; consider each case separately, think of possible consequences and only then make your ethical decision."

Ethical Stages: Going Up?

Opinions abound concerning the development of a moral sense. Are there stages or levels of ethical behavior? If so, what are they, and which ones are most advanced (more sophisticated)? Ethicists (moral philosophers) have always thought about the question of ethical stages, even if they have not dealt specifically with stages in their writings. Some have written about it, however.

Søren Kierkegaard (1813–1855), the brilliant Danish philosopher and theologian and one of the founders of *existentialism,* proposed a very early set of personal-growth stages. (One's level of personal growth relates to the ethical decisions one makes.) The first and most elemental stage he called the *aesthetic,* a prerational, youthful, energetic, restless state of the "sensuous immediate." It is dominated by "self-love" and by spontaneous likes and dislikes. Right and wrong, in this stage, are tied very closely to feelings and intuition.

Kierkegaard's second (and higher) stage is what he termed the *ethical stage*. It is the progression to rationality, where life acquires unity and coherence and is concerned largely with social obligations and public-spiritedness. The person, however, may eventually find this rational or ethical stage too formalistic and cold, too concerned about *reasons* for doing this or that and about self-justification. So, the person progresses to the third and final stage, the highest one for Kierkegaard.

The third stage is the stage of *faith*. This is the stage of believing, feeling, sensation, intuition and emotion. It is similar to the first stage in its nonrational emphasis, except that it is not *self-centered*; rather it is *God-centered*. In coming to this last stage, the person realizes his or her own inadequacy, seeing that reason has failed to clarify things or to bring contentment and finally finds one's self in the Absolute (understood as God). So we see that Kierkegaard's three-stage progression rises from a duty to self, to a duty to others and finally to a duty to God.

Another ethical progression model—this one contemporary—has been proposed by the Harvard psychologist Lawrence Kohlberg. His is a seven-stage model, going from an unsophisticated moral stage to a progressively more advanced one. Here are the stages with a very brief comment, as might be made by a journalist, beneath each:

Stage 1 (lowest): *Fear of punishment; might makes right.*
My program director said to do it, so I will; I don't want to be fired or to get into trouble.

Stage 2: *Hope of reward.*
I will do this because I may win a Pulitzer Prize.

Stage 3: *Peer or community approval.*
I can't put that in my story; I don't want to upset my readers.

Stage 4: *Because it is the law.*
It's my magazine's policy, and I must follow my editor's directions.

Stage 5: *Social utility.*
I'll publish the story because it will help the sanitary conditions in my city.

Stage 6: *Justice and duty.*
I must follow my principles that I feel are just. I simply must tell the truth. I must not break my promise to my source.

Stage 7 (highest): *Being an ideal person.*
I wish to be virtuous, a good person, a person of principle and character. It is not so much what I *do* in this case, but what I *am*.

Kohlberg envisions the person's ethical progress from a childlike fear-impelled motivation, through several intermediate stages, until he or she reaches a final stage in which ethical action becomes habitual and spontaneous. At the last, Kohlberg sees morality as basically concerned with *the nature or essence* of a person more than what he or she might do in a specific situation.

Accountability Mechanisms

Mass media institutions and organizations, however much they manifest a respect for personal or individual ethics, want to have some way of ensuring a kind of common ethical practice. They are led, therefore, in the direction of accountability mechanisms—methods by which mass communicators (and their media) are held responsible for their actions. Guidelines, policies, standards and norms are important. And so are persons and groups who can criticize media, evaluate them and make suggestions to them as to how to act more ethically.

In a society such as the United States, which venerates its freedom, people do not want to think of accountability mechanisms as "authoritarian" rules but rather as voluntary sanctions. Let us look briefly at a few developments in the area of accountability, which is concerned with a more responsible institutional or professional communication practice.

Codes of Ethics

Every mass-communication organization has become interested in ethical codes. The topic of ethics, at least, has come front and center in the world of American media, replacing the older "public be damned" days of media freedom and profit-making. This change does not mean that media are no longer interested in profits and freedom; it simply means that more attention is being focused on media responsibilities and accountability. Regardless of the reasons, media ethics codes are becoming common, and discussion of their content is taking on increasing significance.

Statements of media behavior, couched in inspirational language, go back at least to Walter Williams' well-known "Journalists Creed" of 1908, wherein the dean of America's first journalism school (at the University of Missouri) admonished journalists to act as gentlemen, to be God-fearing, patient, respectful and aware of their "public trust." By the early 1930s, the emphasis on moral responsibility had all but disappeared as journalists enthroned objectivity and editorial self-determinism, concepts not so fuzzy as the statements issued by Walter Williams. The new emphasis: Just give the facts; don't worry about the consequences, and don't worry about outsiders telling you what to do—the press itself will determine what is right and wrong.

This press-oriented concept began to diminish just after World War II, as it was confronted with the growing concern for *socially oriented communication*. A major force in such a confrontation was the report in 1947 of the Commission on Freedom of the Press (the Hutchins Commission). This 13-member group, which had studied the American media during the war, concluded that they were falling short of their social obligations. The Commission urged more concern for ethics, for public service, for a more balanced reporting, for more mutual criticism among media and for more diversity. In short, the Hutchins Commission (chaired by Dr. Robert Hutchins of the University of Chicago) took the emphasis off the press's freedom and put it on the press's responsibilities to society.

Ethics became a more common subject in media discussions and in communication programs in American universities. And, although codes of ethics were already around (e.g., the American Society of Newspaper Editors wrote one in 1923, the Society of Professional Journalists in 1926 and the National Association of Broadcasters in 1937), it was not until the post-war period that a real concern for codes manifested itself. Old codes were dusted off and revised, and new ones were written. Today a wide variety of groups (such as the Public Relations Society of America, the National Press Photographers Association, the Radio and Television News Directors and the American Association of Advertising) have their own codes of ethics.

The common denominator of such codes is a professed loyalty to truth and accuracy and a concern for fairness and good taste. The advertising code (1962), for example, says that there will be "no false or misleading statements or exaggeration" and that there will be no "suggestions or pictures offensive to public decency." And the Society of Professional Journalists code stresses truth as the goal and advises journalists against "pandering to morbid curiosity." The ASNE code asks for truthfulness and accuracy and warns against "pandering to vicious instincts" and publishing anything that is not "demonstrably for the general good." The news photographers' code proposes that all photos be truthful, honest, and objective. And the code of the Public Relations Society of America insists on integrity and truthfulness.

The chief problem with ethical codes is their vagueness and use of glittering generalities that are open to many interpretations. The advertising code even says that its provisions (such as those dealing with public decency and exaggerations) can be differently interpreted. But since terms filled with much *semantic noise* are found in all ethical codes, the assumption must be

In the movie "Under Fire," an American photojournalist covering the Nicaraguan Revolution is asked to fake a photograph of a dead guerilla leader in order to save the revolution. The journalist (played by Nick Nolte) agrees to the request.

CHAPTER 15 Media Ethics

that there is considerable common understanding; otherwise the codes would be useless. The fact is that, in spite of the highly abstract nature of these codes, practitioners have a sense of what it means to work ethically. The codes, at least, evidence a concern for ethics on the part of media and communications organizations.

News Councils and Ombudspersons

In addition to ethical codes, the establishment of news councils in several states and even nationally added weight to the post–World War II concern with responsible communication. In the 1960s, community news councils were created; they were composed of public and media representatives who were to provide a forum for criticism of the media and a way for media people to respond to them. Councils appeared in Oregon, California, Illinois, Missouri, Washington, Massachusetts, Hawaii, Kentucky and Minnesota. (Today only two survive—in Hawaii and Minnesota.)

In 1973, the news council idea went national when the National News Council (NNC) was founded. The NNC was supported by eight foundations and was created to examine the American media and to speak out on press freedom and responsibility issues. Like the community and the state councils, the NNC had no means for enforcing its findings—being able only to have its reports published by cooperating media. This national council was inspired by similar groups that had been created in Sweden (1916) and in Britain (1953).

Media reactions to the NNC were mixed, but the idea of the Council never really caught on. Even the powerful *New York Times* was opposed to it, seeing in it seeds of control and the lessening of editorial autonomy. The News Council went out of business in 1984, citing lack of funds, inadequate staff, insufficient media cooperation and a lack of public visibility.

Related to the news council concept, but more media-connected, was the ombudsman—or "ombudsperson"—an idea borrowed in the 1970s from a Scandinavian practice. A media organization would have a person specifically designated to hear public complaints against it, to serve as the people's advocate to the media managers, to provide internal criticism and to write reports to the administrators and columns for the newspapers.

These ombudspersons would give personal and confidential hearing to disgruntled audience members, would mediate in disputes, would investigate charges, would criticize media personnel and would counsel media managers. The first newspaper to have such a person was the Louisville *Courier-Journal,* in 1967, followed in 1970 by *The Washington Post.* Today about 50 members belong to the Organization of News Ombudsmen (ONO). A first cousin to these "people's representatives" are ethics advisers (or ethics "coaches") who spend from a few days to several months at various media. But it must be said that neither the ombudspersons nor the ethics coaches have caught on in the American media.

Professional Tendencies

Given the post-war emphasis on social responsibility, on ethical codes, ombudspersons and the like, it is little wonder that there is a steady trend toward professionalization among media people. Public service, social obligations and ethical practice force media thinking into a concern for having "professionals" in the business of public communication. Hardly anyone would deny that in the United States there is a tendency today toward journalism's professionalizing—toward its becoming a *profession.*

Many journalists and journalism educators would like to see journalism considered a profession. (The same can be said for public relations and advertising practitioners—and to a lesser extent for motion picture actors, musicians, recording stars and photographers.) But there are some journalists and journalism educators who see such a profession as dangerous. James Carey, former dean of the College of Communication at the University of Illinois, for example, believes that if journalism were a profession it would become more self-centered and less concerned about its public responsibility. And other journalism educators, like John Merrill, Jay Black and Ralph Barney, see a profession of journalism as restricting pluralism in the media and flying in the face of the spirit of the First Amendment.

Since a *profession* is usually thought of by sociologists as having licenses for members, an elite group empowered to expel unworthy members, a code of ethics, minimum entrance requirements and a discrete body of knowledge, it is clear that journalism is not presently a profession. It is, however, what might be called a developing profession. And some public communicators, such as public relations people, have made more progress than others in becoming professionalized.

(For Class Discussion)

1. Have no gods but the God of Success.

2. Create, however, false Gods in order to make the people think they are sharing in your power.

3. Always advocate Truth—your Truth, stemming from your Power and your Purpose.

4. Never tamper with the Truth unless such tampering will enhance your Authority and Power, accomplish your purposes and assure public conformity and stability.

5. Recognize that Justice is the handmaiden of Truth in the minds of the people; so proclaim both constantly.

6. Recognize that the people prize Power even more than the concepts of Truth and Justice, and act accordingly.

7. Recognize that Journalism is really beyond Ethics and that you are not accountable to anybody or anything except Market forces and your own consciences.

8. Never commit plagiarism, except if adequate camouflaging is possible.

9. Obey laws and common morality except if they interfere with your objective.

10. Never admit a moral or legal transgression.

Source: J. C. Merrill, "Machiavellian Journalism," *Journal of Mass Media Ethics,* Vol. 7, No. 2, 84–96.

Media Ethics: A Critique

It is an understatement to say that American media have come under severe criticism since about 1950. Movies have increasingly dealt with newspapers and their ethics; the press puts its spotlight on movies; and television gives mounting attention to both movies and newspapers in talk shows and special PBS forums that bring problems of the media to the audience's attention. Individual media have begun to look at themselves and their ethical problems. This is what the Hutchins Commission hoped for back in 1947, but it must be said that the mass-media establishment (as a whole) is still disinclined to self-criticism and generally has a very defensive demeanor.

Poor Taste

Among huge segments of the public, the media's main ethical shortcoming is the *poor taste* regularly evidenced in publications, on radio and television, in the movies and in advertising. Poor taste, of course, is generally seen as subjective, and the media defenders (purveyors) of the "sleaze-factor" in mass communication—blatant on-screen sex and violence and obscene language, for example—are quick to defend this content by saying that your objection to it is "just your opinion." Also, they plead freedom of speech and press for any form of expression they want to make. Certainly with them, selfish (profit reasons) freedom is more important than ethical concern.

Walter Lippmann, the noted American journalist and political scientist, and present-day colleagues (Walter Berns, a political scientist, for one) have said in their writings that the First Amendment was not intended to protect such magazines as *Screw* and *Playboy* (and other material much more tawdry). These thinkers have viewed the First Amendment as having to do with serious, politically important material that is necessary to the governance and progress of the country.

But such arguments are not widely persuasive, and the controversy goes on. Poor taste may be subjective, but how many journalists would feel that the following journalistic activities (not fictional) are not in poor taste?

- a photo of a baby burning to death in a kitchen
- a TV filmclip of several decapitated bodies lying at the scene of an accident
- specific details of a murder-rape
- a police officer lying in the street, blood coming from a bullet hole between his eyes
- a couple copulating on a park bench
- a story about child molestation with detailed description, possibly even with a photo

Concern About Media Content

The subjectivity of poor taste aside, it does appear that almost anything goes in today's media world. Radio, especially—at least certain portions of it, called "shock radio"—has pulled out all the stops; the aim seems to be to indulge in poor taste as a "policy." Television, too, dumps its violence, sex and off-color satire into our living rooms. Along with violence and advertisements for various personal hygiene products, TV provides the public with sexy soap operas, Rambo-like destroyers and a whole world of crime, prostitution and drugs.

This menu was certainly not the intent of early broadcasters. The Radio Act of 1927, for instance, stated that "no person within the jurisdiction of the United States shall utter any obscene, indecent, or profane language by means of radio communication." Even though modern American society is far different from the one in 1927, there are millions of Americans today who believe that media have gone too far in their freedom and have, in a sense, brought the garbage can into the living room.

Of course, we must note that as anything-goes "shock radio" escalates its flamboyant utterances and vulgarizes its programming, we have the example of dignified and serious radio in NPR (National Public Radio), just as we have serious TV in PBS. But for every serious program dealing with culture, public affairs and the arts, at least 100 are rocking-and-rolling, dealing with sex talk and gossip, churning out "pop" religion and offering amateur psychiatric advice.

Pictures of Pennsylvania state treasurer R. Budd Dwyer's bloody 1987 suicide are widely published and broadcast but considered by some readers and viewers to be in poor taste.

This famous picture of injured childern fleeing an accidental napalm attack on their Vietnamese village draws criticism from some readers when it is published.

When one considers the general level of radio and TV, there is reason for concern about the concept of poor taste. As such programming proliferates in the modern media, it degrades the entire intellectual and cultural underpinnings of the society. "But that's what the people want," say the communicators of such material, shunning completely any thought of *ethical* responsibilities they might have to the public.

For the print media, too, there is a need for moral concern, although their messages may not be as obtrusive as those of the broadcast media. Much trash is also found in publications, and papers like *The National Enquirer* and Rupert Murdoch's *Star* are everywhere in the supermarkets, poisoning minds as people are buying groceries to nourish their bodies. Two-headed babies, visitors from other planets and Hollywood escapades and gossip are constantly available for the harried shopper in the checkout lines. In addition to the tabloids, there are magazine racks almost everywhere displaying publications replete with naked men and women in various suggestive poses. Covers show people being "blown away" by hideous gangsters or green monsters. Spiders entrap beautiful (always skimpily clad) women in their webs. Terrorists secure sticks of dynamite to the neck of an airline passenger. These come not from the mainline, establishment press, of course, but are a form of mass communication readily available through-out our society. We cannot divorce such publishing and broadcasting from *ethical concern.*

Moral Judgments Necessary

What is needed within the media to improve their taste and their content? To start, we need to make moral judgments. One's character can be corrupted by what Ayn Rand has called *moral agnosticism*. The idea that a person should never pass moral judgment on others—that one must be morally tolerant of everything—is pernicious and leads to lack of behavorial standards. (The unethical communicator, or course, is always happy to support such a passive precept.) Pronouncing a moral judgment or an ethical indictment is a big responsibility, but it should be done even when opinions differ—as they usually will. Such moral judgments at least force the principals to reconsider their actions seriously.

When a reporter misrepresents a situation, misquotes a source or fabricates a quote, we often hear that he or she "meant well," "didn't know any better" or was "just careless." What is needed is straight talk—calling unethical activity unethical, not falling back on some euphemistic evasion or complete silence. And the one making the moral judgment doesn't have to be perfect in order to pass judgment; his or her moral status really has nothing to do with the unethical action being pointed out. If an act is unethical, it is unethical regardless of the person drawing attention to it. Journalists who see colleagues being unethical and remain silent (or laugh it off as inconsequential) are moral cowards.

Special Spot

20 Ethical Cases for Discussion

1. The Case of the Unnamed Source
2. The Case of the Purloined Document
3. The Case of the Secret Taping
4. The Case of the Doctored Quote
5. The Case of the Government Junket
6. The Case of the One-Sided Story
7. The Case of the Purchased Interview
8. The Case of the Fictionalized Story
9. The Case of the "Eavesdropping" Reporter
10. The Case of the Reporter's Misidentity
11. The Case of the Resurrected Information
12. The Case of the Staged Photograph
13. The Case of the Unpublished Story
14. The Case of the Avoided Interviewee
15. The Case of the Adversarial Reporter
16. The Case of the Insensitive Reporter
17. The Case of the Accepted Gift
18. The Case of the "Off-the-Record" Remark
19. The Case of the Hidden Camera
20. The Case of "Sexist" Language

Strategies and Ethical Problems

How can we translate theoretical concerns and critique into practice? Ethicists generally agree that one of the best ways to educate people about ethics is through consideration of actual situations. This activity can be enlightening: Given a certain situation, you, your roommate, your friend and your professor may each favor different behaviors, which each of you considers ethical. Such divergence of thought illustrates how thorny a topic ethics can be. In this section, we look at a case to see how loyalties affect behavior, and we list some ethical problems related to the media.

Consideration of Loyalties

When a mass communicator is trying to determine the ethical thing to do, it is necessary to consider basic loyalties. Of course, a person may have loyalties to several different parties. Usually, though, there is a loyalty that transcends others at any particular time.

Let us look at the main loyalties a journalist may have: to the *medium,* to the *audience,* to *sources,* to an *ideology* or *political position,* to the *nation* or to *improvement of status.* Assuming that the principal loyalty of a mass communicator will affect his or her ethical practice, let us take one case and see how it might be handled in view of each of the above loyalties.

A source in the Pentagon gives information to a reporter about a new secret weapon developed and asks not to be named in the story. The reporter and his publisher are staunch Democrats and very liberal, whereas the national administration is Republican and conservative. The reporter is young and new at the newspaper and needs a big story. The newspaper's policy is usually not to print stories with anonymous sources.

Now, let us look at the possible influence of the six loyalties. You may well disagree with these actions below, but they will serve as catalysts for discussion.

Reporter with loyalty to the *medium:* Would print the story if source's name could be withheld.

Reporter with loyalty to the *audience:* Would print the story even if it meant naming the source.

Reporter with loyalty to *sources:* Would print the story without the source's name or would not print the story.

Reporter with loyalty to *ideology:* Would print the story—even without the source's name.

Reporter with loyalty to the *nation:* Would not print the story.

Reporter with loyalty to *personal status:* Would print the story.

Some Code-Suggested Ethical Problems

Innumerable ethical problems exist in mass communication. Whole books have dealt with the wide assortment of problems facing various areas of mass communication. But here we shall concentrate on a few special trouble areas facing mass communicators (the *they* in the parentheses below) that are stressed in ethical codes:

- Relationship with sources. (They must not be compromised by these sources, but at the same time they must protect them.)
- Conflicts of interest. (They must not do anything that might cause them to lose credibility, e.g., "moonlighting" after hours for a U.S. senator.)
- Gifts and subsidies. (They must not accept gifts and financial help—junkets, for example—that might interfere with their unbiased perspectives.)
- Serving the truth. (They must aspire to presenting the truth; it is their "ultimate goal.")
- Serving the public interest. (They must do what is good for the public. But what if that might be *withholding the truth?*)
- Invasion of privacy. (They should not invade another person's privacy. Problem: defining privacy.)

- Prompt and complete correction of errors. (They should quickly and thoroughly make corrections. Problems: What kinds of errors? How quickly and how thoroughly?)
- Fulfilling their "constitutional mandate . . . to report the facts." (They wonder where in the Constitution such a mandate is found.)
- Misusing their "professional status . . . for selfish or other unworthy motives." (They may question their professional status and whether all selfish motives are "unworthy.")
- The bad practice of "lack of thoroughness." (They may find this difficult to correct since such a lack will always be relative.)
- Plagiarism. (They may agree that plagiarism is "dishonest and unacceptable" but may wonder just what constitutes plagiarism.)

Now, for a few more ethical problem areas, not touched on in many ethical codes. For example, what about the ethics of tampering with quotes, even with good motives in mind? And how does one ethically determine which quotes and whose quotes to use? And what about refraining from telling the truth—or hiding part of the truth—in order to satisfy a subjective desire of the reporter? In other words, is full-disclosure reporting (seeking to tell the truth) always the ethical thing to do?

And, what about a practice such as "President Doe was not available for comment" usually tacked onto the final paragraph of a story? The implication given is that Doe is hiding out or has something to be ashamed of. Seldom if ever does the story say *where* President Doe was when he or she was called or how diligent the reporter was in trying to find him or her. And, finally, let's consider the "one-person cross-section" reportorial device whereby one person is quoted as a representative of a whole group or population.

Conclusion

What can we conclude from all of this? Are there definite ethical rules that a communicator can follow in order to be ethical? What should one do in this or that situation? Which of the philosophical pathways should we take? Such questions indicate a normal frustration found in every ethics conversation, conference or seminar. Perhaps we are asking the wrong questions. Could it not be that a *moral consciousness* and an *ethical motivation* (desire to do the right thing) are really the important considerations? If ethical consciousness is being raised and you are developing a sincere moral concern, then something worthwhile is taking place.

Deni Elliott, who has been a leader in the area of communication ethics, has suggested a trinary model for moral decision-making. Her model is based on her reading of Aristotle's ethical views. From this perspective, Dr. Elliott sees the ethical journalist as a person of character who tends to do the right thing out of good motives, sound thought and deep concern for humanity. It is Aristotle's *way* that Dr. Elliott suggests for today's journal-

Meetings of world journalists held in various parts of the world since 1978 have focused on developing some type of international code of ethics. This interest stems largely from a UNESCO declaration dealing with the potential contributions of mass media. Following a consultative meeting (in Paris and Prague, in 1983), the International Organization of Journalists (headquartered in Prague) drew up a 10-principle code of ethics "as a source of inspiration for national and regional codes."

Without the brief discussion of each, which is part of the code, here are the 10 principles:

1. People have a right to an objective picture of reality.
2. Journalists must serve the people's right to true and authentic information.
3. Journalists should consider information a social good and not a commodity.
4. Journalists should have high standards of integrity.
5. Journalists should promote access to, and public participation in, the media.
6. Journalists should respect the right of privacy.
7. Journalists should respect the national community and public morals.
8. Journalists should stand for the universal values of humanism—above all, peace.
9. Journalists should not justify or incite wars of aggression and the arms race.
10. Journalists should promote a new information and communication order for the world.

ists. And when a journalist is able to follow this way, he or she will be in Lawrence Kohlberg's highest and final stage. Three factors play parts in this Aristotelian idealization of a journalist: a respect for the truth, the intent or motivation for the action and a consideration of possible consequences. Often, Dr. Elliott says, it is impossible to have all three of these factors in an ethical decision, but one should want to have at least two of them in order to justify an action.

Actually there is not much more to say about communication ethics. Being a person of character, of principle and of goodwill is the Aristotelian way, and when we have said that, we have come close to saying it all. Ethics is, indeed, a highly controversial field if we quibble over every little case, situation and action. But when we look at ethics from the broader Aristotelian perspective, concentrating on character-building and the formation of intellectually sound habits, we are on much firmer ground. Since mass communicators have great responsibilities to their publics, they need to be persons of good intentions with philosophical and spiritual foundations that will support their activities, even when some of those activities may be questionable. A good character can usually overcome an ill-conceived, incorrect or poor ethical decision.

Jay Black, of the University of South Florida, has posed the question as to whether ethics is the same as moralizing. His answer is no. Ethics, he says, is a branch of moral philosophy—or thinking about morality, moral problems and moral judgments. Moralizing, on the other hand, tends be entail dogmatic, pragmatic and advisory statements about what should or should not be done.

It would seem that in many cases we indulge in moralizing when we think we are conversing about ethics. Certainly courses in ethics should not be courses in moralizing; they should go beyond just giving advice about actions. They should deal with analytical thinking about ethical principles, about why a concern with ethics is important in the first place (meta-ethics) and about various theories of ethics that may be of use to us.

Perhaps we can say simply that moralizing is a kind of propaganda (advice for specific cases) espoused by the moralizer (talker/writer), whereas ethics or moral philosophy deals with principles that, as Dr. Black and others have said, are intellectually based and consists of general advice that is valid over time, from person to person, and from case to case.

Retrospective

Media ethics is a most difficult topic, mainly because it is heavily laced with opinion, with subjectivity, and with general social values. When we talk about media ethics we are considering how media personnel make decisions in the moral or ethical realm. We are concerned with *reasons* for doing *this* instead of *that,* for seeking better (rather than worse) actions in the world of mass media. A *concern* for being ethical is a basic assumption upon which this chapter has been founded.

Every segment of mass communication has its ethical concerns— advertising, public relations, reporting, movie-making, television news and documentaries, talk shows on radio, recordings and various types of magazines and books. Often, for some media people (reporters, for example) ethical concerns tend to conflict with professional aspirations.

Which of several main ethical theories is a media practitioner led to accept? There is a legalistic position (*deontological ethics*), a concern for consequences (*teleological ethics*) and a pragmatic and selfish ends-justifying-the-means ethics (Machiavellianism). And there are others. By and large, communicators want to be ethical and they try—but often they follow different paths with different results. This points up the great relativism (and controversy) in media ethics.

Questions

1. Explain briefly the basic concepts of ethics held by Immanuel Kant and John Stuart Mill. In what way (or ways) might they be considered similar?

2. What is the "categorical imperative"? Can a journalist use it for making an ethical decision about, for instance, withholding the names of a news source from the story?

3. Do you agree with those who say that news councils and codes of ethics are in conflict with the First Amendment? Give the reasons for your answer.

4. How would you define *poor taste* in mass communication? Do you agree that the media indulge in practices of poor taste? If so, what, if anything, would you do about it?

5. What were Kierkegaard's three stages of moral growth? Do you think he presents a logical model? If not, how would you change the order of his progression?

6. How do you feel about Aristotle's concept of "character" (or the "ideal person") taking precedence over doing the ethical thing in a particular case? How does Aristotle's position agree with those of Kohlberg and Elliott?

Suggested Readings

Adler, Renata. *Reckless Disregard*. New York: Knopf, 1986.

Barron, Jerome. *Freedom of the Press for Whom?* Bloomington: University of Indiana Press, 1971.

Berns, Walter. *Freedom, Virtue, and the First Amendment*. Baton Rouge: Louisiana State University Press, 1957.

Carey, James W. *Communication in Culture: Essays on Media and Society*. Winchester, MA: Unwin Hyman, 1988.

Christians, Clifford, et al. *Media Ethics: Cases and Moral Reasoning*. New York: Longman, 1983.

Duska, Ronald, and Whalen, Mariellen. *Moral Development: A Guide to Piaget and Kohlberg*. New York: Paulist Press, 1975.

Elliott, Deni, ed. *Responsible Journalism*. Beverly Hills, CA: Sage, 1986.

Fink, Conrad. *Media Ethics*. New York: McGraw-Hill, 1988.

Fletcher, Joseph. *Situation Ethics: The New Morality*. Philadelphia: Westminster Press, 1966.

Gerald, J. Edward. *The Social Responsibility of the Press*. Minneapolis: University of Minnesota Press, 1963.

Goodwin, Eugene. *Groping for Ethics in Journalism*. Ames: Iowa State University Press, 1983.

Haselden, Kyle. *Morality and the Mass Media*. Nashville: Broadman Press, 1968.

Hulteng, John L. *The Messenger's Motives: Ethical Problems of the News Media*. Englewood Cliffs, NJ: Prentice-Hall, 1976.

Johannesen, Richard L. *Ethics in Human Communication*. Prospect Heights, IL: Waveland Press, 1981.

———. *Ethics and Persuasion: Selected Readings*. New York: Random House, 1967.

Klaidman, Stephen, and Beauchamp, Tom. *The Virtuous Journalist*. New York: Oxford University Press, 1993.

Lambeth, Edmund. *Committed Journalism*. Bloomington: Indiana University Press, 1986.

Merrill, John C. *Existential Journalism*. New York: Hastings House, 1977.

———. *The Dialectic in Journalism: Toward a Responsible Use of Press Freedom*. Baton Rouge: LSU Press, 1989.

———. *The Imperative of Freedom*. New York: Hastings House, 1974.

Phelan, John M. *Disenchantment: Meaning and Morality in the Media*. New York: Hastings House, 1980.

Rivers, William, and Mathews, Cleve. *Ethics for the Media*. Englewood Cliffs, NJ: Prentice-Hall, 1988.

Rivers, William, Schramm, Wilbur, and Christians, Cliff. *Responsibility in Mass Communication*. New York: Harper & Row, 1980.

Swain, Bruce M. *Reporters' Ethics*. Ames: Iowa State University Press, 1978.

Thayer, Lee, ed. *Morality and the Media*. New York: Hastings House, 1980.

Whalen, Charles. *Your Right to Know*. New York: Random House, 1975.

Global Media and Issues

S cientists and exobiologists involved in a search for life on other planets and in other star systems will tell you the question is not "Is there anyone out there?" but rather "Where is everyone?" They maintain that it is both insular and dangerously naive to think of ourselves as the only intelligent life form in the universe. After all, the universe is infinite and the suns and solar systems uncountable.

We have much the same problem of provincial insulation and dangerous naiveté in the study of media. We grow so accustomed to our own media system that we begin to think our way is the only way. It isn't. The world, due in part to technological media advances, grows smaller every year, and national problems are rapidly becoming international problems. As the world seems to shrink, our knowledge of and interest in the world becomes more important. Communication activities of a global nature are especially significant to us, for our media are "windows on the world," and largely determine our perception of other peoples and cultures.

Let's take a general look at some of the international media and how they disseminate information worldwide. As we do, it is important to keep in mind that global communication is changing. The international media picture blurs and mutates rapidly. The cold war is over. The Soviet Union has dissolved. The two Germanies are reunited. New international frictions arise. Although muted in recent years, the controversies between the so-called Third World developing countries and the advanced First World countries continue to strain international harmony. The New World Information and Communication Order (NWICO), so divisive in the 1970s and 1980s, still rumbles under the surface of global dialogue.

Changes in the East

The former Soviet Union, now called the Commonwealth of Independent States (CIS), is switching rapidly from a strict Marxism-Leninism to a hybrid Western-type capitalism. As a result, the old Soviet Union's former serf-states of Eastern Europe are laboriously trying to find their own way through the labyrinth of change. And the media systems of the East European countries, struggling under new and unaccustomed burdens, are trying to adapt to unanticipated new freedoms devoid of government economic paternalism. Just how all this reshuffling and the vast changes that are presently underway will affect the media systems of the region is anybody's guess. It's too early to tell, and we probably won't get a clear picture of the pattern from this volatile part of the world until about 1995 or even 1996.

But the early evidence leads us to believe that many of these new states are developing nationalistic and individualistic media systems that they feel might best reflect their traditional and ethnic diversities. And socialism, though badly damaged, is far from dead. Many of the emerging countries will no doubt retain some of their socialist structure, adding to it the trappings of free-market economy, competition and increased reliance on free expression.

We can be fairly certain the press systems in these former Communist

GLOBAL GLANCE
TASS Is
Gone—Almost

The old, well-known international news agency of the former Soviet Union—TASS—has officially disappeared. In 1992, the TASS news agency—one of the biggest in the world—died. In reality, it merged with another agency, Novosti, to become the principal news agency of the Commonwealth of Independent States (CIS): RITA.

RITA is the abbreviation for the Russian Information Telegraph Agency. But TASS has not completely disappeared. It will remain as a domestic branch of the new RITA agency. Many of the old TASS employees are not happy about this change, and as 1993 began were agitating the new powers of the CIS to reconsider and to reinstate the old agency to its former prestigious position.

---

countries will be freer than they have been in the past. That much is already evident. Media voices in Eastern Europe are energetic and free, in spite of the occasional remaining controls. No longer monolithic and enslaved by government and the Communist Party, these media are increasingly savoring their new-found individualistic voices. Every month brings new changes to the media systems of this vast area; media units are born and media units die, while media barons and media conglomerates from the West rush into the vacuum, intensifying the Westernization of the media.

Western media organizations, universities and foundations have joined the rush to offer help to the newly developing media. One organization, the Freedom Forum (a Gannett foundation from the United States) regularly sends delegations to Eastern Europe to assist media education and to offer encouragement to journalists struggling to shift in the direction of capitalistic journalism. A Freedom Forum delegation reported in 1991 that basic problems facing the emerging media in East Europe include lack of training in media management and marketing, lack of advertising, rising costs of printing and paper, newsprint shortages, difficulty of access to printing presses, lack of press law, circulation problems, scarcity of journalists, the continued licensing of journalists by some governments and lack of journalism schools.

It would seem that most of the problems (not all, of course) facing the post–Cold War countries of Eastern Europe are financial and technical, not political. But instances still persist where governments exercise considerable control over media. The systems are in flux, and old habits and traditions die hard. Some media systems are freer than others. Jozsef Antall, prime minister of Hungary, declared in 1991 that Hungary had the "freest press possible."

Specific newspapers and magazines are hard to identify, since something publishing today may be gone tomorrow. But, in time, some of the current publications will find their niches and will become leaders. A few newspaper titles from the old Soviet Union—such as *Izvestia* and *Komsomolskaya Pravda*—have managed to survive, though in changed form. Western cooperation has led to such publications as a Russian-language version of *The New York Times* (started in 1992 with the help of the weekly *Moscow*

News) and a monthly newspaper called *We,* published jointly by the Hearst Corporation and the Russian newspaper *Izvestia.* Perhaps the leading political newspaper in Russia heading into 1993 was the post-USSR *Rossiskaya Gazeta.* Other serious contenders could be the serious *Nezavisimaya Gazeta* of Moscow (patterned after England's *Independent*) and *Izvestia* (though still in the throes of serious financial problems).

The serious magazines of the new Russia are led by *Literaturnaya Gazeta* and *Ogonyok.* Even these magazines faced economic woes as 1993 came along and were becoming increasingly "popular" by giving more attention to murders, sex and other sensational activities.

The Flow of World Information

A flow of news, analysis, propaganda and entertainment gushes forth from some countries; it floods into some and trickles sluggishly into others. The flow mainly originates in the big information-producing countries of the **First World** (advanced capitalist nations in North America, Western Europe and Asia) and proceeds in uneven fashion into the rest of the world. The so-called **Second World** (advanced socialist nations such as were found in the USSR and Eastern Europe) are no more; they are in a state of flux, striving to find the right formula of economic stability and political freedom. And the **Third World** (developing, economically underdeveloped nations largely in Africa, Latin America and Asia) is primarily a receiver of small amounts of global information and does little to add to the global flow. The result of this unevenness of flow is that certain countries receive far more coverage than do others. This inequity generates much of the Third World's dissatisfaction with First World journalism.

Information flows in many ways: from movies, recordings, books, newspapers, magazines, radio, television and visits by world leaders. Through satellites, information flows to almost every corner of the globe. Many broadcast media and networks, as well as magazines and newspapers, send their correspondents around the world to find and disseminate news. But the bulk of the information flow is in the hands of the big world news agencies, which are primarily in the hands of the First World. This fact alone causes distress among Third World nations, who feel virtually left out, and is a point of contention within large segments of the world community.

In an attempt to balance the situation somewhat, the Pool of News Agencies of the Third World was founded in 1975, using the facilities of the former Yugoslavia's national news agency Tanjug. And in 1986, the North-South News Service was established in New Hampshire to train Third World journalists to write for First World publications. So far, however, such efforts have not made much difference, and the Third World continues its complaints.

Major News Agencies of the World

News and other information usually flow from big city to big city, from well-developed nations to well-developed nations or from well-developed to less-developed nations. Certain global "hubs" play particularly important roles in this news flow. Cities like New York, Washington, London, Paris, Zurich, Bonn, Madrid, Rome, Stockholm, Tokyo, Delhi, Beijing, Hong Kong, Moscow, Toronto, Montreal, Honolulu and Manila serve as sources for some 90 percent of all information that flows among nations. Other cities that are important within their own national borders—for example, Abidjan, Lagos, Tunis, Addis Abbaba, Kuala Lumpur, Poona, St. Petersburg, Nanking, Saltillo, La Paz, Cartegena and Rosario—receive little or no attention in the world press because the big news agencies are usually based in—and emphasize—large cities and well-developed countries. In fact, some five—perhaps only three now that UPI and TASS are in the twilight zone of visibility—big news agencies provide the great bulk of news.

Of course, there are scores of smaller news agencies serving individual nations and regions of the world, but they are usually economically starved, governmentally controlled or extremely provincial and thus are less effective disseminators of information than the large agencies. A few of these smaller agencies, however, are very effective (for example, Kyodo of Japan, DPA of West Germany and Xinhua of China) and serve their many clients well.

The "Big Five" Agencies Plus Two. The main news agencies of the world (if we count all five) once included: United Press International (UPI) and the Associated Press (AP) of the United States, Reuters of Great Britain, Agence France-Presse (AFP) of France, and Telegrafnoie Agenstvo Sovetska-vo Soiuza (TASS) of the Soviet Union. Now, UPI and TASS are mere shadows of their former selves.

In addition to these, there are two TV agencies of international significance that supplement the "Big Five." The world's largest television news agency is VISNEWS (Vision News), created in 1957 by Britain's BBC. It has four regular daily satellite feeds of news—three from London and one from New York. Principal receivers of its services are in Australia, New Zealand, Japan, Hong Kong and South America. The service is extended through videocassettes sent to other nearby TV stations that do not get direct satellite reception. VISNEWS is owned by BBC, Reuters and broadcasting corporations of Canada, Australia and New Zealand.

Another television agency, the main rival of VISNEWS, is UPITN. It is a transnational agency combining the services of UPI and the British Independent Television News (ITN)—resulting in its synthesized acronym. It is growing rapidly, with more than 200 TV stations in some 80 countries using its services. Its transmissions are accessible to some 90 percent of the world. Like VISNEWS, it uses satellites for transmission. It has editorial offices in several important cities such as New York, Washington, Paris, London, Frankfurt, Rome and Hong Kong. And, through UPI bureaus, UPITN has correspondents in almost every part of the world.

It is small wonder, then, that the large agencies dominate the world's collection and dissemination of information. They all have networks of correspondents to gather news in many countries and headquarters staffs to

EXCELLENCE IN NEWS

Reuters, like AFP, is one of the world's "Big Five" news agencies.

edit this news and transmit it to bureaus abroad for local distribution, to national and regional agencies with whom they have exchange agreements and to subscribing print and electronic media throughout the world that use their messages.

Leading National/Regional Agencies. Most of the smaller agencies that supplement information and relay to local clients the big agencies' news have exchange agreements with those agencies or with other national and regional agencies. They play a very important part in filtering world news to the grassroots communities and in adding more local coverage to the main flow of international information.

Some of the national agencies have bureaus and correspondents in the main world capitals, but most of them operate primarily within their own borders. Among the largest and most important of such agencies are Jiji Press and Kyodo in Japan; Novosti in the USSR; DPA (Deutsche Presse Agentur) of West Germany; SAPA (South African Press Association) of South Africa; CNA (Central News Agency) of Taiwan; MENA (Middle East News Agency) of Egypt; and Xinhua (New China News Agency) of the People's Republic of China.

"Journalistic responsibility!" This is a cry that is dying slowly in Eastern Europe and the former Soviet Union. Leaders in this vast area, although dedicating themselves to press freedom, are still nervous. They believe that certain government secrets should be kept and that nosy investigative reporters can endanger national policy. They would agree with Vaclav Havel of Czechoslovakia, when he said in 1990, that he deplored "a press that was always playing detective."

Havel has stated that press freedom is needed to safeguard democracy, "but it is also a sacred cow, largely of the press's own making, that it has nurtured for years to build a protective wall around itself." (*New York Times,* July 15, 1990, E19). This kind of thinking is still extant in Eastern Europe, and the Western concept of press freedom is fragile.

All sorts of problems still exist. Poland seeks a better advertising base for its nascent marketplace so as to ensure financial independence for its press; Hungary worries about growing control of its press by multinational groups buying up media units; Romania attempts to develop media supply and distribution systems free from government control; and Russia is toying with new laws to ensure press freedom.

As this dynamic new "freedom" area of the world nears the middle of the last decade of the 20th century, it exudes much hope for real press libertarianism. But with this hope, there are still the old fears, leftover from the Marxist days, of media excesses and journalistic endangerment to the social stability and national security.

Media Systems and Theories

The *kinds* of media systems found in the world today depend largely on the political philosophy embraced by a particular country. Five main "theories," or media systems, dominate: **authoritarian** (media support the state of authority but are mainly privately owned), **libertarian,** or Western (media are largely autonomous and privately owned), **Marxist** (media are owned and controlled by the state and are cooperating partners with government), **revolutionary** (media are used to subvert the government or fight against foreign interference), and **developmental** (media are seen as instruments for nation-building). Note that the revolutionary and developmental systems are not "pure" in that they are either *supplementary* to another system (the developmental system) or are *temporary* (the revolutionary system).

In addition to these five systems, others have been suggested, such as Robert Picard's *democratic socialist* system (1985) and Ralph Lowenstein's *social centralist* and *social libertarian* systems (1971). Both are modifications of the old "four theories" model of Fred Siebert, Ted Peterson and Wilbur Schramm (1956). The "four theories" model contained (besides the authoritarian, libertarian and communist) what the three authors called the *social responsibility* system, which was not parallel to the other three and which was filled with semantic noise. It has increasingly been challenged. It was Professor William Hachten, in his *World News Prism* (1981), who proposed the "revolutionary" and the "developmental" theories. Hachten's concepts were elaborated on in 1984 by J. Herbert Altschull in his *Agents of Power.*

The world's largest television news agency is VISNEWS, based in London. Here, editors check a "feed" from a satellite.

Whether they accept one of the "four theories" or one of the others mentioned before, all of the world's nations have together spawned amazingly diverse media systems around the globe. Media systems, following their own theories, saturate the globe with information.

Within these various systems, existing in pure or hybrid form throughout the world, there are some 500 million copies of nearly 10,000 daily newspapers and an unknown number (perhaps 50,000) of other newspapers published. The actual number of newspaper readers is hard to estimate, since in many nations the practice of passing copies on to others or posting them in public places is common.

About 90 nations operate national shortwave radio stations aimed at other countries, with programming in many languages. Illustrative of these is the United States' Voice of America. Three radio organizations of the world—the VOA, the BBC of Britain and Deutsche Welle of Germany—account for at least 80 percent of the world's broadcast news flow. Some 1,500 shortwave transmitters are operating throughout the world.

The First World nations are the main exporters of TV programs and films to other nations. The United States dominates in the export of TV

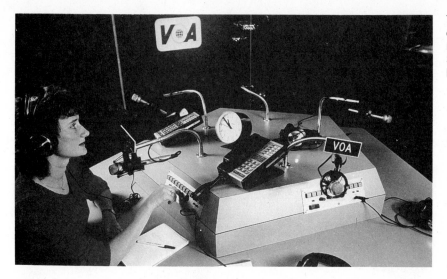

The Voice of America is one of the world's biggest radio news organizations. Studios are in Washington, D.C.

programs and joins with India, Great Britain, Japan and Germany in providing most of the films to the world. More than 80 percent of yearly book publication takes place in the industrialized countries of the First and Second Worlds.

Print Media: Overview

Although not nearly as pervasive as the broadcast media, the print media provide information throughout the world. Because they mainly reach the opinion leaders of various countries, they probably have a greater impact on national and international policy than their circulation numbers indicate. It is really impossible to know how many newspapers and periodicals are published in the world, although the United Nations Educational, Scientific and Cultural Organization (UNESCO) tries to find out from time to time.

At least one-third of the world's periodicals are published in North America. Another third come from Europe, and the final third from throughout the rest of the world. Newspapers everywhere are in difficulty, due to the high cost of newsprint and equipment, restraints on their freedom and problems with trade unions. The world's newspapers are quite diverse in respect to purpose, emphasis and content although group ownership, news agency impact and economic realities are tending to make them more similar.

Media: A Panoramic View

Media development largely correlates with economic development. Therefore, it is natural to find the largest and most modern media in the economically well-developed nations of the world. And these nations are

The world's best known newspapers include both "elite" and "mass-appeal" publications.

found largely on two continents: North America and Europe. It is no surprise that about half of the world's media, and certainly the largest and most technologically advanced media, are found on these two continents.

The average newspaper in these developed countries stresses features, photographs, editorials and essays, columns, letters to the editor, news analyses, comic strips, weather reports, stock market charts, crossword and other puzzles and a variety of other editorial tidbits. In addition, these economically sound newspapers, usually operating in a capitalist system, typically fill from 50 to 65 percent of their space with advertising.

In former socialist or communist nations, newspapers were far more serious, even puritanical, giving little or no sensational news of disasters, crime, sex and the like. Instead, they were usually filled with official pronouncements, news of progress and development and stinging editorial propaganda against the noncommunist world. Although most of these former Marxist nations now appear to be slowly gravitating toward Western-style capitalistic democracies, there are still various kinds of socialism and even extreme communism (China, North Korea, and Cuba, for example) extant in the world.

In Third World countries, the newspapers are often very small and poorly printed and are struggling to keep from fading away for lack of finances. Some papers are much like the capitalist papers, and others resemble those in former socialist countries, depending on which direction the Third World country is leaning politically.

The highest readership rates are found in Sweden, Japan, Britain, Norway, Denmark and the United States. All of these countries have rates of more than 200 copies of dailies per 1,000 persons. For the whole world, the rate is between 90 and 100 copies per 1,000 persons, although there are many parts of the globe where newspapers are never read.

Elite or Quality Papers. Throughout the world there is a small group of "elite" or international prestigious newspapers, furnishing leading opinion leaders at home and abroad with a heavy diet of well-written and serious material. The emphasis in these papers is on international relations, politics, economics, science, literature and the arts and informed analysis and interpretive reporting. These are the papers read by government officials, academicians, journalists and other opinion leaders.

The majority of such papers are found in Western Europe and North America, but there are a few scattered throughout other continents. Typical of such papers in the United States are *The New York Times, The Wall Street Journal, The Washington Post* and the *Los Angeles Times.* In Europe, there is *Le Monde* of France, the *Neue Zuercher Zeitung* of Switzerland, *El País* of Spain, *Il Corriere della Sera* of Italy, the *Frankfurter Allgemeine Zeitung* of Germany, *Svenska Dagbladet* and *Dagens Nyheter* of Sweden, *Berlingske Tidende* of Denmark, *Izvestia* of the CIS and *The Times* and *The Independent* of England.

Elite newspapers in Asia are *Renmin Ribao* of China, *Asahi Shimbun* of Japan, *The Statesman* and *The Hindu* of India and *The Age* of Australia. In the Middle East and Africa, *Ha'aretz* of Israel, *Al Ahram* of Egypt and the *Cape Times* of South Africa have considerable influence. In Latin America, there is *El Mercurio* of Chile, *La Nación* of Argentina, *El Tiempo* of Colombia, *O Estado de S. Paulo* of Brazil and *Excelsior* of Mexico. Canada has the *Globe and Mail* of Toronto.

Most students of the press maintain that there are probably no more than 30 to 50 such newspapers globally. Placing a newspaper in this elite group is, of course, subjective, but there is a general agreement around the world as to which are the "best" newspapers—although their order in a quality list may vary. These newspapers are often not the circulation leaders in their countries, having circulations averaging 200,000. But in some cases (e.g., with *Asahi Shimbun* of Japan and *Renmin Ribao* of China) they also have very high circulations—in the millions.

The Mass-Appeal Papers. On the opposite side of the world's newspaper spectrum are the mass-appeal, or "popular," newspapers. These cater to the tastes of the masses, to those who are seeking some news but who want their reading material to be entertaining and interesting. These newspapers often stress sensational and gossipy material rather than serious cultural and political news and analysis. There is some overlap among the elite and the mass-appeal papers, but not very much.

Rupert Murdoch,
International Press
Mogul

The Australian publisher turned American citizen, Rupert Murdoch, is one of the biggest media owners in the world—with an empire that stretches from Australia to Europe. More than half the newspaper market in Australia belongs to Murdoch, and in Britain, more than a third. He owns 150 newspapers and magazines. His power is felt even in Asia where his Hong Kong *South China Morning Post* is a giant among the English-language papers.

In addition to his newspaper empire, Murdoch owns TV and cable systems in the United States and Europe, magazines such as *Epicurean.* (Melbourne), *New York Magazine* and *TV Guide,* and he has significant interests in book publishing (including HarperCollins). He also owns a large part of Reuters, the global news agency based in London. And his empire includes an airline and a hotel reservation service.

Once a socialist, Murdoch today is a free-market capitalist with political leanings of a conservative nature. He has been described as a secretive, suspicious person who alienates many people—especially government leaders. He grew up in Australia, son of a publisher who died in 1952 when Rupert was in his last year at Oxford University. He served his apprenticeship with London's *Daily Express,* which had the world's largest circulation using a formula of lively page makeup, succinct writing and heavy dosages of gossip and sex.

Most of the papers he has purchased since (such as his first British purchase, *The News of the World*) have reflected this popular journalistic tendency. However, he has kept some of his purchases serious—the venerable *Times* of London and the *Sunday Times,* which he acquired in 1981. He entered the American market in 1973 with the purchase of two San Antonio papers. The following year he created a weekly tabloid, *The Star,* as a competitor to *The National Enquirer,* which was dominating the gossip/movie star/occult/sex market from its racks at checkout counters of super-markets. Today, *The Star* has a circulation of nearly 4 million.

In 1977, he bought *The New York Post* and *New York Magazine,* and in 1985 he created Fox Television, which he saw as a competing network with ABC, CBS, NBC and TBS. Murdoch is truly an international media mogul with ambitions for more acquisitions worldwide.

Media magnate Rupert Murdoch holds a copy of *The Sun,* his biggest daily newspaper. Murdoch owns newspapers, magazines, book publishing firms, television stations and other media-related interests on four continents.

Some of the giant circulation papers (of at least one million) that are also high-quality papers are *Asahi Shimbun* of Japan, *Daily Telegraph* of England, *Renmin Ribao* of China and *Dong-a Ilbo* of South Korea. In the United States, there are three big-circulation "elite" dailies: *The New York Times* and the *Los Angeles Times* (with about a million each) and *The Wall Street Journal* (with about 1.9 million). And then there is the national popular-appeal paper of the Gannett group, *USA Today,* which has a circulation of some 2 million nationwide and daily distribution in about 55 countries.

A Potpourri of Periodicals

The world is well supplied with magazines of all kinds. As is true with newspapers, these periodicals tend to predominate in Europe and North America, but many and varied magazines are published in Latin America, Asia and Africa. In the Third World, many of the magazines are small and poorly printed, albeit lively and often sensational. In the First and Second Worlds, the magazines are thicker, glossier and extremely varied in approach and content.

Many countries have magazines of the arts—cultural magazines of high quality such as France's *Réalités*. And there are many "illustrateds" such as West Germany's *Stern* and *Quick,* Greece's *Eikones* and Norway's *Aktuell.* One of the best news-oriented picture magazines in the world is *Paris-Match* of France.

In some countries there are newsmagazines roughly patterned after *Time* and *Newsweek* of the United States. For instance, the very popular *Der Spiegel* (The Mirror) of Germany is much like *Time* but tends to be more political and opinionated. Other important weekly newsmagazines of this general type are *L'Express* (France) and *Shukan Asahi* (Japan). And increasingly, there are serious newsmagazines with an economics focus patterned after two leaders in this field: *The Economist* of Great Britain and *The Far Eastern Economic Review* of Hong Kong.

Other newsmagazines are usually more pictorial and colorful, exemplified by Italy's *Oggi* and *Tempo,* Egypt's *Al Mussawar* and *Mundo Hispánico* of Spain. In addition, there are many humor-satire magazines and journals; foremost among them are Britain's *Punch* and *The Tatler,* Italy's *Il Borghese,* Switzerland's *Nebelspälter,* Austria's *Igel* and Chile's *Topaze.*

Political magazines and journals are widespread. Typical of the better ones are *The New Statesman* and *Encounter* of Britain. Many countries also have journals dealing with the press, such as India's *Vidura,* Britain's *World's Press News,* and France's *L'echo de la Presse.*

And, increasingly, serious academic journals around the world are dealing with mass communication and journalism. A few of them, offering excellent analysis and insights, are *Publizistik* (Germany), *Gazette* and *European Journal of Communication* (Netherlands) and *Equid Novi* (South Africa). America, however, leads the field with such journals as: *Journalism Quarterly, Journal of Communication, Journal of Broadcasting & Electronic Media, Public Relations Quarterly* and *The Journal of Mass Media Ethics.*

Future Focus Post–Cold War Eastern Europe

Dangers abound in this region of flux and newly found freedom. Nationalist tensions will prolong international problems at least to the end of this century. Indecisive and contradictory economic reforms have already undermined the socialist economies without providing adequate free-market substitutes. Democrats in the region are slow to show effectiveness and authoritarians are impatient. Post–Cold War despair is to be found in every country of the region—in the southern nations more than in those of the north.

Most experts feel, however, that the nations of Eastern Europe will muddle their way toward democracy, and the problems of nationalism, weak economies, emerging class conflicts and political leadership will leave the region in some politico-economic twilight zone between communism and capitalism.

The mass media of the region will certainly gravitate toward more private ownership, but quite likely with considerable government subsidization. The media systems at the end of the century will resemble that of Sweden more than that of the United States. The mass communication situation will improve as the general economy improves. Press freedom, in the Western sense, will certainly take over from the authoritarianism that prevailed for some 50 years and ended in 1990. In spite of many problems, the media picture of Eastern Europe promises to be bright.

As communications research and education make inroads into the world's universities, the number of these scholarly journals is increasing.

All in all, the world is served well by magazines and journals. It is difficult to estimate the number of such publications since they start up and fold with some frequency. But UNESCO has suggested that at least 300,000 appear at any one time globally and that of these at least 100,000 are scientific and technical journals.

World Press Review: Essential Reading

"Must reading" for American journalism and communications students is *World Press Review,* a monthly journal that provides in English actual articles from dozens of top newspapers and magazines of the world. What are foreign newspapers and newsmagazines saying about our new president, about the Middle East, about the changes in Eastern Europe, about the continuing problems in Yugoslavia? *World Press Review* will tell you.

Articles from many of the publications mentioned in this chapter are reproduced in the magazine—names like *Der Spiegel, Le Monde, Svenska Dagbladet, El Pais, Asahi* and *The Hindu* dot the pages, with pungent comments from each.

WPR began publishing in 1974 under the name *Atlas World Press Review* (its predecessor *Atlas* had done a similar job from 1961) and in 1980 dropped "*Atlas*" from its name. The magazine reaches some 70,000 opinion leaders in the United States and many others in other countries. It is a product of the Stanley Foundation, of Iowa, dedicated to providing Americans a variety of viewpoints and kinds of information. The reader of *World Press Review* is privy to editorial cartoons, editorials, political and economic commentary, to a wide assortment of material about science, literature and the arts and to many pieces about how the United States and its citizens are seen from foreign perspectives.

Broadcasting is a potent force in the world. It reaches almost every corner of the globe, diffusing its messages where the print media make little or no inroads, particularly to areas with low literacy rates. Radio, especially, is able to penetrate regions where newspapers and television are virtually unknown. If anything, global broadcasting is even more diversified—in organization and control as well as in programming—than the print media. And it is quantitatively affecting ever greater areas of the world.

Scope of World Broadcasting

More than 150 countries have radio broadcasting, with close to a billion sets available. Transistor and battery sets may well double that number; it is impossible to estimate the total. Television has spread to some 120 countries; there are an estimated half billion sets around the world. Radio, however, is the more popular and accessible medium, and it is a much cheaper means of communication. Nevertheless, for every thousand inhabitants of the developing portions of the world (countries like Mali in Africa), UNESCO estimates that no more than 20 radio sets are available. At the same time, in a country like the United States, every 1,000 inhabitants would have 2,000 radio sets, an average of two sets per person.

The pattern for television saturation is even lower. In the Third World, there are only some 25 television sets per 1,000 people. In some parts of the developing world, the situation is even worse: In the central portions of Africa, for example, there are only 10 sets per 1,000 inhabitants. In the developed capitalist world (First World), on the other hand, there are more

GLOBAL GLANCE
Media Needs in Eastern Europe

In this transition period for journalism in Eastern Europe, some basic and urgent needs have been defined by government and media spokespersons. The most-often mentioned problem areas are:

- Lack of trained journalists
- Lack of capital
- Lack of management and technical expertise
- Lack of press laws
- Circulation and advertising problems
- Poor distribution systems
- Threat of government licensing of journalists
- Lack of journalism schools
- Lack of computer software
- Lack of investigative reporting skills
- Lack of understanding of a free-market system and its strengths and problems

World broadcasting depends upon facilities like this INTELSAT center from which many satellite feeds are received.

than 400 sets per 1,000, with the United States close to 98 percent total saturation of its population.

With the exception of the United States and a few other capitalist countries, the traditional broadcasting pattern has been systems owned and controlled by government. Privately owned commercial broadcasting is found in a minority of the world's nations, but it is slowly growing. Countries like Britain, France, Germany, Italy and Japan now have commercial stations operating alongside their national broadcasting stations.

Britain was a leader in Europe with the creation of ITA (Independent Television Authority) in 1954; its stations compete with the British Broadcasting Corporation (BBC). In Italy, commercial broadcasting came in 1976 and in Germany in the late 1980s. Japan, with a multitude of TV stations and nearly 70 million TV sets, has a thriving pay-TV system. In China, some 50 million TV sets are picking up programs from the country's communications satellite.

Control and Ownership Patterns

Control and ownership of broadcasting around the world is complex, and the standard dualistic manner of looking at it in terms of capitalism versus socialism is not satisfactory. Most systems are merger systems, having some aspects of capitalism and socialism. Countries like Germany may have broadcasting that is basically owned and operated by the government, but such control is decentralized, with authority in the hands of the various states. And other countries—Japan, Britain and Italy, to name three—have government-controlled broadcasting existing alongside private broadcasting. In most Arab countries, broadcasting is under direct government control. Government broadcasting monopolies are also found in most Third World countries (such as Nigeria, India, Malaysia and the Ivory

Tangential, but very important, to the NWICO controversy taking place globally today is the danger many see posed by direct broadcasting satellites (DBS). These high-powered satellites can beam TV or radio programs directly to sets having small antennas or satellite dishes. Stationed some 22,000 miles above the earth, these satellites can broadcast to upward of a million square miles of the earth's surface.

Dr. Nancy Rivenburgh of the University of Washington, who has studied the problem, says many countries see DBSs as posing three kinds of threats: political, commercial and cultural.

The political threat would be largely a problem of *propaganda,* whereby differing political systems could reach people of other systems directly. The second would, in effect, take commercial development of broadcasting out of the hands of an individual government and would interfere with various advertising regulations. And the third, which gets the most attention, sees DBS broadcasting as a threat to a nation's cultural sovereignty, by having foreign values replace indigenous value systems.

Critics of DBS, like Herbert Schiller (U.S.), Kaarle Nordenstreng (Finland), Jeremy Tunstall (U.K.) and many from the Third World believe such broadcasting without prior consent of receiving nations would violate national sovereignty and give certain nations an even greater chance for "communication imperialism."

It is interesting that, in this particular debate, the Second and Third World spokespersons are putting their emphasis on *the danger of communication imperialism* rather than on another favorite issue of theirs—*the need for a free flow of information.*

As the 21st century begins, DBS programming will undoubtedly be widespread around the globe in spite of considerable and continued global resistance to it.

Coast) and in the communist countries (countries like China and Cuba). Finally there is Argentina with a trinary system: state commercial stations, state noncommercial stations and private stations.

Financial support of broadcasting is also varied. About 40 countries support their systems completely by advertising, and about half that number rely on money from general taxes. Nearly 50 countries use both advertising and license fees paid by customers on a regular basis. Countries relying mainly on license fees (Britain, Japan and Germany, for example) have differing systems for payment for radio and television (either for each service separately or for a package deal). And some broadcasting systems like Japan's Nihon Hoso Kyokai (NHK) send collectors out to get the fees, whereas in other countries (such as Britain) the fees are paid through the Post Office.

In concluding this section on broadcasting, let us look at one particularly interesting system, that of the Netherlands. Wanting maximum diversity in broadcast messages for the country, the Dutch government has created what might be called a "forced pluralism" TV system. The government-owned broadcast system allocates air time among various societal groups (such as religious and political), which are charged with providing the programs. Any group with a large enough number of members can, by law, qualify for some air time. In addition, each group publishes a program guide carrying advertising. This advertising and a share of license fee money provide the support for the programming.

Now that we've looked at the general media situation, in print and in broadcasting, around the world, we need to turn to some of the issues that are paramount in global discussions. Although we have seen that some information flows almost everywhere through the world's gigantic media distribution system, there are those critics who feel that the First World (and to some degree, the Second World) have too much domination over international information flow. They ask for a new arrangement, for fresh thinking and rearranged priorities for global mass communication. They are increasingly criticizing the First World's communication assumptions, monopolistic tendencies, journalistic definitions and biased treatment of the developing world. Issues and problems abound. It is well that we take them seriously, for they will likely be with us for a long time.

The NWICO and Global Issues

The Third World, especially, wants a new ordering of information collecting and dissemination, feeling that developing countries are being short-changed in the quantity and quality of communication found in the world today. Since the 1960s at least, Western news agencies have seen the rising tide of Third World frustration and bitterness. And largely through the forum of the United Nations Educational, Scientific and Cultural Organization (UNESCO), the developing nations have mounted a campaign to bring about what they have called a *New World Information and Communication Order*.

The Basic Criticisms

The indictment of the West (First World) by Third World countries is strong and direct. They offer eight prominent criticisms that indicate the nature of the new "order" they desire:

1. The flow of information is unequal, with too much information originating in the West and not enough representing the developing nations.
2. There is too much bias against, and stereotyping of, the developing or "less developed" countries.
3. Alien values are foisted on the Third World by too much Western (mainly American) "communication imperialism."
4. Western communication places undue emphasis on "negative" news of the Third World—disasters, coups, government corruption and the like.
5. Finances are unequally distributed around the world for technology and communication development.
6. The Western definition of "news" (meaning atypical and sensational items) is unrealistic and does not focus enough attention on *development news* (items helping in the progress and growth of the country).

7. Communication and journalism education in universities is too Western-oriented, and too many textbooks used in the Third World are authored by First World writers, especially by Americans.
8. Too much of the world's information is collected by the big news agencies, giving the news a biased (Western) slant.

These are the main criticisms of the prevailing "communication order" in the world, but there are others implied by several Third World suggestions. One, for instance, is that the old structure of global communication is harmful to world understanding and what is needed is a restructuring (or in Russian terms, a *perestroika*) to bring balance and justice to the world's dialogue. Many Third World and Second World (advanced communist nations) spokespersons also want some kind of journalistic licensing for journalists covering other nations, and they have also made a call for an international code of ethics that would give guidelines for global newsgathering. By and large, such suggestions have been scorned by Western journalists who see them as endangering freedom and giving authoritarian governments a rationale to control visiting newspersons.

As to their response to the Third World's general criticism, Western spokespersons note that an unequal flow of information is natural and that nobody should ever expect to see it equalized. To the charge of communication imperialism, the Western retort is that it is a naive and ridiculous one; nobody is forcing Third World nations to accept U.S.-produced messages. And, besides, the Third World even pirates or steals U.S. programming from satellites, hardly a sign of "imperialism."

A VISNEWS cameraman photographs an event in Angola.

Mahmoud el-Sherif
Speaks on New
Information Order

Mahmoud el-Sherif is former president of the Arab States Broadcasting Union and former News Director of Radio Jordan; he has also been an editor of a Jerusalem Arab newspaper and a journalism professor at several mass-communication research centers. He made these remarks at a media conference in 1984 in Tokyo, Japan.

The debate over the media's role is one of the important elements of the New International Information and Communication Order, which has been proposed by Third World countries through UNESCO. This debate has triggered a wave of indignation in the West so strong that . . . some Western countries threatened to withdraw from UNESCO if such ideas continue to be discussed. The argument of our Western colleagues is that giving any role to the communications media will automatically threaten their freedom. The best and probably the most extreme example of this Western outlook was articulated by Mr. Marvin Kalb, when he declared in one of his famous articles that the media should enjoy the right to be "irresponsible." This attitude stems—I am afraid—from the simple fact that the Western media look at the Third World through their own prism, and choose to ignore the great differences between conditions, social and political "climates" and problems and challenges of development that face the two worlds. . . .

The New International Communication and Information Order does not call for the abolition of the press. On the contrary, it upholds the concept of a free unfettered press. It does not call for the governments to control the media. It abhors this; it denounces this. Anybody who thinks that the New Order calls for the control of governments over the media either did not read anything about the New Order or didn't bother to ask questions about it. . . .

The NWICO Controversy

Participants in the worldwide debate over this New World Information and Communication Order have been mainly in two camps. One side is the Third World journalists and government officials, along with their press organizations, which are supported by other important journalist groups such as the IOJ (International Organization of Journalists). The other side is Western journalists and publishers and spokespersons for Western organizations like the IPI (International Press Institute) of London, the IAPA (Inter American Press Association) of Miami and the WPFC (World Press Freedom Committee) of Washington, D.C.

Basic problems were originally voiced in the United Nations by the Third World members. As far back as 1976, UNESCO supported a declaration (proposed by the former USSR) stipulating changes that were looked upon as dangerous to press freedom by many of the Western members. As a result of this disagreement and others of like nature, UNESCO set up a commission, under the chairmanship of the highly respected Irishman, Sean MacBride, to study the problems of world communication. This group (the International Commission for the Study of Communication Problems) is generally known as the MacBride Commission. Its report was delivered at a UNESCO conference in 1980 and has been published both as a report and as a book (*Many Voices, One World*).

The MacBride Report was not adopted by UNESCO. Instead the organization proposed further study of the issues contained in it. Such study is still going on.

Beyond the MacBride Commission

One result of the MacBride Commission's report and the debate on the NWICO has been the creation of the International Program for the Development of Communications (IPDC), which encompasses an assortment of programs, such as First World gifts of equipment and technical training personnel to Third World countries asking for help. Things have slowed down considerably since 1984 when the United States and Britain withdrew from UNESCO, believing that it was not run efficiently and was basically serving as a propaganda forum against the West.

The whole controversy of the NWICO stems from obvious inequities in world communication. And there is really no debate about these inequities —only about how to eliminate them. The big international news agencies, for example, account for almost 90 percent of the global news flow. The industrialized nations produce at least 80 percent of the books found in the world. And, in international shortwave radio, the big nations have a virtual monopoly; at least 90 percent of the usable radio frequencies are in the hands of the Western industrialized countries. Films and television programs saturate Third World nations, and elaborate and glossy Western newspapers and magazines crowd out the poorly printed and less interesting publications of the Third World.

Although the global rhetoric on these issues diminishes from time to time, they are not likely to disappear. In fact, UNESCO is still dedicated to restructuring the world's communication system; Third World nations are still dissatisfied; First World nations remain dedicated to frustrating any basic changes in the communication picture; Second World allies of the Third World remain in the fray; and the whole topic is ideological enough to remain a viable one for many years.

And What About the Future?

American mass media and their journalists and the communication philosophy that supports them face an uncertain future. Within the United States itself mass communication is thriving; media are growing and support activities such as public relations and advertising appear to have healthy years ahead. This optimistic note, however, pertains to the *physical* and *economic* aspects of modern American mass media. When placed in the context of institutional *concept*, rather than *structure*, the situation is not overly bright.

The three main problems facing the American media of the future are *conceptual, ethical* and *international*.

First, the American media are unsure of a number of things: of their purpose in society, their professional status, their relationship to people and groups seeking access, their own limits to freedom and their proper relationship to government. Figuring out these issues is their *conceptual* or philosophical problem for the future.

Second, the media will face increasing *ethical* problems in the future. A more concerned and sophisticated citizenry will challenge the media's performance and their sense of responsibility. Future emphasis will be on *positive* freedom (or media obligations to society) rather than on the older *negative* freedom, which dealt mainly with *media freedom from government.* The media face growing questions about their self-interest, their irritating arrogance, their invasion of privacy, their increasing sameness and their escalating emphasis on advertising and megaprofits.

And, third, the media face an uncertain future so far as their *international* posture is concerned. The entrenched self-righteousness and provincialism exhibited often in recent years by American media leaders is not likely to win many friends around the world.

The future for American media, to a large degree, will be determined by how media adjust to a new global consciousness with its rising demand for increased communication equity among nations. Just how American media will respond to the world of the future is anybody's guess, but the drift of history appears to be against "business as usual" for the future media of the country.

In conclusion, we have seen that American media are powerful and growing more so. Communication theory and research is growing ever more sophisticated, and social and ethical concern seems to be increasing along with global awareness and sensitivity. If this is true, and we believe that it is, then the future of American media can be bright indeed, and the fascinating legacy passed on to this generation will prosper and expand as it is shared increasingly with the rest of the world.

Retrospective

In this post–Cold War period of rapid change and national frustration, a student of mass communication should know as much as possible about communication issues and media systems around the world, not just in the United States.

In the matter of global communication flow, most information emanates from *First World* countries (the advanced capitalist world). This information flows into the *Second World* (developing socialist/communist nations) and also into the *Third World* (developing nations of other political types). Three big news agencies (located in the First World) and a growing number of broadcasting outlets (CNN and Visnews are examples) have made substantial inroads globally. Many regional and national news agencies add to this international news flow.

Theoretical constructs of national media systems tend to be aligned with each country's political/ideological and economic realities. Basically, a nation's media system reflects its cultural and political system. At present, many nations, especially in the former Soviet Union and the newly independent states of Eastern and Central Europe, have political and economic systems caught in the throes of transition.

Most of the important movies, records, magazines, newspapers and radio and television transmissions originate in the First World. Many important issues command attention in global communications circles. Particularly pressing is the issue of unbalanced flow of world news, which is still being discussed in connection with the Third World's demand for a New World

Information and Communication Order. Many inequities, real and imagined, in world communication are begging to be set right. The conviction that this must be done is still limited, and the arduous campaign for a New Order is just beginning.

1. Do you see anything wrong with the three "worlds" (the First, Second and Third Worlds) classification? If so, how would you refer to these different kinds of countries?
2. Name 20 of the main news centers (cities) of the world, and give three reasons why you think they have communication importance.
3. What are the main "theories" (or systems) of the world press? Are they realistic and meaningful conceptual models for describing world media systems? Explain your answer.
4. What are three of the many broadcasting patterns of control, ownership and financing found throughout the world?
5. Can you give five of the main issues (criticisms) of the world communication situation as elucidated by the proponents of the New World Information and Communication Order?
6. In your opinion, what would be some of the reasonable actions by which the United States could defuse many of the criticisms of the Third World and improve the world communication situation? Do you feel the Third World's criticisms are reasonable? Why or why not?

Suggested Readings

Altbach, P. G., and Rathgeber, E. M. *Publishing in the Third World*. New York: Praeger, 1980.

Burke, Richard C. *Comparative Broadcasting Systems*. Chicago: SRA, 1984.

Fisher, Glen H. *American Communication in a Global Society*. Norwood, NJ: Ablex, 1987.

Fortner, R. S. *International Communication*, Belmont, CA: Wadsworth, 1993.

Frederick, H. H. *Global Communication & International Relations*. Belmont, CA: Wadsworth, 1993.

Gerbner, George, and Siefert, Marsha, eds. *World Communications: A Handbook*. New York: Longman, 1984.

Hachten, William. *The World News Prism*. Ames: Iowa State University Press, 1981.

Hamelink, Cees J. *Cultural Autonomy in Global Communications*. New York: Longman, 1982.

Head, Sydney. *World Broadcasting Systems*. Belmont, CA: Wadsworth, 1985.

Kurian, George, ed. *World Press Encyclopedia*. 2 vols. New York: Facts on File, 1982.

MacBride, Sean. *One World, Many Voices*. Paris: UNESCO, 1980.

Martin, L. John, and Chaudhary, Anju. *Comparative Mass Media Systems*. New York: Longman, 1990.

Merrill, John C., ed. *Global Journalism*. New York: Longman, 1990.

Mowlana, Hamid. *Global Information and World Communication*. New York: Longman, 1986.

Nordenstreng, Kaarle. *The Mass Media Declaration of UNESCO*. Norwood, NJ: Ablex, 1982.

Picard, Robert G. *The Press and the Decline of Democracy: The Democratic Socialist Response in Public Policy*. Westport, CT: Greenwood Press, 1985.

Richstad, Jim, and Anderson, M. H., eds. *Crisis in International News: Policies and Prospects*. New York: Columbia University Press, 1981.

Richter, Rosemary. *Whose News? Politics, the Press, and the Third World*. London: Times Books, 1978.

Robinson, Gertrude. *News Agencies and World News*. Fribourg, Switz.: University of Fribourg Press, 1981.

Schramm, Wilbur. *The Story of Human Communication: Cave Painting to Microchip*. New York: Harper & Row, 1988.

Schiller, Herbert. *Communication and Cultural Domination*. White Plains, NY: International Arts and Sciences Press, 1976.

Siebert, Fred S., Peterson, Theodore, and Schramm, Wilbur. *Four Theories of the Press*. Urbana: University of Illinois Press, 1956.

Stevenson, Robert L. *Communication Development and the Third World*. New York: Longman, 1988.

Tunstall, Jeremy. *The Media Are American*. London: Constable, 1977.

GLOSSARY

academic journals Scientific and scholarly publications, often edited and published by university presses, whose submissions are reviewed and judged by a panel prior to publication. (Chapter 7)

account management In advertising, the process of handling an entire product campaign from start to finish, including direct contact with the client and interdepartmental contact within the agency. (Chapter 11)

advertorial Advertising copy designed to look like editorial copy in print media. It may be a commercial message with an editorial approach or a special section containing normal-looking features written by an ad agency to support normal-looking ads. (Chapter 11)

agenda-setting According to McCombs and Shaw, a *powerful effect* of the media in which people learn what to think and talk about from the media messages they receive. (Chapter 4)

anti-change effect A view of the media as supporting the status quo, sustaining a social equilibrium, and reinforcing already existing values. (Chapter 4)

antitrust laws Federal laws used to control economic concentration by preventing any business from monopolizing the marketplace. (Chapter 14)

audience Someone for whom a message is intended. It may be anything from a single person audience in face-to-face conversation all the way to a heterogeneous, scattered media audience. To become a true audience member, one must make an effort—listen, watch, read, and so on. (Chapter 2)

authoritarian press system A media system in which an authoritarian government regulates press units tightly; in such systems, media are generally privately owned and allowed to operate as a special privilege granted by the government. (Chapters 13, 16)

barter-purchase show A type of syndicated show in which the program syndicator finds one or more major advertisers and then markets the show at a low cost to stations, which then sell the remaining commercial time to local advertisers; also called *cash-plus-barter* show. (Chapter 8)

cable television Television service provided by a local company that for a monthly fee offers dozens of wired channels without signal interference; also called *CATV (community antenna television)*. (Chapter 9)

categorical imperative A maxim formulated by Immanuel Kant, which states that what is ethical for a person to do is what the person would want to see everybody do. (Chapter 15)

CATV (community antenna television) See *cable television*.

channel The mechanism by which a message is transmitted; of two types, *basic* (sound waves and senses) and *instrumental* (posters, newspapers, television etc.). (Chapter 1)

classified advertising A newspaper's advertising arranged (classified) by subject. (Chapter 5)

consumer magazines Magazines, sold at newsstands, drugstores and supermarkets, that offer a single subject of broad appeal (e.g., *TV Guide*) or cover a wide variety of topics targeted specifically to audiences with demonstrable demographic differences (e.g., *Esquire, Country Living*). (Chapter 7)

contagion factor Refers to the belief that some audience members react not only to the content of a message, but also to the responses of other audience members. An example might be infectious exaltation at a rock concert, in which the audience reacts as much to itself as it does to the music. (Chapter 3)

copyright The exclusive right to the use of the work of a writer, photographer or artist. (Chapter 14)

correlation role According to Lasswell, one of the societal functions of the media, in which the media offer interpretations and opinions. (Chapter 3)

decoder The intended receiver who interprets a message. (Chapter 1)

demassification As used by Alvin Toffler, the progressive process of fragmentation that has recast a once largely homogeneous U.S. society into a host of special-interest groups. (Chapter 12)

deontological ethics An ethical position that is formalistic, absolute, legalistic and duty-bound; Immanuel Kant best exemplifies a *deontologist*. (Chapter 15)

desktop computer publishing Growing trend in publishing by which personal computers are used to write copy, typeset it, design page layouts, add illustrations and send the product directly to the printer, all on a low budget; used increasingly to publish newsletters, company publications and smaller consumer magazines. (Chapter 7)

development phase In movie-making, the process that starts with a story idea and ends with a movie script, and usually goes through many versions and many writers in the process. (Chapter 10)

developmental media system A media system in which media are seen as instruments for nation-building. (Chapter 16)

direct mail An advertising medium by which flyers, coupons and catalogs are sent to a specific zip code area as third-class mail; has the advantage of total area saturation. (Chapter 11)

display advertising A newspaper's local or national retail advertising. (Chapter 5)

distribution system The part of a cable TV system that amplifies broadcast signals and sends them out to local subscribers. (Chapter 9)

distributors In the movie business, companies that market movies to theaters and other outlets. (Chapter 10)

dyadic communication The simplest type of communication, in which one person attempts to communicate with another. (Chapter 1)

educational books Professional and technical books and college, primary- and secondary-school textbooks. (Chapter 6)

empathy advertising An advertising technique based on the belief that purchases are often made for consciously or unconsciously sexual reasons and that advertising should appeal to such reasons, with which consumers can be expected to identify. (Chapter 11)

encoder The person who formulates (and sometimes sends) a message. (Chapter 1)

ethics The branch of philosophy that deals with what ought to be done, with what kinds of actions are good and with personal values and individual character. (Chapter 15)

exhibitors Theater owners who present movies to the public. (Chapter 10)

Federal Communications Commission (FCC) A regulatory agency, established in 1934, responsible for licensing and regulating radio and television stations. (Chapters 8, 14)

feedback Return messages sent from message receivers to message senders; may be *immediate* or *delayed*, *verbal* or *nonverbal*. (Chapter 1)

First World Advanced capitalist nations such as Japan and those in North America and Western Europe. (Chapter 16)

four theories concept A typology of press and media systems set forth by Siebert, Peterson and Schramm that proposes four government types and accompanying media systems: *authoritarian, libertarian, Soviet press* and *social responsibility*. (Chapter 13)

Freedom of Information Act A 1966 act of Congress that makes it possible for any citizen to challenge classified public records and thereby make the government prove that secrecy is necessary or release the information to the public. (Chapter 13)

gag rules   An order from a judge that bars anyone connected with a trial from talking to reporters without facing the risk of being cited for contempt of court or jailed. (Chapter 14)

general public audience   One of two types of mass audience—very broad and extremely complex, an anonymous, massively heterogeneous and scattered mass of individuals. (Chapter 2)

general semantics   The study of the way people are affected by language, how it causes us to think and act. (Chapter 2)

halftones   Black and white photographs. (Chapter 5)

head end   The antenna tower that captures broadcast signals as part of a cable TV system. (Chapter 9)

house drop   The point in a cable television system at which subscribers receive broadcast signals. (Chapter 9)

image advertising   The advertising technique of giving a product a special aura to make it seem better or more expensive than competitors' products; also called *status advertising*. (Chapter 11)

inferential feedback   A return message that the sender of a message infers from the receiver's demeanor; of questionable reliability. (Chapter 1)

infomercial   Commercial messages for electronic media designed to look and sound like informational or entertainment programs. A common practice is to present a 30-minute program that resembles a game show or a talk show, but is devoted to one product or to a series of products from one sponsor. (Chapter 11)

interpersonal communication   Communication between or among persons; can take place *one-on-one, face-to-face* or can involve *groups,* both large and small. (Chapter 1)

intrapersonal communication   Communication that takes place within a single person; self-communication. (Chapter 1)

invasion of privacy   Violation of a person's right to privacy, in one of four forms: casting someone in a false light, revealing intimate details of someone's life, misappropriating someone's name or likeness and intruding physically into someone's private life. (Chapter 14)

inverted pyramid   Style of newswriting that requires the story's first paragraph to sum up what happened in one sentence, while answering the questions *who, what, when, where* and perhaps *how* and *why;* subsequent paragraphs explain the story in declining order or significance. (Chapter 5)

joint operating agreement   A federally approved merger of all but the editorial departments of competing newspapers. (Chapter 5)

kinesic communication   Communication through physical movements; "body language." (Chapter 1)

libel   A false statement about a living person, which does damage to that person's reputation, causes embarrassment or humiliation or affects a person's ability to make a living. (Chapter 14)

libertarian press system   A media system in which the press is largely autonomous. (Chapters 13, 16)

little magazines   Literary publications, usually edited and published by university presses, whose submissions are reviewed and judged by a panel prior to publication. (Chapter 7)

local origination channel   A cable television channel that offers diverse local programming such as city council meetings and sports events. (Chapter 9)

"magic bullet" theory   A theory that attributes powerful effects to the media, in which messages are seen as bullets which, if aimed and fired properly, reach their targets and accomplish their purposes. (Chapter 4)

market penetration   For newspapers, readership per capita. (Chapter 5)

marriage mail   A form of direct mail advertising in which a mailing service combines many unrelated advertising messages and coupons together in one envelope. (Chapter 11)

Marxist media system   A media system in which media are owned and controlled by the state and are cooperating partners with government. (Chapter 16)

mass audience   In communication, receivers of messages sent through some form of technology; characterized by large numbers and by scattered, anonymous and heterogeneous natures. (Chapter 1)

mass communication   The process of communication in which messages are sent through some form of technology to large groups of people *(mass audiences)*. (Chapter 1)

mass-market paperback   Inexpensive paperback books sold to a mass market at grocery stores, airport newsstands, drugstores and discount stores as well as bookstores. (Chapter 6)

media buying   In advertising, the process of determining where and when to place ads and the subsequent purchase of advertisement space. (Chapter 11)

media dysfunction   The negative or unexpected consequences of media function. (Chapter 3, 8)

message   A meaning, sometimes simple, sometimes complex, that one person wishes another person or persons to understand. (Chapter 1)

message entropy   The tendency of a message to lose information during the process of transmission. (Chapter 1)

minimal-effects theories Theories that consider media messages as only one of many forces acting on peoples' thoughts and actions. (Chapter 4)

monological illusion The misconception that communication is accomplished by simply telling people what they ought to know, concentrating too much on the message itself and ignoring the needs and response of the audience. (Chapter 1)

narcotization A media dysfunction in which a person becomes apathetic and lazy in response to media messages. (Chapter 3)

New World Information and Communication Order (NWICO) Demands of Third World nations to improve the prevailing communication order that such nations see as balanced in favor of First World ("imperialistic") nations. (Chapter 16)

news hole Newspaper space not filled with advertising and therefore available to the editorial department. (Chapter 5)

noises Barriers or disruptors of communication; may be mechanical or semantic. (Chapter 1)

open records laws Legislation on the federal and state levels that (with some exceptions) forces government bodies to conduct their business openly. (Chapter 13)

pay cable Cable television service for which subscribers pay a fee in addition to their basic service charge; networks such as Home Box Office and the Disney Channel are pay cable services. (Chapter 9)

penny press A kind of newspaper, created by Benjamin Day in 1830s, that offered popular news reports and human interest stories to the middle and lower classes in an easy-to-read format at an affordable price. (Chapter 5)

plagiarism The use of another writer's words without giving credit to the source. (Chapter 14)

playlist The list of musical selections to be played during a radio show. (Chapter 8)

positioning An advertising technique that aims one's product at particular market segments. (Chapter 11)

postproduction phase In movie-making, the process of editing and previewing the film, preparation of advertising and, finally, distribution. (Chapter 10)

powerful-effects theories Theories that consider the media to have substantial effects on mass audiences. (Chapter 4)

preproduction phase In movie-making, the process of budgeting and scheduling a movie, including input from various studio departments such as casting, art, camera, wardrobe, makeup, music, location, sound and special effects. (Chapter 10)

press associations Organizations that specialize in collecting and writing news for other news organizations; also called news agencies or *wire services*. (Chapter 5)

prime time A television station's most valuable time, with largest audience size. (Chapter 9)

prior restraint An act of government that is meant to block publication or broadcast of a story. (Chapter 14)

privatization A media dysfunction in which a person made nervous by unsettling news withdraws from news entirely, rather than being stirred to action as was intended. (Chapter 3)

producers The companies and individuals who make movies. (Chapter 10)

production phase In movie-making, the process of rehearsal, set design and construction, wardrobing, creation of music, titles and special effects and the actual shooting of the film. (Chapter 10)

propaganda The technique of influencing human action by use of intentionally persuasive messages, which sometimes are devious. (Chapter 2)

propaganda devices The following seven techniques of propaganda, suggested by Lee and Lee (Chapter 2):
  bandwagon: telling audience members to do or like a certain thing because "everyone else does."
  card-stacking: hiding some or all of the truth by devious tricks such as lying, exaggerating, general distortion or outright censorship.
  glittering generalities: using vague generalizations and "virtue words" to plant in the minds of audience members emotional images devoid of evidence or fact.
  name calling: giving good or bad names to products, projects or candidates without providing substantive data or evidence to support the use of the name.
  plain folks: convincing the audience that the propagandist is "one of them."
  testimonial: getting a well-known person to testify to the worth of something in an effort to persuade the audience to like it.
  transfer: transferring the audience's respect for some symbol over to the propagandist's product, project or candidate.

public relations (PR) An umbrella term for a series of complex activities that include the measurement and evaluation of attitudes and the use of various techniques—including both mass and nonmass channels—to influence those attitudes. (Chapter 12)

pure barter show A type of syndicated show that is largely or completely underwritten by nonlocal advertisers and marketed by a syndicator at no cost to stations; also called *all barter* show. (Chapter 8)

rating An estimate of audience size, calculated as the percentage of households viewing a particular program when compared to all the *potential viewing households* in a market. (Chapter 9)

revolutionary media system A media system in which media are used to subvert the government or fight against foreign interference. (Chapter 16)

Second World Advanced socialist nations like the USSR and those in Eastern Europe. (Chapter 16)

share An estimate of market size, calculated as the percentage of viewing households compared to all the viewing households *currently watching television* in the market. (Chapter 9)

shield laws State statutes that protect journalists from having to reveal news sources. (Chapter 14)

slice of life An advertising technique of using a brief self-contained story in which the product being advertised appears as a natural element in the plot line. (Chapter 11)

small-group communication Communication that takes place in groups consisting of several people. (Chapter 1)

Soviet press system The media system, found in Soviet states, that uses the media to transmit social policy and spread socialist ideals; in such systems, the media are owned and operated by the government. (Chapter 13)

specialized audience One of two types of mass audience—composed of persons who have some common interest, orientation or ideology that causes them to seek similar messages; smaller, more homogeneous and usually less anonymous than a general public audience. (Chapter 2)

spiral of silence According to Noelle-Neumann, a powerful-media theory that contends that people who feel they are of a minority opinion remain silent, thereby reinforcing or enlarging the majority position. (Chapter 4)

subliminal advertising Advertising that uses messages below the conscious threshold of perception. (Chapter 11)

surveillance role According to Lasswell, one of the societal functions of the media, in which the media survey the general environment of society, interpret the signs and report their findings in day-to-day news and in warnings that alert communities to various potential dangers. (Chapter 3)

sweeps Three major annual television ratings periods, which occur in November, February and May. (Chapter 9)

syndicated show A radio or television program leased to many stations in return for a fee from each; the leasing stations recoup costs and earn profits by selling commercial time within the program. (Chapter 8)

syndicates Organizations that supply newspapers with materials ranging from editorial cartoons and opinion columns to comic strips, advice columns and daily horoscopes. (Chapter 5)

teleological ethics   An ethical position that is consequence-oriented; John Stuart Mill exemplifies a *teleologist*. (Chapter 15)

teletext   A one-way flow of televised information, supplied for a fee. (Chapter 5)

theory of social responsibility   A media system that seeks to place ethical and moral restrictions on the press, shifting emphasis from press freedom to press responsibility. (Chapter 13)

Third World   Developing, economically underdeveloped nations located largely in Africa, Latin America and Asia. (Chapter 16)

tiered service   Cable television service that offers basic stations and networks and, *for an additional monthly fee,* satellite-delivered pay cable service. (Chapter 9)

trade book   A book, fiction or nonfiction, aimed at the general public; includes the subcategory of children's literature. (Chapter 6)

trade magazines   Publications targeted to business, agricultural and professional audiences; sold primarily through subscriptions rather than newsstands. (Chapter 7)

transmission of culture   According to Lasswell, one of the societal functions of the media, in which the media transmit social and cultural heritage from one generation to the next by transmitting information about society itself. (Chapter 3)

UHF   Television channels that transmit at Ultra High Frequency, the number of which is established by the FCC. (Chapter 9)

unique selling proposition (USP)   In advertising, the idea that a product can make a specific promise to the consumer, offering some unique benefit to the consumer who buys the product; usually used with parity products. (Chapter 11)

verbal communication   Communication using words, either spoken or written. (Chapter 1)

VHF   Television channels that transmit at Very High Frequency, the number of which is established by the FCC. (Chapter 9)

videotext   A fee-based two-way television system that allows the subscriber to select specific reports or services at the push of a button. (Chapter 5)

wire services   Organizations that specialize in collecting and writing news for other news organizations; also called *press associations*. (Chapter 5)

CREDITS

Chapter 8

166 ScottForesman; **169** UPI/Bettmann Newsphotos; **171** The Bettmann Archive; **176** Kosti Rughomoa/Black Star; **177** The Bettmann Archive; **178** The Bettmann Archive; **181** Sandy Roessler/The Stock Market; **183** Janet Fries/Black Star; **186** Kevin Horan; **187** United Media; **190** The Bettmann Archive.

Chapter 9

196 ScottForesman; **200** NBC Photo; **202** Kobal Collection; **214** Shelly Katz/Black Star; **218** Michal Heron/Woodfin Camp & Associates; **220** Arlene Collins/Monkmeyer Press Photo Service; **221** NBC Photo by R.M. Lewis; **223** Alan Weiner/ Gamma-Liaison.

Chapter 10

230 Universal Studios; **233** Kobal Collection; **235** Kobal Collection; **238** The Bettmann Archive; **239** The Bettmann Archive; **241** The Museum of Modern Art/Film Stills Archive; **242** The Bettmann Archive; **244** Kobal Collection; **245** Kobal Collection; **255** Outline.

Chapter 11

260 Courtesy of Energizer; **266** The Bettmann Archive; **269** (left) The Bettmann Archive; **269** (center) The Bettmann Archive; **269** (right) The Bettmann Archive; **273** Courtesy of Früsen Gladje and McCann-Erickson; **274** Young & Rubicam; **277** (left) Courtesy of Cadbury-Schweppes/Ogilvy & Mather; **277** (right) Courtesy of Hathaway Shirts/Ogilvy & Mather; **278** Abbas/ Magnum; **282** Leonard Freed/Magnum; **283** Gabe Palmer/The Stock Market.

Chapter 12

292 Reuters/Bettmann; **295** Charlie Cole/Picture Group; **298** UPI/Bettmann Newsphotos; **300** Yvonne Hemsey/Gamma-Liaison; **303** Helena Kolda/Photo Researchers.

Chapter 13

314 Gifford/Gamma-Liaison; **318** Larry Downing/Sygma; **320** Paul Conklin; **324** Sebastian Salgado/Magnum; **333** Dennis Brack/Black Star; **334** R. Mims/Sygma; **338** K. Condyles/Impact Visuals.

Chapter 14

344 Gentile/SIPA Press; **349** The Bettmann Archive; **354** Claude Urraco/Sygma; **355** Reuters/Bettmann; **362** Tribune Media Services.

Chapter 15

372 Robert Fox/Impact Visuals; **383** Kobal Collection; **388** (top) AP/Wide World Photos; **388** (bottom) UPI/Bettmann Newsphotos.

Chapter 16

398 Noel Quidu/Gamma-Liaison; **404** Peter Marlow/Magnum; **406** VISNEWS; **407** Voice of America; **408** Richard Nicholas/The Stock Market; **410** Stuart Franklin/Magnum; **414** Burt Glinn/ Magnum; **417** VISNEWS.

INDEX